Information Policy Series

Edited by Sandra Braman and Paul Jaeger

The Information Policy Series publishes research on and analysis of significant problems in the field of information policy, including decisions and practices that enable or constrain information, communication, and culture irrespective of the legal siloes in which they have traditionally been located as well as state-law-society interactions. Defining information policy as all laws, regulations, and decision-making principles that affect any form of information creation, processing, flows, and use, the series includes attention to the formal decisions, decision-making processes, and entities of government; the formal and informal decisions, decision-making processes, and entities of private and public sector agents capable of constitutive effects on the nature of society; and the cultural habits and predispositions of governmentality that support and sustain government and governance. The parametric functions of information policy at the boundaries of social, informational, and technological systems are of global importance because they provide the context for all communications, interactions, and social processes.

Virtual Economies: Design and Analysis, Vili Lehdonvirta and Edward Castronova

Traversing Digital Babel: Information, e-Government, and Exchange, Alon Peled

Chasing the Tape: Information Law and Policy in Capital Markets, Onnig H. Dombalagian

Policy for Computing Infrastructure: Governance of the Cloud, edited by Christopher S. Yoo and Jean-François Blanchette

Privacy on the Ground: Driving Corporate Behavior in the United States and Europe, Kenneth A. Bamberger and Deirdre K. Mulligan

Privacy on the Ground

Driving Corporate Behavior in the United States and Europe

Kenneth A. Bamberger and Deirdre K. Mulligan

The MIT Press
Cambridge, Massachusetts
London, England

MIT Press books may be purchased at special quantity discounts for business or sales promotional use. For information, please email special_sales@mitpress.mit.edu or write to Special Sales Department, The MIT Press, 1 Rogers Street, Cambridge, MA 02142.

This book was set in Stone Sans and Stone Serif by Toppan Best-set Premedia Limited. Printed and bound in the United States of America.

Library of Congress Cataloging-in-Publication Data

Bamberger, Kenneth A., 1968–
Privacy on the ground : driving corporate behavior in the United States and Europe / Kenneth A. Bamberger and Deirdre K. Mulligan.
    pages cm. — (Information policy series)
Includes bibliographical references and index.
ISBN 978-0-262-02998-8 (hardcover : alk. paper)   1. Privacy, right of.
2. Privacy, right of—Europe.   3. Corporate governance—Law and legislation—United States.   4. Corporate governance—Law and legislation—Europe.   5. Data protection—Law and legislation—United States.   6. Data protection—Law and legislation—Europe.   I. Mulligan, Deirdre K., 1966–   II. Title.
K3263.B36   2015
342.08'58—dc23

2015029211

10   9   8   7   6   5   4   3   2   1

KAB: To Michael and Phylis, role models in law and life. And in all ways, to Sara.

DKM: To my one and only.

Contents

Series Editor's Introduction

Sandra Braman

Privacy on the Ground participates in a number of stories. Two have to do with transformations in law-state-society relations: the rise of governance relative to government, and legal globalization. Two have to do with trends in scholarship: the "law and society" movement, and the role of research as inputs into policymaking. Together, the book provides insight into not only macro level social processes, but also why research into such processes matters.

It is among the central thrusts of the Information Policy book series that those concerned about law and policy in the twenty-first century must take into account not only government, but also governance and governmentality—that is, informal processes as well as formal, private-sector actions in addition to those of the public sector, and the cultural habits and predispositions that make all of these possible and sustain them. *Privacy on the Ground* offers a premier example of just why that is so with Bamberger and Mulligan's research on the perceptions of those recognized as privacy "leaders" by their corporate communities regarding how their companies translate data protection laws into organizational practice. The book provides a vivid picture of the roles of private-sector individuals and professional associations in creating workable approaches to data protection that turn the intentions of lawmakers into livable practice. In the course of fulfilling these roles, these individuals and corporations contribute to the development of the law itself.

Of course neither the difference between law on the books and law on the ground, nor recognition of its importance, is new. Many mark the beginnings of thinking about the law from a social science perspective with Oliver Wendell Holmes in the 1880s, and by 1975 legal historian Lawrence Friedman could remark upon the wide consensus that law on the books and law in action are not the same. The Law and Society Association was formed in 1964 to support and promote the development of the kind of theoretical approach used by Bamberger and Mulligan to frame their work. As governance grows in importance relative to government, however, so does the relative salience of this kind of work.

Legal globalization, the harmonization of law and policy across states irrespective of differences in their legal and political systems, is increasingly influential in a growing number of areas of the law. Drivers are multiple, ranging from the UN mandate that has been so influential in shaping counterterrorism laws around the world at one extreme to the development of best practices for fair use in the area of copyright coming out of specific content production communities at the other end of the spectrum. The mutual massaging and spread of ideas via professional associations and personal contacts—such as that reported upon in this book—is one of the more common processes through which legal globalization occurs. Practitioner- or community-driven legal globalization, though, most often still depends upon the leadership of particular individuals. In the case of fair use, Pat Aufderheide and Peter Jaszi, working under the umbrella of Aufderheide's Center for Social Media, conceived of the process and its legal value and deserve credit for its success. In the case of electronic discovery, it was the Sedona Conference that sponsored the conversations through which best practices were developed and disseminated to lawyers and judges around the world. In the area of data protection, this work by Bamberger and Mulligan should accelerate the process of legal globalization by drawing attention to the insights of those widely recognized as privacy leaders and making very clear just what the implications of those insights for law and policy are.

And that brings us to the deontological question of the value of social science research on legal problems altogether. It is useful, of course, to understand how things are working, and why, from a sociological perspective, and for this alone the book not only stands but will continue to have value long after any legal decision making immediately in sight takes place. It is possible, though, to go further. The ways in which research can inform law and policy are themselves complex, muddy, and rarely as one expects, intends, or has seen depicted in maps of decision-making flows. But ideas do matter and research does have policymaking impact; thus the postscript, in which Bamberger and Mulligan speak directly to policymakers, has its valuable place as well.

Acknowledgments

This book has taken several years, spanned five countries and two institutions, and benefited from the time and goodwill of many people. We have, therefore, many people to thank. In the few pages we have it's not possible to convey the depth of our gratitude, so we will do no more than scant justice to those we mention given the outsized nature of many of their contributions.

None of this work would have been possible without the generous support of the National Science Foundation and others who fund the Team for Research in Ubiquitous Secure Technology (TRUST) (NSF award number CCF-0424422); the Berkeley Center for Law and Technology, including funds from a Nokia Corporation research grant; the Miller Institute for Global Challenges and the Law at Berkeley Law; the Privacy Projects.org; the Intel Corporation; the Rose Foundation for Communities and the Environment Consumer Privacy Rights Fund; and the Institute for Information Infrastructure Protection (US DHS grant 2006-CS-001-000001).

But for former Berkeley Law Dean Chris Edley's vision, wise council, and excellent ability to read people, the collaboration at the heart of this project might not have emerged. Edley saw in our related but not yet intersecting agendas the possibility for something bigger and more important. We don't know that we've met his vision, but we are deeply grateful to him for suggesting that we collaborate. It has been a rewarding journey, a solid partnership, and from our perspective yielded our most important scholarly contributions. We cannot thank him enough for the introduction.

The strong personal and professional support we received from Chris, and from Robert Barr, Annalee Saxenian, and Shankar Sastry has been essential to sustaining this project. We are grateful in so many ways.

We have benefited from our broad community at UC Berkeley. Colleagues, Ph.D., Masters, and J.D. students from the law school, the Ischool, the Berkeley Center for Law and Technology, the Center for Law and Society, and the Department of Electrical Engineering and Computer Science, as well as undergraduates, have shaped and contributed to this project. We are particularly grateful for the assistance of several colleagues in developing this project: Chris Hoofnagle, Jen King, Aaron Burstein, and David Thaw.

Our deep appreciation goes to colleagues at Berkeley and elsewhere in the privacy landscape, who shared their knowledge and provided advice, feedback, and constructive criticism along the way: Catherine Albiston, Anita Allen, Colin Bennett, Michael Birnhack, Julie Brill, Herbert Burkert, Jenna Burrell, Beckwith Burr, Fred Cate, Danielle Citron, Mary Culnan, Lauren Edelman, Alex Fowler, Bob Gellman, Mark Gergen, Rosann Greenspan, Leslie Harris, Dennis Hirsch, Trevor Hughes, Bob Kagan, Cameron Kerry, Colin Koopman, Christopher Kuner, Mark Lemley, Toby Levin, Maryanne McCormick, David Medine, Helen Nissenbaum, Anne Joseph O'Connell, Nik Peifer, Shari Pfleeger, Richard Purcell, Joel Reidenberg, Ira Rubinstein, Pamela Samuelson, Michael Samway, Peter Scharr, Fred B. Schneider, Jason Schultz, Ari Schwartz, Paul Schwartz, Viola Schmid, Spiros Simitis, Dan Solove, Jeff Sovern, Rainer Stenzel, Peter Swire, Eric Talley, Omer Tene, Jennifer Urban, Nico van Eijk, David Vladek, Steve Weber, Phil Weiser, and Daniel J. Weitzner.

For critical assistance in Europe we extend thanks to Pascale Gelly, Francoise Gilbert, Christoph Klug, Marcos Judel Meléndrez, Fabrice Naftalski, Eduardo Ustaran, Stewart Dresner and Privacy Laws and Business, Rita DiAntonio and the International Association of Privacy Professionals, and Ulrich Wuermeling and Euroforum.

For excellent research assistance we also thank very much Hailey Anderson, Emily Barabas, Maydha Basho, Marta Porwit Czajkowska, Nathalie David-Warcholak, April Elliot, Heather Ford, Kim Fox, Jonathan Francis, Ilan Goldbard, Cory Isaacson, Lea Mekhneche, Alisha Montoro, Mary Morshed, Parichart Munsgool, Celia Perry, Katy Robinette, Sarah Ruby, Quinn Shean, Tatyana Shmygol, Sara Terheggen, James Wang, Andy Wiener, and for excellent administrative assistance we are grateful to Rebecca Henshaw and Jean S. Hayes.

Portions of our research were presented in "Privacy on the Books and on the Ground," *Stanford Law Review* (2011); "New Governance, Chief Privacy

Officers, and the Corporate Management of Information Privacy in the United States: An Initial Inquiry," *Law & Policy* (2011); and Privacy in Europe: Initial Data on Governance Choices and Corporate Practices," *George Washington Law Review* (2013). Many thanks to the student and peer journal editors who worked with us along the way.

Behind every good book is an excellent editor. This one is no exception. Kerry Tremain stepped in at just the right time to assist us in making hard decisions, finessing prose, and architecting a narrative that is both true to our research and accessible to the range of audiences we hope to reach. We are grateful for his sage advice, excellent organizational skills, structural and technical editing, and, most importantly for the confidence he had in the book, and our project, and his constant reminder that at the end of the day, this is our book.

But Kerry was not alone.

Michael Berger arrived at the Ischool in time to share with us his formidable talents in research, synthesis, and editing. Without his efforts during the last few months of this project our book would have no footnotes or endnotes, no table of contents, or index. Yes, it would not have been noticeable as a book.

Jen King has been at our side helping us wrangle, interpret, and manage our data since day one. She has managed other students, dealt with multiple transcription companies, trained students on Atlas TI, joined us on interviews to provide feedback on methods, and assisted in perfecting our survey instruments. We are indebted to her for the time, organizational skill, and expertise she has put into this project over the past eight years.

This book benefited enormously from the astute comments of three reviewers. It is much improved thanks to the diligence and care with which they considered our work, and the expertise and knowledge they brought to bear on our research findings and conclusions. Given the state and length of the manuscript when they received it, we are particularly impressed by the quality of their advice. We hope they find the book vastly improved by their efforts; we surely consider it to be so.

We appreciate Sandra Braman's early interest in the project, and her feedback and support through the process of going from manuscript to book. Thank you to the MIT Press for working on tight deadlines to bring this book to market quickly.

We are immensely grateful to the chief privacy officers, data protection officers, former and current regulators, privacy lawyers, and other experts who shared hours of their time with us. Of course, without them this book would not have been possible, but our gratitude also runs in other directions. As individuals our data traverses the systems and resides in the databases governed by policies, practices, and technical protections that they—with vision and chutzpah, cunning and skill—create. Most of their work remains hidden from the public it serves. They and their work are mostly known due to failures. Yet we have confidence and admiration for the effort and creativity with which they seek to protect our privacy from the gaping mouth of technology, bureaucracy, and the ever-present bottom line. We thank them for championing privacy in all its messiness in their institutions. They may not always win, and they surely do not always get it right, but we walked away certain that they make a difference in more ways than those on the outside can possibly know. Within these pages we've had to protect their privacy, but we hope that despite going unnamed they understand how thankful we are for their time, candor, interest, and work.

Finally, the most important acknowledgments:

[*From Deirdre Mulligan*] This book was made possible by the vast—seemingly boundless—generosity of my husband, Ben. He has endured my extended absences that left him with carpools to drive, music lessons to oversee, soccer games to coach and watch, and numerous chaotic mornings and bedtimes. He is the heart of our home. I am grateful to Marly and Malcolm for being well mannered and reasonable when faced with my literal and figurative absences, and for providing endless distractions when I needed a break from writing. They are the light. Finally, thanks to my parents—Steve, my most loyal reader, and Peggy, who taught me to answer tough questions—for their ongoing love and support.

[*From Ken Bamberger*] I am blessed with a gifted and generous partner, my wife Sara. Her sage counsel illuminates the clear path when it remains obscured to me. And her labors and leadership created the space in our very busy lives for this project, all with love and good humor. She and our children Max, Isaiah, Niva, Ezra, and Talia make an extraordinary superhero team, and I am grateful to be part of it.

I Introduction

1   Paradoxes of Privacy on the Books and on the Ground

By the time Chinese journalist Shi Tao was released from prison, in August 2013, he had helped to change the world, although not exactly in the way he'd originally intended.

The events leading to Mr. Shi's imprisonment—and to a United States Congressman famously condemning leaders of a major Silicon Valley firm as "moral pygmies"—had begun nearly a decade earlier, with an anonymous post to an online forum. In April 2004, as the fifteenth anniversary of the Tiananmen Square massacre approached, China's Communist Party authorities sent a document to their national media instructing them to "correctly direct public opinion" on the events in a way consistent with "central policies." Probably hoping to call media attention to the censorship, Mr. Shi sent notes summarizing the directive via his Yahoo! China email account to a colleague at a Chinese-language web site based in New York—which posted the notes. When the Chinese government determined that Mr. Shi was the author of the anonymous post, they arrested and convicted him of sharing state secrets, and then sentenced him to ten years in prison.

But how had party officials discovered the anonymous poster's identity?

In the months after his trial, it emerged that the Yahoo! Beijing office had provided records to the Chinese government that enabled the government to pinpoint Mr. Shi as the source of the information in the web post. When pressed to defend its actions, Yahoo! clung to legality, arguing, "When we receive a demand from law enforcement authorized under the law of the country in which we operate, we must comply."[2] That defense led Representative Chris Smith to ask "If the secret police, a half century ago, asked where Anne Frank was hiding, would the correct answer be to hand over the information in order to comply with local laws?"[3] This revelation spawned widespread public condemnation, climaxing in a U.S. congressional hearing in which Representative Tom Lantos memorably castigated Yahoo! CEO Jerry Yang. "While technologically and financially you are giants," said the Silicon Valley congressman, "morally you are pygmies."[1]

Human rights, civil liberties, and journalism organizations also weighed in. One accused Yahoo! of being a "police informant" and another sued the company in federal court. Pressure from these diverse stakeholders was relentless and powerful—and felt in boardrooms throughout Silicon Valley and beyond.

Fast-forward to 2013. In June of that year—coincidentally just a few months before Mr. Shi's release—the *New York Times* reported that in 2007 and 2008 Yahoo! had battled National Security Agency demands to turn over customer information to their warrantless Internet surveillance program. Rather than hide behind a legal paper tiger, Yahoo! had fiercely challenged the government, arguing that the NSA's broad requests were unconstitutional. While Yahoo! ultimately lost the litigation, the company proved it was willing to fight, even in a secret court, for its users' privacy interests.

The Electronic Frontier Foundation, a respected advocate for users' rights, wrote of the case, "Yahoo! went to bat for its users—not because it had to, and not because of a possible PR benefit—but because it was the right move for its users and the company. It's precisely this type of fight—a secret fight for user privacy—that should serve as the gold standard for companies." It awarded Yahoo! a gold star for its resistance against U.S. surveillance programs.

Why the about-face? Why had Yahoo! shifted from its defense of local corporate compliance to a defense of global human rights?

In the intervening years since Mr. Shi's jailing, the regulatory climate had changed little. While congressional hearings on privacy and human rights were held, no significant legislation was enacted. But following the Shi Tao incident, and the groundswell of diverse advocacy it unleashed, the corporation's stance toward its users' privacy "on the ground" shifted dramatically. After "being pummeled by Congress, human rights groups, the media, and shareholders," one expert wrote of the Shi Tao case, "Yahoo! finally shed its head-in-the-sand, lawyer-driven posture and actually took moral responsibility for what had happened."[4] The company formally apologized and quickly reached a private financial settlement with Mr. Shi's family. Yahoo! dedicated more resources to its privacy and law enforcement staff, launched a Business and Human Rights program[5] covering privacy and freedom of expression, and supported several related initiatives outside the company. The company, along with other tech giants, civil liberties and human rights organizations, socially responsible investment firms, and academics, launched a voluntary code of conduct, known as the Global Network Initiative, to protect and advance freedom of expression and privacy in the information and communications technology sector.[6] Yahoo!'s dramatic evolution highlights three questions at the heart of this book:

• What drives corporations to adopt privacy protective practices?
• What role does law play, and what else shapes corporate understanding of privacy's meaning and corporations' obligations to advance it?
• How do those understandings manifest in firm practices?

Mr. Shi's case changed Yahoo!'s understanding of its privacy obligations to users, and it helped open the company's eyes to the forces beyond the law that affect the role of business in society. Placing this local action on the global stage brought into focus the multiple actors and instruments, beyond local law and officials, that influenced the public's view of Yahoo!'s actions. That case and other high-profile revelations about privacy breaches also had wider corporate repercussions. In 2014 alone, an estimated 176 million customer records were compromised at Target, Home Depot, and JP Morgan. Government requests for customer data, at least in large technology companies in the United States, now appear to receive a more thorough assessment by the companies, and certainly more public exposure.[7] Company policy and practices increasingly respond not only to the law, but also to an overarching framework of human rights norms, the sentiment and reaction of a larger set of actors, including users, media and consumer advocacy groups, government, investors, and even employees, across the globe.

Certainly, legislatures, courts, and regulatory agencies continue to play a key role in shaping privacy practices and corporate decision making—after all, Yahoo! lost when it chose to fight and was told to turn over its users' personal information to the NSA. But the center of action has shifted. A broader set of players hold sway over corporations' privacy obligations and hold them accountable for privacy blunders in myriad ways and multiple venues, and at times reward them for efforts at privacy protection, even if those measures ultimately fail in their full effect.

This book springs from an observation of new corporate activity "on the ground." While companies continued to blunder, sometimes in disturbing ways, there are signs of a shift in company attention to privacy. In particular, we noted a steady rise in the number of chief privacy officers at U.S. corporations starting in the early 2000s.[8] This, in and of itself, suggested the possibility of a meaningful shift in the corporate lens on privacy.

Wondering what this development signaled about corporate attention to privacy, and whether it mattered, we initially undertook inquiries to understand how U.S. companies that are considered leaders on privacy organized their privacy activity. What led firms to adopt these new professionals and what factors shaped and influenced their work? How was their work organized and supported within their firms? What tools did they use? Most importantly, did this new corporate attention and dedication of resources enhance privacy protection?

Initial interviews we conducted with leading U.S. chief privacy officers revealed a surprisingly deep chasm between privacy law on the books and privacy practice on the ground. While U.S. privacy law on the books remained sectoral, fragmented, and incomplete, corporate practices reflected a more integrated and robust approach to privacy management. This exposed a rift between the generally accepted story—stronger data protection–style laws and their enforcement (the European model) were necessary to improve corporate privacy performance—and the reality on the ground. The interviews also revealed key non-legal factors and actors that influence firms' understanding and approach to privacy.

These findings in the United States in turn led us to conduct a multiyear, multi-country study exploring privacy as understood and practiced in large corporations under different legal and cultural conditions.

To do so, we interviewed and surveyed corporate privacy officials, regulators, and scholars in Germany, Spain, France, and the United Kingdom, as well as the United States. Although all the European countries observe the EU's 1995 Data Protection Directive, their relevant laws, institutions, and legal and corporate cultures vary widely, and all vary from the American model. Responding to the horrific legacy of the Nazi government as well as East Germany's Stasi, Germany and all of Europe to frame privacy as a fundamental human right. This has in turn impacted the regulatory environment for company's operating in Europe. But in the United States and, to a certain extent in the United Kingdom, corporations more often define privacy protection in terms of fairness to customers and employees, and managing risk. France and Spain have detailed privacy laws on the books and centralized, regulatory agencies to enforce them, while German and American approaches tend to generate greater ambiguity, and thereby responsibility for the firm, coupled with more flexible enforcement by a distributed set of actors.

Despite the enormous and increasing importance to privacy, research about how corporations understand and manage privacy is remarkably thin. In particular, on-the-ground examinations of corporate privacy practices—how corporations handle personal information, how privacy concerns influence product design or market entry, for example—are rare.

One exception is a landmark study of corporate privacy practices in the United States by management scholar H. Jeff Smith published twenty-one years ago.[9] His conclusions were grim. In the seven corporations studied, the privacy arena was marked by systemic inattention and lack of resources. Policies in important areas were virtually nonexistent, and those that existed were not followed in practice. Executive neglect signaled to employees that privacy was not a strategic corporate issue. Privacy decisions were left to midlevel managers who lacked substantive expertise, privacy played a "particularly subservient roles in most privacy discussions," and attention to privacy issues was reactive and piecemeal. Privacy considerations were particularly absent in decisions about technological or business developments. As one midlevel manager lamented: "The top executives rarely ask for policy implications of . . . new uses of information. If anybody worries about that, it's my [midlevel] colleagues and myself. And we don't usually know the right answer, we just try something."[10]

Smith attributed these failures to "ambiguity" in the legal meaning of privacy and the requirements governing corporate management of personal information.[11] In the face of this ambiguity, corporate executives avoided action unless external parties demanded specific new policies and practices. They viewed privacy as a goal in tension with core operational aims. The inherent secrecy around corporate data management worsened the problem. No ambitious executives wanted responsibility for an issue lacking a clear metric of success, especially one that risked constantly pitting them against the corporate bottom line.

Smith concluded that the remedy for corporate inattention to privacy concerns required a "systemic fix"[12] that reduced the level of "ambiguity in the U.S. privacy domain."[13] He argued for comprehensive, credible, and unambiguous external mandates, and advocated a suite of legal reforms aligned with the European approach to privacy protection.[14] This approach emphasized the creation of a dedicated government board to develop and oversee rules protecting individual privacy rights.[15] These steps, he concluded, would force corporations to devote effective attention to privacy.[16]

Smith's concerns and proposals have been echoed loudly for twenty years. While they differ in detail, proposals for legal reform generally advocate a model of protection adopted throughout Europe: omnibus privacy principles in law or binding codes, interpreted and monitored by an independent privacy agency.

But while the recommendations for reform remain substantially the same over two decades, the privacy landscape today would be unrecognizable to Smith's respondents. Corporate privacy management in the United States has undergone a profound transformation. Thousands of companies have created chief privacy officer positions, a development often accompanied by prominent publicity campaigns. A professional association of privacy professionals boasts over nineteen thousand members and offers information-privacy training and certification.[17] A robust privacy law practice, along with other privacy consultants, now services this growing group of professionals and assists them in assessing and managing privacy. Privacy audits are offered across multiple sectors. Privacy seal and certification programs have developed.

And here we detect a paradox. American corporations considered leaders on privacy now devote considerable managerial "time and attention" to privacy concerns, as Smith called for two decades ago. There is evidence of direct privacy leadership within firms and, in those we studied, relatively large and well-resourced staffs. Yet these changes on the ground cannot be attributed to the adoption of European-style regulatory approaches.

In the corporate arena, U.S. law has largely eschewed a commitment to privacy as an individual right. While there have been significant changes in U.S. privacy laws on the books, privacy regulation remains fragmented and ambiguous, siloed and sectoral. And Congress has declined to follow the European model of a dedicated privacy administrator. In the United States, law on the books has not delivered the clear and consistently enforced mandates that Smith and others have called for. We must look elsewhere to explain the profound corporate changes on the ground.

Unfortunately, there is no past empirical study of corporate privacy practices in Europe parallel to Smith's research of U.S. firms. But we can compare how European nations have interpreted and implemented privacy protections differently within a substantially similar legal framework. As it turns out, there is considerable variation on the ground. Despite the formal unity demanded by the EU's 1995 Data Protection Directive, any lawyer or corporate executive doing business in multiple European jurisdictions (and we spoke with many) knows that privacy requirements and the corporate practices designed to address them diverge radically.

As in the United States, formal European privacy laws must be interacting with other forces to yield such different results. Something important must be catalyzing privacy behavior on the ground that extends well beyond privacy law on the books.

Legal scholarship, advocacy, and policy discourse around privacy regulation has almost entirely ignored this paradox. A number of social scientists have toiled to bring the institutions, actors, and instruments of privacy into the account, but their work has not looked deeply into internal firm practices. On both continents, policy attention has focused largely on privacy laws, rather than the granular experience of privacy protection on the ground.

Exploration of how corporations in different countries operationalize privacy protection, and why, is troublingly absent. With the exception of Smith's study, no sustained inquiry has been conducted into how corporations actually manage privacy. The last detailed comparative account of varied international enforcement practices occurred over a quarter century ago.[18] And no one has undertaken a comparative, qualitative inquiry of corporate privacy practices across jurisdictions.

This absence of empirical assessment of regulatory impact on the practice of privacy leaves legal reformers shooting in the dark, without a real understanding of the ways in which previous regulatory attempts have either promoted or thwarted privacy's protection.

This book begins to fill this gap, and at a critical juncture.

Today, policymakers in the United States and Europe are considering tough new corporate privacy regulation. The thirtieth anniversary celebration of the OECD (Organisation for Economic Co-operation and Development) Guidelines in 2010 sparked an international review to identify areas ripe for revision. The European Council is considering a new General Data Protection Regulation that would bind all member states and largely eliminate substantive national deviations. And the U.S. Congress, the Federal

Trade Commission (FTC), and the White House are each exploring legislative models for "strengthening the current consumer privacy framework."

At the same time, revelations of systematic data dragnets, which former NSA contractor Edward Snowden all too starkly brought to life, highlighted the important role corporations played in collecting and aggregating massive amounts of personal information. To many, the privacy laws on the books, whether constitutional sectoral, or omnibus, and the institutions relied on to oversee and enforce them, were proven inadequate to protect privacy on the ground.

Neither data protection authorities in Europe nor their counterparts in the United States have a say in national security matters,[19] and it is equally rare for courts to have a say in these matters.[20] This has created a "wide chasm between what the laws (and governments) say and what really takes place."[21] Given the mounting concern with government surveillance, a key question is how to create a privacy field that protects privacy both in day-to-day corporate practice vis-à-vis its users *and* vis-à-vis governments. Since our current regulatory framework seems ill-equipped to sufficiently protect user privacy, are there alternative legal strategies that could do a better job? Surely, Yahoo!'s actions in resisting the NSA mattered. Despite the company's failure in its legal appeals before the Foreign Intelligence Surveillance Court, Yahoo!'s objections on constitutional grounds to disclosing user data no doubt gave the government pause, sparked deeper review, and ultimately brought important new details about government actions and programs to light fueling the ongoing reexamination of national security surveillance practices globally. The work of corporate privacy and human rights professionals is rarely visible to the outside world. Their hard-fought battles over product design or data collection, storage, use, and disclosure do not often see the light of day. But here we caught a glimpse of how a shift in corporate orientation toward privacy could make a difference.

To examine these questions, our research draws on both historical information and qualitative empirical inquiry. We interviewed and surveyed corporate privacy officers, regulators, and other actors within the privacy field in five different jurisdictions to learn how privacy protection is implemented on the ground. We worked to identify the combination of social, market, and regulatory forces that drive privacy decisions and how these forces interact with formal privacy laws in successful and unsuccessful ways.

We want to be clear about our gauge of success. We did not measure what some might catalog as specific privacy "outcomes"—the number of data breaches, or the relative frequency of specific substantive choices like opt-in defaults.[22] Rather, we assessed corporate behaviors, as revealed in interviews and questionnaires and documented by internal materials, systems, and technologies. We did so in light of a consensus emerging among scholars, advocates, and regulators about approaches to corporate privacy management that demonstrate the greatest promise for vindicating the increasingly expansive definitions of privacy that societies demand.[23]

We also looked beyond analysis of the results from each country to extract insight into how to build the privacy futures we want. Spying on people isn't the same as it once was, and the ways we protect our nation, our commerce, *and* our personal privacy will always lag behind if our approaches aren't proactive and adaptive, and smart. In this book, we propose a new framework for considering how future policy choices can catalyze effective privacy protection. We suggest that the rising number of privacy and data protection professionals presents a promising opportunity to institutionalize privacy protective practices and tie them to a broader social license. This approach may yield corporate practices that defend privacy against the corporate bottom line and against mindless compliance with government demands for user information. Based on these insights, we provide a model for evaluating regulatory choices, and concrete suggestions for regulators and everyone else seeking to protect our privacy now and in the future.

WHAT WE FOUND AND HOW

We focused our research on corporate professionals identified as leading the field of privacy protection. We chose this focus to identify understandings about privacy's meaning, and also the emerging set of privacy management "best practices" among the subset of firms identified as leaders in the five jurisdictions. This group of leaders resides in large firms—a useful cohort for exploring the impact of regulatory forces since they tend to be more sensitive to the external environment.

Both aspects of our sample limit the ability to generalize from our findings. These accounts do not—nor are they intended to—present a survey of general practices throughout any of the countries surveyed.

The differences between the cohorts from each jurisdiction are fundamental and instructive. U.S. and UK privacy leaders generally framed privacy protection as a form of risk management to avoid harm to consumer
expectations. Privacy leaders in the three continental European jurisdictions largely framed privacy as an individual human right and eschewed
the language of risk and consumer harm. While these clusters were predict-
able, we were surprised by the divergent ways in which the leading firms
understood and operationalized their privacy function.

Despite their stark differences in the perceived meaning of privacy, and
their substantive legal mandates and governing institutions, the U.S. and
German firms approached privacy management in much the same way.
The architecture for privacy protection and decision making within leading
firms in Germany and the United States was strikingly similar. Leading privacy officers in both countries share a congruent view of privacy within the
firm as an evolving notion shaped by social negotiation and discourse.
They described privacy protection as a strategic issue implicating concerns
far beyond mere compliance with specific legal rules. And they positioned
privacy as an evolving, forward-looking and context-dependent social
value, rather than as one solely centered on individual consent and control.
These parallel orientations were coupled with commitments of significant
corporate resources and shared management approaches and structures.

The U.S. and German corporations had powerful and relatively autonomous professional privacy officers with access to high-level management.
The privacy officers led their firms in a strategic approach to information
privacy and data protection and reported substantial engagement with
external stakeholders. Indeed, their activities largely involved strategic,
rather than purely operational, issues. And their participation at a senior
corporate level moved privacy from a subsidiary "add-on" issue into one
integrated into strategic corporate decision making. As senior-level employees, they both directed top-down activities, such as employee training, and
communicated directly with the board of directors.

These interviewees also described how ambiguity and dynamism in the
external privacy environment fostered internal reliance on their professional judgment, which in turn afforded them greater autonomy and power
within their organizations. External uncertainties included the interplay
among norms, technical and business changes, and flexible regulatory
authority. Faced with these dynamic external demands on the firms, the
privacy leads reported spending considerable time interacting with external

stakeholders, including regulators and professional peers. Such deep and ongoing external engagement, they report, is essential for assessing the changing state of privacy norms, participating in their construction, and translating them meaningfully into firm practices.

We also found two notable stylistic similarities in how U.S. and German firms operationalize privacy and data protection. First, our respondents in both countries described how framing privacy and data protection as "beyond-compliance" functions enables their integration into core firm values. So understood, privacy and data protection are moved from a cost center to a functional concern, ideally on the level of product operability, manufacturing accuracy, and process effectiveness. At this level, preexisting and highly resourced technological, management, and audit processes for managing risk kick in—powerful systems that would not otherwise be directed toward privacy concerns alone.

Second, within these firms privacy is operationalized through a distributed network that includes dedicated privacy professionals and specially trained employees within business units. These employees are empowered with practices and tools to help identify and address privacy during product design and in the early stages of business development. Distributed mechanisms significantly extend the reach of the privacy officers. Within the firm, they create a bidirectional system for communicating privacy objectives downstream and new issues upward—an architecture that simultaneously enhances the legitimacy and effectiveness of the privacy function. The structure engages business units in defining and tailoring privacy's operationalization within specific corporate environments. And it places responsibility with the business unit senior executives to comply with agreed upon and business-aligned privacy objectives. German firms leaned toward more direct reports, informed by a statutory requirement of independence. U.S. firms favored looser networks of embedded staff. But both sought to position privacy, and accountability for its protection, closer to the day-to-day work of firms.

These shared approaches in the United States and Germany contrast with the accounts of the identified privacy leaders in Spain, France, and the United Kingdom, and the approaches and behaviors in these three countries differed further among themselves. Firms in Spain and France largely characterized their privacy function as complying with fixed legal mandates. French and Spanish leaders described privacy and data protection as meaning specifically what laws mandate or prohibit explicitly, though these leaders expressed considerable doubt as to whether such compliance was even attainable. Respondents in the UK largely shared their continental counterparts' view of the central importance of the law, but were more optimistic about compliance.

Spain, France, and the United Kingdom each lacked key, although different, elements of the U.S./German suite of practices. While the nuance of these differences will be discussed in detail, several are worth noting in broad strokes.

As compared with practices in the United States and Germany, the experience of British chief privacy officers (CPOs) was mixed. They were usually several rungs below their U.S. and German counterparts in their organization's legal or compliance reporting structure. Our respondents accordingly spoke of their frustration about limited access to resources and limited involvement in high-level firm decision making. Thus, while privacy leads in the United Kingdom were often successful in leveraging their risk-management orientation to integrate privacy into general corporate compliance processes, their position within the firm often inhibited efforts to create a robust distributed architecture to raise privacy issues throughout firm units.

Spanish and French privacy leads looked far different from their U.S. and German counterparts. Most were siloed within corporate compliance or legal divisions, and focused mainly on meeting formal data registration, use, and reporting requirements. As a result, privacy processes largely lacked a distributed privacy architecture altogether. Unsurprisingly, interviewees reported little success integrating data protection concerns into the processes of developing products or services.

In countries with compliance-focused privacy leads, regulators generally possess the greater expertise. While the Spanish firms we studied all had a CPO—some of them an important public face for the company—their internal influence was limited, and their orientation more operational than strategic. French privacy leads were often quite low-level, and the functions were divided among compliance lawyers and others. Indeed, at the close of our interviews in 2013, two-thirds of the firms identified as French industry leaders either did not have or had only recently appointed a dedicated chief privacy officer.

While identifying elements neglected in the dominant on-the-books privacy narrative, our findings also begin to tease out elements that shaped best practices in the United States and Germany. Chapters 10 and 11 take up this question directly. Guided by the factors our interviewees identified as important, these chapters look to independent legal and historical sources to develop more robust accounts of the key factors, legal and non-legal, that molded the U.S. and German privacy landscape on the ground.

Our on-the-ground accounts reveal the parallel emergence of a suite of privacy best practices in leading U.S. and German corporations, and suggest recommendations for flexibly replicating these best practices elsewhere, including:

1. *Making the Board's Agenda*: a high level of attention, resources, access, and prominence for the privacy function within the firm;

2. *A Boundary-Spanning Privacy Professional*: a high-status privacy lead who mediates between external privacy demands and internal corporate privacy practices; and

3. *The "Managerialization" of Privacy*: the integration of privacy decision making into technology design and business-line processes through the distribution of privacy expertise within business units and assignment of specialized privacy staff to data-intensive processes and systems.

Likewise, by comparing corporate best practices, we synthesize a set of "properties" of regulatory activity that encourages stronger privacy protection. These three properties embody an approach we call *bringing the outside in*, suggesting the goal of meaningfully infusing privacy protection inside corporations with the expertise and concerns of a wider community of advocates, experts, and professional peers:

1. *Ambiguity with Accountability*: broad legal mandates and open regulatory approaches, activist regulators, and meaningful stakeholder scrutiny fostered dynamism in the face of changes and pushed more accountability onto firms;

2. *A Boundary-Spanning Community*: U.S. and German corporate privacy leads situated themselves in a broad and inclusive community of outside stakeholders, including other corporate privacy professionals as well as those from civil society and government, who both challenge the inside privacy officers and empower their role in the firm;

3. *Disciplinary Transparency*: greater transparency around privacy failures, including data breach laws, enabled nonregulators such as civil society, media and the broader public to become credible enforcers in the court of public opinion, leading corporations to invest greater resources and authority in internal privacy professionals and processes.

Finally, we suggest how current regulatory reform proposals in the Europe and United States advance this "bringing the outside in" approach— and which head down a path that has not proved successful.

HOW THIS BOOK IS ORGANIZED

Chapter 2 gives an overview of the scholarly literature that informed our research and a longer explanation of our methodology and its constraints.

Chapter 3 provides an overview of the law and legal culture in the five jurisdictions studied.

Chapters 4–8 offer granular accounts of privacy on the ground in the United States, Germany, France, Spain, and the United Kingdom. These chapters reflect over fifty-four interviews with corporate privacy officers identified as "industry leaders" in each jurisdiction, as well as another twenty-six interviews and conversations with regulators and lawyers active in the privacy field. The work has been refined in dialogue with numerous subject matter experts from the privacy field, and benefited from feedback at scholarly, policy, and practice-oriented workshops and conferences.

As we discuss further in chapter 9, there is reason to believe that the privacy management practices in the United States and Germany hold promise for privacy protection. They resonate with recent scholarship and policy advocacy to broaden the substantive understanding of privacy values and the related importance of incorporating privacy "by design" into technological and corporate structures. The findings also resonate with the scholarship of organizational theorists more generally regarding the optimal manner of incorporating secondary interests, such as privacy protection, that may be in tension with core firm goals.

Chapters 10 and 11 take up the question of what elements, neglected in the dominant on-the-books-narrative, might have combined to shape privacy practices in the United States and Germany. Beginning with elements our interviewees identified as important in shaping privacy attitudes and behaviors, these chapters investigate independent legal and historical sources to construct more robust accounts of how the U.S. and German privacy landscapes developed.

Finally, chapters 12 and 13 advance this analysis an important step forward: from descriptive to constructive. Chapter 12 moves beyond the identity of the relevant actors and institutions in the U.S. and German landscape, to identify a shared set of properties in the two regulatory fields that fostered, catalyzed, and permitted these robust internal privacy practices to emerge in the firms, and shifted firm orientation to privacy from a question of legality to one of social license.

We conclude, in chapter 13, with a call to action. With novel challenges to privacy, the adaptability of distinct regulatory approaches and institutions has never been more important. As technology and social change have altered the generation and use of data, the definition of privacy that has operated in the political sphere—individual control over the disclosure and use of personal information—has increasingly lost its salience.[24] The common instruments of protection generated by this definition—procedural mechanisms to ensure the perfection of individual choices—have offered an inapt paradigm for privacy protection in the face of data ubiquity and computing capacity.[25] Based on our comparative studies of the privacy landscape in five countries, our recommendations upend the terms of the prevailing policy debate, and offer important insights for policymakers considering reform.

In the last section of chapter 13, we define more specifically which proposals under consideration in the EU and the United States advance or hinder the "bringing the outside in" approach.

This book offers an empirically informed analysis and a new framework for thinking about privacy protection at a decisive moment. Policymakers are now engaged in making important decisions about which regulatory structures to expand in the United States and Europe, and which to leave behind.[26] They are considering how to structure the administrative agencies governing privacy moving forward and the strategies those agencies will adopt regarding legal enforcement. And they are debating how best to develop privacy expertise within the government and corporations and the ways that other participants will or will not be enlisted to shape corporate decision-making and privacy outcomes

We hope our findings, analysis, and recommendations contribute to a better understanding of how privacy laws on the books can galvanize effective protection of privacy on the ground.

II Framing a Privacy on the Ground Approach

2 Literature, Framework, and Methodology

LITERATURE

PRIVACY AND ITS PROTECTION

The "Data Protection" Approach: Fair Information Practices   The foundation of information privacy protection throughout much of the world is "informational self-determination"[1] or "the claim of individuals . . . to determine for themselves when, how, and to what extent information about them is communicated to others."[2] This rights-based conception of information privacy is embodied in the code of Fair Information Practices (FIPs) that provides the backbone for data protection laws in Europe and a key touchstone for American information privacy regulation. First proposed by an influential U.S. Advisory Committee on Automated Personal Data Systems convened to study the impact of computer data banks on individual privacy,[3] the FIPs form the core of the Council of Europe's 1981 Convention for the Protection of Individuals with Regard to Automatic Processing of Personal Data[4]—the first legally binding international instrument in the field of data protection—as well as the OECD's Guidelines on the Protection of Privacy and Transborder Flows of Personal Data,[5] and the European Union's 1995 Data Protection Directive.[6]

The FIPs framework resonated with national European data protection authorities, some of which had existed since the 1970s,[7] and with existing understandings of data protection, animated in part by the experience of European fascism and totalitarianism.[8] These understandings embodied commitments to privacy as a human right and "fundamental value" independent of the existence of risk or harm, limited data processing without legitimate purposes, and assured individuals control over their "automated personal data files."[9]

Yet, while rooted to the substantive principle of individual self-determination, and oriented toward protecting human rights, the FIPs approach often relies on procedural protections, such as providing notice to the data subject and securing consent to informational use.[10] The OECD Guidelines, the most influential statement of FIPs, illustrate the primacy they place on process.[11] The Guidelines articulate eight principles that emphasize an individual's knowledge of, participation in, and control over personal information.[12] They embrace transparency regarding the types of information collected and the way the information will be used.[13] They propose certain limits on data collection—namely that "data should be obtained by lawful and fair means and, where appropriate, with the knowledge or consent of the data subject."[14] They require data collectors to maintain information securely and emphasize the rights of data subjects to access and ensure the accuracy of personal information.[15]

Although the United States and Europe have dissimilar regulatory climates and accordingly have institutionalized privacy regulation in different ways,[16] they have historically shared a commitment to this atomistic, individual-oriented understanding of privacy and to FIPs as its instrumental expression. Whether implemented in an omnibus fashion and enforced by a dedicated privacy agency, as in Europe, or enforced in limited sectors with no consistent regulatory oversight in the United States, FIPs has been considered the only legitimate way to express and protect information privacy for nearly thirty-five years.

From Data Protection to "Privacy"   As privacy has become more salient in the political realm, and as technology has permeated all spheres of life, privacy's meaning itself has become increasingly contested.[17] In particular, the prevalent legal definition of information privacy and its operationalization in institutions has been increasingly criticized as insufficient to address concerns raised by technological shifts, changing societal uses and risks, and globalization.[18]

Some commentators have argued for abandoning privacy as an organizing framework. They find it lacking as a descriptive matter, irrelevant to the experiences and needs of people on the ground,[19] inattentive to the power of large-scale social surveillance,[20] and politically problematic due to its framing of collective experience as an isolated individual problem.[21] They have thus argued for abandoning the "discursive monopoly" of the "privacy regime," arguing that the fixation on "privacy" eclipses real issues regarding surveillance, and fails to help politically or legally when those issues arise.[22]

Others continue to embrace privacy as a useful concept. They critique instead its definition as a means for effectuating FIPs, and suggest new ways of framing its value. For them, defining privacy as "informational self-determination" at once claims too much and protects too little. The notion that law should provide individuals with a common set of mechanisms for vindicating privacy requires that "[i]nformation privacy policy [be] based . . . on procedural, rather than substantive, tenets . . . by which individuals can assert their own privacy interests and claims, if they so wish," and "the content of privacy rights and interests . . . be defined by individuals themselves."[23] Scholars from multiple disciplines have criticized FIPs for reducing privacy to a set of mechanisms to facilitate discrete, often binary, and atomistic decisions regarding the collection, access, or use of data.

Even on its own terms, the FIPs model often fails. FIPs reduce privacy protection to an individual right to "a procedural order, not a substantive guarantee: if the rules are followed (consent forms, warrants, boilerplate notifications) then the objections are null."[24] In Fred Cate's words, FIPs, as "translated into national law" have "increasingly been reduced to narrow, legalistic principles (e.g., notice, choice, access, security, and enforcement)" which "reflect a procedural approach to maximizing individual control over data rather than individual or societal welfare."[25] And while European approaches to data protection have also embodied substantive protections limiting data processing without a legal basis and legitimate purpose, technical and social trends suggest an increasing reliance on consent globally.

Studies find that well-known cognitive barriers, combined with disparities in access to information about potential uses and harms, leave consumers poorly equipped to use consent-based privacy protections meaningfully.[26] The inability of individuals to assess, in advance, the way an organization will actually use their information further compounds problems with relying on notices to protect privacy.[27] Paradoxically, researchers have found that practices that appear to increase individual control over personal information, such as the provision of privacy notices and more granular controls over data use, lead individuals to disclose more sensitive information.[28] Thus inducing corporations to provide more sophisticated privacy controls—for example efforts at layered notices, short notices, and just-in-time control that are in vogue across many jurisdictions[29]—may lower individuals' concerns about the accessibility and usability of information, and lead them to disclose information more freely, and more widely.[30] The procedural approach to privacy also generates prohibitive costs and unrealistic expectations. One study has demonstrated that it would take the average person 81 to 293 hours per year to skim the privacy policy at each website visited, and 181 to 304 hours to actually read them.[31] In real terms, the procedural right is often an empty one.

These shortcomings are further exacerbated by changes in the technology landscape. The ease with which data analytics can reveal or discover personal information post-collection undermines even the limited utility FIPs offers,[32] thwarting the ability of upfront decisions to protect against privacy risks.

Scholars from a variety of disciplines go beyond documenting the short-comings of a proceduralized FIPs approach in providing individuals with meaningful control over their information, critiquing instead the entire definition of information privacy as "informational self-determination." They argue for definitions of privacy that are less wedded to liberal conceptions of the self, and more reflective of privacy's nature as a public, as well as private, good. Protecting privacy, moreover, necessitates an appreciation of the way that it is contextually and relationally constructed.

The Public Good of Individual Privacy   Priscilla Regan has forcefully argued for framing privacy as "a common value, a public value, and a collective value."[33] Regan does not deny the individual value of privacy, but argues "that society is better off as well when privacy exists."[34] Regan claims that we must attend to the social value of privacy if we are to appropriately weigh and balance it with other social values. Regan's examination of legislative battles over privacy in the United States found that privacy was most successful when framed as instrumental to another widely supported social objective; on its own it has a more niche constituency and a weaker chance of success. Paul Schwartz has pointed to the injury caused to privacy as an important element of democracy when informational choices are relegated to individual market choices.[35] In Colin Bennett and Charles Raab's words, privacy's meaning must "transcend that of individual benefit."[36]

Philosopher and theorist Helen Nissenbaum similarly explains that a focus on informational "self-determination" inappropriately limits the privacy calculus to the costs and benefits accruing to an individual decision maker.[37] It thus precludes inquiry as to whether "my act [will] be one of a set of acts that will together harm other people,"[38] ignoring privacy's importance as a social good. Thus it obscures the fact that an individual's privacy can be breached by the analysis of other individuals' information.[39]

A recent news story involving personal genetic testing company "23andMe" illustrates the new genre of privacy challenges facing society, and the limits of models that treat information as a discrete "resource to be assigned" to either a single person or a company.[40] In conjunction with its saliva-based direct-to-consumer genetic testing, the company offered a "predictive relative finder program." Through the program a biologist discovered his unknown half-brother (a product of his father's infidelity), causing a massive family rift ending in his parents' divorce.[41] While opt-in procedures offered the biologist a chance to consider what the test might reveal about him, it offered no protection for his father or his newfound sibling.[42] Genetic information relates to a group of individuals, not just the one disclosing it, posing challenges to the "traditional atomistic, autonomy-based approach."[43]

Privacy in Context   Meaningful privacy protection, moreover, must reflect the way individual understandings of privacy derive from social context. As privacy scholar Sandra Petronio describes, understandings about what an individual can justifiably expect regarding the treatment of his or her information "are coordinated between and among individuals."[44] Similarly, Nissenbaum emphasizes the socially situated nature of privacy, arising from the reality that "we act and transact not simply as individuals in an undifferentiated social world, but as individuals acting and transacting in certain capacities as we move through, in, and out of a plurality of distinct social contexts."[45] Each of these social contexts is governed by a set of norms derived from history, culture, law, and practice about what is "appropriate, or fitting, to reveal in a particular context,"[46] and about whether the information's distribution, or flow, is consistent with expectations of confidentiality and discretion, as well as with entitlements and obligations to reuse or disseminate pertinent information.[47]

Nissenbaum's work points toward the importance of detailed contextual analysis of function and practice. At the heart of her contextual integrity model is a heuristic for interrogating the functioning of privacy in spheres of social life, each governed by its own internally negotiated norms, parsed into a multiplicity of elements: activities, roles, norms, power structures, and values. These norms vary by context and evolve over time but, consistent with the findings of scholarship on decision making,[48] they embody at any one point the situational clues and understandings that inform individual cognition. Thus, as Robert Post has described, privacy norms "rest not upon a perceived opposition between persons and social life, but rather upon their interdependence."[49] When the full circumstances of a privacy decision are upended by atomizing and isolating individual decisions regarding the use of information, it results in unintended and unexpected breaches in "contextual integrity,"[50] and therefore unmoors privacy decisions from social understandings and expectations about privacy's protection, and the appropriateness of information uses.

Decontextualization proves a particular challenge as rapid technology changes and changing business models reduce the individual's power to isolate and identify the use of data that concerns them. As Priscilla Regan explains, "privacy as an individual right . . . provides a weak basis for formulating policy to protect privacy"; because "it emphasizes the negative value of privacy; it establishes a conflict between the individual and society; and it fails to take into account the importance of large social and economic organizations."[51]

Organizations, Privacy, and Context As Regan's analysis suggests, large corporations and organizations are most often the salient decision makers regarding the collection, use, aggregation, and dissemination of personal information. Focusing on information practices at the corporate level often offers the best way to avoid privacy harms. Yet, the framing of privacy as "informational self-determination," Nissenbaum explains, often provides no "decision heuristic,"[52] no substantive touchstone, to guide corporate managers in making systemic choices about the treatment of information that will limit the very choices that a "self-determination" emphasis suggests must be accorded to individuals.

By this understanding, robust privacy protection requires corporate consideration of substantive norms, social values, and evolving community practice, in addition to the existing procedural tools, to instantiate individual autonomy and personal choice. For example, Nissenbaum suggests, the consistency of particular information practices must be understood by considering what users of information services bring to a transaction—the "mental model" they have of information "flows"—and whether a practice is unexpected in light of those understandings and therefore violative of public policy.[53] For Colin Bennett, such a focus on data flows—the ways in which information is actually used in the organizational context—in turn offers promise in creating a more robust conception of privacy values deserving of defense.[54] Together, these analyses suggest that to successfully protect privacy, firms must do more than satisfy requirements to provide formal notice and consent mechanisms to individuals. Rather, they must integrate into their decision making and value structures such collective, contextual, and varied understandings of the ways that corporate use of personal information can intrude on the personal sphere, individual autonomy, and the public good of privacy.

Operationalizing Privacy in Corporations

Integrating Secondary Goals in the Corporate Context   For scholars of organizational behavior, requiring corporations to take into account externally imposed "secondary goals"[55] such as privacy that are at best orthogonal to, and at worst in tension with, the organization's primary mission is a familiar challenge.

The organizational form provides a means of leveraging individual strengths within a group to achieve more than can be accomplished by the aggregate efforts of group members working individually. In particular, organizations provide a means for efficiently overcoming the constraints on the decisional and productive capacities of any single individual imposed by limits of both the human mind and practicality.[56]

Accordingly, firms organize administratively in ways that limit the attention and perception demands on any individual decision maker. Employees are organized into discrete subunits, each assigned a separate set of tasks and subgoals, and charged with mastery of a limited set of information.[57] This distribution of decisional responsibility throughout the firm mitigates any individual decision maker's attention and perception constraints, while permitting the organization as a whole to engage in the wide variety of activities necessary in the modern corporation. Learning from past successes in maximizing core firm goals such as production or profit maximization, corporate operations develop efficiency-enhancing rules for identifying similar situations quickly and providing a regularized response.[58] By storing firm knowledge in this way, routines eliminate the need to reinvent the wheel, and both "allow reuse of solutions to problems"[59] and support the creation of a "collective mind"[60] that promotes interrelated actions in service of organizational goals.

This lens shapes the way that organizations react to demands from their external environment. DiMaggio and Powell describe how firms through a process of "institutional isomorphism"[61] adopt structures and practices from other organizations like competitors, unions, professions, and trade associations that are considered "legitimate"[62] and therefore attract partners to work with them.[63] They will adopt regulatory compliance practices considered legitimate to acquire a necessary business "resource"[64]—the ability to signal to others (including government enforcers, business partners, and the market) that their pursuit of organizational goals is valid.

At the same time, public values and regulatory mandates will predictably encounter systemic resistance when they create tension with the primary substantive goals.[65] Organizational theorists attribute such resistance to the very structures responsible for the strength of the organizational form.

In particular, the division of tasks among subunits with discrete responsibilities creates barriers for ensuring that corporate decision making integrates public goals. Subunits responsible for regulatory compliance have little managerial power to reshape existing routines elsewhere in the firm, relegating legal rules to simply one of a number of distinct and competing claims on decision makers. This undermines the legitimacy of regulatory obligations, limiting the capacity of the responsible unit to "to produce decisions that generally seem as justifiable and capable of enforcement."[66] As legal sociologist Carol Heimer explains, while the "adoption of new structures and practices" to comply with regulation might "smooth interactions" with external regulators, "it may be disruptive to the internal workings of the organization."[67]

As a result, organizations seek to structure compliance by adapting to external mandates in ways that most easily achieve the appearance of legitimacy, while minimizing the dislocation of existing practices. This process can undermine the efficacy of the regulation by focusing on easily visible indicators of compliance, rather than meaningful incorporation into firm decision making. This process of "coercive isomorphism"[68] often results in the "ceremonial" adoption of rules,[69] or a "check-the-box" approach to compliance.

In the employment law context, for example, Lauren Edelman and others have illustrated how firms implement antidiscrimination protections by focusing compliance efforts on creating new legalistic processes. Such procedures signal "legality" but, because they are distinct from other firm structures, avoid fundamental alterations in existing workplace culture. The legal norm is therefore translated into the firm so that the "right to a nondiscriminatory workplace in effect becomes a 'right' to complaint resolution."[70] The right to complaint resolution, notes one sociologist, "is far more superficial and entails fewer disruptions of routines than would a right to a nondiscriminatory workplace."[71]

Legal scholars have pointed to a similar process in the traditional focus on audits as a central means for compliance with securities regulation. While there is no doubt that such safeguards comprise an important component of comporting with legal requirements, the capacity of audits is necessarily limited. They explicitly focus on certain factors that can be measured, such as whether data is presented in a universally recognized manner, rather than on substantive changes to firm practices.[72] Thus, the establishment of auditable controls often provides firms with ways to signal legitimacy without addressing deeper problems inherent in existing routines and structures.

These observations have particular salience in light of the emerging consensus in the literature about privacy's meaning discussed earlier in this chapter. That scholarship suggests that formalized processes focused on notice and consent, access limitations, and registering the collection and use of data—visible legal compliance behaviors that firms can easily adopt—have been rendered largely ineffectual in light of technological developments and changing business practices.[73]

Promise for Secondary Goals in Corporate Decision Making By contrast, what type of corporate behaviors and practices might show promise in directing attention to broader understandings of privacy—understandings include its contextual nature, the social rather than just individual interest in protecting privacy, and the complicated way in which constant data collection, manipulation, and aggregation can impinge on individual privacy?

Scholarship from a range of disciplines has focused on ways to reorient firm behavior toward meaningful integration of public goals into corporate decision making,[74] and to promote what Neil Gunningham, Robert Kagan, and Dorothy Thornton have, in the context of environmental protection, termed "beyond compliance" behavior. [75]

This work emphasizes at once a centralized, high-level management commitment to the public goal, and a decentralized integration of that commitment into the processes that govern decisions in subunits through-out the firm. Together, then, "corporate policies, organizational structure, measurement and control systems . . . and organizational culture"[76] are key elements for promoting the fulfillment of, and even improvement beyond, compliance standards.[77]

Centralized coordination of issues across business units can send impor-tant signals to those units about the importance of the value at issue. It can help ensure that issues are not marginalized and avoid "silo" behavior in which locations and divisions are principally focused on maximizing their own accomplishments, harming the organization as a whole.[78] Gunning-ham, Kagan, and Thornton in particular have identified the manner in which internal perceptions and attitudes of senior management "act as an important filter through which information about the external licenses is sifted and guided"[79] for the rest of the firm. Similarly, systems theory insights suggest public values are more easily integrated into corporate behavior by changing their description from extrinsic "legal" practices that disrupt the existing decision-making logic to "business" or "technology" practices that resonate with them.[80]

Top-level attention to regulatory values, importantly, facilitates their integration into existing organizational structures. Sim Sitkin and Robert Bies[81] contrast the effect of organizational rules that are easily included in the existing chain of command with those that are imposed externally (for example, by lawyers), and violate routinized order and the chain of com-mand. The former, not surprisingly, yield a far higher incidence of success. In particular, scholars of environmental regulation have identified success in contexts where corporate managers demonstrate an organizational commitment to environmental protection by adopting environmental management systems.[82] These systems enable business units to integrate environmental values into ongoing decision-making structures with tools such as environmental impact assessments.

Organizational theory points to the value of pushing responsibility downward into the units whose decisions will most affect the protection of particular goals and interests. Paul Lawrence and Jay Lorsch[83] explain that a decentralized decision-making structure provides the most effective response to an uncertain external environment because it permits individu-als who are closest to the problem to react and make better-informed deci-sions. Research on decision making in the face of uncertainty further reveals that the deep knowledge of substance, people, and institutions that only one close to the problem can achieve is critical to developing and exercising the expertise and the rapid intuitive decision making at its core.[84] It also suggests that making individuals personally accountable for considering certain values in their decisions signals the importance of the value, and fosters a sense of responsibility for the outcome.[85] In such circumstances, decision makers employ more analytic and complex judgment strategies, and perceive the decisions under consideration to be more significant and less reversible should they turn out to be incorrect.[86] When it is made clear at the point of action that an individual is actively responsible for a decision whether to commit fraud, for example (rather than whether to *permit* fraud), the likelihood of misrepresentation decreases significantly.[87] The benefits of accountability in promoting meaningful decision making are especially pronounced where decision makers do not know the socially "acceptable" response—or more precisely, when those decision makers need to explain themselves to others whose views they do not know in advance. This type of accountability motivates people to become more vigilant, complex, and self-critical information processors.[88]

"Boundary spanning" relationships between firms and outside institutions that pursue goals unrelated to—and sometimes in direct tension with—the firm's bottom line can promote both attention to outside values and accountability.[89] "Networked" interactions with organizations that are external to the firm, but cooperate with it, provide bridges to different ways of understanding situations and making decisions;[90] they make visible unexamined elements of firm culture that had remained unexamined within firm culture; and they call attention within the firm to external data points that can be used for benchmarking purposes.[91] Moreover, because of their independence from the firm, the knowledge that outside partners introduce within firm boundaries can claim particular legitimacy among insiders across firm subunits.[92]

Operationalizing Privacy   These organizational insights are reflected in an emerging consensus among privacy scholars, advocates, and practitioners about corporate practices that show promise in protecting information privacy.

Meaningful privacy protection depends on its relocation from the legal domain into that of technology design and business processes.[93] Privacy's traditional orientation as a legal compliance exercise channeled privacy protection toward post hoc intervention, "undertaken well after the main design parameters have been set, an organizational structure committed, and significant costs incurred."[94] This has limited the integration of privacy values: "Clients will rarely welcome a recommendation that an entire project be taken back to the drawing board and fundamentally re-designed, and it is unrealistic to expect practitioners to make such recommendations even where it is obvious to them that a different direction at an earlier stage would have been preferable."[95]

By contrast, privacy must be integrated into corporate decision making from the very beginning of the design of products, business processes, and technology systems, "by design,"[96] and through other integrated approaches to privacy.[97] Studies of the treatment of privacy in organizations identify a suite of structural elements necessary for such an approach: "a culture of privacy that begins at the top" with CEOs and boards of directors;[98] dynamic high-level cross-organizational structures that coordinate and communicate on privacy issues;[99] governance processes that raise privacy issues early in the decision-making process;[100] and the development of distributed expertise embedded within decision-making teams, to identify privacy issues and bring them to the attention of privacy higher-ups.[101]

Privacy by design, one scholar describes, "will only be achieved when the instigators and designers of new systems recognize privacy at the outset as one of the variables that they need to consider."[102] Privacy experts knowledgeable about technological and business choices should be involved "when policies are being formulated and key choices are being made about how to meet organisational objectives."[103] This insight resonates particularly in the design of technology systems, during which decisions are made about the values embedded in computer code. The implications for privacy may remain invisible, and difficult to isolate and change after the system is put into place.[104]

Privacy impact assessments (PIAs) provide a core element of this approach. They provide an organizational tool for evaluating a project's potential effects on privacy, and identifying alternate design strategies or mitigations to avoid adverse impacts.[105] They are particularly effective when built into ongoing decision-making processes.[106] The "ideal privacy impact assessment" moreover, "is prepared by someone from inside the project and with an up-front demonstration of just how it works or is supposed to work."[107] In this way, PIAs "can expose and mitigate privacy risks, avoid adverse publicity, save money, develop an organisational culture sensitive to privacy, build trust and assist with legal compliance."[108]

In this light, scholars, advocates, and regulators have outlined a metric for corporate privacy structures likely to accommodate a broader, contextual, and dynamic understanding of privacy. Such structures emphasize comprehensive information privacy programs[109] that engage in both compliance and privacy risk analysis; employ privacy impact assessments, privacy design processes, and empowered privacy and data protection officers; and require greater attention and commitment to the institutional processes of privacy.[110]

THE REGULATORY "FIELD"

The socio-legal tradition has long emphasized that comprehending law's effect "in the real world" requires looking beyond statutes as they appear "on the books" to law as it operates "in action."[111] In the context of regulation, understanding law's "salience and meaning to legal decision makers and legal subjects" requires inquiry into the range of forces shaping the way that those subject to legal mandates "attend to, understand, or redefine legal rules, rights, and liabilities."[112]

Such inquiry, then, requires consideration of both strategic and substantive choices reflected in legal texts and the behavior of those government actors responsible for applying, interpreting, and enforcing regulation. At the same time, it must also engage "a far broader range of stakeholders" than regulators alone.[113] It must take account of what sociologists understand as the legal, or regulatory "field"—"the environment within which legal institutions and legal actors interact and in which conceptions of legality and compliance evolve."[114]

Regulatory Styles Regulators adopt a variety of styles[115]—reflected in the framing of legal mandates, the choice of regulatory instruments or "tools," and the general approach to regulation and enforcement—that shape their relationship with, and the behavior of, regulated parties.

The traditional "command-and-control" regulatory model envisions a centralized expert government body that promulgates clear and concrete legal mandates that seek to achieve particular outcomes by articulating, specific, ex ante, universal rules requiring certain conduct or the achievement of particular measurable outcomes.[116] The shortcomings of such forms of regulation have been well documented. Specific rules often cannot reflect the large number of variables involved in addressing complex regulatory problems[117] as they arise in heterogeneous firms and varied contexts.[118] Moreover, outside regulators are poorly situated to assess and mediate risks within the workings of individual companies.[119] Finally, static rules perform particularly poorly in anticipating risk created by rapid changes in technology and business models.

At the same time, rule-based regulation systems can have detrimental effects on decisions within the organizations they govern. They lead to a process of bureaucratization that results in "goal displacement," by which compliance with partial but specific rules—originally promulgated as a means for achieving a regulatory goal—becomes the singular end.[120] Moreover, when rules of action are communicated in a centralized top-down fashion, they can disempower those within organizations who are charged with carrying out those policies, constraining internal pressures for greater resources and attention.[121] These effects can lead to routinized "check-the-box" forms of compliance and crowd out meaningful organizational attempts to achieve public policy goals.[122]

Faced with the shortcomings of traditional approaches, regulators have turned to a range of other methods. In particular, scholars have identified a suite of "new governance" approaches that show particular promise when it is difficult to articulate particular measurable behaviors or outcomes. These include "management-based" mandates[123] or "enforced self-regulation,"[124] requiring that regulated firms develop individualized, internal risk-management processes; "soft" or nonbinding approaches such as dialogue with interested parties, speeches by regulators, educational activities, and the issuance of interpretive or guidance documents;[125] activities to promote field transparency, such as the collection and publication of data and information-disclosure requirements;[126] and the strategic use of limited enforcement resources to send signals about evolving regulator understandings of legal requirements. By supplementing, or sometimes replacing, codified commands with more open-ended directives, these methods create ambiguity and uncertainty about the appropriate application of regulatory requirements in particular contexts, leaving significant discretion in their application. Such discretion permits evolving interpretation by administrative agencies themselves, and leaves space for regulated firms to exercise their own judgment and expertise in experimenting with different methods of implementation.[127]

Scholarship on corporate compliance and organizational behavior suggests that this suite of approaches can have profound effects on the behavior of regulated firms. Inside the firm, collaboration with those who have "on the ground" knowledge and expertise can lead to specific management choices that address granular challenges to achieving public goals.[128] Outside the firm, by a combination of coordination, education, and coercive functions, new governance approaches can create pressure on regulated parties to move away from static, check-the-box compliance toward the ongoing development of meaningful internal practices.[129] As Lauren Edelman and Mark Suchman describe, "ambiguous mandates and uneven enforcement may actually heighten law's cognitive salience, as organizations struggle to make sense of legal uncertainties and to develop shared definitions of acceptable compliance."[130]

Most importantly, such approaches can shift the locus of privacy expertise to the corporation itself.[131] Uncertainty and dynamism in the meaning of legal requirements, combined with the shadow of legal enforcement, can encourage firms to invest in subject matter experts charged with legal compliance, and enhance their influence[132] and autonomy.[133]

The Social License to Operate   An understanding of the regulatory field, moreover, must appreciate not only top-down constraints imposed by government, but "all processes of governing, whether undertaken by a government, market or network, whether over a . . . formal or informal organization or territory and whether through laws, norms, power or language."[134]

In the corporate context, such broader normative forces combine to create a "social license to operate"[135] that constrains behavior, reflecting "theories that emphasize the importance of a firm's social standing and in particular its economic stake in maintaining its reputation for . . . good citizenship."[136] Such a social license is comprised of a combination of legality, market pressures, and the concerns of social actors. It is not static, but is "interactive," "open to interpretation, negotiation," and "amendment."[137]

Scholars examining environmental protection have identified how the social license intersects with the insights of public choice theory about the difficulties in creating a political constituency when the number of affected parties is large, and individual economic interest is small or uncertain, as is the case with privacy. In particular, participation by a variety of stakeholders—including advocates, professionals, consumer groups, and others—in the governance dialogue can aggregate otherwise dispersed market pressures to produce forces that scholars of corporate regulation flag as important to "beyond compliance" behavior: visibility, community concern, and threat to economic investment.[138]

Studying governance through the lens of the regulatory field illuminates how formal national and state regulators can shape firms' social license by enlisting and empowering nongovernmental forces, promoting transparency about corporate behavior, creating fora for nongovernmental actors to discuss policy, and collaborating with relevant parties to shape evolving best practices when traditional approaches are insufficient. Thus it reveals "sets of formal institutional and informal linkages between governmental and other actors structured around shared if endlessly negotiated beliefs and interests in public policy making and implementation."[139]

Policy Diffusion A focus on governance further includes elements that transcend, and transmit the diffusion of norms across organizational and national boundaries. These include international networks of regulators and other government officials collaborating on approaches to global problems.[140] They also embrace private governance forces, including networks of activists and stakeholders formed around issues,[141] the media,[142] industry bodies, and professional associations that shape and transmit notions of best practices. These forces are critical to developing the "self-regulatory instruments"— codes of practice, standards, and privacy protection seals—identified as particularly promising in protecting privacy.[143]

Professionals constitute a particularly robust force in shaping norms and behavior within and across organizations and nations. By one influential account, professionals comprise the "most influential, contemporary crafters of institutions."[144] They create cultural and epistemic frameworks for ordering knowledge, they "devise and promulgate principles specifying what individuals, groups, organizations, and states 'should' do"; and they often oversee and enforce these rules.[145] Professionalism's normative power underlies its strength as a source of organizational change.[146] The degree of professionalization, moreover, influences the ability of an occupation to promote the diffusion of knowledge and practice.[147]

Scholars have identified two distinct professional models: the "social trustee model of professionalism" that "stresses the altruistic, civic-minded, moral aspects of professional status";[148] and the technical expertise model, where skill and knowledge are the defining attribute. The combination of those roles can strengthen the professional's capacity to transmit external norms within an organization,[149] reflecting the ability to influence both norms and practices, in both hard and soft ways.[150]

Privacy Governance   Comparative privacy governance scholarship reflects these socio-legal insights about the importance of regulatory style and the mix of public and private governance forces in the construction of the privacy field. David H. Flaherty's five-country analysis of the implementation of privacy laws in the United States, Europe and Canada,[151] and Colin J. Bennett's study of privacy regulation in the United States and three European countries,[152] underscore the critical way that legal frameworks are mediated through government institutions, policy styles and regulatory choices.[153] Charles Raab and Bert-Jaap Koops emphasize the importance of going beyond "nam[ing] the parts" involved in a privacy regime to "comprehend their relationships and contributions toward producing a regulatory output and outcome."[154] A closer examination of those "actors," and their "roles" can, among other things, identify gaps in the regulatory regimes.[155] Together, they demonstrate that despite a common set of substantive and procedural principles, the implementation of privacy protections has diverged significantly between countries; and they illuminate the importance in identifying convergences and divergences between national regulatory approaches, and the elements producing them.

Further scholarship builds on these themes by identifying additional elements salient to privacy governance. Bennett and Raab catalog and assess "policy instruments" employed in the governance of privacy, extending from legal instruments adopted by regulatory agencies to transnational policy instruments, self-regulatory instruments, and technological tools—and the way they combine in various "privacy regimes."[156] Individually, Bennett has documented the rise of an international network of civil society privacy advocates, whose success in various jurisdictions differs.[157] Abraham Newman and Francesca Bignami have each developed important multicountry accounts of privacy's comparative development[158] that emphasize both national approaches and transnational networks,[159] which

Newman in particular argues have converged on European regulatory forms. Nick Doty and Deirdre Mulligan describe the way that processes enabling multistakeholder participation in "co-creat[ing]" privacy norms that play the important "boundary-spanning" role of bringing in a range of perspectives, which is particularly useful when technical and social changes pose new challenges.[160]

Policy Reform and Legal Culture   Finally, the socio-legal insight that regulation operates through the interaction among institutional, social, and normative forces "in which conceptions of legality and compliance evolve," combined with privacy scholarship documenting the meaningful divergence between national privacy regimes, together frame a caution for the normative project of policy prescription. The project of law reform, by necessity, often involves attempts to "transplant" legal approaches deemed successful from one jurisdiction to another, or to "harmonize" regulations across national boundaries.[161] Yet the fact that the operation of such approaches or regulations is mediated by "legal culture"— defined by Lawrence Friedman as the "social forces constantly at work on the law"[162]— can alter their operation in significant, and unexpected ways. Thus law reform proponents have often despaired at the difficulty of changing legal frameworks.[163]

This is not to say that such efforts are doomed to fail. Legal cultures are not static, and formal legal changes, shifts in regulatory approach, and pluralistic inputs into the regulatory field all contribute to that dynamism. Indeed, scholarship on the European Union has identified both convergence in member states' approaches to a range of substantive legal areas,[164] and the emergence of a new "European legal culture."[165] At the same time, the challenge posed by legal culture counsels more detailed study of what Friedman called the "impact" of the legal system on behavior in the "world outside," which is "usually overlooked, assumed, or ignored," but then provides feedback that can affect "the system itself."[166]

FRAMING A RESEARCH INQUIRY IN LIGHT OF THE LITERATURE

Since Smith's study more than two decades ago (discussed in chapter 1), no one has conducted a sustained empirical inquiry into the manner in which corporations actually manage privacy, and what elements of the regulatory "field" motivate them.[167] Further, no one has ever conducted a comparative inquiry across jurisdictions.

This is not surprising. For a variety of reasons, Robert Kagan explains, "[w]hile most socio-legal studies of regulatory enforcement have sought to *explain why* implementation style varies, there has been less research concerning the *consequences* of variation in enforcement methods—that is, how regulatory style affects the day-to-day responses of regulated entities."[168]

Our project takes seriously the notion that understanding legal regimes requires a granular appreciation of institutions, styles, approaches, and tools. At the same time, it seeks to expand the inquiry deeper into the privacy landscape, adding to appreciation of top-down governance elements consideration of the corporate privacy practices that have emerged in the shadow of different legal choices.

We embarked on a wide-ranging project, across five jurisdictions in North America and Europe, to collect qualitative and quantitative empirical information documenting privacy's operationalization "on the ground." By examining five distinct jurisdictions the project took advantage of variations in national implementation of data protection and information privacy to conduct a comparative, in-the-wild assessment of their efficacy and appropriateness.

The privacy and governance literatures frame our research questions. Privacy scholarship explores the challenges created by revolutionary technological change and emphasizes the necessity of a move from a "data protection" framework to a "privacy" orientation that reflects context, social meaning, and the public good. Academics, as well as policymakers and professionals possessing greatest familiarity with privacy in the corporate context, have converged on a set of prescriptions regarding the best practices in privacy's "operationalization." Together, they generate important questions regarding whether at least the leading corporations in different jurisdictions have adapted their understandings and practices accordingly:

• Are those firms' internal operations focused primarily on compliance with concrete legal mandates regarding data protection and information privacy? Or do they reflect more expansive understandings of the ways privacy can be harmed?

• Have they developed practices oriented toward vindicating such understandings, such as embedding processes that actively surface privacy implications early in product and technology development?
• Do they have a culture of privacy?

The scholarship exploring governance tools, styles, and actors that comprise a regulatory field expands the lens wider. That research underscores the importance of inquiry into a range of forces that "regulate" corporate behavior. In the privacy context, it generates important questions about the ways in which those forces have, or have not, combined to shape corporate understandings and practices.

• Which approaches have regulators employed?
• To which have firms responded?
• What other factors have shaped the corporate construction of privacy's meaning, and the means for its protection?

Finally, the literatures on comparative privacy governance offer analytic direction:

• What does the behavior of corporations in different jurisdictions suggest about differently constructed national privacy fields, and different national regulatory styles?
• Might the comparative analysis of privacy fields and the behavior of regulatory targets offer lessons for policy reform?

METHODOLOGY

Central to this project was the execution of semistructured qualitative interviews with fifty-three privacy "leads"—corporate managers or officers in charge of the privacy function within their firms—in the United States (nine), Germany (nine), France (twelve), Spain (twelve), and the United Kingdom (eleven). The four European jurisdictions were chosen because, as discussed in chapter 3, although they are all governed by the EU Privacy Directive framework, they diverge in both the history and timing of the institutionalization of their privacy laws, and the different regulatory styles for which they are known. The privacy leads interviewed are referred to in this book as "chief privacy officers" (CPOs) or "data privacy officers" (DPOs). Using a snowball-sampling technique, they were identified as regional leaders by domain experts—leading members of the privacy field (both lawyers and nonlawyers) including academics, legal practitioners (in-house and firms), members of trade groups and advocacy groups, and regulators.

To conduct our research, we had to gain the trust and confidence of high-level professionals in five countries. They shared private, and sometimes proprietary and confidential information about their day-to-day work, their successes, and their struggles, as well as details about firm organization, policies, processes, and tools. Key to their participation was a promise of confidentiality regarding their identity and that of their firms, as well as their responses. By operation of this commitment, this book presents certain types of information about our interview cohorts, but not others. Because of the elite nature of the experts and the attributes of the firms, it would otherwise be too easy for others in the small field to identify them.

In each country, our informants came largely from firms headquartered in the relevant jurisdiction. In the United States and Germany, all the firms were domestically based. The French, UK, and Spanish samples also included several privacy leads at domestic subsidiaries of foreign companies (two of twelve in France, two of eleven in the UK, and four of twelve in Spain).

Moreover, with two exceptions, all were large firms—indeed, at least 50 percent of the domestically based entities in each cohort appear on the "*Forbes* 2000" list of largest global corporations.[169] This is not surprising. Large entities are most likely to be targeted by regulators and plaintiffs, to have the greatest compliance capacity,[170] and to have strong interests in establishing a positive reputation for compliance.[171] At the same time, because of these attributes, they "can be viewed as sensitive receptors and reflectors of differences in the demands actually made by different regulatory and legal regimes." In short, large companies "provide a unique perspective on some ways in which differences in law and regulatory practices really matter."[172]

Beyond size, our respondents came from companies that are heterogeneous. Some claim global presence, others only a domestic scope. Some include highly diversified business lines, while others are focused within a single industry. Many focus on technology-intensive products and services, while others engage in more traditional lines of business. Moreover, those interviewed have varied personal characteristics—some are lawyers, others come with a technology background or from business units—and work in different settings. For example, some work under the auspices of the corporate legal department, while others work as freestanding officers.

Initial interviews, running an hour-and-a-half to two-and-a-quarter hours, were conducted (with the exception of two telephone interviews) in person between 2008 and 2013; European interviews took place from 2010 to 2013. Follow up inquiries with the U.S. respondents were conducted in 2012 and 2015 to ensure the continued validity of their responses. The interviews followed an interview protocol that focused on the duties of the privacy lead; privacy's meaning within the corporation; external and internal factors that have driven the company's privacy practices or policies, corporate implementation, evaluation, and policymaking around privacy; and the role of the companies in participating in, or shaping public discourse and policy. Foreign-language translators were provided when requested. Interviews were recorded and transcribed.

Our interviews probed how corporations defined "privacy" in their work. To avoid influencing the discussion by prompting respondents with, or directing them to, particular constructs of privacy, we avoided the terms "information privacy" and "data protection" in our questions. We phrased questions more broadly in terms of privacy to allow respondents to define and narrow what work of the firm fell under that definition. When respondents introduced either term, or others such as "consumer expectation," "private life," or "fairness," we used their terms, but also reverted back to the privacy terminology regularly to see if other definitions or constructs were provided. Similarly, we framed questions about "law" broadly, again to avoid narrowly focusing our subjects' responses on information privacy and data protection laws, and instead inviting them to speak more broadly about whatever laws and regulations influenced their privacy work.

Throughout our research, we were conscious of both the strengths and limits of our selection methods. Because snowball sampling relies on social networks, it provides a particularly useful method for investigating small populations of individuals who possess unique information because of their experience,[173] especially when such experts are both difficult to identify and access because of their elite status, and the nonpublic nature of their work.[174] Additionally, because it identifies participants with thick social networks in a field, this sampling method provides a means for capturing the way in which "key informants" at the center of the privacy field reflect the broader privacy discourse of which they are a part.[175] At the same time, such a nonrandom sampling method does not produce findings that can be statistically representative of any larger population. Our interview data cannot support unqualified generalizations about the understandings and practices of privacy officers or firms broadly. They must be understood as the responses of the particular set of privacy officers identified by others to us as leaders.

Focusing on interviews of "elites"[176] raises additional issues regarding the motives of participating subjects.[177] Whether consciously or not, elites can skew their answers in one direction or another, or subtly take control of an interview, in order to use the researcher for their own ends or protect themselves from criticism.[178] Thus such interviews raise the concern about accepting, without further consideration or deeper probing, responses that may represent simply "well-practiced narratives."[179] This underscores the importance of examining other material, including compliance materials and corporate records, in addition to corporate interview subjects' evaluative opinions.[180]

With this in mind, our research did not end with these initial interviews. Each firm was asked to complete written questionnaires about the background and qualifications of the interviewed privacy lead, as well as the history, size, and scope of their internal privacy program. Follow-up interviews were conducted in person, by telephone, and over email to collect additional information about corporate practices and procedures, and confirm the continued validity of the data. The firms' policy and practice materials—including employee training materials and internal organizational charts—were shared both in person and remotely, by access to intranet resources, and over the Internet. Where possible, we met with other firm employees, including engineers and managers responsible for policy implementation, and viewed (sometimes after signing nondisclosure agreements) process documentation and technology systems.

We also conducted an additional twenty-six interviews with leading members of the privacy field, including former and current regulators, academics, lawyers, and other privacy professionals. Most of these unstructured interviews were recorded; the remainder were captured through detailed notes. These interviews were instrumental in contextualizing the responses of the privacy leads.

Those latter interviews were central to the development of the detailed descriptions of the U.S. and German regulatory fields that will be presented in chapters 10 and 11. As described in chapter 9, our initial interviews with privacy leads revealed parallel developments in the corporate operationalization of privacy in those two countries, but not the other three. These developments were identified as promising, evaluated in light of the emerging consensus regarding privacy best practices described in the literature discussed earlier. Drawing on these interviews, as well as on legal and historical materials, we engaged in richer case studies of the privacy fields in those two countries,[181] focusing on the elements of the regulatory field identified as important by the interviewed privacy leads in those jurisdictions. That in turn permitted us to highlight different elements in each jurisdiction that played similar roles in constructing the privacy field, and in turn, offer "grounded" suggestions as to how parallel elements might be encouraged in other contexts.[182]

III Privacy on the Ground

3   Background Law

THE UNITED STATES AND EUROPE

Europe moved first to institutionalize Fair Information Practices robustly and in a consistent manner. In 1981, the Council of Europe adopted its Convention for the Protection of Individuals with Regard to Automatic Processing of Personal Data recognizing privacy as a "fundamental value," granting individuals safeguards to control their "automated personal data file," and articulating limits on transborder data transfers.[1] The European Union's 1995 Privacy Directive,[2] moreover, reflects the notion that a full implementation of the FIPs requires two institutions: (1) omnibus laws governing information collection and use regardless of type and sector; and (2) to administer these laws, a strong, single privacy enforcement authority that "knows exactly when to use the carrot and when to use the stick, and who is not concerned with balancing data protection with other administrative and political values."[3]

These omnibus protections reflect a commitment to self-determination enforced uniformly by a dedicated privacy agency, and typify what Abraham Newman has termed a "comprehensive" privacy regime.[4] Shaped in its detail by regulatory networks within Europe, it is an image of a privacy governance scheme that, as Newman describes, has spread globally,[5] and reflects the influence of the 1995 European Union Data Protection Directive's limit on the transfer of data to parties in third countries that do not provide an "adequate level of protection."[6] It has served, moreover, as the dominant metric for assessing the adequacy of U.S. regulation.[7]

In general, commentators have found the U.S. privacy framework lacking in comparison to the European approach.[8] "[I]n contrast to the approach in many other nations," one scholar explains, "it is unusual in the United States to find any comprehensive privacy laws . . . that enumerate a complete set of rights and responsibilities for those who process personal data."[9] U.S. privacy regulations target "specific, sectoral activities," such as credit reporting (the Fair Credit Reporting Act, or "FCRA"[10]), health care (the Health Insurance Portability and Accountability Act, or "HIPAA"[11]), and financial institutions (the Gramm-Leach-Bliley Financial Services Modernization Act, or "GLBA"[12]). Accordingly, numerous different laws govern informational privacy, setting forth divergent requirements for the treatment of information by type and business sector. These laws are administered by multiple government agencies—GLBA alone gave authority to eight federal agencies to administer and enforce its Financial Privacy Rule[13]— or sometimes by no agency at all.[14] The Federal Trade Commission[15] and states' attorneys general[16] have taken an active role in privacy regulation pursuant to their consumer protection mandates. Companies doing business abroad, moreover, face the restrictions of European regulation. While the U.S. regime has not been determined to meet the "adequacy" standard, a "safe harbor" framework permits individual U.S. firms to self-certify their privacy practices, thereby allowing transfers of personal information from European countries.[17]

The policies behind U.S. statutes also vary considerably. FCRA and the Privacy Act of 1974,[18] which regulates the collection and use of data by the federal government, reflect the FIPs' "informational self-determination" rubric, and include a full range of safeguards based on the principles of notice and informed consent.[19] In contrast, more recent privacy measures have developed in response to the concerns of individuals, as well as concerns about threats to other interests. Such concerns highlight privacy as an instrumental means of promoting social goals, such as the efficacy of doctor-patient relationships or of commercial exchanges, including the notion that "privacy laws might promote confidence in Internet commerce, with benefits both for surfers' privacy and companies' sales."[20]

Such instrumental justifications, and the approach of balancing privacy with other values, were reflected in formative decisions regarding the governance of privacy on the Internet. Limited government mandates were to be supplemented by significant reliance on "self-regulation" by industry players.[21]

In short, as one scholar has described:

[T]wo dominant models have emerged, reflecting two very different approaches to the control of information. The European Union . . . has enacted a sweeping data protection directive that imposes significant restrictions on most data collection, processing, dissemination, and storage activities, not only within Europe, but throughout the world if the data originates in a member state. The United States has taken a very different approach that extensively regulates government processing of data, while facilitating private, market-based initiatives to address private-sector data processing.[22]

This focus has undergirded a widespread and coherent critique of U.S. privacy regulation. Many argue that the "patchwork"[23] nature of U.S. privacy laws leaves the United States with gaps in data coverage, confusion among regulated entities and consumers, and a tapestry of specific laws typically tied to specific technologies and business practices[24] Critics describe U.S. protections as "FIPs-lite,"[25] a less robust approach than the FIPs-based protections in European mandates.[26] Self-regulation, they argue, is bound to fail in the absence of external incentives for information protection.[27] Moreover, by adopting market-oriented rationales for privacy protection, critics contend, the United States devalues the moral weight of privacy and its role in a democratic society.[28]

THE EU MEMBER STATES

While approaches to privacy regulation differ significantly between the United States and Europe, the shape of such regulation also varies significantly among the four EU member states we studied: Germany, Spain, France, and the United Kingdom. The 1995 directive, like all EU Directives, was addressed to member states, but was not legally binding on citizens until "transposed," or implemented through national laws. As a result, while each EU member nation complied with the general floor set by the governing framework, they diverged in important detail, reflecting distinct histories of privacy regulation, agency models, enforcement approaches, penalty structures, and even formal rules.[29] This in turn led to the evolution of different means of exercising enforcement authority and different definitions of privacy in light of each nation's political culture and social context.

GERMANY

Germany is often credited with being the birthplace of data protection. In October 1970, the state of Hesse enacted the world's first data protection law, which governed the use of data in the public sector.[30] After five years of vigorous debate during which other states pressed for national action,[31] data protection was extended nationally, and to the private sector, with the passage in 1977 of a Federal Data Protection Act (BDSG).[32]

These developments reflect an important aspect of the country's legal system: its federalist structure. Article 30 of the German Basic Law[33] provides that Germany's states, or *Länder* (which now total sixteen) have default legislative and administrative competency, except to the extent prescribed elsewhere in the Basic Law. While the national government has sole competence for subject matters such as defense and immigration, jurisdiction over other issues is shared between the *Länder* and federal government. Under the BDSG, data protection is governed by both federal and state laws, and supervision and enforcement regarding the private sector is delegated to the supervisory authorities—data protection authorities (DPAs)—in the states.[34] The federal data protection commissioner, by contrast, has only jurisdiction over the public sector.

Notions of privacy and data protection received their strongest grounding as fundamental rights in the German Constitutional Court's 1983 Census Decision (*Volkszählungsurteil*). In that case, the court articulated a right to "informational self-determination" (*informationelle selbstbestimmung*) in the German Constitution, based on the express rights to human dignity and personal liberty through the associated right to develop one's personality.[35] The right of personality, the court held, is a broad notion, the content of which is "not specified ultimately" in legal practice. It includes "the authority of the individual to decide himself, on the basis of the idea of self-determination, when and within what limits determine what information about his private life should be communicated to others and to what extent."[36]

In the context of this constitutional commitment, the BDSG has imposed requirements of fair information collection, processing, and use. It also established a requirement that automated processing procedures be registered with the competent supervisory authority in advance. This requirement of prior "registration," or "notification," is characteristic of European approaches to regulating data privacy. Yet as a practical matter, registration plays a reduced role in Germany, unlike the situation in many other EU countries.

The relative unimportance of registration arises from a waiver of the law for firms that have appointed a *betriebliche Datenschutzbeauftragter*, or data protection officer, which was required in many contexts. Specifically, any company or organization employing more than four employees in its automated personal data processing operations, employing more than twenty employees in manual personal data processing, or that processes especially sensitive data or use complex systems,[37] must engage a DPO. The DPO is either a direct employee of the firm or an outside expert,[38] tasked with monitoring company projects that involve the processing of personal data. The DPO's aim is to fulfill the provisions of federal and state data protection laws.[39] To ensure an officer's independence, the BDSG requires that the officer report directly to the company's management.[40] The company must fund continuing training for the officer and not discriminate against him or her.[41] The officer must have access to all relevant documents and data-processing locations, and be included in data-related projects and decisions.[42] Companies, and individual managers may be fined for failing, intentionally or through negligence, to appoint a DPO, appointing an unqualified individual, or failing to provide the DPO with adequate resources.[43]

Thus, as comparative law scholar Francesca Bignami describes, Germany had a well-developed set of rules, institutions, and practices already in place that influenced the transposition of the 1995 EU Directive through the amendment of the federal law in 2001.[44] These included, on the one hand, a commitment to the fundamental nature of privacy rights and their embodiment in principles of informational self-determination, as well as "more precise and legally binding" directives.[45] On the other, they involved the institutionalization of enforcement in a multiplicity of regulators situated in "a political system based on consensus and compromise."[46]

This orientation is reflected in what Bignami documents as an "open-ended"[47] and "managerial"[48] regulatory style characterized by a combination of openness to "organized interests,"[49] reliance on self-regulatory instruments through delegation of some standards-making and standards-enforcement authority to industry groups,[50] and "negotiated compliance."[51] These institutions and data protection practices reflect what others have characterized as Germany's belief in individuals' and industry's capacity to act appropriately, and to identify and conform their behavior to the law[52]— seen as well as the limited sanction authority initially accorded the state authorities.

Amendments to the federal act enacted in 2009 have augmented the DPAs' enforcement authority and ability to impose penalties,[53] adding "deterrence-oriented enforcement"[54] to their regulatory toolbox.

SPAIN

While Germany was the first in the world to enact a data protection statute, Spain was the last in the jurisdictions we studied. This timing reflects broader political developments, arising from the country's late experience with fascism, and its post-Francoist transition to democracy in the late 1970s and early 1980s. As late as 2010, an OECD study of regulation in Spain reported that the "corporatist legacy and legal traditions stand in the way of a more modern approach, especially in terms of improving transparency and instilling a more economically-aware perspective into the rule-making process."[55] Notwithstanding, that report described Spain's "profound transformations over the last two to three decades," noting that "public administration has undergone a profound remodeling to fit the new context of democracy and decentralization."[56]

In 1978, the country adopted a new constitution, which stated, "the law shall restrict the use of informatics in order to protect the honor and the personal and family privacy of Spanish citizens, as well as the full exercise of their rights."[57] The country's first data protection act was enacted in 1992, which established a system by which anyone who created an automatic data file must first file a notification, and set forth principles governing the use of personal data.[58] A national data protection authority, the Agencia Española de Protección de Datos (AEPD), was established the next year by Royal Decree.[59]

A 1999 law, the Ley Orgánica de Proteccion de Datos de Caracter Personal (the PCP or LOPD), was enacted to transpose the 1995 EU Directive.[60] The LOPD preserved the structure of the 1992 act, and as amended again in 2008, and has been characterized as creating one of the toughest privacy regimes in the European Union.[61] The AEPD has robust interpretation, investigation, and prosecution powers, including the authority to impose large fines.[62] It has grown in recent years, measured along any dimension—staff, cases, and penalties.[63]

Several attributes of the Spanish data protection regime reflect a unique orientation. First, the "prior notification" or registration process differs in Spain from elsewhere in the EU in its detail and scope. Instead of maintaining a register of all data controllers, Spain "maintains a register of all databases containing personal information. Therefore, a single data controller can have multiple registrations."[64] By 2007, 1,017,266 databases were registered with the Data Protection General Registry.[65]

Second, infringing the law at any level can lead to significant penalties. Infringements are classified by category: minor, serious, and very serious.[66] Minor infringements include failing to submit a required notification to the AEPD, or failing to provide notice to an individual before the collection of personal data, for which penalties range from 900€ to 40,000€.[67] Serious infringements include "failing to implement adequate security measures,"[68] for which penalties range from 40,000€ to 300,000€. Very serious infringements include transferring data without prior authorization to countries that do not provide an adequate level of protection, which can trigger penalties from 300,000€ to 600,000€.[69] Fines can be adjusted upward or downward depending on damages, benefit obtained from infringement, and level of culpability.[70]

Fines have steadily increased in Spain—in 2007, the AEPD imposed 399 sanctions with a total of €19.6 million in fines; in 2012 those numbers were 557 and € 21.1 million respectively.[71] The most inspected and sanctioned sector is what the AEPD calls the "telecommunications sector," followed by video surveillance, financial/banking, Internet, and commercial communications.[72] In 2012, that sector accounted for 71 percent of the fines levied by the AEPD, and 289 of the 863 agency infringement decisions.[73] Of note is the recent €900,000 fine levied against Google for failing to provide users with sufficient information on its data collection processes.[74] The total penalty, made up of three separate €300,000 fines, demonstrates how the AEPD can aggregate fines for each breach within a single case to reach very large total fines.

Together, these elements have reflected a data protection regime focused on regulatory filings, an aggressive enforcement agency, and harsh penalties.[75]

FRANCE

Modern French law reflects its orientation as a "civil law" jurisdiction, to the extent that the French Civil Code of 1804 has been credited with structuring the country's development "from its traditional to its modern form."[76] As a substantive matter, the Napoleonic code integrated into the civil law principles of freedom and equality. Procedurally, it institutionalized a "disciplinary centralized state."[77]

A recent OECD study of regulation in France describes the modern instantiation of these civil law characteristics.[78] It depicts a public governance regime characterized by strong central government; professionalized public servants chosen by a competitive examination system, a relatively "closed attitude" toward outside input into policymaking, and a mass of regulations which are not conducive to smoothness and flexibility."[79]

The report describes how the use of "new laws and the symbolic force of the law" as a "means of communication" about values, and as a response to "crises, professional lobbying, and public opinion," still "permeates French culture."[80] At the same time, the employment of law in this manner creates a "massive reliance" on regulation, described by some as the "French malady."[81]

French privacy law has reflected this combination of substantive and institutional characteristics. The country's early adoption of its data protection act[82] in 1978 was indeed spurred by a crisis. As with the German state of Hesse's pioneering data privacy law, the French act targeted a program of government data collection that triggered public outrage—in this case, an attempt by the French government to create a centralized database of personal data allowing French citizens to be personally identified by different government agencies, known as "SAFARI."[83]

The law established a strong, independent, data privacy administrative body, the Commission Nationale de l'Informatique et des Libertés (CNIL), whose duties have traditionally reflected the centralized licensing and approval model. Pursuant to the law, as subsequently amended, the CNIL keeps an inventory of data processing operations in the private sector through a three-level system of "notification" and pre-approval—depending on the type and level of automation of the processing—to ensure that individual rights regarding that data, such as rights to access and inspection, are vindicated.[84] The agency is, in turn, vested with powers of advice and consultation to ensure that individual firms comply with these requirements and protect these rights. It also has the power to inspect and audit corporate practices and punish noncompliance with fines of up to EUR 300,000.[85]

As Francesca Bignami describes, the CNIL's centralized approach has traditionally reflected the tendency toward procedures "determined by bureaucratic elites."[86] While privacy is considered a fundamental human right, vindication of the right is not left to individuals but rather to public servants.[87] Operationally, moreover, while the authority had both "licensing, registration, and rulemaking powers,"[88] and "considerable investigation and sanctioning powers," CNIL officials traditionally used only the former in a robust manner.[89]

The 2004 amendments to the data protection act,[90] Bignami described, shifted emphasis from forward-looking licensing to "deterrence-oriented enforcement,"[91] involving the investigation of privacy breaches and the punishment of offenders.[92] They also provided a method for streamlining firm interaction with the regulator by creating the position of a correspondant informatique et libertés (CIL).[93] The CIL is a data privacy officer or "correspondent" position that firms can voluntarily designate to assist the organization with respect to data privacy compliance, and to serve as a means of communication between the firm and the CNIL.[94] The appointment of the CIL provides compliance advantages to corporations by exempting them from many CNIL notification processes and placing the duty of ascertaining compliance on the designated agent within the firm.[95] Designating a CIL also facilitates the conveyance of administrative advice and guidance into the firm. CILs have access to a designated office within the CNIL for CIL communication that offers resources such as an extranet site dedicated to these DPOs and that provides "a platform for preferential exchanges, fora, Q&As, form specimens, and training material prepared by CNIL departments."[96]

THE UNITED KINGDOM

The British regulatory style reflects multiple approaches to governance. Traditionally, Michael Moran describes, "the British have been reluctant to codify rules in details, and correspondingly reliant on trust and implicit understandings," as well as on the involvement of "private associations," in "the life of self-regulatory systems."[97] Against this background, however, the British system of governance has, since the 1980s, integrated "increasing institutional formality and hierarchy, where the authority of public institutions has been reinforced . . . by substantial fresh investment in bureaucratic resources to ensure compliance."[98]

The changes have shaped a British regulatory system characterized by governance approaches that combine several "hybrids of controls."[99] This hybridization inevitably embraces modes of governance in tension with one another. As an initial matter, the system reflects transparency and openness to outside forces. It makes "systematic information accessible both to insiders and outsiders," and employs "reporting and control mechanisms that offer the chance of public control."[100] It emphasizes "accountability and transparency of public services," which requires public oversight.[101] This, in turn, has led to significant growth: total staffing in public sector regulatory bodies grew 90 percent between 1976 and 1995 alone.[102]

At the same time, the British regulatory state is characterized both by increasing formalization of rules and regulatory institutions, and "higher investment in oversight regulation (compounded with performance measurement),"[103] including "technologies of regulation, most notably enforced self-regulation and meta-regulation"[104] that limit the role of the state in direct management.

British regulation of privacy and data protection reflects these competing impulses, which may explain why it rests more uneasily within the European framework than the other studied jurisdictions. The UK, which does not have a tradition of fundamental rights or a written Constitution, first enacted a data protection law in 1984,[105] in response to the 1981 Council of Europe Convention.[106] As Francesca Bignami explains, the legislation was driven by UK policymakers' fear that failure to join the Convention would undermine the competitiveness of British industry. Accordingly, "[i]n the regulatory practice that followed, data privacy was conceived largely as a matter of good corporate practices and responsible management of information systems, not as a question of individual rights."[107]

The act's framework included registration of databanks with a formally independent Data Protection Registrar (later called the Information Commissioner's Office, or "ICO")[108] But it also included the development of industry-developed voluntary codes of practice, and administrative dispute resolution. The regulator was accorded only limited investigative and enforcement powers, and had no authority to inspect premises or compel information without a court warrant.

The law was expanded in 1998 to implement the EU Directive.[109] While the 1998 act was "tighter and more comprehensive" than the earlier law, a 2010 European Commission study described it as "quirky" and "extremely complex."[110] That report opined that the UK act "still, in many ways, fails to fully implement the requirements" of the 1995 European framework.[111]

Such critiques focus on narrow interpretations of some of the act's language by the ICO and in judicial opinions[112]—interpretations that reflect, in more sympathetic terms, a "pragmatic" rather than "excessively legalistic" approach.[113]

One particular area of debate involves the ICO's view that consent to the use and processing of data can be "implied."[114] In the ICO's view, "it is better to concentrate on making sure that you treat individuals fairly rather than on obtaining consent in isolation,"[115] reflecting what Bignami has characterized as the ICO's "especially flexible" approach to regulatory standards.

While the ICO has not characteristically engaged in vigorous enforcement,[116] it was granted expanded powers in 2010, including the ability to impose criminal penalties of up to £500,000. Since that time, the ICO has markedly increased its enforcement activities, through fines, enforcement notices, and prosecutions.[117]

These national variations in defining and implementing privacy protection offer a living laboratory in which to explore the specific outcomes of regulatory choices. The regulatory diversity provides an opportunity for an assessment of privacy "on the ground" that explores the way that formal legal frameworks and regulatory choices combine with social forces to shape the behaviors of the corporate targets of regulation.

4   Empirical Findings—United States

In the United States we interviewed nine chief privacy officers identified as field leaders. Our interviewees came from firms that included those governed by all the major sector-specific privacy statutes (health, financial services, credit) and from unregulated sectors; those both global in scope and only domestic; and those both with highly diversified business lines and with a single industry focus. Even those firms in more traditional lines of business use data and technology intensively. Half are part of the technology sector.

The CPOs themselves had varied personal characteristics; six were women and three were men; seven were lawyers, two had business degrees, several had operational or technical expertise and educational background; three had worked in government, while most had exclusively private-sector careers. All but one was the first person to hold the CPO title within their firm. Most had been in the position for several years, but two had recently joined their companies (both coming from long tenures as CPOs at other institutions) and been in place for approximately a year.

The interviews yielded important insights regarding perceptions about privacy's meaning, and the ways that privacy is "operationalized" within leading firms, largely reflecting a variety of forces beyond formal statutes and regulations governing privacy. Specifically, our findings suggest the development of a framework for thinking about privacy that is focused on maintaining consumer trust, rather than attending purely to legal rights, and that is tied to the potential risks privacy missteps pose to firm reputation. They further describe two important trends in the architecture of internal corporate privacy management that are perceived as integral to this risk management orientation. First, companies need a powerful and relatively autonomous professional privacy officer at the top level of management, one whose job includes substantial engagement with external stakeholders. Second, firms require architectures designed to distribute privacy decision-making throughout firm units. This is most notably achieved by (a) including privacy in existing risk management processes and (b) embedding privacy decision making within business unit structures. This embedding involves placing responsibility for setting and meeting privacy objectives on high-level business unit managers, as well as integrating into business lines a network of specially trained employees who can identify and address privacy concerns during the design phase of business development.

THE MEANING OF PRIVACY

THE LIMITED IMPORT OF THE "RULES-COMPLIANCE" APPROACH TO PRIVACY

In response to open-ended questions about the "external factors" shaping their corporations' privacy practices, respondents articulated a consistent view of the role of compliance with specific legal requirements—arising both from the United States and in the U.S. sector-based regimes. They described specific legal rules as important in establishing a floor and shaping certain "compliance-oriented" measures. At the same time, respondents indicated that legal rules played only a limited role in animating corporate processes and practices more broadly.

The Role of Legal Rules   When asked about the external or environmental forces that shaped particular practices in their firms, each respondent identified particular U.S. sectoral statutes as relevant to their firms' compliance efforts. Four, moreover, described specific actions they had taken to facilitate data transfers from European Union member countries consistent with the EU Privacy Directive, steps that included certifying to the U.S.-EU Safe Harbor program.[1]

"[O]bviously," stated one respondent, specific "statutes and regulations" shape particular privacy practices. Others described them as the "starting point," "the backing" of an approach to privacy, or the "bottom" of the "privacy triangle." They were attentive to the reality that "[p]rivacy has parts of that, which is you have to comply with some of these laws that are out there." Compliance, then, "has driven the issue to some extent," in that companies must "always meet the legal compliance."

Moreover, several cited compliance with high-profile and highly speci-fied regulatory regimes as a means for signaling privacy leadership to con-sumers, businesses, and foreign regulators. As to the first, one respondent explained, there is some benefit "from the consumer perspective, even though they don't understand HIPAA, to know that there is some federal law that makes it criminal if they misuse data. . . . [O]ne thing I think that HIPAA does well is it helps, in whatever fashion, tell the consumer, look, you're protected in this sphere. I don't think they understand it but I think it helps."

A respondent in the business-to-business sector explained that participa-tion in the U.S.-EU Safe Harbor program plays a similar signaling function for business partners. That CPO described the firm's decision to participate in the program, as opposed to enforcing privacy safeguards through con-tracts with outsourcing, as "driven to a large extent by customers who started asking us, 'Are you members of the Safe Harbor?'" This customer push arose, then, because a firm's Safe Harbor certification represented a "checkbox," indicating to others that a company met privacy adequacy standards.

The Shortcomings of Rules for Privacy Decision Making   At the same time, every respondent—whether in highly regulated industries or not—spoke about the way that specific legal rules played only a limited role in shaping the understanding of privacy they attempted to embed in the firm. One might have expected much more significance to be attached to the require-ments imposed by HIPAA and Gramm-Leach-Bliley as well as other sector-based requirements. Yet those mandates, remarked one CPO, "enforce the minimum," and then, as another continued, "we build from there."

Our respondents emphasized especially that procedural rules informed by a commitment to principles of "informational self-determination" are irrelevant to many decisions that companies must make. Specifically, they described the failure of such rules to offer a touchstone for guiding privacy decision making in new contexts, as new types of products, technologies, and business models evolve. New products and services may derive their value from information sharing between companies and consumers. Com-panies may be unclear as to whether they can reuse and repurpose con-sumer information. And in some cases, they may be able to manipulate and profit from data supplied by consumers without violating the letter of the law. Formal compliance with laws shaped by traditional concerns about security and access, and notice and consent, provide insufficient guidance for decisions about the reuse and repurposing of information when companies can manipulate huge amounts of data willingly supplied to them by consumers.

Respondents spoke about potential privacy issues arising out of evolving product or service offerings or innovative organizational structures at their firms. Several examples illustrate the shortcomings of static laws in dynamic business contexts.

The most wide-reaching example discussed arose from the societal shift toward "ubiquitous computing."[2] Devices such as smartphones that are always connected to various networks tax the limits of traditional notice and consent models. Respondents explained that the very fact of a communication or interaction may reveal information about an individual: that they are an account holder, or user of a particular product or service, or that they have a disease and are involved in ongoing medical treatment, or are in a specific location. They also pointed to the privacy threats created by data flows coming in and out of a home on a "smart" energy grid—data that may be shared to enable energy management by the traveling homeowner, the utility, or a consumer service. The computing and communication capacity in this setting resides in mundane everyday objects that lack the interfaces necessary to support a robust notice and consent approach to privacy. Yet the data can nonetheless reveal significant information about the activities of the inhabitant.[3] Explained another way, previously unproblematic policies, such as monitoring communication to audit the quality of customer service, take on new meaning as personal information is revealed to third parties uninvolved with the service provision itself. In each case, a customer might have been made aware of the privacy practices consistent with FIPs, and the firm involved might have complied with all legal requirements, yet reasonable concerns about the integrity of privacy protections might nonetheless be triggered. In such new and changing contexts, existing regulations frequently fail to provide a clear path for navigating between "value information flows and being technology-enabled" on the one hand, and "privacy-centric" or "trust-generating" concerns on the other.

Respondents thus identified the shortcomings of a "compliance-based" approach in a variety of contexts where technology supports the trend toward ongoing remote communications with a product or service provider. Such technologies include, for example, remote transmission of data and information regarding software updates, and sensor technologies that convey usage and performance information back to manufacturers—information that consumers would, for some purposes, very much want corporations to have.

In discussing this issue, one respondent noted their commitment to FIPs: "We are an informed consent company. That's been my mantra. Informed consent is something a hundred years old. We can draw our little common-law hooks around it." Yet, the CPO noted, this is an area in which FIPs' rights-based notions of privacy fails to provide guidance: "Opt in and opt out drives me crazy, especially when you talk about peripheral devices. How do you 'opt in' to a [product] telling [the manufacturer] that it burned out? And do you want to? Probably not."

Indeed, many new business services in the United States involve open-ended and ongoing corporate use and reuse of information in ways that shift over time. These services focus on the continuing manipulation of data to provide a "value proposition" to the "person who is giving us the information so they see some value coming back."

A number of respondents identified healthcare as one sector operating in this manner. Nontraditional medical providers—such as pharmaceutical companies and medical technology firms—play an increasing role in ongoing oversight and monitoring of health practices and outcomes. One respondent described these shifts in their own company, which now both "provid[es] IT systems for hospitals" and "make[s] all sorts of machines that you would see in a hospital" such as "diagnostic and interventional medical devices" that "go into the body." While these lines of business certainly require "thinking about HIPAA [the health privacy statute]," the respondent explained, they also require deeper assessments about personal privacy unaddressed by either rights-based or process/access notions of privacy: "When you obviously get into the body," this respondent noted, "you've got all sorts of different healthcare privacy issues."

Another privacy officer brought detail to these additional privacy issues. That respondent spoke about the related challenge of personalizing medicine, and explained that there are "different tumor types," "different types of diabetics," and that patients have "different kinds of diseases so they need different types of interventions." "[A]s you start to personalize," the respondent noted, "[t]his requires more interaction with consumers. Moreover, we may need to try and figure out how to work or partner with another entity that has a tissue bank or we may need to figure out how to get access to a significant database that will allow our research to go forward. And the figuring out has to take [the ethics] into consideration . . . what are the privacy issues around doing that?"

Consumers may be fully informed about a company's privacy practices. They might also be truly interested in reaping the value resulting from the exchange of sensitive personal information. But as another CPO explained, entirely new privacy issues, outside of traditional informed consent, are raised by the "fits and starts in the healthcare industry about its adoption of IT and the true connection of the different elements of that ecosystem."

Finally, respondents spoke of potential privacy issues arising when two types of third parties—outsourcers and the government under its law enforcement powers—are accorded or seek access to personal data. In both instances, while privacy is potentially compromised, existing legal rules might offer no protection or remedy: sharing information with outsourcers might be justified by compliance with governing legal rules such as Safe Harbor requirements; and there may be no legal obligation hindering the release of data to a government agency. In light of subsequent revelations about U.S. National Security Agency practices with regard to personal information held in the corporate sector, this limitation on existing privacy rules appears especially problematic.

Accordingly, respondents uniformly rejected an understanding of privacy as a compliance function. In part, their point was that the law didn't answer specific questions posed by the day-to-day activities of the firm. "[T]he law in privacy," one respondent summarized, "will only get you so far." Despite all that "privacy" requires, said another, "there's no law that says 'you have to do this.'" Thus broader principles have to be developed that can guide privacy decisions consistently in a variety of contexts—privacy must be "strategic, part of the technical strategy and the business strategy."

AN ALTERNATIVE FRAMING OF PRIVACY
The U.S. interviewees also described significant changes in how corporations have approached privacy. Almost uniformly, they explained that corporations consider privacy issues in a variety of contexts, with an eye toward understanding and meeting consumer expectations. Such expectations

evolved with changes in technology and consumers' methods of interaction with it. These changes require privacy practices that are dynamic and forward looking. This approach, moreover, stressed the importance of integrating practices that prevent the violation of consumer expectations, focus on avoiding harm, and go beyond policies rooted exclusively in formal notice and consent models.

Company Law As an initial matter, citing both operational and strategic reasons, respondents stressed the importance of developing "company law"—consistent and coordinated firm-specific global privacy policies. These company policies ensure that a firm complies with the requirements of all relevant jurisdictions and acts concordantly when dealing with business issues not governed by any particular regulation.

Respondents explained that European law plays a large role in shaping such company-wide privacy policies.[4] As already noted, the influence of U.S. law was evidenced by specific activities such as Safe Harbor certification and the adoption of binding corporate rules (BCRs). "[W]e end up defaulting to the highest common denominator," explained one, "which really right now is Europe, and enforcing a fairly European looking code of conduct when it comes to privacy and information protection."

However, interviewees noted that these global policies at times extend beyond compliance with specific legal mandates and focus on outcomes that, even if technically legal, implicate privacy. The aim of such beyond-compliance policies one stated was to be "consistent with our global corporate values, and consistent with evolving customer expectations."

Privacy Measured by "Consumer Expectations" Every one of our respondents identified consumer expectations as a touchstone for developing corporate privacy practices, including the "company" definition of privacy. Over the past several years, respondents reported, privacy has come to be defined in large part by respect for what consumers expect regarding the treatment of their personal information. In the words of one CPO: "Your customers will hold you to a higher standard than laws will, and the question is: Do you pay attention to your customers? Do you care about your customers?"

The expectations approach was framed in relational terms and expressed in a normative language of "values," "ethical tone," "moral tone," and "integrity"; in experiential terms such as "secure," "private," "reliable," and "consistent"; and, most frequently, in fiduciary terms, such as "respect," "responsibility," "stewardship," and "protect[ion]." On a fundamental level, respondents repeated, privacy "equates to trust," "correlates to trust," and is "a core value associated with trust."

Privacy leaders varied in their articulations of "consumer expectations," but sounded several consonant themes. Each emphasized the customer's experience, including "think[ing] about how this feels from the customer perspective, not what we think the customer needs to know." The privacy leaders described adopting an orientation that put themselves in the customers' shoes. In so doing, one respondent reported: "[Y]ou run it by your friends, you run it by your family; ask your mom, ask your granddad, ask somebody who doesn't live in this world or doesn't live in technology or the leading technology companies. What's the reaction? Do they laugh? That's one set of problems. Do they get the heebie jeebies, you know? Is it kind of creepy? So, the creepy factor, for lack of a better description, is good."

Respondents noted that consumer expectations also arise from the representations and actions of firms themselves, the "discrete behaviors that are going to be objectively put out there, subjectively put out there and then met," and the ability to "deliver those consistent experiences, compliant experiences, you know, that's trust."

Consumer expectations stem, further, from concrete market pressures. One interviewee recalled that a number of years ago, "we talked to customers and said, 'How high on the radar is [privacy] for you?' and most of them [replied] 'not at all.'" Yet "now we're seeing it pop up in RFPs [requests for proposals] in almost every selling instance. . . . And so these go on and on and that's something you never would have seen back in 2000." Another described how "six, seven years ago, there was a change in the marketplace." Before then, "no customer" was demanding security in their solutions that handle personal information—"they were demanding product features, and the more that you can ship me and the more that you can give me the capability to use, the better." This lack of market pressure drove corporate practices accordingly: "[W]e're a product company [and] product companies produce what the market wants. [If t]he market doesn't want security, then you don't spend a lot of time thinking about security."

Finally, a consumer-expectations approach was described with regard to outcomes, rather than particular rules or practices: "[T]he end objective in my mind is always what's the right thing to do to maintain the company's trusted relationship with our employees, with our clients, with any constituency in society that has a relationship to us, which is probably pretty much any constituency." "[H]ow likely," for example, "is that customer going to be comfortable using online banking in the future or any other new online service that the bank offers, and how many friends is he likely to tell?" Or, will "they start wanting to shut down the relationship, in other words shut off the information, complain to the FTC, send nasty letters and threatening lawsuits about email and that kind of stuff"?

The fundamental implication of this definition of privacy, one respondent explained candidly, is that "it's not necessarily beginning from a privacy-as-fundamental-right point of view," but rather reflects the notion of "privacy as important to what we do for a living."

The Implications of a "Consumer Expectations" Framing: From Compliance to Risk Management Defining privacy through a "consumer expectations" metric, the interviewees explained, has important implications for how firms need to think about privacy protection, and, accordingly, how privacy protection is operationalized within the corporate structure. The interviewed privacy officers sounded a consistent theme: the definitional ambiguity inherent in privacy regulation requires companies to embrace a dynamic, forward-looking outlook toward privacy. "[I]t's more than just statutory and regulatory," said one, "it's such an evolving area." "We're really defining [privacy as] 'Looking around corners . . . looking forward to things that are a few years out.'" "We are all still learning," described another, "because the rules change. Customer expectations change and the employee expectations change. The world changes periodically too on top of that and I look at what we're doing as something that's really important from any kind of a personal and values perspective and from a business perspective."

In the words of a third: "[B]est in class is comparative, and it's also subjective. . . . [T]hat bar changes and it's different by industry and it's different by moment in time." A fourth echoed the contextual nature of the "external environment" shaping privacy, including "how the regulations or even the perception of the public changes." Accordingly, explained a fifth, corporate leaders must focus on "[w]hat's the next thing that's coming down the pike, because if you get caught unawares, you're behind the ball and you're spending a lot of money."

This conceptualization of privacy issues, other respondents described, has shaped the way their companies have understood and operationalized the corporate privacy function. As rules compliance provides an increasingly inapt mindset for privacy management, privacy is increasingly framed as part of the evolving practice of risk management. "[W]e're all talking about risk," said one interviewee, "[a]nd how do we mitigate risk at the same time we're . . . protecting information." Privacy, then, must be approached with the questions: "What do I need to be worrying about today? What am I missing?" As a result, "I want to keep changing the way we're doing business so it is dynamic, so we are . . . trying to mitigate the risk of the day while keeping our core program in place. And so we're changing." Privacy, by this view, is "a journey, not a destination," a process by which "we . . . try to get everybody together to say, how do we mitigate risk?" and constant inquiry into "what's the next thing on the horizon?"

Accordingly, as follows,[5] our interviewees describe that they are incorporated into risk management structures at the highest management level, and privacy discussions have been moved out of compliance offices into the processes throughout the firm by which new products and services are developed.

INFLUENCES ON THE FRAMING OF PRIVACY
This new emphasis on consumers and markets, the interviewees described, arose in the context of several intertwined phenomena central to development of a new privacy definition. In particular, they pointed to two regulatory developments—first, the Federal Trade Commission's expanded application of its consumer-protection enforcement authority pursuant to section 5 of the Federal Trade Commission Act in the privacy context and, second, the passage of state data breach notification statutes. They also pointed to societal and technological changes that strengthened the role of advocates and the media, and to the professionalization of privacy officers.

Legal Developments   While respondents generally downplayed the role of compliance with legal rules in shaping corporate approaches to privacy, every single respondent interviewed mentioned two important regulatory developments they believed central to shaping the current "consumer expectations" approach to privacy: the behavior of the FTC, and the enactment of state data breach notification statutes.

The Federal Trade Commission   Respondents uniformly pointed to the FTC's role as an "activist privacy regulator" in promoting the consumer protection understanding of privacy. As will be discussed,[6] since 1996 the FTC has actively used its broad authority under section 5 of the Federal Trade Commission Act, which prohibits "unfair or deceptive practices," to take an active role in the governance of privacy protection, ranging from issuing guidance regarding appropriate practices for protecting personal consumer information to bringing enforcement actions challenging information practices alleged to cause consumer injury.

For three of the privacy leaders included in our study, the FTC's enforcement power held particular salience, as their firms had previously been subject to privacy enforcement actions by the FTC or were currently governed by its consent decrees. One of the privacy leaders owed their CPO title and responsibilities, in large part, to the FTC's action against their firm. The other leaders gained stature and access due to the FTC action. Yet respondents from firms uninvolved with previous FTC proceedings joined those three in describing the threat of enforcement under the FTC's broad authority as critical to the shaping of consumer-protection, rather than compliance-oriented, approaches to privacy. As an initial matter, they said, state-of-the-art privacy practices must reflect and take into account both "established real black letter law" and "FTC cases and best practices," including "all the enforcement actions [and] what the FTC is saying."

Perhaps more importantly, several respondents stressed, a key to the effectiveness of FTC enforcement authority is the commission's ability to respond to harmful outcomes by enforcing evolving standards of privacy protection as the market, technology, and consumer expectations change. This is the very opposite of the rule-based compliance approach frequently embodied by regulation. In acting against unfair and deceptive consumer practices, one respondent explained, the FTC has "moved the bar over the last couple of years" toward enforcement actions charging that firms had engaged in unfair practices, "[a]nd in the land of 'unfair,' [standards can be] pretty foggy." Under the unfairness standard, "there [are] always new situations that require an interpretation," in that "'unfair' is much more subjective, and the FTC has been pretty clear that they will figure out what it means at the time."

Others suggest that the unpredictability of future enforcement by the FTC and by state consumer-protection officials in parallel contribute to more forward-thinking and dynamic approaches to privacy policies, guided by a consumer-protection metric. One of those respondents in a firm subject to FTC oversight explained the ways in which the enforcement action against that company transformed the understanding of privacy, in their firm and others, from one centered on compliance with ex ante rules to one animated by the avoidance of consumer harm. That respondent explained that, at the time of the privacy-compromising incident leading to the enforcement action, the firm had both security technology and privacy statements in place that were "fairly standard in corporate America" and "consistent with the best practices at the time."

Yet the FTC determined that these "best practices" failed to conform with what should be expected of firms holding themselves out as privacy-protective. As the CPO explained: "[W]hat we didn't have was the comprehensive program and the FTC, with our case, for the first time, looked at the privacy statement and said, 'You know what? You can't say that you respect privacy and then not have a full privacy program with training.'" At the time, the CPO said, "[W]e did our walk around with the FTC commissioners, I went with my general counsel, and it was a completely eye opening thing for [the GC]. . . . [T]here were exchanges with the commissioners where . . . they basically said that . . . what we did was similar to . . . a nuclear warhead being dropped. . . . [T]he significance of that statement from a regulator who had the power to really hammer us hard . . . stunned my general counsel. Now, however," the CPO says, it's "fairly fundamental," that companies must develop a "comprehensive program behind the website statement."

Even those respondents not involved in previous FTC actions cited incidents involving ChoicePoint, Microsoft, Tower Records, GeoCities, and other "FTC governance-type issues," as instigators for their firms' decision to hire a privacy officer, or create or expand a privacy leadership function— although at least one of those companies had a CPO at the time of the FTC action. One described the threat of FTC oversight as a motivating "Three-Mile Island scenario"—the equivalent of a corporate nuclear meltdown. Several reported that the prospect of an enforcement action enhanced their credibility within their firms. "You can't really go in and build I think solely from an appeal to the . . . greater good," one explained, "because it's not as tangible. It's longer term, right, and it's hard to do things in corporate America that are purely longer term." By contrast, the threat of losing trust, and being subject to prosecution, created an important "fear aspect" or "risk aspect." Similarly, another respondent described, "I walked in [to firm officers and said:] '[L]ook at what happened to them. This could be you. Be lucky because it's not just because they're bad guys.'. . . And it was the FTC oversight [of other firms] and the length of scrutiny and the cost of [the] audit that they had to submit to that I think was the dollar lever that started to open that box for me."

The very unpredictability of future enforcement can lead, a different respondent noted, to "good dialogue" with regulators. "I think," that CPO said, that "companies are often reticent to expose what they're doing for risk that they will be, you know, investigated or somehow found lacking. I would rather have the conversation now than have it during an enforcement action." Indeed, yet another suggested, FTC enforcement actions under a "loose framework of Section 5" create an "extra layer [that] I don't think any privacy officer wants to skirt." Accordingly, it changes the focus from the "strict compliance line" to "what can we do above and beyond that's appropriate."

Similarly, another respondent remarked on the differences between the firm's relationship with the FTC and the relationship companies in Europe (and Canada) have with their regulatory agencies, and how the uncertain threat of FTC enforcement affected U.S. businesses:

You find out someone who practices in Europe has a different outlook on how you comply than you do. And sometimes it's that they want to have a form that looks right but they don't care so much about the practice . . . it's kind of funny in Europe where they get all kooky about the Americans who want to dot every "i" and cross every "t." . . . [But] my enforcement agency . . . is the Federal Trade Commission [and] they enforce...the black letters, the spaces, the semicolons, the periods; all those things . . . I don't have this wink, wink, nudge, nudge, paragraph four, who cares.

Security Breach Notification Statutes   In addition to the changing role of the FTC, every single respondent mentioned the enactment of state security breach notification (SBN) statutes[7] as an important driver of privacy in corporations. These laws, the first of which took effect in California in 2003, require that companies disclose the existence of a data breach to affected customers, usually in writing.[8]

Such laws, respondents explained, have served as a critical attention mechanism, transforming the effects of media coverage, and heightening consumer consciousness. "[A]ll the news around security breaches" is "[a] large focus," reported one respondent. In the words of another, "the breach news in the states last year was so—the drumbeat was so loud—that it didn't take much to get the attention of our senior executive on data security."

This mechanism has called attention to the potential downstream effect of corporate treatment of consumers' personal information. Specifically, as one CPO described, it "has heightened more people's understanding of the stakes inherent in managing data," by shifting the analysis of risk from "the risk of losing data or IP or financial information," to the effects on the "poor individual." Previously, one might think, "I just lost a credit card file, who gives a hoot? . . . [I]t's capped, so no big deal." Now, however, the response is "[H]oly moly, I lost somebody's Social Security number and now there's liability associated with it for the company and they have to worry about it."

The public attention triggered by notification requirements has been critical, several respondents reported, in strengthening the privacy function more generally. Notification legislation, reported one, "enriched my role; it's putting more of an emphasis on leadership internally in a very operational sense as opposed to just policy setting and management of that sort." Indeed, explained another, "The external environment has helped that tremendously. And that's everything, . . . from what the CEO reads in the newspaper to the number of breach letters that our own employees and executives get from other companies saying, 'Oh, my gosh, I don't want this to happen to us. I don't want to see one of these with [our company's] logo on it.'"

The media pressure on this issue has accordingly given that CPO "the opportunity, internally, to say, 'Well, it's not just data breaches, it's not just laptops, it's a responsible overall program about how we take in, and use, and process and secure data. . . . [It's] the tip of the iceberg [of] what privacy challenges are, and the privacy program should be.'"

Further highlighting the distinct impact of the SBN laws, a respondent who oversees privacy at a global company reported a perception that many European companies, despite their more rigorous FIPs compliance requirements, are far less sensitive to the problems of compromised data when they outsource business functions. They "don't think about it very much," that CPO said, because "[t]hey don't have security breach notification," which "changes behavior." Another noting the absence of a general SBN requirement in Europe said, "Don't you think tapes used to fall off the back of trucks all the time? Does anybody know? Was anybody harmed? Nobody knows. If it happened in a country like Belgium or Switzerland, tapes fall off the back of a truck, what's going to happen? Nothing. Nobody will know."

Media, Advocates, and the Court of Public Opinion   Our respondents explained that the high-profile activities of the FTC and the disclosures mandated by security breach notification laws were particularly important because they dovetailed with already-occurring social and technological changes fueling privacy consciousness. This rise in consciousness both germinated, and was in turn facilitated by, the growth of media interest in privacy, and the development of what one called a "privacy community"— including journalists and advocates—that pressed privacy as an issue.

All of our respondents discussed the importance of the media on their work, particularly noting the way it galvanized firm attention at the more senior level. The major newspapers in the United States have consistently both covered and broken privacy stories. Reporters have been nominated, and in some instances won, the Pulitzer Prize for privacy reporting.[9] One study exploring the relationship between the media and public awareness and legislative efforts on privacy found over three thousand articles in the *New York Times*, the *Wall Street Journal*, and the *Washington Post* on privacy issues related to advanced technology in the public or private sector between January 2000 and December 2010. As one interviewee observed, "[C]ustomer expectations are really important," and they "are driven by the media, by advocates."

Respondents thus described the way in which the "court of public opinion," as well as regulatory attention, is shaped by "a nice, closed loop that is the media advocate." They stressed the importance of "what the CEO reads in the newspaper" to the "external environment." As one explained, "Right now, you see the P word all over the place. [I]t used to be like once a week I'd cut out an article and say, 'Look, they're talking about privacy in the paper on page twenty-two of the *Wall Street Journal*.' And now it's pretty much every day. So I think we've won the battle of actually being noticed."

Indeed, said another, "I think seeing other big brand names take a hit on the issue certainly raised awareness." These developments, in turn, reflect what a third termed a "growing sensitivity by particularly senior executives to [privacy] things that are going on in the marketplace." This sensitivity, in turn, pushes companies to "[t]ry to avoid the breaches and the problems and the brand tarnishment issues and promote the ability to use and flow data in a proper way and make it a competitive advantage."

The role of advocacy organizations was also consistently noted. Advocates played multiple roles. They were feared for their ability to shape public opinion: as "true believers" their ability to "tell their stories" about privacy threats is "very compelling, and they are very sound-bite-able." Thus one CPO recounts: "I always am watching [a particular privacy advocate's] website."

At the same time, advocates were viewed as an important sounding board, providing input on corporate practices. Our interviewees reported spending considerable time building community and connection with advocacy organizations, thereby "being part of it, and learning from it and carrying back what are the new issues, what are the emerging issues." They described "informal and more collaborative" relations, and spoke of direct engagement in policy development and information sharing.

Professionals   In addition to emphasizing the development of an ambiguous and dynamic understanding of privacy through the interactions with regulators and advocates, and the role of the media in enhancing the corporate attention accorded privacy, the U.S. CPOs point to the importance of the increasingly professionalized community of privacy officers in instantiating a dynamic, consumer-expectation-oriented approach.

As one CPO explained: "Part of the privacy office challenge is what I call demystifying privacy. . . . Typically your boss and your boss's boss don't have a good, you know, pre-established idea of exactly what the program will look like except that they want a good one. That's what my bosses said, we want to have a wonderful privacy program and you tell us what that means. I think that's not an unusual experience."

In defining what "a wonderful privacy program means" in the face of a quickly moving regulatory target, the interviewed privacy leaders described a deep reliance on peers. They highlighted the role that professional associations and communities of practice play in "filling in the details" of a fluid consumer-expectations privacy mandate. In particular, they cited the importance of the IAPP, the large privacy trade association described in this book's Introduction, and discussed later in chapter 10. The association's publication and dissemination of information about best-practices approaches, and its capacity to provide a space for "networking" and "getting to see the other privacy offers," one respondent said, is about getting "drenched in the culture." Respondents reported that a nontrivial component of their job duties involved collaboration with other members of the privacy sector. Information sharing about accepted best practices, guidelines, and policies among the CPOs we interviewed was widespread.

Information garnered from peers provides privacy officers with leverage as they advocate for certain privacy practices within their own firms. It's also an important cost-savings technique that enables CPOs to draw on the information and insights generated by better-financed peers. Information sharing, one CPO stated, "is really helpful for very resource-strapped groups. . . . [I]f there's a change in privacy, it's so ill-understood outside of our little enclave that for me to say, 'I need five hundred thousand dollars to do a research project based on opt in,' it ain't happening." To fill the knowledge gap within the constraints of the corporate budget, CPOs report learning from those they perceive as leaders. "So, with other corporate leaders, you know, the Microsofts and the Acxioms and the P&Gs and others who really have phenomenal programs, there's a lot of, I think, of sharing that goes on."

At times, the peers themselves were literally brought into an intrafirm conversation. Strikingly, one CPO reported, "I've been on the phone with [other firms'] executive committees, telling them about [our company's] experience because it helps the other company['s] privacy office to have me tell their people because they've told them and they don't believe them. So when they hear it directly from me, that has some advantage and I've done that with a number of different companies. And we just see that we have to go down this path together. It's very important."

While respondents view doing privacy "well" as a strategic advantage in the marketplace, they are also cognizant that a peer's mistake risks tarnishing the entire sector or worse by drawing regulatory or public attention. For this reason, CPOs reported that helping competitors make better privacy decisions was in their interest. Helping "my competitor at XYZ Company do better," one described, is not "about competitive advantage." Rather, "[t]hat's about doing the right thing because if they screw up . . . it screws up all of us."

Similarly, another respondent attributed a willingness to share information about privacy policies and practices freely to the belief that privacy offers more value to an industry than to an individual firm. This perceived lack of competitive value created tremendous latitude for information sharing: "I think most companies have the belief that the best practice, the good privacy statement or the training materials [or] a process for handling a security breach isn't going to give you a competitive advantage . . . so you share these things pretty freely. We are pretty much an open book. If I had created it, then I'm very happy to share it pretty much with anybody, regardless of what it is, for the most part."

OPERATIONALIZING PRIVACY

Our U.S. interviewees further described two important trends in the architecture of internal corporate privacy management. They understood both to be integral to the risk-management function, the ambiguous and dynamic nature of privacy's meaning, and the link between information privacy and consumer expectations: (1) a powerful and relatively autonomous professional privacy officer at the top level of firm management, whose job includes substantial engagement with external stakeholders; and (2) architectures to distribute privacy decision making throughout firm units, by both including privacy in existing risk management processes and embedding privacy decision making within business unit structures.

PRIVACY LEADERSHIP FROM THE TOP: THE ROLE OF THE CPO

Our interviews add depth to the portrait of leaders in this professional group and the ways in which their power, function, and role reflects new elements governing the regime in which they function. The interviews highlight two key elements of this role: the centrality of the CPO's location and policymaking autonomy within the corporate structure, and the way in which external engagement shapes the CPO's substantive focus.

The Structure of the CPO: Location and Autonomy   The privacy leads we interviewed occupied positions within their company structures that reflect the increasingly central role that privacy plays in corporate decisions. Each was either located within the c-suite or reported directly to a c-level executive. Several reported directly to the chief executive officer (CEO), while others had less direct but nonetheless significant reporting structures. For example, one reported to a strategic vice president, and another "ha[s] a dotted line to the CIO, a dotted line to the chief compliance officer and a solid line up to the general counsel." Every firm, moreover, had instituted some form of formal reporting of privacy issues to the corporation's board of directors. Many of the CPOs we interviewed described substantial interaction with board subcommittees, or the body as a whole. "Either I or somebody makes a presentation around the privacy-related thing every time [the board] meet[s]," said one interviewee, while in another firm, "[t] hey tend to hear about privacy probably three or four or maybe half a dozen times a year." Thus, because "data management inside the company [. . .] has enormous implications [as] to how effectively we're going to manage the privacy of our customer's information[,] it's talked about at very, very senior levels . . . [including] presentations to the audit committee and board of directors on where we're at with privacy."

More subjectively, respondents described the professional deference they were accorded in developing approaches to privacy. Such a phenomenon is not surprising. Organizational scholars have long pointed to the importance of professionals who interpret and mediate uncertain external environments for the firm,[10] and explored the ways in which individuals important to shaping access and control to necessary external resources— like legal legitimacy—become increasingly powerful internal firm decision makers.[11]

Indeed, the interviewees explicitly make the connection between the development of a norm-dependent, contextual, socially driven conception of privacy in the wider legal field and their own professional autonomy. Top executives recognize the centrality of privacy protection; in the words of one CPO, "privacy is to the information age what the environment was to the industrial age. You know, it's our big impact on our environment to misuse data in a way that environmental resources were misused earlier in the industrial age. And we'll be paying this cost if we don't get this right now. . . . The data Valdez." Another described the effect of regulator's

criticism of what firm executives had assumed were sufficient privacy practices as "similar to, you know, a nuclear warhead being dropped." Thus,
"the company has this almost insatiable, undescribed vision" about privacy. Yet the dynamic, multifaceted nature of privacy pressures obscures
clear solutions for top managers. CPOs consistently linked this uncertainty
to the wide latitude accorded them to define and structure their organizations' privacy agendas at both the policy and implementation levels.

The External Orientation of the Strategic CPO   In light of the latitude
accorded top privacy professionals, CPOs described their roles and responsibilities as heavily strategic, as opposed to operational or compliance oriented. Their function, one described, was "to take a much more forward
look" aimed at identifying solutions "that are not even on perhaps the
drawing board right now." They sought processes by which they no longer
had to "rely on the development process to catch [privacy issues]" because
the firm structures were designed "to understand how to do this with privacy built in right from the onset." Accordingly, CPOs reported spending
substantial portions of their time on strategic planning—"looking over our
priorities, understanding where our business is going and the kinds of privacy related issues or challenges that we either face or will face."

They also described the ways that the location of the CPO function
within the corporate structure facilitates this strategic role. It permits participation in high-level strategic decision making and ensures that privacy
concerns are integrated in strategic firm decisions rather than addressed as
an "add-on"—or never considered at all. One CPO speaking about inclusion in high-level conversations stated, "I liken it to going up to the bridge
of Starship Enterprise and hanging out. Big picture thinking, CEO thinking." CPOs reported extensive participation in formal leadership committees that establish firm strategy. Participation in such committees was
viewed as a source of internal power, while positioning privacy as a strategic
consideration in a wide range of business decisions. "The fact that I sit on
the . . . Chief Executive Council with all the GCs, means I get to hear about
new programs," described one CPO. "And just also having the privacy
leader sitting there at these meetings means people go, 'Oh, yeah. I wonder
if there's a privacy aspect to this.'" Thus, from the very highest levels, CPOs
discussed the importance of integrating privacy concerns throughout decision making about firm goals, products, and services by ensuring a voice on

privacy matters is heard at the table. The practice of placing employees responsible for privacy throughout operational units, to be discussed further, is also important.

The very uncertainty about the external environment governing privacy that enhances CPOs' stature, autonomy, and strategic role within the firm, however, complicates their privacy management task. In the words of one CPO, "[W]e're all still learning." Because this uncertainty results from the interplay among norms, technical and business changes, and flexible regulatory authority to mediate between the two, CPOs say, such learning requires deep and ongoing external engagement. They all described substantial interactions with external stakeholders, including regulators and civil society members. For each CPO, somewhere between one-third and one-half of his or her job focuses on external engagement. This engagement, moreover, was distinct from lobbying, which, if done, was carried out by other firm participants, albeit with substantive CPO input.

Such an outward orientation is essential, many explained, for guiding appropriate internal firm behavior. "I don't think you can be a good privacy officer without knowing the external environment," said one, "I really don't." This knowledge was cited as an essential source of input to the CPO's professional judgment, as well as a source of power within the firm. As another described, "Not only can you then come back to the organization and say what you think is important and here is why, and here's how other companies tackled it, but you can also help strain that, shape it, and go work with policies makers, etc. Absolutely critical, you've got to spend a significant amount of time outside the organization."

The CPOs discussed their ongoing engagement with regulators, ranging from relationship building, to education, to pre-product launch briefings. One CPO, for example, described "go[ing] door to door . . . to maintain good relationships with [privacy regulators], and be part of the kind of dialogue about global privacy." Others discussed regular interactions with the FTC and privacy advocacy groups in which they sought feedback on contemplated policy changes and on new products and services. Another discussed a two-day meeting to educate a specific regulatory agency about the mismatch between the privacy regulations and the firm's business model in an effort to identify substantively equivalent models for compliance. And, of course, the interviewees participated in numerous legislative hearings and agency-sponsored workshops.

Finally, respondents noted the importance of their professional community. They emphasized the importance of the IAPP and other venues for exchanging information with peers. They also reported participation in multistakeholder initiatives focused on advancing privacy in contexts outside the regulatory sphere. Some reported bringing external privacy stakeholders—such as members of advocacy organizations, academics, and former regulators—into the firm to increase their own and the larger firm's understanding of privacy. They all participate in conferences and workshops that bring multiple privacy perspectives to the table, such as the IAPP annual conference, the annual international conference of privacy and data protection commissioners, the Computers, Freedom and Privacy Conference, and the Privacy Law Scholars Conference. Participation in external privacy discourse through informal and formal interactions fosters the CPOs' sensitivity to privacy in the face of new risks and contexts.

The CPO's effort and engagement with external stakeholders also was identified as a means to mitigate substantive privacy failures, because conversations with advocates can identify potential privacy objections prior to the release of a product or change in policy. Respondents moreover viewed collaboration on policies to guide novel technologies as a valuable tool for addressing and managing privacy risks proactively. Maintaining connections with advocates was also viewed as useful in case things went wrong. As with regulators, the CPOs reported that meeting and developing a relationships with these groups under less adversarial conditions than those in a crisis was viewed as a best practice.

Regardless of motivations—which are undoubtedly mixed—the role of the CPO as described by our respondents involves a dual orientation. On the one hand, they gauge the privacy climate, share information about firm policies and practices, and participate in the privacy discourse. On the other hand, they use that information to shape internal corporate strategy at a high level, translating it for deployment within the firm.

OPERATIONALIZING PRIVACY THROUGHOUT THE FIRM

While our interviews explored the leadership aspects of the CPOs' roles, they also revealed a variety of ways in which privacy has been operationalized across and downward in the respondents' firms. These developments fall, roughly, into two categories. First, they involve leveraging existing risk-management functions to align privacy with other core firm goals. Second, they involve distributing expertise—through embedded experts, training, decision-making tools, and the assignment of responsibility—throughout business units.

Leveraging Core Firm Processes: A Strategic Risk Management Focus   To the extent privacy governance requires the dynamic, "learning" approach that many of our respondents described, privacy is increasingly framed as part of the evolving practice of risk management. "[W]e're all talking about risk," said one interviewee. "And how do we mitigate risk at the same time we're . . . protecting information."

Such a risk management focus has permitted privacy's inclusion in enterprise-wide governance activities, including enterprise risk management and audit. The CPOs viewed this development as significant for several reasons. Some emphasized this phenomenon as a means for adding privacy to the list of issues considered in setting the overall policy and strategic direction of the firm. "[T]he real sort of policy governance is going to happen . . . [at] the enterprise risk-management policy group. . . . I'm in that group, our head of IT security is in that group; we have an ethics compliance and a risk officer in that group."

Many noted that such integration made greater resources available for addressing privacy issues through economies of scale. For example, one CPO discussed the adoption of a single "fundamental governance model" establishing a "compliance process, an oversight process . . . a risk-management [process]" and a crisis-management process that was applied across privacy and other disciplines. The CPO noted that this integration was valuable because it built a process and architecture that would be expensive if pursued independently. The use of a consistent process across risk categories also reduced the overhead for the business units. Similarly, the CPO discussed privacy red flags included in the technology system that tracked every product and process, from creation to production. Just as individual workers were required, at various junctures, to sign off on questions intended to flag production, cost, performance, and other operational risks—which would then be exposed and highlighted for the relevant managers to address—they were likewise asked questions to determine whether the product-implicated concerns related to the treatment of personal information.

A second CPO discussed "an inspection readiness toolkit that helps [business units] implement the policies" across the firm and the use of server configurations to establish and maintain marketing preferences. Several others discussed the use of access controls to manage personal information, while still others pointed to "product lifecycle" management tools that provide a "deep understanding of what that data is that goes on the systems" during product development.

As a component of overall risk management, moreover, CPOs have leveraged the resources and attention available for information privacy and security by integrating additional risk-management activities. "[T]he way that we've even approached an organizational risk management," summarized one CPO, "is merging security and privacy together." CPOs reported close collaboration with chief information security officers, including joint management committees, regular meetings, joint educational and audit activities, and other informal and formal means of integration. Other CPOs discussed the ways in which the integration of privacy and security concerns permitted the allocation of resources for special crossing-cutting standing committees, organized efforts to consider risks of specific new initiatives, and short-term task forces.

Finally, in every firm we considered, treating privacy as a manageable risk permitted privacy officers to profit from system-wide audit activities, including those reported to the board. Two firms reported regular external privacy audits. The CPOs discussed their participation in defining the set of auditable criteria and the role this plays in affirming business-line accountability on privacy metrics. CPOs reported audits of privacy training goals, business design documentation, and customer preference management.

Many CPOs conveyed a sense of achievement in having won a seat for privacy at the audit table. "[W]e've worked to make privacy reviews a part of every single internal audit," one explained. In the assessment of another, integrating an auditing function was "probably the most significant move" they accomplished, noting, "We have four full-time privacy auditors." CPOs indicated the utility of audits in focusing the attention of senior executives within business units. In one CPO's opinion, "[internal] auditing changed everything." Explaining the significance of audits in establishing accountability, another CPO stated, "audit identifies the issue, gets management to agree on a set of action plans, they're documented, published, and my oversight role . . . is to make sure that . . . those action plans [are] realistic, that they're not missing what we really do, and then quite frankly make sure that it's being followed up."

Distributed Expertise, Responsibility, and Accountability The harnessing of effective auditing and risk management capacities is particularly important to the privacy officers we interviewed because of the way it facilitates a separate aspect of privacy's operationalization. Specifically, every CPO we interviewed described internal privacy structures that relied on a distributed network of privacy professionals and specially trained employees within the different business units, enabled by practices and tools that assist with identifying and addressing privacy during the design phase of business development.

As our interviewees describe, this distributed form of privacy management takes a number of forms and is designed to further multiple goals. It begins with the collaborative development of policies and practices. Authority for setting high-level policy about the corporation's goals and commitments regarding privacy, and formulating guidelines for the treatment of personal information, rests with subject-matter experts under the CPO's direct authority. Yet business-line executives are directly involved in the development of the specific privacy policies and practices that will govern their domain. While dedicated privacy officers, together with the legal team, often conduct the initial drafting, the privacy leaders we interviewed all viewed meaningful business unit participation, as well as feedback from other functional areas, such as security or enterprise risk management, as important to ensure "buy-in." As one CPO explained, "[W]e will consult with lines of business that are affected by those aspects of the policy we're reviewing. And we'll say 'Review this, tell us whether it does everything you need it to do.'" Another described a model by which privacy policies were developed by "a cross-functional team that had representation from all of the lines of business."

This engagement, in turn, establishes the basis for holding the business-line executives accountable for achieving privacy goals. Indeed, the majority of the firms at which our interviewees worked situated primary responsibility for privacy with senior executives in the business units, in the same way that they are responsible for such core measures as productivity and profits. Describing how such distributed responsibility works in action, one CPO explained, "If there is an issue . . . it's the accountability of the vice-president of marketing, not of me. You know, my role is to help them understand what it is they have to do but then their role is the implementation so that accountability is very important for them to understand."

As another CPO put it, "my team is not responsible for compliance, they're responsible for enabling the compliance of the business," and "if what we hear is bad, I'd say . . . 'Go audit these people.'"

The U.S. privacy leaders we interviewed considered policies of holding business-line executives responsible as essential to the success of privacy management because of the weight this direct line of accountability carries within the corporation. As one leader commented, "[T]he executive management saying they're accountable is, I think, very powerful." In describing this power, another analogized it to their experience in sending out a privacy survey,

"We [the office of the CPO] sent out ninety surveys, we got seven responses. Once the guys who wrote them the check sent out the surveys, we got ninety-eight responses . . . isn't that special!"

As another explained more directly, "[Y]ou know, their own executive directors or VPs in that area will say, 'Now, why are we doing this? Because we don't really see the benefit of this activity.' And so they can speak with that authority that you can't as a privacy officer, you know? They don't give you credibility and say you know the business but, when their own executives look at it and you help them understand the privacy risk, then they look at that and say, 'You know, it's not really worth it to do that.'"

Another critical method for distributing the privacy function throughout the firm involved "embedding" employees responsible for privacy management within business units, and then empowering them through a mix of privacy decisional tools, technical decision-guidance mechanisms, and appropriate training. These responsible employees—personnel with a variety of training and expertise in privacy, who may or may not handle privacy issues full time—offer privacy officers a means for expanding the depth and breadth of privacy's "tentacles" within the organization. One firm whose CPO we interviewed employed twenty people "fully dedicated to privacy," and *three hundred* who worked on the issue globally, through relevant business units. Another reported between thirty and forty full-time employees as well as four hundred part-time employees. A third reported approximately eighteen employees working full time on privacy management (not including privacy lawyers), with privacy focal points in each business unit at the senior executive level.

The structures for such embedded personnel vary by firm. The corporation with the most centralized structure assigns to specific business units privacy leads that report directly to the CPO. In this structure, the privacy leads were viewed as integral components of the business unit's decision-making process and took part in the design and rollout of new products and services. The CPO of this firm described "realigning my staff along the lines of supporting our business . . . match[ing] expertise, skill sets and /or interest" in an attempt to move the privacy orientation of the organization away from "a minimum reactive, late in the game" approach to a "strategic and best-in-class" approach.

Several other firms also have full-time privacy subject-matter experts in each business unit or product line, some with an overlay of privacy experts assigned to countries, geographic regions, or countries similarly situated with respect to stage of development of the privacy field, the firm's business interests, or types of risk. Unlike the first firm, these subject-matter experts often report directly within the business line and only indirectly to the CPO.

In still other instances, firms assigned a "lead" privacy expert, with a direct report to the CPO, to business units, and added a range of second-tier employees responsible for privacy who report fully within the business unit itself. For example, as one CPO described, their corporation had "full-time people in each of the business units, and then we have" privacy advocates "that are embedded in each part of the business. So we have a requirement that there be a privacy lead in every single subsidiary, every single marketing organization." Another said, "I have privacy officers in each area that report to me on a dotted line but they're a solid line into their own business area. So—we have a marketing privacy officer and she has a dotted line to me and a solid line to the V.P. for marketing."

In each of these models, the embedded privacy staff engages in a variety of activities, depending upon their relative level of privacy expertise. At the low end, embedded privacy staff identify items for consideration by others acting as issue spotters or triage personnel. At the high end, they are full privacy professionals with responsibility for developing appropriate business-level policies through coordination with the CPO, other privacy professionals, and the business unit senior executives. In some organizations workflow and design documentation and technology are used heavily to provide "self-serve" privacy guidance to nonexperts making business-line decisions. For example, one firm utilizes a suite of self-help tools for the businesses to assist them in passing privacy "checkpoints" and a privacy impact assessment tool that integrates internal privacy requirements and external compliance issues into a dynamic set of questions based upon projects and data. The results are reported and audited. In others, by contrast, privacy documentation is used primarily to surface issues to be referred to experts rather than to direct their resolution.

Regardless of the nature of the reporting structure, the CPOs we interviewed viewed the embedded privacy experts as enormously important. They valued their ability to leverage existing staff members within the business units by providing them with specialized training and decision tools to assist them in surfacing privacy issues and identifying alternatives ways to reduce privacy risks. This leverage was considered an important tool for positioning privacy as a design requirement rather than a legal matter—for "translating the world of privacy into regular business language." Moreover, the distributed system of expertise and tools facilitated the organic consideration of privacy, like other requirements, from the start of a business-planning process. These methods are, in the words of one CPO, an invitation to "get engaged [with privacy] right in the outset, because the organization wants to understand how to do this where privacy is built in right from the onset."

The CPOs cited the devolution of responsibility for privacy implementation and accountability as a strategically important means to reorient the relationship between the privacy officers and the business units. As one CPO explained, "[If] I had a 20-person group that all reported directly to me . . . I'd be imposing, I'd be demanding and imposing and, you know, cajoling. . . . [But in this decentralized structure] they're coming to me and saying, 'Hey, you got to help us, you know, we're coming to privacy stuff, you've got to help us. I'm accountable for this but I'm not comfortable.'"

Another described the dynamic as follows: "[It] was initially a lot of effort and work, now, thankfully, it's gone pretty native. So the questions that we get back from our marketers are much more sophisticated than, 'Do I need to have a notice?'"

And in the words of a third, "[It's] insinuating yourself further and further into the planning. . . . So making sure that we're consulted."

SUMMARY

These accounts shed new light on the U.S. privacy field. They describe a robust understanding of privacy's meaning that does not track legal mandates. They focus attention on two changes in the legal environment with seemingly high impact on corporate privacy practices that, until recently, had received scant attention from privacy scholars. The interviews emphasize the importance of nonstate actors in shaping corporate understandings of privacy, and corporate decisions about privacy-related business choices. In particular, they reveal the significant role of professional associations and peers in defining corporate practices. Finally, our respondents identify a set of corporate practices across these leading privacy programs that situate privacy at a high level, build it into corporate practice through integration into firm processes and distributed staffing, and buttress it by resting accountability on responsible firm managers.

5 Empirical Findings—Germany

Our work in Germany revealed a nuanced picture of how the rich mix of regulatory institutions and privacy professionals combine with other aspects of the regulatory and corporate culture to manage privacy. This work generated our most surprising, and perhaps even counterintuitive, finding: interviews with the tier of German privacy identified as leaders reflected internal corporate privacy management approaches remarkably akin to those we documented in leading U.S. firms. This is somewhat startling given the vast and obvious differences in regulatory substance and structure between the two countries. In global debates, Germany's legal commitment to privacy protection is held up as representing one end of the spectrum, while the United States is placed at the other end.[1] It is also remarkable given that we found the definitions of privacy at work within the two countries' firms to be similarly distinct.

To be sure, there is overlap, substantial in some areas, between U.S. privacy protection principles and those reflected in the EU Data Protection Directive and related instruments. But privacy in the United States is infused with key regulators' consumer protection objectives in a manner that makes achieving privacy obligations a more forward-looking and dynamic task, our respondents noted.[2]

By contrast, in Germany, privacy efforts center on compliance with data protection law, as they do in Spain and France.[3] However, according to our German interviews, data protection is also more solidly and specifically influenced by other ethical frameworks that, as with consumer protection in the U.S. context, require data protection officers to more actively engage in sorting out privacy's meaning with divergent stakeholders. The atrocities committed during World War II, enabled in part by personal data collection, have firmly nested privacy issues in a broader ethical framework of human dignity. Furthermore, the strong position of workers' interests within the German economy—including representation within firms and their boards—and ongoing workplace privacy issues combine to create a second ethical framework that infuses fairness and respect for employees and indirectly customers into privacy work.[4] These broader ethical frameworks provide additional institutional structures—including the work councils and their representatives on corporate boards—and a richer language that DPOs leverage to engage the firm leadership and move beyond a compliance mentality.

DPOs are strategic players within German businesses. This is reflected in the mix of internal and external activities they reported as well as the structures they have put in place to embed privacy throughout firms. As it has in the United States, the less fixed and regulator-defined definition of privacy at work in German firms empowers the DPOs. What is perhaps most interesting about the role of the DPOs, however, is the recent accretion of power, authority, and resources. This can't be explained alone by the statutory framework, which has long required DPO positions in German firms.[5] Our interviews suggest that the statutory command was sufficient in many—though certainly far from all—instances to establish a data protection office with some clout. But it took risks to firm reputation caused by increased publicity stemming from penalties and data breaches to fully catalyze the current character of the DPO role.[6]

THE MEANING OF PRIVACY

THE IMPORTANCE OF COMPLIANCE

The definition of privacy that emerged from our conversations with DPOs reflects the heavy influence of data protection law. Within German firms, the force of data protection is strong. The "set of rules . . . the legal regime," and "the data protection laws" were routinely cited as the "fundamental" source and "really the starting point" for defining the meaning of privacy and firms' obligations. For all interviewees, a key goal was "to try to do [the firm's work] in as compliant" a manner as possible. All firms thus strongly aligned privacy with data protection.

NESTING COMPLIANCE IN BROADER ETHICAL FRAMEWORKS

Yet, German privacy leads emphasized, the meaning of privacy within firms goes beyond legal requirements of data protection and is tied to the broader concept of privacy and an overall human rights framework. While DPOs focused predominantly on data protection, the related concept of privacy embodied in the European Charter of Fundamental Rights[7]—the right to respect for private and family life, home, and communications—informs corporate perspectives on data protection obligations, particularly with respect to employees.[8] DPOs reported using the broader concept of privacy as a tool to go beyond the compliance mentality associated with data protection alone. As one reported, "I use privacy to have more room to explain different concepts. But from the content, it's driven from the requirements by law, which is basically the EU Data Protection Directive and the relevant national laws."

Our interviewees explained that two additional ethical frameworks inform German corporations' understanding of privacy, one borne of history, the other of the political economy. In several instances, the compliance-oriented meaning of privacy was situated in broader ethical obligations on firms and the government stemming from World War II atrocities, in which some corporations were complicit or active participants and beneficiaries.[9] In some industries, such as healthcare, the connection between ethical behavior generally and privacy loomed especially large. As one interviewee explained: "That comes mostly from the Nuremberg Codex[10] of 1947 . . . that was ages before someone thought about 'privacy,' but it was the same idea . . . you have to be transparent to the people, you have to explain to them which data you collect for which purpose and what will happen with the data; so more or less the same [as] you do in the privacy field . . . if we violate privacy laws, then it's very close to violat[ing] this ethical obligation to be fair."

Additionally, DPOs explained that notions of workers' rights shaped the meaning of privacy within firms, and sometimes portrayed these notions as representing the interests of society broadly. As one explained, "the issue of data protection is very much influenced by work councils"—elected employee bodies that, pursuant to German corporate law, participate in "codetermination" with management on a variety of issues, including legal compliance and workplace issues affecting employees, such as intrusions on employee privacy.[11]

Thus, as a second DPO described, "It is written in the collective labor law that the works councils have to become involved whenever monitoring employee accounts [comes] into . . . play. And that involves quite a few privacy matters."

Because of this structure, dialogues with works councils shape firm understandings of privacy more generally. Another DPO explained that the company works to ensure "that our employees can trust our processes," to "bring more awareness to our employees in the handling of personal data" more broadly. Codetermination is important as well because it allows firms to say to the public "these are our processes, these are our regulations, we have discussed it with the works council."

Accordingly, one respondent explained how the nexus between privacy and workers' rights facilitates "a discussion around . . . the values of the company," which another specifically connected to "trust and motivation" on the employee side. The nexus also generates a broader conversation about the balance between individual rights against company and societal interests. One DPO told us: "I would argue that privacy is balancing the rights of the individuals where we collect and then process data with the interest of the company to use that data, to deal with that data, be it in our own interest or because we are obliged to process that data by regulators of whatever kind."

Others connected this privacy conversation to broader questions of corporate social responsibility. One interviewee stated that "in Germany or in Europe [generally] . . . the customer wants to be sure that the company also is very . . . correct and very responsibly acting as far as . . . personal data are concerned." Another spoke clearly of his company's current shifting perspective around privacy, his role in it, and the key driver of globalization: "[P]art of that process is to rearticulate and reposition the policy first and foremost as a customer value because its background tends to come from compliance and law and risk . . . which is important but it's not the whole story and certainly for the kind of business we are—heavily consumer-focused or focused on individuals and the services we deliver, connectivity . . . being the trusted guardian of information and privacy is a critical factor for our success."

That data protection officer went on to explain that a consumer focus is "really the aspiration and I am in discussions with my executive board sponsor about this new set of principles, which really encapsulates this point of the value of privacy, specifically talking about going beyond compliance." By contrast, "where we are today predominantly comes from a compliance background," we're "steeped in the complexities and vagaries of European data protection law." While a legal-compliance focus was beneficial in some ways, as it had given the firm "a sensitivity towards the issues," it did not offer a strong basis for shaping business practices outside Europe. "Privacy in markets like India, it means nothing there. Compliance in what? There's no law that deals with privacy, so what does it mean? In part, re-articulation is [meant] to actually encompass markets that don't understand the concept . . . to present [privacy] as being about the value to the customer and preserving that value, and enhancing and maintaining the trust that we need to be successful."

The strong regulatory structure in Germany and the EU creates a platform for DPOs to engage other company executives in a conversation about making privacy a value commitment as the company enters new markets, some of which have no privacy laws. As one interviewee described in the context of negotiating binding corporate rules: "[W]hen we introduced our first BCR, binding corporate rules . . . we had discussions on what the exact scope of the binding corporate rules should be. Should we only use them to protect what we were legally [bound] to do; protect European data that gets transferred to non-European states? . . . Or should we have a broader scope and protect all data? And I think that was the first time when we had this discussion around values."

That DPO described a board-level debate between those who said, "well, this could harm our business because we do more than we are legally required to do," and others who asked how to explain to an employee or a customer in Africa "why we treat him with less respect and why we treat his data less seriously." In sum, that privacy officer described, "I think that was the starting point, at least the first time that I realized "not only [that] . . . we need to do privacy because it's prescribed by law but to focus on that kind of more and more ethical and value-oriented way."

Another DPO similarly captured the connection between ethical corporate behavior and privacy, saying that it would be "unfair" to approach data differently in different regions, "only with the argument that, 'well, there's no privacy laws . . . so we could do whatever we like.'" That, he explained, "would be really unethical." So one has to "find a good balance between what is good for the business and what is also important to have a good ethical standard."

While legality is the overriding definition and objective of privacy within German firms, then, the language of privacy is laced with references to other ethical and social constraints. These are born of specific German experiences, including the Holocaust, the representation of and respect for workers and their interests in firm decision-making, and the general European connection between data protection and human rights during a time of globalization.

OPERATIONALIZING PRIVACY

Despite the divergent legal frameworks and definitions of privacy used in the two countries, the internal structures we found in German firms were largely similar in function to those in the U.S. cohort. We next discuss the role of the DPO, which, as with CPOs in the United States, we found to be high-level, strategic, and forward-looking. As in leading U.S. firms, German firms, with some nuance reflecting the legal requirement of the DPOs' independence, operationalized privacy by distributing privacy accountability throughout the firm, and by integrating privacy into existing risk management functions.

THE ROLE OF THE DPO

From its inception, the German system has placed much responsibility for privacy within the firm. The principle of corporate self-monitoring is evidenced in the overall structure of German data protection—which scholars refer to as an "advisory model."[12] A clear expression of the importance of self-governance in the German regulatory scheme is the legally mandated position of the DPO.

The Internal Focus DPOs reported spending between 5 and 40 percent of their time on compliance activities, and an additional 10 to 30 percent working with legal affairs. This emphasis is not surprising. As a legal matter, the DPO is envisioned as an extension of the regulator, placed within the company with access to data and decision makers, but with overriding obligations to regulators and the law. The DPO's legal duties, accordingly, are generally aimed at supporting compliance and are internally oriented.

As one described: "[W]e spend most of our time in consulting the organization [on] what is necessary to be compliant. So our function is really a consulting role and a training role and also an auditing role. So these are the three main areas we have. We have to explain the requirements that come from the law. And we challenge all the ideas we come across in order [to see] how can they be further developed.

Moreover, a DPO is not legally charged with implementing privacy, but rather with advising on its implementation. As one DPO explained, "compliance with data protection is the ultimate responsibility of management, either the managing director of [a] legal entity or in our case, the corporate board." By contrast, the role of the DPO and "all the people in the data protection organization is to give advice." Thus, by law, while the DPO leads the development of policies and processes, responsibility for their ultimate implementing lies with the business unit.

The DPOs identified two complementary legal elements as important levers for their work: (1) the requirement of independence, and (2) the requirement that the DPO report to a board member or other senior executive. One DPO explained: "The independence . . . makes it possible to just judge in a very neutral way. It's very important that the function is neutral. . . . We have to be able to stand up against it and say, "[n]o, we read the law like this and we interpret it like this," and we say it has to be done that way. And they, then, have to tell their people how they have to do it so that the real responsibility for keeping data protected and secure is with the respective management."

Another especially valued the DPO role's balance between insider and outsider, explaining, "In the end you are part of the company. You get paid by the company like the works councils do." Thus the data protection officer is both an "independent function," and "also accepted here in the company." The respondents spoke, moreover, about how their location outside the usual firm reporting structure permitted them, and their privacy staff, an important vantage on the systemic use of data, and access across firm units.

Expanding the Internal Role   At the same time, these privacy leads described attributes that exceeded what they considered to be the traditional role of the DPO, reflecting a broad notion of what might be understood as "compliance" activity. This is reflected in the comments of one, who divided his DPO responsibilities between (a) "compliance-related work," which he described as "deal[ing] with human resource records, dealing with contracts, dealing with . . . companies' processing costs and data to all of this legal work, and also support[ing] our IT people by understanding what the local laws mean concerning their protection measures," and (b) acting "more like an internal consultant who work[s] to help [the firm] understand [its] responsibility."

As a functional matter, then, although the DPOs are not responsible for operationalizing privacy within the firm, all reported exercising leadership on developing privacy policies, systems and processes, and collaborating closely with those responsible for their implementation—including business unit heads, managers, and technologists. As will be discussed further, this integration was most often reflected by a distributed architecture of individuals responsible for privacy, along similar lines as seen in U.S. firms.

As an institutional matter, moreover, the DPOs we interviewed sat very high up in the firm structure. Their titles ranged from senior executive to vice president. Many reported directly to a member of the corporate board. Every DPO reported regular interaction with the board; some reported to their board quarterly, others yearly. One discussed conducting "deep dives" on privacy with the board. Another reported on specialized training for board members and other senior managers, including all business team leaders—totaling seventy members of the firms' most senior members: "[They all have to] go through a data protection training with me personally for one hour, because all of the very high[ly] paid people from all over the world are not aware of the conditions we are playing in, and it really makes sense to try . . . to start with this top-down approach."

Access to the board was described as a source of leverage and power for DPOs, and was often described in terms that reflected a role in firm strategy. For example, one DPO reported working with the human resources board member in the wake of several scandals to develop an innovative program to train the heads of all business units. Other DPOs reported more frequent and sustained interaction with a board subcommittee responsible for privacy. Such subcommittees, along with specific board members responsible for privacy or employee interests, were viewed as an important source of influence on firm decision making. As one DPO explained, although he reported directly to the CFO, he also had ongoing contact with a board member responsible for "privacy, legal, and compliance." This, he explained, had significant effect on the board's focus: "They are number driven there and now we have someone . . . asking 'wait a second; let's think about the other thing,' and this really helps."

Developing an External Orientation   Despite German law's focus on DPOs' consultative role inside the corporation, our subjects described spending an increasing amount of time on outward-facing activities, as a means of better informing the firm on privacy. For example, one DPO reported spending "40 to 50 percent outside," on matters ranging from data protection conferences to trying out "audits." A second, estimating the job's time allocation, reported, "I would say it's 50-50 [external/internal]."

A third described the DPO job as having two parts. One, taking "60 percent to 65 percent of my time" was spent "focusing on internal projects, mostly managing my team doing the privacy work in the company." The other involved focusing on "external third parties like data protection authorities, attending conferences, speaking at conferences, working with industry associations with data protection, professional associations and meeting with peers from other companies."

Regulator Consultations   The most consistent outward engagement involved interactions with regulators. All the DPOs reported routine meetings with relevant data protection authorities, either to discuss new issues or on a somewhat regular basis to merely check in.

In the words of one DPO: "We try to be proactive and we meet authorities. Not all of them but let's say all main authorities . . . on a constant basis, . . . we meet them two, three times a year to talk generally about developments. We tell them, '[l]ook, there's [a] new product we are planning to roll out.' Or from earlier incidents where we know that they have a high interest in knowing about changes related to certain issues, then we discuss that with them. And that has been very, very helpful."

The extent of proactive engagement varies depending upon the regulatory interest or public concern generated by issues faced. As a second DPO described: "This really depends whether there is an interest of the authority or the public discussion related to it. For example, if the authority, or also the Article 29 working group has . . . issued recommendations for a certain topic like RFID technology . . . then of course . . . we proactively try to introduce our planning, our product to them. It's not in a sense of an approval, because we're not forced to go through an approval, but we want them to understand what we are doing there."

DPOs also attempt to educate regulators in order to mitigate the risk posed by the introduction of a potentially controversial technology or practice. One reported that "we do a risk analysis to find out if we launch the product, could it be that there would be press reactions on it, which automatically would go to the authorities." If so, "we try to avoid that by informing them" in advance, "and "during the discussion we find out whether they have any kind of" issue.

Another DPO pursued interactions with regulators in order to sensitize them to the challenges facing industry: "[I] go to governments, go to the European Commission, go to data protection authorities, go to conferences and try to explain [to] all of these people where we have original problems." These interactions were generally between the individual company and the regulator. For example, a third described: "I'm in regular contact with the leading authorities in Germany . . . where we discuss—on a very concrete basis sometimes—our solutions for the mass market we have. . . . It's very important to discuss it with [them] before so that we know if [they] accept it, or could accept it, this would be a very good support in the public discussion later on."

A fourth respondent reported "very intensive contact" with the lead authority, reporting meetings "about every six weeks to two months . . . to discuss specific projects or to discuss politics, policies and so on, sometimes also complaints." And a fifth said, "[I]n general we have close contact with them . . . in case we have some special things we are always discussing." Interactions can reportedly range from merely informative discussions to negotiations.

Sometimes DPOs will use the data protection authority to provide additional weight to their advice to the firm. As one described it, "I will go [to the authority] . . . with the head of the responsible department in my area and sometimes if there are managers in the operational area that do not want to understand what we tell them, we take them with us.

Our interviewees further reported infrequent (closed-door) regulator meetings based on industry sector: "[S]ometimes the authorities themselves offer certain kind[s] of venues. They do that from time to time . . . in the telecommunications sector. Then some federal state authorities do kind of yearly get-togethers with data protection officials, which is also important to see what they're working at and where they have pains."

While our respondents all seek regulators' advice and input, however, they emphasized that it is advisory, not binding: "The German authorities always argued the law doesn't provide for a formal approval [and that] 'we can tell you where we are fine with what you do and how you implement that but no formal letter stating that we have accepted this.'"

Advice "is of course something that must be taken into account by a company if it is relevant," one respondent explained. "But still then, you do not have really a binding thing. The only thing that is binding is what a judge decides."

Finally, several of our respondents described external engagement aimed at shaping the regulatory environment, including influencing new laws. For example, one DPO claimed that he is "actively engaged" in legislative debates, and described how his position as an independent actor within the company allows him to "say something critical" about the privacy issues distinct from the way the firm's business representatives addressed cost issues. This high level of independence appears to be a novel component of the German privacy environment.

Peer Engagement   Regulators were not the only external constituency identified by the DPOs we interviewed. Interaction with peers and professional groups was routine and valued by the DPOs. Most reported regular participation in meetings, workshops and conferences held by professional associations, as well as less formal interactions with select peer groups. As one explained, "[w]e interact informally, we exchange knowledge. We discuss issues and of course . . . [there] are a lot of organizations that spread information, that try to create certain standards and understandings." The DPOs we spoke to viewed both German organizations like the German Association for Data Protection and Data Security ("GDD") and the Bavarian Society for the Protection of Personal Data, and international organizations, such as the IAPP, as essential venues for sharing information and generating best practices.

In addition to interacting with professional privacy peers generally, the DPOs also reported regular interaction with those in their particular market sector. For example, one reported being head of the "Workgroup on Data Protection" of a sectoral industry association. The activities of these professional associations and networks run the gamut from highly informal meetings to formal workshops and events that include regulators. Some associations are purely focused on information sharing, while others engage in lobbying or other actions aimed at influencing policy. DPOs view professional networks as particularly important for smaller companies, because "many of them are the only privacy function in their respective companies. . . . And that's why . . . the industry associations are quite strong in organizing that exchange of views. We try to share and help each other as much as we can."

DPOs identified peer interactions as valuable because they assist with managing risk by providing access to information and practices of similarly situated organizations. These interactions are useful in clarifying what others think the often ambiguous law requires. As one said, "[I]t doesn't make sense to reinvent the wheel. . . . It's a question of benchmark, or in other words, it could also be the question of what is the proper defense line. The law doesn't give all the answers you need."

The DPO Role and the Limits of the Law   Notably, the privacy leads we interviewed underscored the fact that, while the legal requirement of a DPO could be credited with the *existence* of their position, it was not responsible for the *contours* of the DPO role they played. The law, then, was not sufficient to explain their robust strategic as well as compliance orientation, their ability to access and leverage resources within the firm, and their expansive external, as well as internal, duties.

More specifically, they described the robust privacy officer model they represented as a relatively new, and somewhat limited, development. Although the legal requirement of a DPO had existed in some form for decades, the empowered role they commanded arose only in the past ten years, in the wake of notable privacy scandals in prominent German firms, laws requiring companies to disclose security breaches, and greater publicity generally about corporate privacy failings—as well as resulting laws enhancing DPA enforcement authority.[13] Explaining that the contours of their role were unlikely to be indicative of German DPOs generally, one respondent explained, "quite often companies prefer [an] external one (DPO), because they believe they could [more easily] get . . . rid of them if they cancel the contract," and many firms do not comply with the requirement to appoint an internal DPO because it is not aggressively enforced and, if discovered, is "not a big risk."

OPERATIONALIZING PRIVACY THROUGH DISTRIBUTED EXPERTISE

In Germany, as in the United States, we found a near-uniform decision to both integrate privacy into other firm risk management systems, and distribute expertise and accountability throughout firm decision making.

The only noticeable distinction in overall corporate strategy for privacy management between the two countries was some adjustment to retain centralized control over policymaking consistent with the independence requirement placed on DPOs by German law.

As an initial matter, our German interviewees all described attempts to embed privacy in larger systems designed to manage corporate risk more broadly. Every DPO we interviewed drew on both the internal and external audit functions of their firms to monitor compliance. Though most adopted audits during the 2000s, one reported that their firm has been using them since 1994.

While the DPOs discussed standalone privacy decisional tools and processes—such as privacy impact assessments, guideline documents, privacy audits, and others—these were later integrated into larger corporate structures, leveraging additional resources. As one DPO said, "privacy is part of risk management and also privacy . . . is part of compliance . . . and . . . a compliance risk catalog and there we also feed in." Another described the benefits of integrating privacy into the firm's preexisting process for software development: to "implement that on your own . . . is almost impossible if you don't find this kind of process where you just plug in." Still others reported linking privacy to security, reporting close cooperation and regular interaction with chief information security officers, including joint boards and reporting structures, shared assessment tools, as well as ad hoc committees as needed to address emerging issues.

All of the DPOs further described a strategy of placing ultimate accountability for privacy on business leads, and a robust program of personnel with specialized individuals trained in privacy working with business units. This was combined with an emphasis on maximizing expertise within the DPOs office, often reflecting the legal requirement of DPO independence. Thus one DPO described the importance of having technologists within the privacy unit itself, to better understand the impact of privacy policies on decision making elsewhere in the firm. Moreover, while most DPOs, as in the United States, relied on a mixed strategy of direct and indirect reports within business units to bring privacy work into day-to-day processes, one DPO chose a different model because of his interpretation of the legal requirement of independence. He adopted many of the same processes for promoting the integration of privacy into decision-making processes, but emphasized the importance of "collect[ing] all the people that have some privacy responsibilities under the data protection officer" as direct reports in a "central data protection unit," with only a few "decentralized people." The members of that unit work with members of other firm units to "check business models and IT applications," and give "reliable statement[s] of compliance." This structure, the respondent believed, was necessary in light of the legal requirement of DPO independence from management supervision. "In Germany," that DPO explained, "it makes a difference because we are the only ones who can say . . . what you are doing [is okay]."

Looking more broadly at all nine firms studied, the number of employees who report directly to the DPO on privacy ranged from four to seventeen. By contrast, indirect reports and other personnel with privacy training who report to a business executive ranged from four to three hundred. Direct reports were typically responsible for business segments or geographic regions. In some instances they were dedicated to a highly sensitive data-processing system or process, or to a particular horizontal function such as human resources. The other personnel with responsibility for privacy work in various layers of business units, as well as in cross-cutting functional units. Some reported only to the business lead, while others also had indirect reporting responsibility to the DPO. As in the United States, these embedded players were not necessarily devoted full-time to privacy, but were valued because of their ability to address issues in an integrated fashion as they emerge.

The distributed-expertise model was supported with specialized training. All firms reported regular training, and some firms reported "trainings for specific areas" including "HR," "IT security," "IT developers," "procurement," and "business security." They also oversee training for employees generally, holding workshops and other forums devoted to privacy training, and using the firm intranet to provide access to privacy assistance, guidelines, and other privacy educational materials. All of the firms provided some basic, generally web-based training for all employees.

As one DPO described: "[We train] in order to make people able to ask that question, to be aware . . . that there is a topic and I have to react on that and I have to make sure that I have seen all the issues around that. Therefore we train the whole organization."

The DPOs we interviewed found embedding personnel essential to the operationalization of privacy within business units. One vividly contrasted this approach with his experience as a young compliance lawyer. "I was very alone in an office in the headquarters," he recalled, "and I started to write policies and guidelines. I had one day. I wrote fifteen guidelines and policies—so wonderful!" But, he continued, "they had absolutely no effect, because I had no people to help me to implement . . . [them] and to live it, and this is the most important thing." By contrast, "The people give you the power and the ability. . . . If I want to penetrate business a bit, only a little bit with privacy ideas, I must have people for that, and the people will generate . . . additional ideas, like defining a new process and new procedures, discussing [requirements and writing] them down."

The DPOs reported that their ability to leverage a distributed set of embedded privacy experts was useful both for staying abreast of developments that raised privacy concerns and for implementing solutions. One DPO said his privacy team works with indirect reports "from the sector or business" in an early stage of development, noting that "we have a system, a risk management system, where we try to identify risks, privacy risks, and that includes kind of formalized meetings and discussions with business representatives in order to, on one side, give feedback on the last cycle. What risks have we identified together with business? How were they dealt with? How were they mitigated?" Similarly, this DPO added, his office holds cross-sector "regulatory and policy meetings" to "discuss what is going on, for example, in data protection or in regulation of medical devices."

The DPO's office provides guidance and tools to facilitate privacy work by the indirect reports and other privacy experts within the business units, including "templates, processes, checklists, guidelines" and "privacy impact assessments." Interviewees viewed these tools as crucial to ensuring privacy in a large corporate enterprise. One DPO reported, "[P]eople are engaged. They've got the tools. They understand where they're trying to get to. And they've got the right kind of competencies to apply them. In that way, we think that's the best way to work with a distributed community of people, professionally competent and tasked with performing this job locally without going across a whole bunch of policies and so on."

DPOs, moreover, discussed efforts to address privacy during technical design. Such efforts were supported by staff with technical expertise, who used tools such as privacy impact assessments to facilitate an "iterative process" around privacy "where we understand what the product is, we understand its impacts and we find ways to mitigate those impacts."

One respondent gave this description:

We always have two guys, a legal guy and a technical guy. And when we talk about a problem like web tracking, for example, then the technical guy says, "okay it's about permanent persistent cookies. And you don't have to do that". . . . [T]hey're doing consulting in this area the whole day . . . they know what the real technical problems are. And they know the language of the programmers. And so, with this knowledge, they can write down, really, requirements for standardization. And this can be reused every time a web application, for example, is programmed and there is a chance of web tracking . . . [Then the programmers] can say "Oh I don't have to use persistent cookies," or "I have to do anonymization.'"

As in the United States, German DPOs who have pursued a more integrated approach believe privacy benefits from integration. It allows DPOs to be proactive and solution oriented rather than solely concerned with compliance and viewed as the "no" person. An officer we interviewed who utilizes an integrated approach described the DPO position as "one of the most creative jobs in the world. . . . [W]e try to solve these problems and for this you must really have some creative potential I would say."

SUMMARY

Corporate approaches to privacy management in Germany and the United States were surprisingly similar, despite differences in both corporate understandings of privacy's meaning, and the relevant laws and institutions. While the actions of German firms were driven more specifically by data protection law and a human rights orientation, privacy was positioned within broader ethical frameworks that gave them greater force and the DPO leverage. The interpretive responsibility vested in the DPO, by law, was a source of power. The interviews further highlighted the importance of works councils—and the broader societal interests that the works councils are perceived to channel—in shaping corporate decisions about privacy-related business choices. They revealed the significant role of professional associations and peers in shaping corporate understanding of legality and bringing corporate DPOs in contact with a larger field of privacy professionals. Finally, they identified a set of corporate practices across these leading privacy programs that situate privacy management at a high level, build it into corporate practice through integration into firm processes and distributed staffing, and buttress it by resting accountability on responsible firm managers.

6 Empirical Findings—Spain

Our interviews with Spanish privacy leaders, and survey of their responsibilities and practices, reveal a tumultuous external landscape that interacts with Spanish firms' internal attributes to shape privacy management. Compliance with a strict and strongly enforced data protection law and, in the shadow of the perceived futility of such efforts, managing compliance risk drive all firms' privacy activities. The Data Protection Agency (DPA) is viewed as operating largely unilaterally to establish what is required of corporations.

This overarching definition of the task of protecting privacy is reflected by an initial set of shared structures and practices across the firms. These structures and practices are predominantly subsumed in broader legal compliance activities and internally focused. Within these broad contours, however, we found greater variation across firms than in the other countries under study.

Interviewees agreed that compliance is the primary objective, and also that it was difficult to achieve. Interviewees' perspectives diverged on exactly what complicated their efforts to comply, and whether the complicating factor(s) can be effectively managed. The difference in viewpoints led privacy leads in one set of firms to have a greater external orientation, while in another it led to somewhat more extensive efforts to move privacy throughout the firm with decision-making tools akin to those found in U.S. and German firms.

One set of firms reporting a higher level of external engagement described a very unpredictable environment where a largely political agency wielded power to exact fines from firms within easy geographic reach. Further complicating the work of the firm, the Data Protection Agency's power could be invoked at the whim of consumer groups, unions, or other civil society organizations as part of a larger battle against companies. The other set of firms emulated the privacy structures and expertise they attributed to colleagues in the United States. These firms expressed dismay at the growing bureaucracy they faced in the privacy area, but did not view privacy as politically volatile. As a result, these firms are more practically oriented and are busy setting up processes and structures to manage their exposure. A final set of firms can be described as having a largely inward-facing data protection staff that struggles with the intricate maze of specific rules set by the DPA, compliance with which they view as unfathomable and unattainable.

While our sample size is too small to generalize, we note that these different perspectives related to specific features of the firms.[1] Firms in industries with high consumer contact perceived the external privacy environment as highly volatile and somewhat political ("Group 1"). They doubted their ability to thoroughly address concerns raised through the regulatory process, in part because the complexity of the rules leaves ample opportunity for mistakes, and in part because the privacy field is at times invoked to address other concerns raised by the powerful DPA or other constituents. Firms in highly regulated industries perceived privacy as bureaucratic, but subject to erratic and sometimes punitive use. They had no doubt that they would be found in violation of some arcane rule if a regulator chose to examine them ("Group 2"). Finally, companies loosely grouped as "high-tech" were prone to be pragmatic in their approach to privacy, viewing it as a legitimate social concern that could hamper their business if not appropriately handled. This last group appeared less driven by the particular proclivities of the Spanish regulatory environment and instead focused more globally on the ongoing dialogue about privacy in a networked society. They were more connected and driven by the practices of their peers around the globe, particularly those of professional associations ("Group 3").

As one would imagine, a firm's perspective on the external environment distinctly imprints on the corporate form. While across-the-board privacy infrastructure was well below that found in Germany and the United States, in some firms—those in Groups 1 and 3—the DPOs interviewed were working to bring privacy out of the shadows of the legal shop and seeking to exercise greater influence over business practices and processes. Those in Group 1 engaged regulators more proactively, seeking to build relationships that would temper the consequences—fines and public approbation—that result from complaints and investigations. They responded to a volatile environment through greater engagement with the Data Protection Agency. This occurred despite limited opportunities and a lack of historic participation and collaboration with the DPA. In contrast, the firms in Group 2 viewed privacy relatively narrowly as a compliance matter. These firms did not seek to alter the settled model of privacy work, which viewed privacy as a legal affair addressed in the course of business through the work of the general counsel's office. Finally, the DPOs in Group 3 sought to integrate privacy into the activities of business units to avoid being the "no" person and to reduce the costs of retrofitting due to legal requirements. The DPOs in this category were often empowered by a CEO and were more connected to professional associations, which they drew upon to develop practices and policies. Thus, unlike Germany, France, and the United States, where leading firms presented more consistency in behavior, Spain presented a fractured picture, reflective of a jurisdiction in transition.

In general, the status of the DPO is lower in Spain than in Germany and the United States. Staffs are smaller, connections to the board are weaker, and connections to firms' functional and business units are attenuated at best. Even those firms seeking to push a more integrated approach to privacy are very far from achieving the staffing, infrastructure, and buy-in required to reproduce what their German and U.S. peers command. While a few of the firms have overarching privacy policies to guide corporate behavior, the law, rather than broader company policy, remains the focus of the privacy task. There is little effort to decentralize privacy decision making or to empower employees to identify and address problems during the work cycle. While some training is provided, it is not necessarily provided to all employees, nor is it usually coupled with broader awareness or educational programs. Generally only a small staff of experts, often in legal affairs or compliance, is responsible for privacy issues.

PRIVACY'S MEANING

Compliance and, given its difficulties, risk management animated the DPOs. Unlike in France and Germany,[2] there was little reference to human rights, or to the broader concept of private life. Although some viewed consumer organizations and unions as involved in pressuring companies on privacy issues, that rarely translated into a definition of privacy within the firm that focused on those constituencies. This seems to reflect the belief that consumers and employees invoke privacy opportunistically to turn relatively more mundane customer service and employment disputes into broader battles that engage a powerful regulator and stir the public's imagination. A few DPOs identified loss of consumer confidence and the market as motivating factors, but it was in a more generalized, amorphous, and political sense than in the United States or Germany.

The focus on compliance with data protection law was ubiquitous. As one DPO stated, "I am responsible for data protection, as it is known in Spain." Elaborating, another DPO explained that compliance must be assured in internal processes as well as external relations: "[M]y job is mainly to comply with the Spanish law and to deal with the problem of international transfers: . . . two different . . . roles. One is in the backdoor internal management of workers' documentation and information, and the other one deals with external products, clients, customers, and so on."

This compliance mentality, according to the DPOs, produces a reactive mindset toward data protection. One reported that the firm hired a DPO "[b]ecause we were going to be fined. It is the main reason in Spain to appoint somebody to data protection. 'We have a problem and we are going to be sanction[ed], so. . . .' It is a reactive manner of hiring someone." Another DPO said that "in Spain, breaches of privacy are very heavily punished according to law and there are serious monetary . . . consequences. So obviously we spend lots of time so as to avoid any claims on breaches." Some were hired as a direct result of a breach: "I was hired for this specific case and then they decided to continue, because I held training sessions with the executive board and explained to them these issues about privacy and data protection and that we have to comply, and they agreed."

Even within the firms that were moving beyond a strict compliance mindset, DPOs emphasized that compliance was the first motivator. For example: "[Compliance] was the first step because when we joined the company, the most urgent, the most—the most dangerous factor that we have to handle . . . was compliance on data privacy because as you know probably in Spain we have one of the . . . strongest data privacy law[s] in Europe."

One DPO explained that while they strived to move the company away from a compliance mentality, they had not yet succeeded: "I think that historically compliance [has] . . . been the driver of information security.

. . . I would like to say another thing, that now the maturity level of the company [has] push[ed] this company to make a lot of efforts to protect data. [But that] is not all the truth."

Despite a compliance-oriented definition of privacy, and the best efforts of the firms, there was a widespread belief among the DPOs that "[i]t's almost impossible [to comply] 100 percent with all of the requirements of the law." Another simply stated that despite "doing everything," it "is difficult to avoid a fine." For some, the futility arose from the complexity and density of the rules. As one DPO said: "There is only one little article in relation to software, but it is very diabolic, as you have seen as regards the Spanish law. And it states that every software for the management of personal data has to comply with security measures, and we have a list of security measures. And I do not know of any company in Spain that complies with it. I repeat, in our training sessions, I challenge the assistants and tell them: if you find any Spanish company that complies with it, just tell me."

For others, the dense nature of the law meant the following: "[I]t's impossible to comply with everything because in math risk, zero risk is cost infinite. . . . So we [[evaluate]in this what percentage of risk we decide to face, and what are the risk[s] that of course the company, not us, the company [will] accept, too." Another DPO described a very clear way in which this risk was managed: "[I]n the dashboard for data protection we have a thermometer where we can see [how] we are comply[ing]— . . . we're right now [at] 82 percent that for me compare[s] . . . with the benchmark which we have [which] is . . . pretty good, but it's 82 percent, so we know that we have another 18 percent [for which] . . . we are assuming risk. This thermometer "match[es] business process with [the] article of data protection law."

Another DPO explained that the lack of consistency across European jurisdictions compounded the problem: "At the end, it is impossible to comply with everything because the structure, your infrastructure, your technology, is not so flexible that you can scratch all you want. You want red, red, for you, green, for you, yellow. Then I'm expected to manage this?"

DPOs expressed concern with the situation in Spain. Some claimed that the law undermined the competitiveness of Spanish firms: "In Spain, you cannot do business if you want to comply 100 percent with Spanish data protection law. So this is a barrier, a competitive barrier for us if we want to—if we compare, as we say, other non-European companies that target

European citizens. . . ." His colleague responded: "Yeah. That's an important thing. You can do business within Spain but to . . . compete with people outside of Spain is where the law becomes a big problem." Another officer, discussing the registration and authorization requirements for international transfers, combined these sentiments, explaining: "[T]he European system is absurd. The European system is very hard. Our system is not adapted to current times and the pace of technology [in the international transfer procedure] . . . you have to explain everything continuously . . . it is not clear to them and they ask for more documentation, and you could make all this with a simple click. DPA [Data Protection Agency] uses a long time to authorize you for something that could be done with one click. That is the reason why most companies do not declare international transfers. They take the risk."

For others, the futility of compliance rests in the broader political and social context in which it is invoked. As one officer remarked: "I would say that in Spain we are—there is a bad . . . use of privacy. What I'm trying to say is that sometimes people see in privacy an opportunity to get compensation, to get money compensation." DPOs questioned the motivations of consumers and consumer protection organizations and viewed the regulator as sometimes reluctantly complicit. As one DPO explained: "[T]here are some claims that in one way or another one can easily see that the reason [behind] consumer[ ] association[s] . . . is [to] tak[e] advantage of a mistake in order to obtain money compensation. The Data Protection Agency is at the same time aware of this, of this manipulation, but they have to comply and work within the law."

Another noted that the political and bureaucratic nature of the DPA's office is problematic: "the Director is a political appointee and people working there are public servants and they are not passionate about data protection. They do administrative work."

The extent to which DPOs considered compliance a realistic metric for success was heavily influenced by external factors. Corporate conceptions of their ability to achieve compliance with data protection law varied dramatically depending on aspects of the firm's history. Those that were high-touch, business-to-consumer businesses were far more sensitive to pressures from labor and consumer protection organizations. As one DPO told us, "[i]t's our global protection to the consumer but this protection goes from attending personally [to consumers] and . . . to inadequate protection of the [consumers'] information." Expanding on the connection between customers and the vagaries of enforcement, another DPO said: "[T]here are some companies that you know [will be targeted], like telecommunication providers, banks, insurance companies. They are the usual suspects. When you have ten million customers, you get complaints. They go to the DPA. There's investigation. And typically there's a finding." From his perspective, the sheer numbers combined with the mass of rules meant that "those companies . . . tend to . . . typically pay, it's like a tax . . . they know that they have to allocate some money at the end of the day because there's no way you're not going to mess up if you . . . have ten million customers and you're doing all sort of things with their data."

Another DPO explained that privacy was taken up in the context of consumer organizations that "focus on different sector(s), for example, telecommunication, electricity, gas, [a]irline. . . . They are very aggressive in the policy." This further explains why different industries perceived privacy as more or less politically driven.

Subsumed in broader consumer and labor squabbles, the corporations viewed privacy claims as, at best, weakly correlated to actual public concern with privacy. They were viewed as unavoidable and generally not substantive, at least with respect to privacy. The lack of moral weight attributed to them gave these claims little salience within the corporation. This is evident in the lack of influence they have had on privacy's definition within Spanish firms. The actions of civil society groups, unlike in the United States and Germany,[3] neither nuanced nor broadened privacy's definition or the DPOs role. The activities of civil society groups did, however, inform the companies' general stance toward compliance—feeding into a more risk-mitigation or tax-like mindset within the corporations that perceived privacy complaints and penalties as inevitable. Unlike in the United States, where the activities of privacy and consumer organizations, along with the media, played out against a legal backdrop that centered on consumers and their expectations in the question of compliance,[4] or Germany, where the works council was viewed as legitimately addressing privacy concerns,[5] in Spain, consumer organizations did not have a forum through which to influence corporate perception of privacy's definition. Regulators did not convene multistakeholder groups to discuss privacy requirements or new threats. As one respondent explained, the role of consumer organizations was in activating the regulator—"the consumer association has big power, and they have a very close relationship with the administration . . . the local regulative administration . . . because . . . [they have] the capacity to initiate the process . . . before the administration, etc., etc." Their role is not in defining the substance of the law.

SHORTCOMINGS OF THE COMPLIANCE MENTALITY

Compliance dominated the perception and practice of privacy, which the DPOs viewed as problematic for several reasons. It keeps the DPO, and privacy, at arm's length from the company, frustrating efforts at achieving deeper, systemic integration into firm processes. And it leads firms to choose simple solutions under the law, rather than engage in more meaningful analyses that could lead, according to the DPOs, to better and more cost-effective solutions.

FRUSTRATING EFFORTS AT INTEGRATION

Some DPOs believe the compliance orientation relegates them to the role of legal technician, hindering efforts to protect privacy:

The problem is that . . . companies think of data protection first as compliance, and second . . . [as driven by] the lawyer. And the lawyer is inside his office, and I always give the same example. I know a lot of lawyers who do not know the software . . . they have to go out of their rooms and go and see. But the concept is this: it is a lawyer thing . . . and we do not care about it. It is very frustrating. And maybe that is why we do not develop good privacy like in the . . . [United States], because we are lawyers we do not get out of our offices to see the business and the thing is that privacy has got more implications than comply, comply, and comply.

The DPOs reported compliance as problematic because it allows privacy issues to be easily dismissed by the business units. As one officer explained "normally, you don't do any more than the law requires. . . . Okay. Because . . . you want to sell products." Compliance also fostered a negative perspective on privacy's relationship to firm objectives: "You want to make easy the life of [the firm]. All of . . . [the] requirements of the law normally [say] . . . stop it, stop it, stop it. No, no, no you don't have to do it. No, no, no stop wait I have to check it. No, no, no, oh my God this is impossible, stop it now."

A DPO from the high-tech sector aptly explained the downside of being in the legal department: "[I]n other companies in Spain legal is no one. You never go to the legal . . . if you go . . . he's going to say no, impossible. And that's why . . . my boss put me in the senior management team because it's the first time that I . . . [saw] a chief privacy officer and a legal in this team. And that drove home to people the importance of privacy for the company, the fact that the CPO was at the highest level of the company."

This DPO attributed his elevated position within the firm to American influence. As that DPO explained, "maybe that's why . . . the title was [chosen] by the CEO. . . . He said, I want you to be 'chief privacy officer.'" The DPO also detected American influence on his prior employer, where the focus of privacy activities extended beyond compliance. This suggests some level of isomorphism, as policies diffuse in the private sector from the United States to the EU private sector.

FRUSTRATING SYSTEMIC APPROACHES TO PRIVACY
Some of the DPOs, particularly those in the high-tech sector, reported that the focus on detailed external rules reduced the obligation companies felt to wrestle thoughtfully with privacy. One reported: "Many companies . . . just sign on the dotted line and you have compliance designed. Now in other countries where the rules are not so clear, then you have experts . . . thinking in terms of security; so this is [what] . . . we want to achieve." One DPO offered the different specificities of the German and Spanish laws as a case study:

[T]he security provisions in the German law, that's an appendix to the law. . . . It's just like ten bullets. It's much less detailed than the Spanish rule. . . . You spend more time discussing about security in real terms with a German customer than with a Spaniard. . . . In Spain the tendency is typically you just agree to comply with the law and I don't want to hear how you do it. I don't really want to see your security document. I don't want to enter into details. You said you would comply, that's all I want. Germany I would say it's by far the country [where] we get more and more discussions, more detail and thorough[ness].

Echoing this concern, another explained that with law and the lawyers leading, "the privacy discussions can become endless." As a result, "I don't think that they [the business people] really understand why . . . this [is] so important. They just feel it's lawyers talking about stupid things." In response, he said, businesses look for simple solutions to complex challenges such as cloud computing: "So when they realized there was going to be a data center in Europe they said 'Okay, our problems are solved. Finito. It's done.' No more privacy issues. The data is in the European Union, you know, finish[ed]." He pointed out that this focus on legal compliance elides serious issues, noting that cloud computing did not in fact resolve the privacy issues: "[We had] Indian engineers, Egyptian engineers, Chilean engineers, American engineers accessing the system. So instead of going to the United States they go to [country X] but the problem is the same: [d]ata might be accessed by people outside of the European Union, the same people . . ."

He blamed the compliance mentality for steering his company toward an inefficient and less privacy-protective—but easily understandable—solution.

In one particularly detailed discussion of the drawbacks of a lawyerly approach to data protection, an interviewee compared company behavior across jurisdictions, explaining that "in the UK . . . large companies . . . bring in a specialized law firm. They don't have this person in-house. They are ready to spend a significant amount of money [on] an external law firm to participate in the privacy discussion. That's something you can also see in Germany."

In Spain, by contrast, they rely on "clear written rules," which "does not amount to better privacy or better security" because it provides "a false sense of protection. . . . Customers are very happy with just saying to you, comply with this. . . . That's all I want from you. The law says you [must] comply with it, and we are all happy with it."

OPERATIONALIZATION OF DATA PROTECTION AS COMPLIANCE

While Spanish firms were overwhelmingly oriented toward compliance-focused data protection structures predominantly situated within the legal and audit divisions of the firms, the variables discussed earlier—high tech, or close contact with consumers—consistently exerted some force on the shape of privacy's institutionalization. In particular, within high-touch business-to-consumer companies, we found DPOs to be slightly more senior and externally oriented. Within the high-tech sector, we found DPOs more actively attempting to diffuse privacy throughout the business units as part of daily practice rather than relying on episodic interaction with the small team of privacy lawyers. However, lacking the seniority of their German and U.S. counterparts, their efforts were relatively nascent and modest.

ROLE AND POSITION OF THE DPO

As with our U.S. cohort, the privacy leaders interviewed come from firms that are heterogeneous on every metric except size.[6] Most have a global presence, although the extent of their international operations varies. Some are highly diversified, while others have a single core business. Most of our interviewees come from data-intensive businesses.

Unlike our U.S. cohort, where privacy leads had somewhat varied backgrounds and training, the majority of our Spanish interviewees were lawyers by training. All but one DPO had a legal title of some sort. Some reported to a lead legal counsel while others reported to a senior corporate officer at the vice president level or above. Despite the reporting structure, which was somewhat similar to the United States and Germany, the titles of the DPOs[7] were generally less senior. This lesser status was evidenced directly by less access to the board and less involvement in strategic decision making.

Unlike German law, which requires the appointment of a DPO and tasks them with both educating employees on data protection and providing compliance advice to the firm,[8] Spanish law has no affirmative requirements that direct employee training. We found that training is still prevalent, although less robust and tailored than in Germany and the United States. Some firms bundled privacy training into information security training conducted by another department; one outsourced it to a vendor that provides overall employee training. Notably, the high-tech companies reported more tailored educational offerings, such as providing training for specific job classifications. One DPO reported, "I have a complete system for every employee. Every employee has a specific program of data protection adapted to their job." Another, explaining his layered approach to training, said: "When a new person is hired, since we have a general training plan in place . . . everyone who enters the company receives their own training on privacy, for instance, people from marketing. They are the most dangerous boys . . . because they are continuously sending emails and doing telemarketing."

One high-tech sector DPO credited his interactions with U.S. colleagues through a professional association for expanding his perspective on privacy education: "As regards training, I learnt from IAPP. The [Spanish] law does not oblige you to have a training plan, so . . . what I do here in my job is not typical."

Spanish DPOs' relatively weaker position was evidenced by their infrequent interactions with the board of directors and little direct knowledge of how often the board discussed privacy issues. One explained: "Normally, the person who reports to the board of directors is the general counsel. And if there is a technical issue, [it] probably is the CFO or directly the IT director [who] report[s] to the board of directors because, just below the board of directors, there are different committees." Again in the high-tech sector, more interaction was reported. For example, one DPO explained that yearly four-hour training sessions and a monthly newsletter were used to increase the firm's awareness of privacy issues.

The DPOs credited information about breaches and fines for raising the profile of privacy concerns and their salience with corporate boards: "[T]echnology and information security . . . are very, very out of the range of the executive culture . . . which is the composition of the boards. . . . The best way to sell to this person is with [an] example, [a] practical example that happened in the real [world]—and that you have read in the newspaper."

Another DPO echoed this strategic use of press reports stating, "[S]omething like WikiLeaks for the data leak prevention project is very, very useful because board[s] understand the importance, the criticality of that." Likewise, one DPO explained that news was an important determinant of whether the board heard about privacy at all, explaining that in general "[t]hey are thinking, the board, in other things, not in privacy" unless it is "in the news when something wrong is happening." He said that "[t]hey just want to avoid the penalties and . . . not be exposed to the press . . . [for] doing those bad things with their customers." Another, who attributed his hiring directly to a complaint against the company, said the key thing for the CEO was "[t]o get rid of the problem. . . . He told me: '[I]f I could destroy it immediately, I would destroy it. If I could press the button, here, I would press it.' It was in this room. But the first task was to get rid of that problem at that moment."

He went on to explain that the fine was not what mattered; rather, "the impact in the press would have been bad." He then generalized about Spanish companies: "[They] have to comply, but [not] only in order to avoid sanctions [or] fines. They do not want to be in the newspapers. I think that is the only reason right now in Spain . . . it is because of the public sanction [i.e., reputational harm]. Because they have enough money to pay [the fines]."

RULE BOUND AND ISOLATED

Unsurprisingly, given the definition of privacy and the placement of DPOs within the firm, the Spanish DPOs reported spending much of their time on legal or audit-related work. Many of the DPOs we interviewed are legal counsel who spend only part of their time on privacy issues. Of their privacy responsibilities, most DPOs reported spending from 10 to 50 percent of their time on compliance and another 10–50 percent on legal affairs. This sits in stark contrast to Germany, and especially to the United States, where the CPOs we interviewed were supported by legal counsel who specialized in privacy, freeing up the CPOs' time for high-level strategic activities.[9]

As part of the legal counsel unit, most of our interviewees reported relying on the general legal review required for new products, business relationships, and other corporate changes to identify and address privacy concerns. DPOs described their firm practices in the following ways: "Whenever there is a new project they are obliged, according to procedures, to report to me, to inform me." As another DPO summarized: "[T]he normal process . . . the communication department or sale department . . . they consult [at a] . . . very, very preliminary stage . . . about this idea. . . . [I]f the minimal requirement[s] according to the law are accomplished, the second step is to consult with the IT department . . . to develop . . . different tools to implement this idea. . . . [Then] probably the matter [will] come back to the legal department."

The DPO explained: "We have internal procedures. . . . I am informed whenever he decides to . . . develop the product. I am completely into the assessment during the process." Describing the work of his office, one DPO said: "[W]e must try to understand all the requirements of the [law]. . . . In each country we must comply, and we must translate this requirement in operative requirements . . . with the legal department of each—of [each] central legal department, corporate legal department, and with each . . . local legal department."

Very few firms had formal processes, separate from the standard legal review, to address privacy concerns. In a striking departure from the norm we found in the United States and Germany, where a key element of corporate privacy management was adopting and operationalizing a set of overarching corporate privacy principles,[10] the DPOs we interviewed in Spain rarely mentioned corporate privacy principles. Those who used the term did so in a vague and aspirational way. For example, one said: "I always say

I am always *away from the law*, not because I [do] not follow the law. . . . The law is getting really old for me, so I have to follow principles."

One Spanish DPO working for a subsidiary of a U.S.-based company explained in a roundabout way the benefit of overarching corporate principles given the state of the law: "[W]hen we receive these policies [i.e., overarching corporate principles], we adopt [them] in relation with internal rules in Spain and the law in Spain . . . but it's [not] very easy because the internal policies in the [United States], in [country X] . . . are more intensive."

DISTRIBUTED ACCOUNTABILITY

Despite the relative lack of business units' involvement in defining privacy objectives, or means to achieve them, accountability for privacy, as in the United States and Germany, is the responsibility of business leads. But in the United States and Germany, there appear to be more efforts than in Spain by DPOs to establish a shared view of requirements through conversation with the business.[11] In Spain, the DPO generally acts as a lawyer telling the business units what they may and may not do. One DPO in the high-tech sector described a distributed system of responsibility coupled with technical detection mechanisms to identify bad behavior: "The Director of the Area . . . has to comply with the instructions . . . we have a whole system prepared to detect the possible violations, like sending emails with information . . . We help them with technical systems . . . But directors and managers are [still not] completely sure about what their responsibility is."

Acting predominantly as lawyers, the DPOs realize that the ultimate decision is not theirs to make: "This is a business. Sometimes the best friend of the business is not the regulation, okay? Probably if they decide to implement new products, it's not sure that the final result will be according to the law. We try to advise them, 'Okay, there is a risk but . . . it's a business decision.'"

BEYOND-COMPLIANCE INITIATIVES

Beyond-compliance models of privacy integration were evident in some firms. Uniformly, they were attributed, at least in part, to substantial high-level buy-in: "[I]t's really, really important, and the CEO, of course, thinks that it's really, really important. . . . If we don't have the support from the

CEO, we would not be able to work." The two DPOs whose companies took a more expansive view of privacy's place in the firm both pointed to a significant U.S. connection to explain it. They were also both in the high-tech sector. One DPO explained the influence of his firm's American connection on how the firm thought about privacy: "This is one of the pillars of the company. [Senior management] believes that the protection of the user's data, of the privacy rights of the users is the most important thing of the company. As a matter of both business and privacy matters. Because we cannot do anything for the business if the privacy of the users is at stake."

The interviewee, perhaps unsurprisingly, reflected definitions and goals more aligned with those of U.S. firms. The interviewee's operation and practices, however, were more consistent with Spanish firms. For the other firm, the arrival of a senior U.S. employee was viewed as seminal: "I think North Americans are more sensitive to privacy issues and he was in [an American Company] and [the American Company] was one of the first companies to have a chief privacy officer. So the CPO role really came when you brought him in. And so it's kind of a vision from the top."

High-Tech Companies Beginning to Adopt Strategies to Socialize Privacy

Although the high-tech companies engaged in activities beyond compliance shared the small and centralized staff of other firms, they were more aggressively attempting to produce privacy guidance documents and decision-making tools directed to various parts of the company. One high-tech DPO described the maze of documents his firm has generated to drive compliance throughout the organization as "a castle" housing "a lot of documents, documents that have developed our law and . . . regulations. As we have a specific law on e-commerce, for instance, not only data protection, and we have also to comply with it and it is all mixed."

He explained: "In the castle, I have different documents that I sen[d] to different departments . . . to the marketing department, or to R&D, and these documents are continuously being revised. . . . Everybody knows there is an instruction and everyone knows, for example: if I am a marketing person I have to follow this instruction." This DPO was attempting to create a set of tools that would spread privacy thinking throughout the firm.

The DPOs in the high-tech companies communicated a strong belief that effectiveness is tied to understanding the company, which required them to get out of the law office. One explained that regularly interacting with the business units was the difference between an expensive retrofit to address legal compliance concerns and a product built with privacy in mind. Discussing his interaction with the firm's research and development department, that DPO said: "I had to present myself and say: 'Hey guys, we have some rules to comply [with] and your products are the machines that treat data and so I ask you to take me in the first stage of your development . . . of your ideas,' because it is very difficult for us to adapt a product once it is finished. In 2007 we had this problem, we had to open it and work back . . . now, we take that into account. We follow the rules, and it is very easy."

Another DPO explained: "I use[d] to loose [sic] or miss a lot of details that were important and now . . . [I attend] technological meetings and for me it is very important. It is one of the best experiences I have had here: knowing the software and knowing how it works. It is very, very interesting. And I assess them to [ensure they] comply with the law."

While Spanish firms are still oriented toward compliance, these interviews reflect efforts to integrate privacy into firm activities at a deeper level. These efforts are in part driven by a desire to avoid the costs of retrofitting products and processes, and to avoid being the "no" person.

ENGAGEMENT WITH THE PRIVACY FIELD

In contrast to the United States and Germany, privacy protection as a professional field is far less developed in Spain. Some DPO's reported little to no interaction with other professionals in the field. One interviewee lamented, "[I]t is very strange having only 200 people who are associated [with privacy associations] in a market of two million companies, only 200 people, it is frustrating." Some expressed concerns about the lack of professional standards for the DPO/CPO role: "[T]here is no standard definition. . . . And it is scary. I am scared of this because they need to explain more in detail how it works."

Despite the relatively low level of participation in privacy professional associations and sparse reliance on peers reported generally, DPOs in high-tech firms are tightly connected to an international network of privacy professionals. Their efforts to develop beyond-compliance models for privacy work within the firm drew upon knowledge gleaned from professional contacts. They found regular interactions with their peers crucial to their work: "It is very helpful because we share the same frustration and we have a lot of ideas." DPOs found information from peers particularly helpful due to the political, rather than expert, nature of the director of the DPA. As one said: "We have the problem that so far none of the Spanish Directors of Data Protection [Agency] were experts in the field. They were political appointees." For those who reported information sharing among peers, they considered it key to understanding issues and developing corporate responses.

EXTERNAL FORCES EXPANDING THE DPO'S ROLE

While our interviewees considered a forceful CEO an important predicate to moving beyond compliance and out of the law office, external forces also raised the level of attention a firm devoted to privacy and created more latitude for the DPO. Interviewees credited the increase in the fines that can be assessed by the DPA with raising the significance of privacy and the stature of the DPO within firms. As in the United States,[12] the monetary loss was viewed as less important than the potential injury to the brand caused by negative publicity.

One DPO explained, "[I]f [the company] has trouble regarding data protection [that damages] their reputation, the damage could be very, very [real]. So I think [the firm is] willing to make an important effort to develop a good product." The increased fines garnered significant press attention, thus raising the potential impact of a breach or violation on the company's image. Another DPO stated: "This is a very important topic for the name of the company because . . . not only is [it a] very expensive penalty. But there is an immense damage for the company because [customers feel] you don't take care . . . [of their] data as [a] customer. . . . So we are very [careful] to maintain the legality o[f] our business about data protection."

While there was a widespread sense that the increased fines contributed to firms' improved attention to privacy within the firms, knowledge of other companies' problems was most actively used by those DPOs trying to break out of the compliance mode. DPOs explained that publicity about a privacy failure in any country was useful, particularly if the company being taken to task was a competitor. Said one respondent: "When you can show something that's happened to your competitor, on one side you enjoy it, and you say, 'Yes, better him than me,' but then . . . [y]ou mind about it because yes, but if this happened to my competitor that ha[s] the same structure, environment, business, this can . . . happen to me."

Our interviewees also attributed positive investment in securing data in Europe to U.S. security breach notification laws. As one DPO told us:

I would say that's been most driven by . . . U.S. evolution, rather than by EU evolution. . . . [We have] many companies that either are subsidiaries of U.S. companies or have significant operations in the United States and they are very sensitive to all, for example, all the changes in the little landscape in the United States around data breaches. And this has created [a] sort of feeling that failing to protect the data can really cause problems. I think that [in] Europe, and we know that there is [sic] some changes coming probably soon due to the [draft EU regulation], but in Europe typically, if there was a breach it was something kind of kept within the company, not disclosed to third parties, managed internally, little noise. The regulators were not able often to know about them [breaches] because . . . they have scarce resources and as a result chances [are] . . . you can do it wrong and get away with it. . . . Now in the United States things are changing. Now the companies realize—and I would say that there is, and especially in some industries like financial insurance, there is a growing concern. As a result, there is a growing pressure on suppliers and all the companies around that supply services to them to be more demanding. I mean they are definitely more demanding in terms of security warranties."

INCREASED EXTERNAL ENGAGEMENT

External forces raising the publicity of privacy failures had the largest impact on DPOs at high-touch B-to-C companies. The increased publicity fed the activities of the consumer and labor organizations that were already focused on these firms. As a result, the firms developed a slightly more strategic perspective, and, in particular, engaged regulators more proactively.

As one might imagine, providing legal advice and participating in auditing functions generally keep the Spanish DPOs highly internally focused. While all DPOs discussed interactions with regulators, the accounts varied widely across interviews. For most, interactions were relatively perfunctory and at arm's length. The DPOs reported the DPA as interacting with firms in three ways: "by specific inspection, from a complaint from a client or something like that, or from a specific review of [something] in the insurance market or [on the] Internet." Importantly, the regulators, "don't call to you [and say] hey, we are thinking about chang[ing] . . . the process." The DPA is viewed primarily as an enforcement agency: "DPA does not intervene in policies. They only act as police." The "DPA issues opinions . . . if you do not comply . . . and somebody tells them, you will be automatically fined."

But increased publicity has altered this pattern for high-touch business-to-consumer firms, as evidenced by their reports of more frequent interactions with regulators and other external players. This set of companies reported more proactive engagement with regulators, for example, about new products. One of the respondents gave this scenario: "For instance, you tell the [regulator] 'I am going to put this product in the market' and they say: 'yes, no problem, come here and we will talk about it.' Then you explain your situation to them regarding your product and they try to help you."

These DPOs saw their value to the firm as partly derived from their ability to alter the relationship with the regulator. As one DPO explained, "[W]e are working together with—not just with the—with the government. We are working together with other governments about the privacy [issues and] international confidence. We share information . . . or ideas about the privacy[issue]."

These DPOs viewed proactive engagement as beneficial to their companies:

[A]nother element could be the relationship with the data protection authorities [that is] good and friendly. . . . Because they are able to see the authority like a friend, not like an enemy and so sometimes we check with them [on] any matters without any problems, to help and so the people are more comfortable to ask different questions because they don't see a problem. They see a solution. It's a mix of the different elements. . . . The relation, the role of the authority, the innovation, different channels to sell their services, the pressure from the different administrations. It's a combination of different elements.

Another DPO, explaining why early meetings with regulators were of value said, "[A] big company like this one has to be really creative . . . in the beginning of new projects and everything."

The relationship between DPOs and the regulator was indicative of the politically infused nature of privacy noted before, and the relatively immature state of privacy professionalization coupled with little domestic history with self-regulation. While one DPO did report that the regulator contacts them proactively, primarily to use them as an example of best practices, no one reported being offered a participatory role in the governance process. The words of one DPO captured the sentiment of many: "Normally, they don't ask for the involvement of the entities. Normally, they . . . go their own way. They don't look to the sector for input. They make up their own mind and then impose it on the sector."

INCREASED INTERNAL AUTHORITY

Increased publicity of privacy failures has also provided an impetus for internal improvements. For example, one DPO was actively developing and advocating a formal privacy infrastructure for an organization, which included hiring a data protection officer and establishing binding corporate rules for privacy. This interviewee explained the focus on those efforts by saying, while the organization was taking care of privacy, "It's more operationally. It's not formally." The DPO thought that the formal title and structure was important for the company, and went on to explain that efforts to integrate privacy would "make them [employees] conscious of . . . [privacy] all over the corporation." This respondent also discussed efforts to use shared software and systems that support activities throughout the company and subsidiaries as a means to address privacy and confidentiality issues. Yet, while clearly taking a more strategic view about meeting compliance goals—organizing and simplifying corporate policies and practices and using it as an opportunity to educate employees about the meaning of privacy—the effort remained tightly oriented toward the law. It was not used as an opportunity to discuss corporate values or principles, the way some of our German interviewees described. In an interesting juxtaposition, this DPO discussed using the adoption of binding corporate rules (BCRs) as an opportunity to speak to the corporate leaders about privacy in an expansive way. This was done by tying the issue to their personal lives, linking it to various roles and experiences in society:

And you try to tell them as people . . . [or] as an employee. That I would use your name and your daughter's name and your economic story and send it all over the world without control, without limit and to give [it to] my suppliers, my big ones for them to send you commercials? You don't like that? Okay, our customers don't, our employees don't, and . . . we have the obligation to maintain that in a correct standard. They say okay and they start to understand and they have influence . . . within the organization because if this is important for them, it will go down.

But, at the end of the day, although the DPO spoke of privacy internally as part of the relationship with various constituencies, the definition of privacy as operationalized in corporate practice retained its focus on the law. When asked about the content of the BCRs, that DPO said: "Actually it's . . . binding corporate rules we have to follow very much like the standard of what the Spanish law established. . . . And taking into account that the Spanish [law has] . . . a very high level of requirements, I would say that if we comply with Spanish [law] we would be perfect as a group."

SUMMARY

Spain presents no single archetype. Corporate privacy programs are oriented toward the law, and DPOs shared frustrations about the impact of this orientation on both business innovation, and integration of privacy protection into firm processes. Some viewed compliance as burdensome, others as impossible for reasons ranging from the sheer density of regulation to the volatility of consumer and employee relations in which privacy was often situated. Efforts to manage privacy were predominantly legal, with some firms attempting to develop processes that push privacy into practice.

7 Empirical Findings—France

The French privacy leads we interviewed portrayed a privacy landscape distinct in important ways from each of the other studied jurisdictions. More than privacy professionals in any of the other three countries, they articulated a historical understanding of privacy protection as synonymous with compliance and with concrete and specific requirements—largely regarding the registration of databases and their use, and the international transfer of data. This compliance function reflected, moreover, a largely settled understanding that one source defines privacy's meaning: the French data privacy authority, the CNIL.[1] French corporate privacy professionals generally understand their role to be comprehending, translating, and helping firms fulfill the CNIL's mandates.

This understanding, and the singular role of the CNIL in defining privacy, is reflected in the operationalization of privacy within firms. Even in those firms identified to us as leaders in the field, managers working on privacy issues were few in number and often worked less than full-time on these efforts. Many recounted their struggles to focus attention on privacy, and integrate privacy into firm decision making. In particular, they faced the challenge of ensuring that their role was not simply relegated to raising data protection issues ex post, after resources had been committed to a project and actions undertaken. Moreover, they described privacy functions that were, in many cases, historically weak and limited, and, in most, highly centralized and siloed from other firm functions. Most strikingly, while each of the firms studied had sought to ensure, through their legal or compliance departments, that they fulfilled key requirements regarding registration of databases and notification of data subjects regarding information use, in more than one-third of the firms, firms either had not created a single firm-wide privacy officer position at all or had done so only very recently—although each firm was working on remedying that structural absence. A number of these firms had not yet formally designated a data privacy officer, or CIL[2]— despite the administrative flexibility such a designation confers under French law.[3]

The privacy landscape in French firms differed markedly from that of German firms, despite apparent similarities in regulatory structure (the dedicated DPA/CNIL and, much later on, a similar but not mandatory DPO/CIL) and substance (a shared commitment to informational self-determination, and a social commitment to avoiding past abuses of data in Europe). French privacy operationalization bore some resemblance to that of Spain, in that firms in both countries approached privacy first and foremost as a matter of complying with regulator-determined requirements and therefore placed responsibility within the legal unit. French DPOs faced challenges in gaining influence similar to those articulated by their Spanish colleagues.

The characteristics of our French cohort were far more diverse. They hailed from operations and IT backgrounds as frequently as they did from legal, and the reasons they achieved reputations as field "leaders" were far more idiosyncratic. These differences often indicated far less about systemic aspects of privacy regulation, the privacy field, or the privacy dialogue in France than they did about elements particular to the firm, its industry, or the experience of either the particular privacy officer or a high-level executive or board member.

The French interviews painted a consistent portrait of historically low levels of privacy operationalization within firms, with only idiosyncratic efforts beyond compliance. But they also reflected a nearly uniform story of recent and ongoing transformations of corporate privacy practices in response to shifts in the external privacy landscape, which, until recently, had remained strikingly constant since French privacy governance began nearly forty years ago. These transformations partially reflect new regulatory approaches. Notably, those interviewed often mentioned the importance of increased transparency and the frequency of audits and enforcement actions brought by the CNIL, as well as a recent change in CNIL leadership. These developments signal changes in attitude toward the challenges of changing technologies and resulting threat models, as well as alterations in the decision making necessary to address them. Interviewees also noted that the CNIL's new emphasis on designating a CIL creates an entry point for regulators to more deeply influence the firm—although they recognized the shortcomings in the French regulatory definition of this DPO function, especially in comparison to its more robust German form.

Despite their recognition of the limitations of the new CIL requirement, the privacy leaders interviewed credited it with opening channels for a number of extra-regulatory influences to affect their firms' understanding of privacy. Specifically, it has facilitated exposure to best practices for robust privacy operationalization from other jurisdictions—including the United States and Germany—through professional networks that have developed in France and internationally. Though these connections have not supplanted existing French understandings of privacy, or the importance of the CNIL in shaping norms, they have begun to expand the dialogue regarding privacy.

THE FRENCH UNDERSTANDING OF PRIVACY'S MEANING AND THE LIMITED PRIVACY FIELD

The French interviewees articulated, in the strongest terms, the social importance of privacy protection. They emphasized that strong privacy laws "protect the liberty of the people to have their private life," and are considered a "cultural" value arising "from very long history," and a "deep and specific sensitivity about privacy and data privacy." This sensitivity, they claim, arises from the experience of the *Shoah*—the Holocaust—and the use of data and databases in deportation and persecution during the Nazi period.[4]

This strong articulation of privacy's cultural importance and historic roots translated into a rather specific understanding of how privacy must be protected: by focusing on individual rights and databases. The CNIL itself was created through France's early privacy law, enacted in 1978 (and amended in 2004)[5] in response to national outrage at an attempt by the French government to create a centralized database of personal data known as "SAFARI."[6] The CNIL's mission tracks this model. It keeps an inventory of data processing operations in the private sector through a three-level system of "notification" and approval—depending on the type and level of automation of the processing—to ensure that individual rights regarding that data, such as rights to access and inspection, are vindicated.[7] The agency is, in turn, vested with powers of advice and consultation to ensure that individual firms comply with these requirements and protect these rights. It also has the power to inspect and audit corporate practices and punish noncompliance with fines of up to EUR 300,000.[8]

The interviewed privacy leads articulated an understanding of privacy protection as compliance with these CNIL-specific mandates. As one described, privacy is "mostly a legal question," and "we don't have so much the kind of situation in France" in which corporate behavior is legal, but people object "because the law is normally . . . kind of strong." Indeed, another explained that the CNIL tries to leave little flexibility as to the rules regarding data processing and rights protection, producing "very detailed and exhaustive checklist[s] of what you need to do in order to be compliant." As a third described: "It's not principles that they put there. It's for a given purpose in a given situation you have to [do this or] that . . . it goes to the details, you have to put these sentences [in] a consent form. You have to give access only to the people who do accounting and not to the people who do reporting and it's really going to be more detailed."

In the words of a fourth interviewee, discussing requirements regarding the format of stored data:

The CNIL would like to give precise instructions . . . for example, when there's an authorization, they'd like to list the type of data one by one. You're allowed to use the last name, the first name, gender. This is very difficult for us, because we have a lot of data. So we prefer that the CNIL give categories of data. Data of identification, instead of listing it one by one, because they'll be missing some. And if they're missing some, we're not in accordance with what they said. We want them to stay within concrete principles, but not too detailed, because then there's always a discrepancy, and that's not progressive.

As a fifth privacy leader we interviewed described, "There is a risk that the CNIL [will] be too specific" in an unnecessary manner, so firms "will not be in a position to do [their] . . . day-to-day work." As another privacy lead described, however, "In the end, it's the CNIL that decides."

The CNIL is structured to provide detailed guidance not just in categories of similar cases—for which they have also developed "simplified" notification procedures—but also as individual questions arise within firms. Interviewed privacy leads describe using this consultation from monthly to yearly. "[O]ften, when I have a case [that's] a little complicated," explained one privacy officer, "where I'm not sure I'll have the authorization of the CNIL, I go see them . . . to have their recommendation. This has, honestly, always gone very well."

"This company wanted to create this treatment of data, it went to [me as] the CIL," described another lead of a recent experience, continuing: "Based on the data we're collecting, we may have to get an authorization from the CNIL. So we set up a meeting at the CNIL, we explained what we wanted to do, they told us, this is okay, this isn't. So the [firm] integrated in the contract what needed to be done, and today, the contract works."

Many of our interviewees also mentioned CNIL workshops and conferences, during which the agency explains appropriate ways to handle particular recurring situations, as well as guidance published on the CNIL website.

As many of our interviewees explained, these modes of communication have been further streamlined by creation of the CIL position in 2004.[9] As one respondent described, "[T]he CNIL put in place a unit dedicated to interfacing with CILs. So when we have a question to ask the CNIL, as a CIL, instead of going through an administrative process, we have privileged answers, with a quick turn-around time."

The CNIL's role as the source of detailed rules regarding privacy's meaning in particular implementations, moreover, contrasts with the negotiations about privacy's meaning in other jurisdictions. The dialogue over privacy in the United States involved a variety of parties including advocates and regulated parties as well as the FTC.[10] Germany's privacy "field" includes robust roles for workers' councils and strong DPOs within the firm,[11] and Spain's landscape incorporates labor unions and consumer groups in enforcing compliance.[12] Such nongovernmental forces, however, are largely absent in the accounts of French firms. Our interviewees explicitly rejected the importance of "advocacy groups," "consumer organizations," and "labor unions"[13] in the dialogue over privacy's meaning. One did suggest that the involvement of workers might be changing, describing how unions "do ask more and more for information that concerns them. And this is very new. That's because the press talks a lot about this subject. So the unions are starting to ask us a lot of these questions."

One interviewee directly attributed the contrast between the French and German workers' role in the privacy dialogue to specific legal differences in the structure of the workers' councils. While such institutions exist in both countries, the privacy officer explained:

[T]hey . . . only they have limited rights [in France], much more limited than in Germany. In Germany you have to remember the board of director[s] of German companies is made half a representative of the employee[s], half a representative of the shareholders, which means that they have a very strong weight. . . . [S]o basically when a company wants to do a major reorganization, sell part of the company or buy part of the company, they have to be involved, the workers. In France they don't. They have to inform people of this change but they don't have to follow their opinion. In Germany works councils can decide, they can block the use of [a] system or block a process in the company.

Our interviewees made a similar distinction between the structure of the German DPO and the French CIL. While both are designated pursuant to law, many of our interviewees described the French version of the position as far less influential because it lacks the job-protection provisions accorded its German counterpart. It also lacks the same sense of independence in reporting noncompliance.[14] Those interviewed did, however, credit the CIL position with increasing access within the firm to the corporate board, and thereby enhancing attention to privacy as a subject.

As one respondent described, "They are not so protected [as they are] in Germany, so I do not see a CIL calling the CNIL to alert about misconduct." In the words of another, "[I]t's not in our culture to go denounce our company." One European lawyer, contrasting their experiences in a number of jurisdictions, explained: "There is a specific dedicated department from the CNIL to help the CIL, but the CIL is very cautious because the CIL wants to avoid audits from the CNIL. So if you say too much to the CNIL, it'll be interested either to better understand the industry, or to know more, so they are cautious with the CNIL."

Summing up the importance of this distinction, one French CPO specifically connected it to the multifaceted network of privacy governance in Germany and the greater government role in France. The CPO summarized, "They don't do a lot of inspection in Germany. Because they have the DPO basically report to them all the time so they have people in-house."

Finally, our interviewed privacy leads explained that, despite the opportunities for communication with the regulator, regulated firms played little role in shaping policy.[15] "[I]t's more when we're working on concrete cases," said one, "it's not at the point where we're discussing the doctrine with them."

"I think in the future, it may be something we are interest[ed] in," said another privacy lead, but "for the moment, now we are [focused on] our day-to-day business."

OPERATIONALIZING PRIVACY WITHIN THE FRENCH FIRM

The privacy officers' opinions differed somewhat on the effects of a governance model centered on the regulator's detailed requirements. One explained that such rules provided the sense that "we have the means to be in conformity . . . [so] we don't consider it to be one of our top five risks." Others found regulations at this level of specificity "extremely cumbersome." Like their Spanish counterparts, they reported that a focus on top-down rules makes it "completely impossible to be 100 percent compliant."

But in every case, the interviewed privacy leads described consistent effects of this regulator-centered model on the firm's management of privacy. Most notably, their accounts reflected the ways in which this model of governance consigned privacy efforts to lower-level lawyers, or to compliance units reporting to the general counsel, which they described as the natural site for responding to the CNIL's mandates.

The French DPOs' backgrounds were diverse. As one interviewee accurately described the group of French privacy leaders, "We say that there are three types. . . . There's the more technical profile, there's the more judicial profile, and there's the conformity/audit profile." And their stories of how their firms came to develop a designated privacy function, and to allocate the resources that go along with it, were also far more varied than those of privacy officers in other jurisdictions.

For two interviewees, a single board member in each of their firms recognized the growing importance of privacy, and made the case for the allocation of additional resources. In one of those two firms, that board member went so far as to try to use privacy leadership as a market differentiator. Other privacy leads already held positions within the firm—for example, in information security or audit—that commanded significant resources or a direct board report, both of which benefitted privacy when it was added to the executive's existing portfolio. Some had worked at firms in industries that dealt with sensitive information and were governed by other relevant legal frameworks that required them to develop expertise in information management compliance. In still other cases, advances arose when privacy was integrated into the consideration of preexisting, robust, and unrelated risk management systems, such as information security, or a well-developed "code of ethics," or other information management and audit systems. As one interviewee working in an otherwise highly regulated industry explained: "If, let's say if privacy aspect[s] were not considered originally, and very often they were not, it is easier to just add a few provision[s] in the existing methodology; it's the best way to ensure that the system that will deploy will have been assessed for privacy and data protection and that the people will follow the rule in practice."

In the words of another interviewee with an information-security background, by adding privacy into security frameworks governing the approval of new IT systems, "I can just push my different ideas inside so we could be able to do some 'privacy by design' more easily than if we did not have a formal process already in place." And in the case of a third privacy officer: "[P]rivacy is part of the whole package, so we have an ethics code, and privacy is part of it, but it's much larger than that. So that means that you fight corruption, illegal interests, conflict of interests, you fight [corruption] and [it] is more or less the same and then you promote equal rights for women or minorities and so on, so this is the whole package and within this package you have also privacy and personal data protection."

Despite individual accomplishments in piggybacking privacy onto other, better-developed firm functions or positions, the size and general privacy focus described by most of our interviewees diverged sharply from those of their German and U.S. counterparts. With the exception of one CPO who coordinated the efforts of designated CILs in multiple subsidiaries within France, few French privacy leads described an operation within their French firm that involved more than one or two professionals working full time on privacy. More than half of the identified privacy leaders we interviewed, moreover, were not dedicated to the issue full time. Some spent as little as 15 or 20 percent of their time on privacy. Most were the first privacy officers in their firms, and most received their privacy duties within the past four years.

A number described the steep hill they have had to climb in making the case for a standalone privacy officer in their firms. One of the longer-serving privacy officers described the experience of initiating a privacy function a number of years ago: "You have no clients and you have no boss, you know. And you are alone in the desert. . . . Nobody cares, nobody wants [it], it's a burden to everybody." Another said: "When I started my job . . . we ha[d] many projects which [raised privacy issues] and it was a difficult time because I had to say 'no.' 'No, it's not possible.'" And a third stated, "sometimes it's very difficult [in] meetings, because I say, 'this, we're not going to do."' Even those at the more fully resourced end of this narrow spectrum headed a centralized privacy operation that was generally not well integrated operationally within the firm. While a few described the designation of a privacy "correspondent," or interlocutor, within diverse business units, none described the embedding of dedicated privacy experts.

For many, their work focused on education efforts about the importance of privacy, attempts to increase awareness of privacy mandates, and, especially, the translation of legal requirements regarding data processing. These requirements were conveyed through training—in person and online—and written materials for firm workers. As one CPO described: "[W]e gave a lot of presentations to train people on the protection of data. We prepared presentations in the form of questions. We put together pamphlets to raise awareness on the important points of the law. I wrote procedures to explain to people how to analyze whether their handling of data conforms [to the law]."

Another privacy lead described in detail how privacy officers develop policies governing data for other firm units:

At first we come up with points that we think are important to develop internally—it can be the right of access, the requests of third parties—because we are very much solicited, not necessarily by clients, to obtain information about our employees. . . . They come to see us asking for information on so-and-so. . . . So we had to teach our colleagues how to respond to this sort of request. Also, how to react when we have a request for a right to access a person's personal data. We [wanted] to develop a framework for this. So we develop the idea, we prepare a notice, and after we have it validated by either marketing to have it placed on our website—a tool for the candidates to explain to them how they can access their data—or a notice that is worked in collaboration with the legal team to be published in our legal reference on the requests of third parties and how to respond in these sorts of cases.

As a third privacy lead described their duties: "[W]e give the law. And then we say . . . here's what you have to do, what we must not do, what's not allowed. And if you do it wrong, here are the sanctions. We explain to people how to work, while respecting the law. So that's the first thing, we make guides. We made some for HR, we made some for everything that is archive[ed]. . . . So we made a guide for each type of work, saying for each type of data, how much time you must keep them. The law says this, and we, CIL, recommend this."

Others explained that building personal relationships with the leads of other units such as marketing and IT makes them institutionally well placed to guarantee consultation as new projects and technology systems are rolled out. "[S]lowly and slowly," one explained, "that's mainly my job. Teaching, making rules, convincing, making bridges all over." This was ensured in some instances not just informally, but also by company policy: "I'm involved at the beginning of [every project that comes from the central part of the company]," explained one CPO. "It's in the technological procedures. In projects, before passing the first step, they must come see me so that I can tell them, here's everything that needs to get done."

At least three of those interviewed—all in firms that had recently developed or revamped their privacy functions, and all of whom came from either core firm operations or IT—had developed a CPO profile that more closely resembled their German counterparts in a variety of ways. This suggested a new model of privacy lead in the diverse mix of the French experience. They appeared especially integrated into core firm decision making by their intimate knowledge of the personnel and their relevant functions. In two cases, the privacy lead served on a high-level trans-substantive corporate committee developed to integrate various firm interests into project planning.

At the same time, most of the privacy leads, including the aforementioned three, described a largely centralized approach to developing privacy policies in these consultative contexts. In describing this orientation, and the decision not to develop a privacy expert within different departments, one explained: "[T]he goal of the game is to discuss this with all of our colleagues. The idea behind our system is for each individual to have the right reflex. As a result of discussing with everyone, it sets the right reflex, and the next time, they'll come consult with us out of their own reflex. So no, there's no point of [a] contact in the marketing department."

In the words of another privacy lead, "[W]e prepare [our policies] by ourselves, our team. And after, we solicit experts, we ask them questions. But in general, we have the knowledge to make the guides, so we don't have too many issues. Then we distribute them."

Even those two CPOs, however, recognized that such centralization is both "an advantage and an inconvenience." As one explained, "There's a risk of missing something. But from our end, since we have the expertise, it's more interesting and constructive to have the marketing expert to explain to us their problem, and we'll work with them to go in the right direction, as opposed to diluting." The second privacy lead stated: "We diffuse within the enterprise that when there is something new, they must alert me. . . . For the big projects that are expensive, I am aware, because it's something that is important in the enterprise, and for that, I'll oversee what is implemented technologically, and say, this is possible, this isn't possible. But for cases that are less important, that can be serious if they're not well done."

SUGGESTIONS OF TRANSITION IN THE FRENCH PRIVACY FIELD

The French interviews showcased the generally low level of privacy operationalization within firms and the shortcomings of efforts beyond compliance in firms with privacy leaders. They also revealed a privacy landscape in the midst of a transition affecting corporate privacy practices.

SHIFTS IN REGULATORY TOOLS AND APPROACHES

These transformations partially reflect a shift in regulatory tools and approaches utilized by the CNIL. Indeed, while the interviewed privacy leads noted that the agency's practices in the past may have reflected an evolution of existing practices, such as the adoption of simplified notification policies for standard uses of data, they attributed more revolutionary change in the privacy landscape to several recent shifts in approach.

The first involves an increase in the frequency and transparency of inspections and enforcement actions. As one CPO explained, by reducing the administrative burdens of notifications, the CNIL has "replace[d] it by commitment to follow a certain methodology or apply a certain simplified rule. . . . This allows them to free up resources to do more inspections. . . . In the past you had to notify or ask for the authorization for everything which of course is a huge [amount of] paperwork for very little . . . benefit . . . [a]nd they were dealing with paper mountains accumulating in their offices."

Now, that privacy lead explained, "they have an approach which is . . . closer to the Anglo-Saxon way of doing these things: This is a rule. That's what you have to comply with. You don't have to notify but we will come and check. And they are doing that more and more."

Indeed, every respondent we interviewed mentioned the enhanced attention to privacy protection spurred by the increase in the CNIL's surprise inspections and audits, which the agency indicated grew by 50 percent in 2012. Moreover, these actions, and any sanctions to which they lead, can now be publicized[16] as a result of the "Defender of Rights" Act, an amendment to French privacy law passed on March 29, 2011.[17]

In particular, our interviewees noted that the agency's articulation of its upcoming audit criteria grabbed people's attention and focused firm priorities. Indeed, 60 percent of the firms studied reported having been the subject of a CNIL inspection in the last several years. The practice of publishing the audits, and their results, was noted as particularly important. In the words of one CPO whose audit was "pretty positive," the audit marked "a success that we could transmit to our CEO, to tell him that it went well, that we got remarks, but also compliments on our tools." Another reported that after an audit, the company decided to elevate a privacy professional within the firm to the position of CIL.

The interviewed privacy leads credited the rise in enforcement actions with increasing firms' attention to the issue of privacy, and how privacy failures can lead to a serious risk to the firm's reputation. Several privacy professionals mentioned, in particular, the CNIL's 2010 ruling against the private tutoring firm Acadomia, a decision posted publicly[18] and widely covered in the press,[19] as a turning point. One explained: "This played a large role [in] the awareness of organizations on the risk of reputation related to IT law. It allowed us to bring awareness to our teams of the risks that can result if there's a negative audit of the CNIL." A second agreed, stating: "[T]here was this reputation risk that was identified, and so I talked to the CEO about it, who said, 'Okay, let's put together the means to remove this risk.' That . . . [meant] an investment in information technology to add popups in the comment fields, investments to do automatic audits. There was a decision made, let's make an investment to deal with this."

Another described the importance of informing the firm's board about the public sanction of a French bank, which involved "a fine plus [a] specific article in the news," as well as about "other examples for other companies, and . . . show[ing them] . . . that [the] CNIL was doing [inspections] inside our own company."

A third spoke of systemic enlistment of this type of publicity to generate support for recent changes within the firm. As the lead explained: "It helps me. So, more and more, there are scandals that are revealed by the media. So that helps me to pass the message internally that this is a real subject. Every month, I send out a press review to all the big bosses, with decisions made world-wide, from the . . . [United States], from England, with big scandals, to try to make them aware. . . . Yes, there are some who have told me that it's starting to interest them. But it's recent."

In the words of a fourth interviewee, "reputation is important for the company. We have shown that other French companies, banks and other types of companies had specific controls from the CNIL regulator and they had either penalties to pay or they had to write specific articles in the newspapers and so in terms of image it's not a good thing."

While several privacy leads suggested that the CNIL needed to increase its actions even further in order to intensify public pressure, they generally recognized that the CNIL's expanded enforcement actions have already affected the public's awareness. For example, while one said, "I think it's not enough," another warned, in light of the CNIL's new decisions, "we have to be sensitive to what we call in France '*l'opinion publique,*' public opinion."

Interviewed CPOs cited a second key regulatory development: new leadership that changed the CNIL's approach to privacy. Several cited public remarks by the then-new CNIL president, Madame Isabelle Falque-Pierrotin, as an indicator that the CNIL intends to use more ex ante guidance, to rely less on formalities, and to credit firms for developing robust privacy systems, even when breaches occur inadvertently. In the words of one CPO, "I had the feeling that we were at a major turning point in France. And that we were in the middle of going from this approach of nonconformity to an approach of the management of risk."

Other interviewees mentioned two other CNIL changes that have led to shifts in the privacy field: the integration of a team of technologists into the CNIL's staff, and the development of a new CNIL Department of Innovation. One privacy lawyer we interviewed described how these new units function: "There is a team dedicated to innovation, which works with academics, sociologists, engineers. They have a big meeting on innovation. There's one department dedicated to technology, with engineers, who will work on the new regulation. But there is also a new department dedicated to prospective innovation. And they work with all types of stakeholders dealing with innovation."

"It's really very open," that privacy lawyer continued. "It's no longer just lawyers and IT providers, it's all types of people who think about the evolution of privacy [including] consumer associations [and] representatives of the education industry." According to our interviewees these developments reflect a broader change—a greater level of overall flexibility in those responsible for coordinating privacy compliance in various arenas. As one CPO described it: "The people of the IT department are very business oriented, very open minded, but the civil servants who are working on the day-to-day notification, they are less open, they are . . . strict[er]. So when you want the CNIL to evolve or be more business oriented, you need to escalate past the first level. The top level is more business oriented than the people who handle the day-to-day."

A number of interviewees cited the new CNIL department as providing greater opportunities for stakeholder involvement, including discussions about policy between the CNIL and outside groups representing specific data-intensive industries like health care, banking, and insurance, as well as privacy professional groups. As one put it, "[T]he professional organizations are more efficient in discussions with the CNIL . . . [and] the CNIL prefers to collaborate with professionals when it's working on a specific subject. It'll discuss with banking organizations when it's on a banking subject, and it'll discuss with health professional organizations when it's working on health data, but I think that it prefers this because it has people who know what they're doing."

In particular, at least one lawyer explained that although companies might not feel comfortable "lobbying" the CNIL themselves, given their position as a regulated party, these industry groups might now be able to present important perspectives in a more secure manner. When I "intervene in the regulatory lobbying" through a professional or industry organization, explained one CPO, "[I]t's not as a representative of [my firm], it's as a professional." Describing the work of the French privacy professionals' organization, another phrased the issue more strongly: "[F]rom time to time, we work on certain subjects where we'd like to remain anonymous. So the work group arrives at a conclusion. And it's this group with only anonymous people, in other words, under the cover of the association, that goes to present the case to the CNIL."

MATURATION OF THE CIL POSITION

A number of interviewees suggested that the maturation of the position of the CIL is an important, albeit recent, development. To be sure, the CIL position has officially been on the books for a number of years. Yet the comments of some privacy leads, especially those who recently assumed a formal privacy lead position, suggest that the availability of the CIL designation has more recently helped generate a more influential privacy professional presence, and a more robust internal privacy practice. Those designated as CILs earlier in the position's life cycle spoke less about the position's capacity for heightening influence and independence within the firm. But the accounts of several more recent CILs suggest a strengthening CIL role in France. Sounding very much like a counterpart in Germany might, one recently designated CIL described confidently, "I'm independent, by the law. The French law says that when a CIL is appointed, he is independent. That means, that it's written in the law, that no one should tell me what to do, nor how to do it." Key to that independence, in that privacy lead's view, was access to the corporate board. "[R]eporting to the CEO is in the law" as is the duty to alert:

If there's a functional problem in the company, for example, data that was accessed by people who shouldn't have, and I'm aware of it, and my colleagues did not do as they were supposed to, I must alert. So I have a procedure that I put in place, where I [send] the alert. First to the director who should know in the enterprise, pretty high up in the enterprise, to tell them, here is the problem, here is the law. What will you do to correct this? When will you correct this?" [And] when I do an alert, I do two or three per year; it's corrected in the month that follows.

Several other interviewees described the designation of a CIL as an organizing event for their companies to completely rework the privacy function, with new structures, resources, and enhancements to the privacy lead's legitimacy and involvement in firm decision making. More specifically, two CILs spoke of the way in which the formalization of their title and role involved their placement on "transversal" committees—either ongoing, or assembled as new projects arose—that handled development from a corporate project's nascence. This ensured that privacy requirements would be articulated, and guidance given, throughout a project's life cycle.

Finally, the rise of CIL designations coincides with the development over the past few years of institutions to support privacy professionalization in France, the subject of the next section. Professional networks can now provide support, guidance, organization, and information about best practices that can shape the views of designated internal corporate privacy leads. One brand-new CIL described a cutting-edge privacy practice as integrating privacy into existing technology systems, enabling his firm to "do privacy by design and implement in this process . . . specific items for [a] privacy impact analysis." When asked how he had derived this notion of privacy, the CPO responded, "It's because I've attended the IAPP conference in Brussels and I've heard a lot of it and I . . . [saw that] it would be coming in the next regulation."

PRIVACY PROFESSIONALIZATION AND BEST PRACTICES INFLUENCES

The preceding quote points to the recently expanded role for privacy professional organizations generally. Every privacy lead interviewed described how they and their peers were becoming "important players in the dialogue about privacy." Together, the interviewees gave an account of the robust role that such overlapping organizations—in particular, the French Association Française des Correspondants à la Protection des Données à Caractère Personnel (AFCDP) and the U.S.-based IAPP—are coming to play in evolving understandings of corporate data privacy. As one interviewee described, participation in these groups "brings us to the forefront, to the new topics. It allows us to meet colleagues. Because if one day we have a problem regarding health, we can contact the CIL of a hospital. Since we have clients with various jobs, it creates a network of diverse expertise. We really have to spend time externally to acquaint ourselves with the news."

The move toward professionalization also creates a network to "get information first," respondents said, about how new technological issues should be conceptualized and the "legal obligation we have in this respect." And, in the words of one active participant, "we define best practices."

This information is disseminated through association websites, conferences, lunches, webinars hosted on association extranets, work groups, online discussions, "knowledgenet" events, and lunches at law firms. The existence of a professional network, along with international conferences such as the IAPP summits on both sides of the Atlantic, and the annual Privacy Laws and Business gathering in Cambridge, England,[20] bring models from a variety of countries across jurisdictions. "I'm attending a conference on next Monday to get more information on the situation and I've talked also to some people from . . . the [United States] who worked on this," said one interviewee. Another stated, "[W]e've been inspired by what's going on in the [United States]"—while noting that "simply, we don't have the same culture." "[F]or me it's great," said one new privacy lead, "because I enlisted in the IAPP last October to attend the conference

and to be in the network of privacy professionals on the international side."
Indeed, that CPO anticipated getting from the IAPP "all the feedback I
would need to implement my activities and defend inside the company
some good practice to implement." In short, explained another respondent, "to be a good CIL, you have to be a part of an association."

SUMMARY

Corporate management of privacy in France is in flux. Shifts in the CNIL's
approach, specifically an emphasis on cultivating firm leadership through
the CIL program, and enhanced dialogue with corporations, are generating
responses in the field. The privacy professional community within France
is beginning to shape its own perspective on what a robust privacy program
should look like, and the roles of a cohort of DPOs are beginning to change.
Their efforts are informed by the programs in Germany and the United
States, and accordingly, look to move privacy outside its historic position
in legal compliance. Despite these movements, corporate privacy management, at the time of our interviews, was a largely regulatory agency–driven
affair.

8 Empirical Findings—United Kingdom

In the United Kingdom, our interviews with privacy leaders revealed a privacy field that straddles the Atlantic in a deeply liminal state: one foot standing on American soil and one foot firmly planted on the Continent. British firms are legally constrained by compliance-oriented domestic and European legal regimes that are themselves in transition. Yet they are also influenced by other legal and extra-legal regulatory forces through their operations outside Europe. Globalized and globalizing British firms seem to be on a trend toward the operationalized privacy practices identified in the United States and Germany, but are not yet quite there. This trend is much less evident in firms that are domestic-facing or smaller in operations or focus.

The privacy executives that we interviewed all expressed a rhetoric of privacy and data protection that was rich in notions of risk management in addition to simple compliance—a view that is closer to that of their peers in the United States than those in continental Europe. This perhaps reflects growing isomorphism and knowledge transfer among privacy professionals through the spread of global professional networks. When it comes to actually operationalizing such notions in the firm, however, those firms we examined are less robust, lacking the twin mechanisms of a powerful, external-facing CPO and a distributed network of privacy expertise and practice. Despite the will and effort of the privacy professionals to marshal resources, executive support, and stakeholder buy-in necessary to reach a higher level of privacy operationalization, they face multiple external and internal challenges to execution.

The recently enhanced coercive powers of the national privacy regulator —the Information Commissioner's Office (ICO)—and its willingness to use them, are partly responsible for the palpable sense of transition. We sensed a fear of falling behind among respondents. They worried that their firms were in danger of becoming the next headline. Many desired more corporate resources, as well as the license and authority from upper management to think and act more strategically in the rapidly changing regulatory, technological, and operational environment.

British corporate privacy leads, on the whole, used U.S.-style rhetoric to describe privacy within the firm. The touchpoints were principles of consumer protection and fairness, beyond straight-up compliance with legal requirements. Many were explicitly dismissive of what they characterized as an overly compliance-oriented approach on the Continent. The respondents expressed a view that consumer protection and fairness principles were valuable for their own sakes. But many explained their value primarily in terms of impact on the bottom line rather than as an element of a wider human rights or ethical framework. Many described privacy protection as providing a direct competitive advantage to their firms, or as an indirect advantage in building trust with consumers and regulators.

Whether framed in terms of competition, market position, or business necessity, these themes aligned privacy's meaning with a risk management approach, and led us to expect similar practices to those in United States and German firms. However, what we found in the United Kingdom was at best a partial implementation. The rhetoric and thinking of privacy leads was out ahead of company investments, although the privacy leads were actively working to transition toward the level of operationalization found in Germany and the United States.

The external environment was more similar to France and Spain, with a limited cast of privacy players and venues. Interviewees characterized the UK ICO as a progressive, business and consumer bridging regulator that worked at shaping privacy as a set of consumer protection principles and processes rather than a set of rules. But until recently, the ICO lacked significant enforcement power. Historically, firms in the United Kingdom had only limited positive interaction with regulators, civil society groups, academics, and other stakeholders in the tussle over privacy's meaning.

British CPOs were not as powerful or well-resourced as their U.S. or German equivalents—most stood two or three steps below the general counsel and for the most part did not interact directly with the board of directors. They generally had smaller teams working directly under them, or had spent the last few years building up their firms' privacy infrastructure from scratch. Without adequate resources, they found themselves less able to delegate routine tasks and focus on forward-looking strategy or the process of translation from the regulatory field to firm operations. Many were consumed in the day-to-day minutiae of compliance, policymaking, and corporate capacity building. However, most were quite explicit that they desired more power. They were actively engaged in efforts to strengthen their privacy office, build their distributed teams, and move themselves toward a more strategic role, in accordance with their already well-formed understanding of privacy as risk management. They were deeply skeptical of the draft omnibus data-protection regulation working its way through the European Parliament, finding the regulations to be, at best, compliance oriented and, at worst, unworkable. They feared an onslaught of needless compliance matters that would overwhelm their resources, such as inter-jurisdictional data transfers. Yet paradoxically, many said the binding corporate rules creation and approval process, which emerged out of these data transfer requirements, had helped strengthen their firms' privacy practices.

While United Kingdom privacy officers find themselves reluctantly bound by the compliance-oriented approach, their notion of data protection is set within a broader risk framework attached to market position and a sense of social license—although in practice social license doesn't appear to play a role. As in the United States, UK CPOs leverage the rhetoric of consumer expectations and fairness, as well as the coercive powers of the regulator, to engage the firm. But these efforts are weakened by their tenuous and sporadic access to leadership. The broader definition of privacy at work in British firms has empowered British CPOs, but on a much slower trajectory than in German and U.S. firms. The recent accretion of power, authority, and resources found in German and American firms has not been realized in British firms, although more global companies boast structures and best practices that resemble their German and U.S. counterparts. This has contributed to a lag in developing strategic CPO roles and rich structures of privacy integration, despite the publicity, penalties, and security breaches that pose increasing risks to firms' reputations.

PRIVACY'S MEANING

For our British respondents, like their European neighbors across the Channel, privacy "principally derives from the law." For their firms, compliance is the starting point. "[T]here's an element of legal compunction" noted one, "that fear of compliance, you know, having to report something to the board . . . and the possible sanctions." Compared to Germany, the United Kingdom has a much more centralized data protection regime. It is also more "relaxed," to the extent that in 2010, the European Commission (EC) found the UK Data Protection Act of 1998 to be "blatantly in violation of the EC Directive" in certain areas.[1] While the text of the UK act appears to correspond with the 1995 EU Data Protection Directive, the ICO and the UK courts have interpreted some of its language more narrowly than elsewhere in the European Union.[2]

Although there has been some data protection legislation in the United Kingdom since 1984, it was not until 1998 that the comprehensive Data Protection Act was enacted specifically to implement the EC Directive.[3] The United Kingdom has also implemented the e-Privacy Directive (Directive 2002/58/EC) by passing the Privacy and Electronic Communications (EC Directive) Regulations 2003.[4] The Data Protection Act and the Regulations are enforced, along with the Freedom of Information Act (FOIA, which applies to government entities), by the ICO (Scotland has its own legislation and a separate agency handles access to information). Some of our respondents were in heavily regulated industries, such as banking or health, where laws protecting patient or customer confidentiality were well established long before the EU Directive in 1995. For some respondents based in large, diversified, or geographically dispersed firms, other regulatory regimes swayed privacy's meaning as well. It depends on "which silo you're talking to, because they're all interested in slightly different things." In other words, "which law's going to be most important" will vary "depending on their activities."

Despite detailed national law, the 1995 EU Directive was considered by our interviewees as the fountainhead for privacy law in the United Kingdom. This may in part reflect firm sensitivity to the perception of the Data Protection Act as a weaker implementation. As one respondent put it: "[W]hen I'm looking at UK legislation I quite often look back to the Directive and how other countries may have implemented that Directive, especially when it's areas that are slightly gray."

As another interviewee related: "[M]y default basis is always: 'What does the Directive say? What is the wording of the Directive?' And I will always start with the Directive."

For companies with broader operations than the United Kingdom alone, the focus on the directive was enhanced due to concerns with harmonization. Some respondents cited the mechanism of binding corporate rules as a harmonizing source of privacy law for their firms' multi-jurisdictional activities. "[P]rivacy policy," noted one, "really was an attempt of [the company] to very early say to the regulators, we will abide by these global high-level uniform rules of engagement as how we handle our data . . . and therefore you should allow us to share data because we apply these rules." In these globalized firms, as in similar U.S. firms, we noted a convergence on a pan-global set of company principles oriented around the EU Directive, which could then be customized, applied, or translated into the requirements for individual jurisdictions of operation.

Another interviewee spoke about the "core issues" common to data protection laws in Europe and around the world: "[Y]ou can still see the same principles at play, informed consent, transparency, the security which I was just talking about. These are the core issues . . . you talk about where Europe has the most sophisticated data protection law, but when you're to the heart of things, it's all about the same thing isn't it, about confidentiality and informed consent and choice, security. . . . I guess it is the law, but within the law there are particular things, you know, there are privacy principles that you try to implement in a practical sense."

In the face of the varied, complicated, and sometimes conflicting rules in the European Union, many CPOs found that taking a compliance approach was not successful within their organizations. One related that "if you stopped most people within [the company] and said 'What does privacy mean?' they would say 'It means an additional layer of compliance headache.'" Another explained that "[i]f you start talking privacy to people, they'll die of boredom and honestly they won't read—in most instances it's not particularly intuitive. Particularly the European stuff is very difficult [to get] onboard and to interpret." This respondent ended up reducing the complex rules into a broad set of principles:

So rather than tell them "these are the data protection principles," what does that mean? "You must process data fairly."

[To which the response is]: "Well, I think I'm doing it fairly." But what does *that* mean? And so when you hear about their project, you say . . . "Why do you want to do this? Why is this a good idea? . . . Are we collecting only such information as is necessary or are we also collecting a whole bunch of other stuff because it might be really useful and this is a good opportunity to do it? How long are we keeping it for because we must only keep it for so long as it's necessary, so we need to build that in now." . . . [T]here's no magic in it. It's the same criteria we use every time and it covers . . . every single data protection principle.

Thus, in contrast to our respondents in Spain and France, who characterized privacy law as a complex, ever-changing set of rules that were next to impossible to comply with fully, British privacy leads were more sanguine about their ability to meet the standard by distilling abiding, cross-cutting principles. As one remarked, "[T]o be perfectly honest it's a bit of practical common sense, if you will."

This pragmatism, and focus on principles, made for a notion of privacy that moved toward a "compliance-plus" or "risk management" approach. One respondent set out this orientation: "We use both terms [data protection and privacy]. And I try and differentiate. Data protection is a clear, if you like, legal obligation. . . . But privacy for me is a broader concept. It's not just fulfilling the black letter of the law but looking after people's ideas, people's data, people's—the stuff of their lives, if you like, in an appropriate manner."

When asked what privacy meant, another respondent articulated this "compliance-plus" mentality: "Well, I think there's an awareness of doing the right thing. So . . . you can argue about whether technically your terms and conditions enabled you to do things or whether conduct wasn't necessarily illegal, but was it the right thing?"

For some of our respondents, privacy was simply risk management. One claimed: "[W]e are all in my team I would say risk managers, it's what we do. We partner with the business but then try to assess how do you remediate risk." Another used similar conceptualization, saying that "privacy both in terms of the approach that you take within the organization itself, and also the regulatory and sanctions coming from the data protection authorities should be targeted at where there could be most risk and harm." This respondent added: "You can try and shut down those opportunities for harm. That's where I think privacy is at its best and most effective. As opposed to me sitting in my office and writing wonderful policies that look great but no one ever reads."

The notion of pragmatism that undergirded privacy's meaning in the United Kingdom was echoed by key informants. One described it as "a cultural deeply engrained approach of the British governing class, if you like. I think pragmatism is seen to be a national virtue of which we're very proud. That's the starting point." The ICO, he continued, "will take a down-to-Earth, common-sense approach, which helps those organizations who want to get data protection right, to do so . . . [and they'll] take tough action against those who don't want to get it right." In addition to being pragmatic, such an approach has legal grounding, as consideration of consumer expectations is an explicit part of the fair and lawful requirement of the UK Data Protection Act.

Our respondents cited the business advantages that an approach based on consumer expectations could engender for their companies, as well as the significant financial *disadvantages* that came with a failure to do so. These factors drove their firms' adoption of a privacy program, and became the primary values undergirding privacy policies and decision-making processes. One tied consumer expectations to the legal requirements, stating: "It's an extrapolation from the fairness or unfairness test, the first principle in the DPA. Having made the assumption . . . that what we're doing is lawful, but then is it fair? And for me one of the tests of fairness, not necessarily the exclusive or the primary test, is what was the expectation of somebody when they gave you that data? Because if they didn't expect it to be used in this way, then the chances of it being fair are going to be more limited."

Still another summed up the principle succinctly: "Your customer or the individual about whose data you're processing, rule of thumb, they should never be surprised by what you're doing. That should be absolutely transparent to them and clear and expected."

As in the United States, privacy leads used emotive or empathetic notions related to consumer feelings to explain the expectations orientation. One stated "I think it's really the basic gut test. If I'm a customer and this is going to happen to me, how do I feel about that?" Another reported framing the question within the firm as, "Well how would you feel if this information would be disclosed about you to these people? It may not be strictly against your privacy law, it may be borderline with our privacy policy, but is this fair?" Another explained that "privacy [was] almost as an emotional issue as opposed to a strict legal and regulatory issue . . . you can get everything absolutely right by the law and you can still receive some very bad publicity."

Digging deeper, we encountered a dominant theme behind firms' adoption of a consumer expectations and fairness principle of privacy:

respecting this principle would benefit the company's bottom line, whether positively (by creating a competitive advantage and building consumer trust), or negatively (through the avoidance of regulatory fines, poor publicity, or the loss of customer trust). With respect to increased competitive advantage, one of our respondents noted that "when customers ask us about these sorts of things, . . . when you come back with an answer straight away and an assurance it makes the negotiation so much easier. It's far more likely to differentiate us from our competitors." Another, looking into the future, wondered, "how do we incorporate [privacy] in our offerings so that they're competitive and so that they don't make further issues for our clients? I think that's going to be really key to us." Finally, another noted with respect to the banking industry that "every bank wants to be the first to surface from this, to be the bank that is no longer under major regulation. . . . That it's getting things right. That it's doing the right things while these evil bad banks at the moment, there's nothing to distinguish [them] and I think everyone is trying to move themselves forward. To say look, we are trying to be better than the rest."

However, not all of our respondents were in agreement with the proposition that privacy could provide a positive competitive advantage. One, speaking about the telecommunications industry, argued: "I don't think consumers quite see it in that way. So yes, in the future maybe things will change and maybe there are opportunities to differentiate. It's certainly very damaging if you get it wrong, but to differentiate yourself just by getting it right—there's no evidence for that at the moment."

There was wide, but not unanimous, agreement on the potential negative consequences of a failure to meet consumer expectations. "The market, then, becomes much more of a threat to your continued existence than any regulator will," noted one respondent. Another agreed, saying "it's going to be very difficult to sell products that are going to put our clients in breach or that may have backlash from privacy advocates." Still another repeated, "[C]lient data is core to our business, right, so if we get it wrong we will not be able to sell our products, frankly, very easily. We will lose the reputation of our clients, we will lose these very lucrative deals which make our profits and keep our shareholders happy."

One respondent in the health industry also agreed: "[I]f you do things wrong in privacy, if you lose patient data, if you suffer some security breach or you are prosecuted by the privacy regulator in a certain country you might get a slap on the wrist, you might get a fine. But this is terrible publicity. . . . And if you fall afoul in terms of confidentiality then this is going to be terrible in terms of your perception against your competitors and within the marketplace . . . that is the thing that worries them the most . . . the biggest driver in terms of the resource[s]."

However, one respondent from a firm in the energy sector—not traditionally an information-intensive industry—illustrated how not all companies are sensitive to negative publicity surrounding a data breach. The respondent remarked that when an employee laptop was lost with several thousand Social Security numbers: "[T]hat's our worst privacy disaster and our share price didn't budge. Our share price is not sensitive to privacy issues. We're not Google, we're not Facebook, we're not LinkedIn. We're not WhatsApp."

These disagreements aside, what we found was that when privacy requirements were aligned with business or individual needs, privacy was an "easy sell" for our respondents. "It's very easy," said one, "to forget that when you come into work, and it doesn't have to be [this company], it's any organization, that the majority of the people are driven by performance contracts. We all want a big bonus at the end of the year, right?" Although noting that this profit motive had recently been giving way to notions of corporate responsibility, this commentator also opined that it had nevertheless "been a long journey . . . for privacy to suddenly get onto the same page as accounting standards." Another respondent explained how firm management only became more "engaged" with record retention and destruction policies once the cost-savings aspects were illustrated. Finally, as another explained in the context of the financial sector:

[T]he good thing about doing privacy at a bank is there is a general understanding that you have to protect people's money. We're not going to have a terribly robust model if we don't do that. And along with that goes a lot of information, because it's not just cash. It's the monetary, financial transaction side of things, . . . and even if there wasn't the legal requirement of a bunch of this stuff that we have to do this anyway, . . . [T]here is a business case to keeping it safe, to keeping it accurate, to keeping it up to date. . . . So whilst there is a legal framework which helps . . . I think if you took that away it's quite an easy sell.

Thus, while they cited goals of fairness and meeting consumer expectations as key to their understanding of privacy's meaning, as in the United States, the UK privacy leads were more likely to tie privacy to purer market advantage. In contrast, their U.S. peers felt there was little competitive advantage to privacy performance.

The privacy leads also connected trust and privacy. Both consumer and *employee* trust were mentioned, echoing the German experience. Corporations engender greater employee and consumer trust by protecting both, because employees identify with consumers' privacy concerns. As one respondent put it: "[P]rivacy is actually a very personal individual thing. Not only to the individuals who've entrusted [the company] with their information but also to the individuals within [the company]. So we very much have educated our employees on the premise that all the privacy expectations that you have as an individual . . . are the same expectations that individuals who've given [the company] their information have of [the company]."

Broader ethical frames of human rights and private life were largely absent in the United Kingdom. Only one of our respondents explicitly identified human rights as a factor in shaping a personal understanding of privacy law. Neither was a concept like "respect for home and family life" specifically indicated, in contrast to Germany and France. However, some respondents cited individual scandals—hinting at the influence of these wider frames in practice—as catalysts for broader changes in their privacy policies and practices, or even their compliance practices generally. For example, phone hacking scandals in the news media sector, the LIBOR scandal in the banking sector, and various data breach incidents such as the loss of personal information by the national tax authority, were all described by our interviewees as key wake-up calls to senior authorities in their organizations.

Another external factor more muted in the United Kingdom than other countries was the role of the national data protection authority—in this case the ICO—in shaping individuals' and firms' understanding of privacy requirements. Unlike in the United States, the ICO had not taken on the same activist role that the FTC had done in the field of privacy until far more recently. Nor did the ICO have or use the same coercive measures, such as the broad investigative or disciplinary powers of the FTC. Similarly, the rigorous compliance requirements of other European data protection authorities, or the huge fines meted out by authorities in countries such as Spain, had only limited effect on companies' operations that were specific to the United Kingdom. Although the ICO has a relatively large staff among jurisdictions studied,[5] it has not been the most effective regulator. Some commentators question whether it is sufficiently independent from the government to satisfy the requirements of the 1995 EU Data Protection Directive.[6]

However, since 2010 the ICO's mandate has strengthened, partly as public reaction to the high-profile scandals. The ICO now has a greater fining capacity, an increased focus on the private sector over the public sector, and a stronger audit power. It has largely ceased granting immunity to firms that self-report data breaches. The ICO is turning from a "toothless tiger" to a "force to be reckoned with" and a "driver of change" in its jurisdiction.[7] As one of our respondents described:

The relationship with the ICO has changed. We have had some issues and we're probably as close to the line of enforcement as I would think [we have] been for a very, very long time . . . as opposed to sort of historically when no one really cared. So I think that's a real sort of sea change and these regulators have teeth. If the regs come through, we all know that we're potentially looking at two percent [of revenues potential fines]. . . . I think the ICO with its fining power, its publicity and particularly the U.S. fines on the horizon, people are starting to see this as a regulator that's going to increase in power and the harm it can do for the bank. So this is again a good time to get ahead of the curve.

Another commentator told us that the ICO regulators "are much more public and open and will be on the news the minute there's some kind of breach attempting to sort of push compliance and whatnot, and their fines are very deliberately . . . looking to increase." When asked whether an increased fining and enforcement capacity was a key driver of that firm's understanding and behavior in the privacy field, the same commentator replied: "Yes. Like I said, everyone's very sensitive to regulatory action at the moment because there have been so many and there's so much public outcry."

Another commentator agreed, citing a high-profile enforcement action against another company as a driving force of change within the commentator's firm:

The recent Sony fine, for me, is probably one of the most useful things the ICO has done in a long time. It's not the fine, per se, it's the fact that they've been transparent about how the fining process works. So to turn around and say, "Why we fined Sony at this level was because Sony said, 'We had security.' We said it wasn't good enough. It was out of date." Then, looking at Sony's turnover and saying, "Had you been a company which was not making so much cash we might have been more lenient with you, but you make lots of cash, therefore, you can afford to have, going back to the law, state of the art systems." And you can see how this is now actually incredibly useful when you're having internal business discussion, and people are transfixed on what is the risk, which is fine, but we have to say now, that's not going to cut it with the ICO . . . to invoke broad standard security . . . It just won't work anymore. So that has been incredibly useful.

A key informant also noted the importance of increased sanctions, explaining that the ICO's powers "were so weak. The only sanction . . . was called the enforcement notice . . . essentially what you would call a cease and desist. But it was so complicated, it was so convoluted that [the ICO] did very, very few . . . everyone knew at the end of the day all it said was 'You've done wrong. Don't do it again,' where you get your wrist slapped."

The ICO undertakes other activities that affect the UK regulatory field. Some of our British respondents credited the regulator for advancing their understanding of privacy with online materials, including open-access privacy branding and awareness tools, data protection and security standards, guidance on ambiguous terms, and generic policies that could be used as precedents. Nor was interaction with the regulator limited to its website. The ICO commissioner and staff also served as external contact points for several of the CPOs that we interviewed. In contrast to the ICO's past soft touch in punishing companies, interviewees described the agency's newly progressive, systemic, and process-oriented approach to deciding when a firm had the appropriate policies and procedures in place needed to protect privacy, especially regarding data breaches. As one noted, "when they look at data breaches, . . . [t]he first question is around what policies and processes do you have in place? So they're really looking for systemic errors or issues. . . . And it's a similar approach to the courts here as well. They'll always look at, you know, is it a systemic issue or is it a one-off?"

The respondent said the ICO generally acts "where there's obvious weaknesses in the organization around policy, training, awareness—the real fundamental sort of things I'd considered as good corporate governance: having proper processes and procedures and policies in place, having training and awareness activities, not just on privacy but generally." Finally, this respondent praised that approach:

[W]e do benefit from a regulator that . . . takes a realistic approach to the way organizations behave and need to act . . . probably less focused on enforcement rather than if there's an issue. . . . Over here what the information commission people are doing is really working with business to help change understandings, help change cultures in the organization behaviors to make us—well, at the end of the day, to make us more compliant, but also for us to understand some of the reasons why we should be compliant, not just from the legislation point of view, but engendering consumer trust and all these sort of things.

OPERATIONALIZING PRIVACY

Our findings from the United Kingdom present an interesting contrast to those from Germany and the United States. The rhetoric of privacy— consumer trust and expectations, risk management over compliance, and so on—and orientation toward principles rather than rules were similar to the United States. The degree of operationalization of privacy that we observed in British firms was not nearly as high as in either Germany or the United States, yet it was a clearly expressed aspiration. Although British firms had decentralized and embedded privacy personnel to some extent, as in the U.S. model, we found these structures to be less extensive than in the United States. Where UK firms adopted a more centralized approach, as in Germany, the central privacy offices tended to have fewer resources, and fell lower in the executive matrix than their German or American counter- parts. The CPOs had only a limited ability to engage in high-level, strategic, and forward-looking activities. Accordingly, the operationalization of pri- vacy expertise and accountability in UK firms, and their integration into existing risk management functions, was several degrees below that found in Germany and the United States.

THE CPO
Legal Basis for the CPO   The privacy rules, institutions, and practices in the United Kingdom were not as well developed as those of France and Germany at the time the directive was adopted and implemented. As a result of the general British preference for individuals' and organizations' to self-regulate, responsibility for privacy protection has been placed largely on firms. This policy preference reduced the influence of the directive in guiding privacy practices in the United Kingdom. Unlike in Germany, firms (specifically data controllers) are not legally required to appoint a data pro- tection officer.[8] The rise of the CPO or privacy lead is not driven by regula- tion, and there are no legislative provisions setting out duties, core competencies, or the stature of the role. Except in the case of a few specific

industries, trade associations do not play a large role in shaping regulatory requirements through dialogue with regulators.

Title and Position within the Firm   For consistency's sake, we have referred to the highest privacy manager in British firms as a CPO, but only one of our interviewees in the United Kingdom actually went by that title. Others had titles indicating management, subject matter responsibility, and at times compliance-oriented roles. The privacy leads we interviewed ranged between two to four steps below the "c-suite." Only one of our respondents had a de facto reporting line to company executives; officially the privacy lead remained separated by several reporting levels. Most of our respondent CPOs were in the legal department, reporting to either the general counsel or an in-house lawyer one or two steps below. Some were situated within the compliance and risk departments, and one sat in the employee department. In comparison to the United States, Germany, and Spain, the UK privacy leads held more junior positions.

Our respondents reported little direct interaction with the board of directors. One respondent found the prospect "a bit frightening." Another explained that such interaction generally does not occur "unless there's been a major issue." Another never had reported to the board or an executive committee. One had frequent board interactions when initiating privacy structures in the firm (approximately quarterly), but noted those had dwindled to less than once per year. One had semi-yearly interactions with the executive committee. Our most actively engaged respondent reported to the board every month or two. A few interacted only indirectly with the board, through their managers. Some hoped to change this. "I think that may happen, we're looking at that," said one, while another described looking for openings: "I guess the key thing for me is to . . . raise the profile when there's an opportunity." One privacy leader expressed an interesting and contrary view: "I've only spoken to the board once. And that's, frankly, as it should be. They shouldn't be hearing about privacy from me, they should be hearing about it from the businesses."

Among our British respondents, there was little consistency as to whether the CPO's advice on privacy issues was binding or advisory. One noted that "our board member is the head of Legal and so when he says 'this needs to get done' it has some authority." Another described "some projects where we've had to restructure them, and some projects where we've had to abandon them, because, you know what, we just can't make it work . . . [and what they] want to do is so inconsistent with our data protection obligations that we can't make it work."

However, another explained: "[U]ltimately, I don't have a right of veto. Interesting, very few chief privacy officers have the right of veto, and the ones I know who have it have described it as a career changing moment in the sense of it's like having your finger on the button for the nuclear missile. You have to think twice and very hard if you're going to fire that missile or not, because the knock-on effects [are felt] throughout the business. You can still be overruled at the top, but you have to be absolutely sure that the advice you're giving in that circumstance is going to be business critical, but almost off the scale."

Another described the CPO role as basically advisory: "If the business wants to operate more in the gray areas to achieve a particular business objective it'd be my role to point out what the risks are, regulatory and legal risks, but also point out some of the consumer-type issues as well. . . .Then they can make a judgment call."

Levers for Change Other nonlegislative factors have fostered the rise of the privacy lead, increased corporate resources directed toward privacy, and led to more distributed networks of privacy personnel. Though from a weaker position than those in the United States, British privacy leads have tried to drive these changes by utilizing networks of social and professional capital to build support for themselves.

In Germany, the United States, and the United Kingdom, we noted that the CPO/DPOs rely on similar extra-legal levers to drive the organizational changes needed to operationalize privacy. One common lever was the potential impact of a data breach on reputation and consumer trust, corporate liability, and personal accountability for officers and directors. Like their counterparts, British CPOs used examples of privacy disasters at other similarly situated companies as leverage with management. As one respondent reported: "[W]atching how they [competitors] choose to react actually is quite interesting internal conversation, but what would we do if we were in that position? Would we come out fighting and say ultimately we're here to [just] make money . . . for the shareholders. Or would we be taking a much . . . wider picture of [risk], of what's the lasting damage here. Could we survive that kind of interest?

Another agreed: "I think 'reputational' stands amongst the highest [risks]. . . . I mean, data security is a key one there. . . . So if the consumer business has a big data security breach, I mean, . . . it's an absolute disaster [for the firm's reputation]. If it's on the corporate side and it doesn't enter the public realm you've still got to go to your customers and tell them what happened and why it happened and how you're going to fix it."

One respondent indicated how reputation risks could be used as leverage within the firm: "I need to take advantage of that as much as possible while people are very willing to listen to me, get in there and change things. The organization wants change because it has to reestablish a brand. . . . So it is that reestablishing trust with the population, the government regulators and consumers, and everybody else. So the company here is ripe for a culture change and so as a privacy person, I need to take advantage of that, so as part of the culture change, data protection is very much a part of [it.]"

Or, as another privacy lead related: "If there's a good story about an amazing fine that FTC has imposed on somebody else, well I'll leverage that absolutely a lot. Always sending to the relevant people, relevant stakeholders. . . . I need that stuff in order to be able to progress the whole topic at [this company] as well because if nothing happens people will stop paying attention, really."

For one of our respondents, industry-wide reputation hits, sometimes unrelated to privacy breaches, elevated the perception of risk in the privacy realm: "[T]here's an awareness that we are exposed because we are an industry that people want them to go after. The minute there's a mistake. . . . [people say,]'You need to go after them and fine them.'"

With respect to individual accountability, one of our respondents explained that a risk management approach has replaced the "historical[ ] —excuse my French—[ ]"cover your ass" approach to privacy, by which "if someone escalates something to me I send it on to someone else." By contrast, "[T]here's a real huge focus now on 'if someone escalates it to you, what are you going to do about it? You own that . . .' So I think there's now a feeling from a number of individuals: 'This is on my watch.' And technically as a general counsel or a head of compliance people are going to look to me. I have some personal accountability. I have some skin in this game, and I have nothing. . . . I don't have experts. I am very exposed."

Challenges to Execution   What was causing the British firms we observed to fail to operationalize privacy to the same extent as their German and American peers? To be sure, there were several external factors, such as a later start on privacy protection or a weaker regulator, but the CPOs we interviewed also reported several internal challenges.

Some reported difficulties in overcoming the perception among internal stakeholders, especially in business roles, that privacy was a stymying rather than an enabling force. "You're perceived to be a barrier," one respondent remarked.

Another respondent had problems with capacity:

The problem is we're so under-resourced that all the divisions are very reactive, . . . they respond to stuff that comes to them and nothing else, so they aren't able to really look [at] risks, so I'm the only one really focusing on the new regulation, which obviously impacts everybody, but I'm the only one really able to sit and read and look. No one else is doing any of that. . . . [N]o one in the businesses really has time to look at that [new U.S. regulation], nor do they have time to do any kind of deep dive or assurance testing or anything, so it's literally just responding to what comes in.

Still another felt that the role of the CPO was not yet properly demarcated, showing a lack of maturity in the privacy field:

I really do get frustrated in the sense of we have a lot of discussions with other regulators, yet they stumble and they struggle with giving me a sensible answer to how [privacy] is this different from anything else. . . . There are policies. There are expectations. There is monitoring. How is that different from health and safety? Is this health and safety for data? You can flag it in different ways, but I think we do need to get back to fundamental basics in saying, what is this role of the privacy officer, be it chief or director of privacy, what should it be doing going forward? Because I do believe . . . this role could be much more of a data governance as a whole of which privacy is just a piece.

Echoing back to Smith's findings, this same respondent noted that ambiguity made organizations reticent to talk about what they do: "My commitment to [the company] when I was offered the role was we don't want to be standing at the conference this week going, "We are the best. . . . I'm not going to . . . set [us] up and . . . get hammered.""

THE EXPANDING ROLE AND RESPONSIBILITIES OF THE CPO

The Basic Role of the CPO   The privacy leads in the United Kingdom do not view themselves as an extension of the regulator. Although they facilitate compliance, many reported being "brought in to . . . look holistically at . . . privacy across the group as a whole, as opposed to . . . in-country compliance." The role is more internally than externally oriented, with less external activity than in Germany and the United States. As described by one interviewee, the CPO's role is to, "establish internal standards . . . facilitate compliance . . . provide training and awareness . . . provide guidance and advice on a daily basis . . . verify compliance with our audits, and we network internally, very important, and externally." The level of strategic versus implementation-oriented activities varied widely, however, ranging from none to requiring a bit over half their time.

All interviewees were responsible for policy development, although practices varied widely. Some take a collaborative approach, and others require business units to pull the laboring oar. One respondent noted that policy development presented an opportunity to build social capital within the firm: "[W]hen I arrived somebody said, 'You're nobody in this organization [unless] you have a policy,' so . . . I wrote [a global data protection policy] and then 'socialized' it, again, around the organization in terms of people who had a vested interest."

As in the United States some created broad, principle-based policies to simplify work in a global organization and move away from a compliance orientation. Discussing the process of policy creation one explained: "You . . . look at the panoply of what's available . . . things like OECD principles . . . really do help, because they survived the test of time. . . . So I've got my principles. . . . They're at a pretty high level. And then I put a little bit more meat on the bone through some of the laws and regulations. . . . But . . . to stand the test of time [and provide] flexibility . . . I gotta stick fairly close to those principles and allow for some gray area where judgment is sort of exercised. . . . [W]e [are] actually going from a rules-based culture to a values-based culture."

Educational and Career Background The UK CPOs were split between legal (about 50 percent), and nonlegal backgrounds. Interviewees agreed the position can be hard to pin down. Said one respondent: "I've gone to a lot of effort to try and position this not as being a legal discipline . . . to sit at the intersection of a range of functions . . . public policy and legal, social policy, consumer attitudes and perceptions and technology; so [the job involves] working with the R&D folks and a wider global technology organization." A second CPO said: "The privacy officer skill set really is [an] incredible mixture." Another noted that historically, data protection was often handled by "nonlawyers, people who'd got sort of thrown into" the role. Some suggested that nonlawyers tended to be "very, very literal" taking a "black-and-white type approach" too privacy—compliance-oriented. While, legal skills were not sufficient for an ideal CPO, many believed them necessary. As one stated, "I'm not a lawyer . . . [but] I've invested a lot of time into . . . understanding our legal obligations. . . . But . . . I can also understand the business. . . . I can talk in language that the business understands." Echoing this sentiment, another respondent, who was a lawyer, stated: "I think you need both skill sets . . . legal advisory . . . compliance, experience of oversight assurance," but also management understandings which are "not a lawyer's strength in my experience."

Still another explained: "[L]egal skills are really important. . . . Now, is that the only skill? Absolutely not . . . understanding of technology . . . understanding of policy, where is privacy going, what are the next trends for the global companies, being able to influence that . . . really engaging with regulators, educating regulators. . . . Ability to communicate and empathize with people . . . I mean you almost act as an ombudsman as well. . . . Government relations, certainly we would have to have those skills as well, being able to kind of work multiculturally across the borders . . . being somebody who can actually engage the business as well and make sure the business consults you."

External-Facing Activities Our British respondents devoted a significant portion of their time to external engagement with the privacy field, but that amount on average was slightly less than that of the Germans and far less than the Americans.

Although many of our respondents reported regular interaction with the ICO, the form varied significantly. Engagement ran from specific projects such "as part of the binding corporate rule process, sometimes it's a daily phone call to see where we are" to "the usual notifications and registrations." But for some engagement included an "open line of communication. 'Hey look, we're thinking about doing this. What do you think? What do you think about this? Can we do this? How do you feel about that?'" Some reported sharing information in both directions, and jointly exploring problems: "It's us informing and educating them. It's them coming and informing and educating us. It's about working through the gray areas together." Others reported more arms-length relationships, describing them as "a strategic liaison sort of contact" where "we try to every six months [see] what does the ICO care about." Others reported irregular interactions with regulators at privacy events or industry conferences. None reported multistakeholder forums.

A few proactively engage with regulators in advance of introducing new technology. One respondent reported such engagement only if the new project "were sufficiently big." Our respondents were, however, alive to the benefits of such engagement. In advance of the potential creation of new regulations on a piece of technology that was a significant source of new business, one respondent took the lead in proactively "talking to regulators and policymakers about what we think the right kind of framework should look like, and . . . talking to [other] companies to say 'You need to think about this, too.'"

Some respondents used proactive engagement to establish trust with the regulator. As one described, "I make sure that they see that we are proactive and that we're doing all the good stuff so that when people complain about us, whether or not those complaints are merited, there's a relationship of trust." Another opined that with regular meetings, "the regulators get to see that you're interested, involved, educated and take [privacy] seriously as an organization." A third mentioned that the privacy regulator would often be invited to an important industry conference to "shake their hands, and . . . kind of show them that we're good people." Still another described similar benefits: "You put in their mind that your company is a good privacy player just in case you have an issue one day . . . what you want is them to have a good perception of you as a good privacy player."

Several emphasized the role of translator between the internal and external environments, as well as among legal and regulatory and technical functions. "I think I'm very much a translator. . . . [I] understand and appreciate the technical and complex privacy landscape outside and then translate that for my company . . . global privacy officers or chief privacy officers play the role of refiner or translator." Translation went both ways for several of our interviewees, who reported interpreting business requirements into legislative and policy requests through lobbying and working to shape public opinion. "[T]here's a huge component to my role about being the face of privacy for [the company]," said one, "part of that is sort of communicating to the rest of the world and contributing to the broader privacy discussion about where we should be, where we shouldn't be."

A few described lobbying in the narrower sense: "I've gotten very much into the game in Brussels trying to advance sort of the health care agenda in the new regulation. . . . [I am] heavily involved in lobbying, engaging a 'lobbying team' and a 'public policy team.'" This privacy lead spends lobbying time totaling 15–20 percent depending on what's going on. Several of our other respondents engaged in regular lobbying primarily as part of larger industry associations.

External engagement was considered essential to the CPO's translation role. As one respondent put it: "There's a lot of noise and in order for any company to focus and not absolutely tear itself apart trying to hear everything, you need somebody to sort of refine [it]."

Respondents reported regular interactions with their peers, both "under [their] own brands" and "under industry groups." Several belonged to privacy associations and reported regularly attending conferences and seminars. They also reported membership and attendance at various other privacy forums and workshops led by law firms.

They relied upon both formal and informal networks of similarly situated professionals in their day-to-day work. As one noted: "[T]hat kind of informal network . . . is invaluable. . . . I'm not ashamed of ringing people up and saying 'What are you doing in this space? I've got this problem. How have you done it?' So there is a huge informal network of people. I probably take one call a week from somebody in a completely different industry."

Respondents described setting up a privacy consortium to share in-house materials across firms, and more formal industry-specific bodies that enabled resources, competencies, and bargaining power to be shared. Peer interaction was valued for several reasons, including to build clout and influence in the broader privacy field. One respondent said, "[I]f . . . you want to have a voice, if you want to influence, whether it's internally or externally, you have to have a relationship, and hopefully one of trust." This interaction was also felt to provide valuable insight into policies and practices within similarly situated organizations, and was a source of comfort while working in the shadow of ambiguous laws. Another respondent reported: "[I]t's really useful to know where the benchmark is, what your peers are doing and understand best practice." And still another: "[Y]ou respect the practical experiences of your peer group . . . I do try to attend the conferences and seminars to . . . hear and speak to people that work and have the same practical experiences and the same problems, who have to do the same things on a daily basis."

Sharing information and practices was in part fueled by self-interest, as one respondent remarked: "It doesn't matter that we have perfect systems. . . . [I]t's in our interests to try and help the other guys like us, because we'll all suffer if one of us gets it wrong."

They also viewed their professional network as an effective means of spreading ideas and practices: "So the fifteen most senior people in privacy from the fifteen largest [companies in a particular sector] in the world get together . . . somebody will say, "Oh, we've just written a policy on the handling of [data from that sector]." "Oh, so you've got a policy. That's interesting. Maybe we should have a policy." Professional networks were tied to institutional isomorphism in much the same way we observed in other countries. For example, respondents lifted ideas from one another, such as data-flow mapping. In an interesting sign of a heightened sense of professionalism, a respondent described a peer system for anonymous benchmarking and inquiries about privacy requirements, which aggregated responses from others.

Peer interaction was also a development strategy, since privacy leads viewed their interactions with their counterparts at clients' firms as useful: "It's very good to actually have a relationship with [the] Chief Privacy Officer there and be able to do something about it and it has been, you know, we have had cases where there was a little breach . . . [the] privacy officer of the company would come and deal directly with me and we would sort of—between two of us we would kind of forge some relationship and help things speed up."

Finally, peer interaction facilitated more unified positions before regulators, raising the chance of winning positive outcomes. As one respondent noted: "[W]e'll ask the ICO to send a representative to talk about the following six issues which we as an industry body are concerned about, and we'll all write down our questions ahead of time, put them in a hat, no names added, and then we'll ask the regulator." Echoing this sense, another stated: "[W]orking with other industry players is about . . . find[ing] common grounds on some of these issues, and also [communicating it] to policymakers."

The privacy leads reported less interaction with academics and civil society, and were dismissive of some advocacy groups that some sought to avoid: "We're very guarded as to what media says about us, what the privacy advocates probably would say. So we're not targeting them in any shape or form. We are sort of trying to not be visible and be silent."

With respect to academics, there was some interaction, but not a great deal. One respondent reported consulting with ethicists, scientists, and data privacy lawyers when coming up "against an issue which . . . legally I think we're fine, but emotionally . . . may be more difficult for certain people." Another respondent employed business school PhD students to perform a literature review on consumer perceptions and behaviors around privacy.

THE OPERATIONALIZATION OF PRIVACY IN THE UNITED KINGDOM

Operationalization within British firms lagged behind their CPOs' mindset and orientation. It was clear that most if not all of our interviewees strove for richer institutionalization of privacy, but had not mustered adequate resources and institutional support to advance the cause. For example, many recognized that integration with risk management structures was key to operationalizing privacy. They positioned it as "behaviors that are applicable to everybody in the firm," connected with other risks ("doesn't stand alone"), and integrated with other practices ("always in connection with something else"). One respondent called it a "hearts-and-minds thing versus the tick-box thing"—everyone in the firm had to understand privacy at a normative level. Still another echoed these convictions: "The key to privacy often is to encourage the creation of processes within the organization of which you then get like a gateway in." Despite these statements, the extent of integration was less than in Germany and the United States.

Distributing Privacy Expertise and Accountability in the British Firm   In previous chapters, we described the dichotomy between a centralized and a distributed structure of expertise, where the German model is more centralized and the American more distributed. For British firms, the pattern fell somewhere in between. As one respondent explained: "[W]e're kind of federal in structure . . . our role is more strategic, because most of the operational stuff is happening on the ground. But to make sure that we don't do different things in different markets for different reasons . . . we needed a consistent approach."

Another CPO pointed out the drawbacks of an overly centralized privacy team: "[W]hen you have a very large central function the rest of the business has a tendency to cede the responsibility to that central function because they can sort of say, 'Well, you have the people, you do it.'" The CPO explained that within their firm "the business owner of the data, user of the data, processor of the data, maintainer of the data—[are] the ones that get audited against the privacy requirements so they 'own' any corrective actions."

Although not all the UK organizations adopted this exact "federal" model, we did note a familiar structural pattern to privacy's functional distribution. In many firms there was heavy reliance on indirect reports within the business units who took on a privacy role. One CPO described utilizing so-called "semi-formal points of contact," individuals who had no official privacy role or reporting requirement, but served as a "kind of a conduit" into other parts of the organization. The CPO cultivated relationships with them, and used them to convey information to units. This same CPO utilized a team of approximately fifteen "notification stewards" to accomplish the more quotidian, compliance-oriented tasks for other European jurisdictions that involved notification, registration, and other similar procedures.

British CPOs recognized the role of distributed experts in "baking [privacy] in." In an interesting twist, some positioned culture change as a goal that could be pursued separately, or at least prior to, formally instituting practices. The respondent explained, "[Y]ou're trying to get the value of privacy built in . . . people talk about privacy by design . . . as a process. . . . I also like to talk about it as a culture . . . you can build in privacy by design as a culture even before you've got the processes." Similarly, another remarked that with a properly distributed network, the CPO could simply say, "here are the values. Here are the principles. Go forth and do privacy." For another the tools were essential: "They've got the tools. They understand where they're trying to get to. And they've got the right kind of competencies to apply them . . . that's the best way to work with a distributed community of people . . . locally without going across a whole bunch of policies."

Direct reports were modest with several having fewer than five and none more than nine, and indirect reports and distributed personnel with privacy training ranged even more with several reporting zero and on the high end, one reporting thirty. As in Germany, direct reports were usually responsible for business segments or geographic regions, and were located in various layers of business units or in cross-functional units.

Tools to Facilitate Privacy Work by the Distributed Privacy Officers British CPOs used privacy tools similar to those of their German and U.S. peers. This included training, branding and promotion, policies, standard procedures, and controls.

Privacy training was generally mandatory. It appeared tied to risk management stemming from regulator attention to employee education after a data breach. While some struggled to require mandatory training for all employees, they prevailed in part due to their ability to spell out the risk posed by its absence. However, the CPOs also viewed training as part of building and sustaining the embedded network. In some firms training was bolstered by privacy "branding" and "awareness" campaigns which helped "make privacy interesting, manageable, [and] accessible . . . to the population." Such activities raised the profile of the CPO's office as well as privacy awareness. One reported that it was "kind of how the company came to know of my existence and the service that I could provide."

There was an art to policy creation and, as in the United States and Germany, CPOs led with values and principles. One explained that having broad, simple policies "[allows] for people to navigate through situations and empowers them to make those judgments on their own." Another explained his philosophy of adopting "relatively simple . . . plain language [policies] . . . [that] put some limits on what they do, but give them flexibility for future projects so I can actually work with them and flex the policy accordingly." Espousing a similar philosophy, another described his company as " privacy policy light" and explained that he drafted "very targeted" policies to address areas of " the most risk and harm" on the belief that if inundated with detailed policies employees "won't take any notice." Others shared this sentiment, noting, for example, "I'm not heavily into prescriptive policies. We have a global privacy policy. Then we have targeted policies where they are most required." The process of creating policies involved, for several of our respondents, talking to the group leads in the business units and soliciting their advice and feedback. For one organization in the finance sector, the process of creating a policy was itself the subject of a formal policy, with a set procedure and standards to follow. Technology was used to disseminate privacy policies, but some suggested that sneakernets were more effective than intranets: "[W]e have a site where our various policies are but people tend not to think of going there." The interviewee noted that the experience and awareness of colleagues were more important than just telling employees "here's a book."

Lines of accountability varied, but the majority of our respondents reported a distributed model, with the CPO and privacy office acting in an advisory capacity and accountability for privacy policies lying with the business units, or individual employees. "If the policy is wrong then it will be me," said one CPO. Another explained: [My] responsibility . . . is to promote the best practices for managing personal information in compliance with the code of conduct, the rules and any local obligations. . . . I do that by making sure that the business has all the tools which it needs to make privacy compliance live and breathe within their segment or function or business usage or process." Contemplating how the separation of accountability would work in practice, another said, "in terms of someone not complying at a frontline level that would be dealt with within a business." Another noted that accountability could be illusory "because it's not real," as in his experience "[t]here are very few instances where any firm is going to hang an individual out to dry [for a privacy violation]." This was echoed by another respondent who said, "We haven't to date been able to . . . scare people. . . . It will probably be taken as part of performance management, their boss will be told about this, but would it be systematic? Not really quite yet." Despite reservations about the relative lack of teeth behind delegations of accountability, respondents thought they advanced privacy nonetheless, because "if it becomes their problem then they'll do something about it."

CPOs also used "controls" set up to "catch" privacy issues before they became errors. Controls could be formal and structural, including technological mechanisms such as online tools, questionnaires, checklists, or forms. According to other respondents, controls were informal or behavioral—"more of a mindset, culture type thing," as one described it. "It's a drip, drip of data protection awareness and privacy awareness-type activities."

Our respondents were unclear on how success should or would be measured. Some pointed to process measures—such as "the number of programs that go through our data protection office and . . . [t]he way in which they're changed is to make sure that they're compliant"—or similar metrics such as determining: "Are we up to correct levels of training?" Others suggested more substantive measures, such as measuring—"How many breaches have we had? Are they going down, or, at least, are the severity of them going down?"—or counting the "[the] number of complaints . . . the number of people making access requests." However, at least some felt that these metrics were far from ideal: "[I]t's very difficult and I'm not sure how to measure success at the moment."

Like our U.S. and German interviewees, UK CPOs "like to get into the weeds." Most respondents claimed to use some form of privacy impact assessment. Many sought to integrate privacy tools into larger risk management structures including audit. They also sought to coordinate and to some extent integrate their efforts with those of the chief information security officer, through processes such as two-way consultations and sign-offs on policies and individual projects. They valued these structures and processes because they "challenge" others in the firm "to think in a different way about the design [of] things. . . . So that to me is a win."

SUMMARY

The British CPOs we interviewed find themselves with an increasing profile and mandate, and a widening informal and formal professional network upon which they can draw. But they report a lag between their aspirations and their position and access to resources within the firm. Many have adopted a more strategic, external-facing role, but most lack strong supporting institutional structures to spread knowledge and practices throughout the firm.

9 Identifying Best Practices: The Promise of U.S. and German Privacy Operationalization

The five accounts in part III address different national understandings about the meaning of privacy for corporations. Perhaps their most striking aspect is the variability of corporate behavior, structure, and commitment in integrating privacy into firm decision making, organization, and culture. Germany and the United States—countries with radically different formal legal mandates—clustered along one end of the spectrum. Firms in those two countries demonstrate similar internal practices. The level of the privacy function within the firms is high and broadly integrated throughout their decision structures, both through the personnel responsible for privacy, and the technologies and processes geared to raising and incorporating privacy concerns.

More specifically, these accounts document the emergence of a parallel suite of best practices in leading U.S. and German corporations. These shared practices include:

1. *Making the Board's Agenda*: a high level of attention, resources, access, and prominence for the privacy function within the firm;

2. *A Boundary-Spanning CPO*: a high-status privacy lead who mediates between external privacy demands and internal corporate privacy practices; and

3. *The "Managerialization" of Privacy*: the integration of privacy decision making into technology design and business-line processes through the distribution of privacy expertise within business units and assignment of specialized privacy staff to data-intensive processes and systems.

By contrast, this combination of factors was largely absent from the accounts provided by privacy leads in Spain, France, and the UK. Spanish firms relegate privacy expertise to a centralized, generally legal, staff. French firms apply inconsistent levels of attention and structure to the privacy function. Firms in both nations focus on compliance with specific formal reporting requirements, yielding apparatuses ill equipped to weave privacy into businesses or deliver the sort of early interventions that go beyond "the margins." And while UK CPOs had achieved some success at developing decentralized and embedded privacy personnel, those structures were less extensive, and central privacy offices tended to have fewer resources and less authority, than in U.S. and German firms.

The practices described by U.S. and German CPOs show particular promise in light of the scholarship on privacy and its governance discussed earlier, in chapter 2. They reflect a broad, substantive understanding of privacy values that must be protected, rather than a "data protection" orientation. They incorporate privacy "by design" into corporate structures. In sum, these three elements of privacy's operationalization offer working prototypes for the sort of internal privacy arrangements that scholars, regulators, and advocates are encouraging the private and public sector to adopt, and that researchers of privacy and of organizational decision making suggest demonstrate special capacity for protecting privacy.

U.S. AND GERMAN BEST PRACTICES

MAKING THE BOARD'S AGENDA

Establishing privacy as a corporate priority is a key challenge to its protection. While privacy polls strongly, and privacy gaffes can cost companies dearly, there is general agreement that privacy does not drive sales. Neither standalone privacy products nor products differentiated by additional privacy protection have fared well in the marketplace. There is a general sense that privacy failures by one member of an industry undermine trust in the whole sector. This vulnerability to other companies' privacy lapses, and the inability to demand higher prices for privacy improvements, create disincentives for corporate investment. Privacy protection has little proven ability to secure profit, little certainty about what success requires, and no shared metrics of evaluation. As Smith concluded twenty years ago, this is a mix of problems from which senior management runs.

Yet in the leading German and U.S. firms we considered, privacy has been taken up by the upper echelons of management. The U.S. privacy officers we interviewed are part of senior management, often within the "c-suite." They often enjoy access to corporate boards, and were routinely involved in strategic decision making. In Germany, such access was even more uniform, buttressed by a regulatory framework that ensured the CPOs' independence and access to the board.

In both countries the privacy professionals were able to bring privacy concerns to the attention of high-level decision makers, and offer suggestions about privacy protection in the face of changing threats. Indeed, privacy officers in both countries considered access to the board a crucial source of leverage and power—and even more so when coupled with their immense latitude to stipulate privacy's requirements. In Germany the autonomy of privacy professionals flowed directly from the regulatory framework, while in the United States it appeared to emerge from uncertainty over how to define or measure success. In both cases, though, the privacy officers described the combination of high-level access with the autonomy to define institutional privacy priorities as significant contributors to effective privacy structures within the firm.

For the privacy leaders we interviewed, these factors permitted proactive and strategic privacy management. When CPOs are integrated into high-level strategy, they reported, they can promulgate policies and practices for managing privacy cohesively and consistently throughout the firm.

These practices directly reflect the lessons of scholarship on the successful integration of social goals, like privacy, into corporate decision making, and the promotion of "beyond compliance" corporate behavior.[1] Management commitment in the form of top-down corporate policies, organizational structure, and measurement and control systems send powerful signals about the importance of privacy to the members of the firm as a whole. They facilitate the integration of those values into existing organizational structures. They deter "silo" behavior by making privacy protection a goal across firm units. Together, they promote the consideration of values in a holistic, rather than atomized case-by-case manner, reducing routinized check-the-box compliance, and promoting beyond compliance corporate behavior.

A BOUNDARY-SPANNING CPO

Beyond their internal roles, our interviewees described a CPO model that included a significant external orientation. This external engagement is a direct expression of the interpretive work required of the privacy professionals we interviewed. Across both the United States and Germany, privacy leaders were vested with the authority to routinely and directly engage with external stakeholders. In doing so, those privacy officers brought out-side perspectives on evolving privacy norms into play within the firm. These perspectives inform and enrich firm decision making, in the best cases avoiding costly and embarrassing privacy gaffes and retrofixes. Priva-cy's dynamic, contextual, and volatile nature increases corporate reliance on the privacy officer's ability to interpret and translate outside perspec-tives—and with this reliance, they explained, comes greater autonomy.

These phenomena, too, resonate with lessons from the literature.[2] The corporate privacy focus they describe, then, is not tethered to compliance, but rather tied to the broader "social license to operate." Privacy was not narrowly confined to data protection or information privacy rules and processes. It includes issues of legality, market pressures, and the concerns of social actors. It is "interactive," "open to interpretation, negotiation," and "amendment."[3] This new orientation places ethics and social obliga-tions—as defined by noncorporate actors—within the scope of firm consideration. A social license approach inclined CPOs to ask whether the firm's activities were appropriate, rather than simply defending them as legally permissible.

The combination of access to high-level management on the one hand, and external engagement on the other offers promise for internal decision making in several important ways. It permits CPOs to better serve as the "filter through which information about the external licenses is sifted and guided." Unlike prescriptive rules, norms reflecting a "social license" are dynamic and at times contradictory. They can diverge both up and down from the law on the books, and vary contextually.

When the meaning of privacy is determined by negotiation among a variety of actors in the field, then, regular outside interactions with diverse privacy professionals is especially important. Participation in the external privacy discourse assists in developing a CPO's own judgment as to the state of external demands on a corporation. A sustained presence in the ongoing negotiations about the meaning of privacy and its enforcement can permit the acquisition of the tacit knowledge and expertise to address new privacy issues in high-stakes, time-pressured situations.

These dual aspects of U.S. and German CPOs' role thereby tethers the firm's success in implementing privacy to the translation of evolving pri-vacy norms. This "boundary-spanning"[4] role serves both to build the cred-ibility of the privacy officer's voice in corporate decisions, and to reinforce the identity and commitments of the privacy professional against a corporate culture primarily focused on efficiency and profit. The boundary-spanning role brings the outside in. By feeding the CPOs' "privacy mindset," it facilitates their forceful engagement with the collaborations and conflicts required to maintain privacy in the face of competing pressures.

THE "MANAGERIALIZATION" OF PRIVACY

The U.S. and German respondents described how privacy is "managerialized" within their firms in three ways that further suggest particular promise for integrating privacy as a core value in the face of competing corporate goals.

First, our respondents described incorporating privacy measures into existing risk management and audit systems. By building privacy into those systems' processes, firms harness significant resources in the service of privacy protection and place its value and treatment on a level with other fundamental management concerns—thus enhancing its legitimacy while limiting costs.

Second, they described how involving and assigning responsibility to senior business unit executives for tailoring and implementing plans—and for accountability in the case of privacy management failures—facilitated their own efforts to embed privacy in firm priorities. In this way, CPOs gained access to high-level decision makers and participated in high-level strategy setting, sending a strong signal to employees of privacy's value to the enterprise. Blending privacy issues into business-unit decision making from the beginning also helped transform privacy management from simply a cost or limitation into a function to be integrated with other core specifications into the product or service.

Third, the privacy leads stressed the importance of embedding staff with privacy protection expertise and personal responsibility for privacy—typically through indirect reporting mechanisms—into the business units. They viewed this as particularly important in institutionalizing privacy considerations in large decentralized organizations. Ensuring that privacy was a responsibility of a member of the business unit helped integrate privacy issues into the regular workflow. Embedding staff created opportunities for identifying win-win solutions, and helped avoid privacy work from becoming polarized and politicized between subject matter experts and the business unit. Our interviewees stressed the importance of maintaining some distance between the politics of privacy, which must be fought at the strategic level, and the practice of privacy management, which is ideally perceived as an apolitical business requirement. Embedded staff members were perceived as bringing privacy into discussions in a more organic and collaborative manner, raising the odds of integrated privacy solutions. Finally, the German and U.S. privacy officers we interviewed pointed to providing routine privacy training and decisional tools to employees that prod them to consider the privacy impact of their design choices, business strategies, and information flows. This corporate infrastructure gives employees a language to surface, discuss, and debate privacy issues in their day-to-day work, normalizing it as a legitimate priority of firm business.

In three ways, these practices track closely the leading consensus of scholars, regulators, and advocates, discussed in chapter 2, about how privacy should be understood and operationalized in corporations to maximize its protection.[5]

First, the architectures that our respondents described reflect the insight that organizations cannot successfully protect privacy as an ad hoc after-the-fact matter, but must integrate consideration of privacy systemically, through institutional processes. A "privacy-by-design" approach employing privacy impact assessments, decision-making tools, and process audits ensures that a business decision's effect on privacy is surfaced from the start. This is especially important in the technology context, in which intended or unintended value choices with significant consequence for privacy often remain hidden until harm occurs, or it becomes burdensome to unravel the source of the threat. Integrating privacy concerns into existing management and audit systems intended to monitor important risks provides a particularly effective means to assimilate privacy considerations smoothly, without disrupting established firm routines and evoking resistance.

For these reasons, such practices are more likely to embed privacy in firm practices, not just policies. Our respondents reported that policies, training, and decisional tools give privacy-minded employees a language to express their concerns, a bully pulpit from which to speak, and an audience of senior personnel awaiting privacy red flags to surface from below. For those less privacy-minded, the same tools pull them out of their standard decision-making processes to remind them to focus on privacy at various stages of work. They thus provide communication structures that surface rather than mask risk.

Second, the practices of distributing privacy responsibility and embedding personnel described in the United States and Germany draw on the combined benefits of decentralized decision making, and the assignment of accountability known to foster responsibility. Decentralization permits individuals who are closest to the problem to react and make better-informed decisions. As one leading privacy scholar describes, "the ideal privacy impact assessment of any project is prepared by someone from inside the project and with an up-front demonstration of just how it works or is supposed to work."[6]

Developing a distributed network of privacy experts empowered with training materials and decisional tools moves their expertise into firm processes organically and meaningfully. Like the integration of privacy into risk management processes, it mitigates siloing along functional lines.

Distributing accountability in this manner, moreover, draws on methods demonstrated to promote effective decision making by individuals. When the attention of business-unit executives and the embedded privacy staff is directed toward privacy, it becomes something they "own" and for which they bear responsibility. The expertise of unit leaders in integrating privacy successfully into existing workflows and decision structures is enlisted in a manner that respects their autonomy, which can foster commitment to implementation of policies—policies that, after all, those managers themselves helped create and champion.

By embedding privacy experts and giving business-unit employees greater privacy authority, firms are building privacy-sensitive receptors into components of the organization with no natural inclination to either feel or respond to such stimuli. This distributed architecture leverages the normative commitments handed down by a CPO with expertise drawn from context.

Finally, these practices reorient firm priorities from the "legalized" goal of documenting data use and providing processes for individuals to use in making decisions about their information, to the substantive goal of preventing harm. The managerialization of privacy reported in our German and U.S. firms reflects the reality that, in an era of "surveillance," "big data," and "ubiquitous computing," information use has become more complex and opaque, and decisions at the corporate level often provide the best and sometimes only way to avoid privacy harms. By providing a requirement and means for considering the use of information throughout corporate decision making, such practices engage employees at times and in venues where privacy concerns can influence technical systems and business practices. Accordingly, this form of managerialization responds to a need to contextualize understandings of privacy, and privacy harms.

These practices distribute responsibility across more actors (not just the individual) and more tools—not just policy, but technical designs, defaults, and configurations. They make firm personnel far more likely to perceive "set[s] of acts that will together harm other people['s]"[7] privacy, than individuals faced with a set of disjointed choices, spread across services and time. In sum, they move the burdensome work of privacy from beleaguered individuals to corporate professionals.

The privacy practices in the leading U.S. and German and firms we studied are not of consequence simply because they are similar. Rather, they are worth focus because scholarly literature about, and policy debates over, privacy protection suggest that they embody principles and understandings reflective of current best practices.

The convergence of practices in jurisdictions with divergent formal laws and institutions also direct our inquiry to the broader regulatory fields that have catalyzed them. How have the U.S. and German fields been constructed, in both purposive and unintended ways? Despite apparent differences, what aspects of the two fields combine to operate in similar fashion, and spur similar behaviors? What lessons can be drawn for privacy reform? The book's remaining chapters take up these questions.

IV Placing the Law in Context

The interviews with privacy leads provided important answers to "how" and "what." They offered accounts of corporate privacy practices in five jurisdictions, and the understandings of privacy motivating them. They further supplied important information as to "why," identifying a number of forces to which they attributed their privacy orientation and behavior.

Yet, the similarity between privacy's operationalization in the U.S. and German firms we studied, and the apparent promise of such behaviors, raises critical questions the interview responses alone cannot answer: What can explain the appearance of such a similar set of practices in two jurisdictions with such different laws? How did the other elements of the privacy field in both countries combine to catalyze such similar best practices?

Answering these questions can illuminate the process by which various forces can combine to shape desired corporate privacy behavior, and offer insights for policy reform. The remainder of our book addresses this inquiry, and lessons that can be drawn from it.

With special focus on the elements identified in our respondents' accounts as important, the following two chapters draw in a range of legal and historical sources to provide detailed accounts of the U.S. and German privacy fields.

The United States has not altered its approach to legislating privacy. It has held fast to its piecemeal approach to federal privacy legislation during this period, and eschewed the adoption of an omnibus privacy law and data protection agency. Our interviews of U.S. privacy leads, however, point to other atmospheric, institutional, and substantive developments that track the changes in the logic and practice of corporate privacy management. Specifically, they suggest a constellation of changed regulatory phenomena, including the emergence of new activist federal regulators, new information-forcing state laws, and the increased visibility and influence of privacy advocates in the regulatory landscape. The regulatory changes fostered legal and market connections among privacy, trust, and corporate brand and, combined with the professionalization of privacy officers, have heightened attention to privacy management within corporate America.

In light of these suggestions, this chapter explores those regulatory phenomena at a granular level, and details the history of their development. This account reveals a history of purposeful interactions among regulators and other actors across the U.S. privacy field.

THE ROOTS OF A CONSUMER-FOCUSED LANGUAGE OF PRIVACY

The privacy leaders we interviewed unanimously articulated a non-FIPs-based definition of privacy as driving activity within their firms. They portrayed privacy as an expansive concept: privacy "equates to trust," "is a strategic initiative," and is "a core value associated with trust, primarily, and integrity and respect for people." They described the concept in terms of broad principles: "apply[ing] information usage to new contexts" in a "very contextual" manner. And the implementation of these principles required ongoing expertise: "[T]he company . . . understands that trust plays a key part . . . but isn't able to kind of codify what . . . trust looks like." So "the idea that there's going to be a one-size-fits-all privacy practice is, I don't think, possible." Thus "you don't really have a practice that is uniformly developed on the back end because it's also a judgment call." Finally, privacy was tied to corporate reputation: "[T]he biggest value to privacy is it's a part of brand."

This way of framing privacy reflects a discourse that first arose in the mid-1990s, a transformative period for information and communication technology use and policy in the United States and globally.[1] The birth of the Internet as a commercial medium and the need to respond to privacy challenges created by its global and data-driven nature altered the political discourse about privacy protection. Specifically, in both the United States and in the European Union, arguments about the importance of privacy protection were no longer voiced exclusively in the language of individual rights protection.[2] Instead, they also reflected a desire to facilitate electronic commerce and the free flow of information by building consumer trust. While tension between the European Union and the United States about how to protect of privacy was high, they increasingly advanced a similarly instrumental rhetoric about privacy's value, stating that electronic commerce "will thrive only if the privacy rights of individuals are balanced with the benefits associated with the free flow of information."[3]

By 1996, the rhetoric of consumer trust as a reason for business to attend to consumer privacy had become "something of a mantra" internationally.[4] That year, the OECD issued the first in a series of reports indicating that "privacy interests" needed bolstering, not only for human rights reasons, "but also [to ensure] that the right balance is found to provide confidence in the use of the system so that it will be a commercial success."[5] In preparation for the U.S. Conference on Global Information Networks in Bonn in July of 1997, German Economics Minister Günter Rexrodt and U.S. Commissioner Martin Bangemann wrote: "Building confidence by achieving efficient [privacy] protection is essential to allow the positive development of these networks."[6] In the same year, the OECD's report "Implementing the OECD 'Privacy Guidelines' in the Electronic Environment: Focus on the Internet"[7] concluded that "consumer confidence is a key element in the development of electronic commerce," and that enforcement of privacy policies serves to bolster that confidence.[8] On the domestic front, the

Clinton administration released its white paper "Framework for Global Electronic Commerce," which stated that e-commerce "will thrive only if the privacy rights of individuals are balanced with the benefits associated with the free flow of information."[9]

Scholars in this period identified "an emerging international consensus" in the public and private sector "on the importance of trust and confidence in modern information and communication technologies and their application to online transactions."[10] The dominant reason advanced to protect privacy in high-level government statements on the global stage was the promotion of electronic commerce rather than individual privacy rights.

THE U.S.-EU DIVERGENCE: THE TIMING OF INSTITUTIONALIZATION

While this instrumental expression of privacy's value in a networked world spanned the Atlantic, it encountered divergent regulatory climates in the United States and Europe. In Europe it encountered a developed framework and growing set of institutional players committed to conceptualizing information privacy through a lens of "data protection."[11]

By contrast, the information privacy landscape in the United States was more of a tabula rasa. Its patchwork system reflected no deep commitment to a specific implementation framework and no institutional authority vested in defending a specific approach. Against this backdrop, the expression of privacy's value in terms of promoting consumer trust proved influential in the United States in a way that rights-based arguments had not. Historically, successful legislative efforts, with a few notable exceptions, were mounted in response to specific and egregious harms or to protect highly sensitive information. Advancing privacy as a matter of individual rights across the corporate sector generally had little legislative or regulatory traction. But legislators and regulators were relatively quick to join a conversation about addressing privacy risks to advance electronic commerce.

Consumer confidence and trust became a central theme of arguments both for and against new privacy regulations in the United States. On the one hand, consumer advocates employed such arguments to promote a regime of new privacy laws. Advocates claimed that in the absence of robust privacy protection, individuals would be "more fearful to disclose information"[12] and would retreat from shopping or banking online.[13] Consumer groups warned that "the full economic and social potential of global electronic commerce will only be realized through its widespread use by consumers," and "[s]uch use will only occur if consumers become confident and comfortable with the online world."[14] Business groups, on the other hand, employed this new rhetoric to support a self-regulatory agenda, stating that "building consumer confidence is a key issue for the development of electronic commerce"[15] and claiming "there is a business advantage to be gained by companies that safeguard consumer interests."[16] When the Federal Trade Commission sought public comments in preparation for a consumer protection workshop in 1999, sixty-nine companies, nonprofits, and individuals responded—some in favor of self-regulation, and others arguing for new rules, but nearly all stressing the importance of consumer trust.[17]

Repeated consumer pushback after corporate privacy blunders underscored the links between privacy, trust, and commerce. Companies announced information-sharing deals only to cancel them once masses of consumers made their objections known.[18] In July 1997, AOL scrapped a plan to sell subscribers' phone numbers to marketers.[19] Other high-profile reversals followed: In 1998, American Express pulled out of a partnership with KnowledgeBase Marketing that would have made the personal data of 175 million Americans available to any retailer that accepted the credit card.[20] In 1999, Intel reversed a plan to activate an identifying signature in its Pentium III chip when faced with advocacy filings to the FTC, pressure from industry partners, and a boycott.[21] And in 2000, DoubleClick, the dominant network advertising service, planned to combine clickstream information with personally identifiable information in a massive customer database it had acquired, to deliver highly customized and targeted advertising. However, the project was shelved due to public pressure.[22]

While disputes over the optimal way to build trust continued—with consumer advocates backing a regime of new privacy laws and the Clinton administration and industry groups calling for industry self-regulation—all players increasingly framed their arguments in favor of privacy protection in instrumental terms. They cited the crucial role privacy played in enabling electronic commerce and e-government. This fit well with the Clinton administration's predilection for market-driven solutions, the FTC's efforts to stake out its regulatory agenda in the privacy space, and pragmatic advocates' promotion of reforms via available regulatory fora.

REGULATORY DEVELOPMENTS AND THE CONSUMER-ORIENTED PRIVACY FRAME

THE FEDERAL TRADE COMMISSION AND CONSUMER PROTECTION DISCOURSE

In this context, the Federal Trade Commission emerged,[23] in the words of one of our respondents, as an "activist privacy regulator," engaging the broader privacy community in a conversation about privacy's meaning through its consumer protection lens.[24] "We recognized," explained former FTC Chairman Robert Pitofsky, speaking about his time at the commission, "that the Internet was a vast new marketplace that could provide great benefits to consumers and to the competitive system. The idea was to protect consumers without undermining the growth of electronic commerce. A special dimension of commission activities related to concerns about online privacy."[25]

The impact of the FTC's actions, while not well documented in the scholarly literature until recently, was decisive. Those outside industry have often discounted the impact of the FTC due to its inability to fine companies unless they violate a company-specific preexisting consent decree, and to the lack of precedential force that consent decrees have on other companies.[26] Recent scholarship has placed the importance of the FTC's actions in a clearer light and, consistent with our findings, documented its forceful influence on corporate behavior.[27]

Jurisdictional Entrepreneurship This development was not predetermined by the terms of the FTC's statutory mandate to police "unfair or deceptive acts or practices."[28] As Jodie Bernstein, director of the FTC's Bureau of Consumer Protection from 1995 to 2001, remarked, "It didn't quite fit into 'deception or unfairness' for us to say, 'Everybody out there ought to be required to protect people's privacy.'"[29] But the substantive imprecision and procedural breadth inherent in the FTC Act gave the commission the space to play an increasingly important role in framing the debate. Beginning in 1995 with a public workshop to identify the Internet revolution's consumer protection and competition implications, and continuing with similar programs over the following several years, the FTC began to chart its own privacy agenda.[30]

These initiatives were strengthened as the EU Data Protection Directive's effective date of 1998 loomed, and the issue of the "adequacy" of U.S. law became a pressing trade matter. In light of the Directive's prohibition on the transfer of data to companies in jurisdictions that failed the test of "adequacy"—which included the United States[31]—U.S.-based multinationals, other firms with a global presence, and substantial foreign markets feared the economic consequences. These fears led to negotiations to develop a "safe harbor" framework, by which individual U.S. firms could sign on and thereby self-certify privacy practices sufficient for trade with European partners.[32] These negotiations culminated with the European Commission approval of the "Safe Harbor Privacy Principles" (Safe Harbor Agreement) in July 2000.[33]

Throughout the extended and contentious process of negotiating the Safe Harbor Agreement, there was heavy pressure on U.S. industry to demonstrate its capacity to self-regulate and for the United States to provide meaningful oversight, enforcement, and mechanisms for redress. The United States struggled with the need for credible oversight and enforcement structures for privacy, but was unwilling to craft either omnibus regulations or to push for the creation of a data protection authority. Faced with limited industry support or participation in self-regulatory activities with credible enforcement, the Clinton administration and industry turned to the FTC to fill this gap. A critical component of the Safe Harbor Agreement was the FTC's commitment to enforce privacy statements and to prioritize complaints by U.S. citizens.[34]

With the Safe Harbor's signal, the FTC was now relatively insulated against suggestions that its nascent privacy activities were beyond its inherent authority. The FTC became a laboratory of privacy norm elaboration, seeking through its own and outside expertise to measure, investigate, and sustain stakeholder engagement. The FTC took on the role of the leading consumer protection agency in shaping and enforcing practices to respect privacy.

The FTC was neither bound to, nor enabled by, traditional conceptions of data protection. By contrast, it had substantial discretion to define which practices were unfair and deceptive.[35] The commission possessed wide latitude as to the institutional methods available for shaping the perceptions of legal requirements. In the privacy arena, it employed this authority to convene FTC Advisory Committees[36] and workshops,[37] request[38] and issue[39] reports, and to work with and place pressure on industry to develop self-regulatory codes of conduct and transparent privacy practices,[40] and safeguard personal information.[41] In all, the FTC leveraged its doctrinal latitude and institutional breadth to facilitate a dialogue about corporate data practices, consumer understanding and expectations, and consumer harms.

Developing a Consumer Expectations Metric: Nonenforcement Regulatory Tools, Public Visibility, and Transparency   Central to the FTC's emerging role as privacy regulator was its employment of regulatory tools outside the enforcement context. The agency used publicity, research, best-practice guidance, the encouragement of certification regimes, the enlistment of expert input, and other deliberative and participatory processes promoting dialogue with advocates and industry.[42] These tools furthered three types of regulatory goals.

First, they greatly increased the transparency of corporate privacy practices. Through "sweeps" of both child-directed and general audience websites, the FTC documented and assessed information practices. Its fora encouraged stakeholders to do the same, fostering the production of additional surveys and research. This iterative documentation of corporate practices pressured industry to improve. The emphasis on best-practice improvement in turn bolstered trade associations and self-regulatory organizations that sought to stave off regulatory action. While the invisibility of corporate data practices had, as noted by Smith's 1994 study, made them largely immune to regulatory and public pressure, FTC initiatives brought corporate practices and their import for consumers' expectations into the light. This fueled a sustained debate about appropriate norms of behavior on an issue that was only previously addressed episodically, at best, by legislators in response to high-profile corporate privacy failures.

Second, the FTC employed its bully-pulpit power to motivate two important developments. Its calls for credible self-regulatory efforts were largely responsible[43] for the creation of two self-regulatory privacy seal programs[44] as well as a technical standard designed to reduce the transaction costs associated with privacy decision making through standardization and initially automated negotiation.[45] Furthermore, FTC persuasion was critical in encouraging companies operating online to post privacy policies. As will be discussed, the publication of company policies making representations about practices with respect to personal information became central to the commission's initial exercise of its section 5 enforcement jurisdiction. The least controversial manner for the FTC to exercise authority in the privacy area was to address factually misleading claims.[46] The increased visibility into corporate practices facilitated evaluation by legislators, advocates, and the press.

Finally, the FTC's participatory fora empowered privacy advocates. Never before had privacy claimed a domestic institutional home as well resourced as the FTC. The advocacy community quickly took advantage of the commission's heft, filing numerous complaints about business practices,[47] participating in FTC advisory committees[48] and workshops, and engaging in agenda setting through the production of independent research[49] as well as interactions with FTC staff and commissioners. The commission's policy fora provided low-cost, relatively high-profile opportunities for advocates to shape the discourse about corporate data practices. Indeed, several privacy organizations and advocates appeared on the scene in the mid- and late-1990s focusing much, if not all, of their energy on FTC engagement.[50] Workshops accorded an opportunity for advocacy organizations to convey their views to a Washington, D.C., audience of reporters, Capitol Hill staff, trade associations, lobbyists, and industry executives. Through a compelling FTC complaint, an advocacy organization could leverage the resources, expertise, and investigative and enforcement capacity of a formidable agency.[51] These contexts provided a valuable stage for advocates to express concerns about privacy risks faced by the diffuse and broad-based population of consumers nationwide.[52]

These processes thus worked in two directions: Through them, the FTC built support for its work and gained an ongoing awareness of the ways in which consumer harms can arise from the breach of expectations wrought by the increased capacity and regularity of data collection. Simultaneously, advocates had a singular opportunity to shape an ongoing stakeholder dialogue in which the links between privacy, trust, and consumer expectation were nurtured. They gave content to the imprecise rubric of privacy as consumer protection.

The FTC's methods produced a detailed public record of factual data about privacy-impacting technologies and related business practices, and how these practices in turn related to consumers' expectations and privacy concerns. This record greatly increased the transparency of corporate privacy practices, where before companies were largely immune to regulatory, media, and market pressures, and shielded from sustained public debate. The transparency trend was reinforced with the enactment by forty-seven state legislatures, beginning with California's in 2002, of legislation requiring notification to affected parties of security breaches involving personal information.[53]

Developing a Consumer Expectations Metric: Bringing Investigation and Enforcement Powers to Bear Evolving consumer-oriented notions of privacy protection, in turn, were ultimately given force through the FTC's enforcement authority. The commission's early cases focused on the accuracy of privacy notices, targeting business claims that were actively misleading under the FTC's jurisdiction to regulate "deceptive" practices.[54]

Progressively, however, the FTC broadened its enforcement focus to practices deemed "unfair"[55] and to transactions that were on the whole misleading, despite legal disclosures. This change in regulatory approach unraveled settled understandings of the commission's requirements regarding corporate privacy practices. If earlier enforcement actions aimed at holding companies to their word provided some precision as to rules of conduct, the new legal standards employed by the FTC to protect privacy were far more ambiguous, evolving, and context dependent. This was highlighted by the commission's actions to address two phenomena: spyware and security breaches.

Spyware—a type of software that is typically installed on a computer without the user's knowledge and collects information about that user—presented an important conceptual challenge to the FTC's policing of privacy. Spyware also challenged industry players intent on distinguishing the good actors from the bad through adherence to procedural regularity. Companies distributing spyware often relied on the same fine-print legal disclosures as other companies to inform consumers of their data practices. But their practices diverged even further from consumers' expectations of the bargain they were striking than those of other market participants, and therefore put consumers at risk. Providing a legal disclaimer and click-through "consent" screen could no longer suffice to evade FTC scrutiny.

Through a series of actions against companies that downloaded software without appropriate notice and consent procedures,[56] the FTC began to breathe substance into the process of consent. The majority of these cases involved "bundled software,"[57] where formal disclosures in end-user licensing agreements (EULAs) were found insufficient to provide notice of hidden software that eroded consumers' privacy in an unexpected manner.

Typically, the cases involved pop-up advertisements collecting information about consumer's online "clicks," or engaging in another insidious data collection technique. Through its spyware work, the FTC broadened the range of practices that trigger privacy concerns to include software that collects and transmits information about users, their computers, or their use of the content,[58] in addition to information narrowly considered "personally identifiable." This signaled that satisfying the formalities of contract law, which courts may accept as an affirmative defense,[59] would not preclude a deeper privacy inquiry or stricter requirements.[60]

FTC actions against companies for breaches of personal information similarly abandoned a legalistic, notice-bound analysis. In these actions, the commission brought unfairness claims against companies that had not made representations regarding data security.[61] While these and other security cases settled quickly, the resulting consent orders have established a de facto obligation to provide a "reasonable" level of security for personal information.[62] The reasonableness standard is fluid, evolving, and open to constant reinterpretation.

The ambiguity developed through FTC practice as to what privacy protection requires of corporations mirrors the sense of ambiguity articulated by the interviewed privacy leaders. It is easy to understand why these leaders believe that managing privacy requires "looking around corners" to anticipate ways in which new technologies and new practices comport with consumer expectations regarding information usage. The commission's move away from a limited notice and consent analysis has let loose a renewed conversation about privacy issues and what firms must do to treat consumers fairly and to meet their expectations in the electronic marketplace.

STATE SECURITY BREACH NOTIFICATION LAWS AND THE HARNESSING OF MARKET REPUTATION

If the FTC sought, through a variety of "soft" and "hard" regulatory approaches, to publicize privacy risks and to link legal standards to consumer expectations, the state security breach notification (SBN) laws provided a single concrete mechanism for strengthening the link between privacy protection and consumer trust. As discussed in chapter 4, these laws—forty-seven have been enacted since 2002—require corporations to notify individuals whose personal information has been breached. The laws work to tie corporate privacy performance directly to reputation capital.

The breach notification laws embody a governance approach that emphasizes "informational regulation," or "regulation through disclosure."[63] Such tools require the disclosure of information about harms or risks as a means of "fortify[ing] either market mechanisms or political checks on private behavior."[64] In this case, disclosure requirements seek to prompt both. And while disclosures have provided important factual predicates for FTC enforcement, they have also subjected privacy outcomes to market and consumer discipline in important ways.

The breach notification laws transformed previously unnoticeable corporate lapses into press events with deep brand implications. Privacy advocates have exploited media coverage of breaches to keep privacy and data protection on the front burner. Thus the Privacy Rights Clearinghouse maintains a chronology of security breaches,[65] while U.S. Public Interest Research Group and Consumers Union have leveraged the steady drumbeat of security breaches to build momentum for the proliferation of model laws across states.[66]

Notification laws lead corporations to "[t]ry to avoid the breaches and the problems and the brand tarnishment issues and promote the ability to use and flow data in a proper way and make it a competitive advantage," explained one respondent. While reported security breaches involving personal information result in both an immediate short-term impact on firms' stock prices[67] and direct remediation and litigation costs[68] (recently calculated at $201 per record breached[69]), the bulk of the penalty to firms arises from lost business—a phenomenon that increased more than 15 percent between 2013 and 2014.[70] Lost business represents the costs related to customer "churn," or turnover, as well as increased costs of customer acquisition. These costs directly reflect consumer pushback arising from perceived failures in protecting personal information.

Without the laws' notification requirements, it is highly unlikely that customers would know about the breach and put market pressure on companies to improve security practices. The consumer expectation rubric revealed in our interviews reflects an increasing reality connecting trust, brand image, and privacy prompted by the SBN laws.

Finally, the SBN laws created an incentive structure that drove companies to develop internal processes to manage risk.[71] The laws provided CPOs with a performance metric, both internally and with respect to peer institutions.[72] The CPOs we interviewed summarized news reports about breaches at other organizations and circulated them to staff with "lessons learned" from each incident. They reported that the breaches at other organizations helped justify expenditures for implementing new protocols within their own organizations. In the words of one respondent, "the breach news . . . was so loud that it didn't take much to get the attention of our senior executive on data security, kind of as part of the privacy program." Another reported, "[the security breach laws] enriched my role; it's putting more of an emphasis on leadership internally in a very operational sense." The visibility of privacy failures thus enhanced internal resources. As one CPO described: "We're now in the process of rolling encryption across all of our laptops. It's the right thing to do and I'm very glad we're doing it but, if it wasn't for the security breach laws in the U.S., we wouldn't be doing it. I don't think any company would be. It's what drove it."

THE TURN TO PROFESSIONALS

The rhetoric of privacy as trust was no doubt appealing to corporate privacy officers trying to gain traction within their organizations, as it was for regulators attempting to motivate industry to take privacy seriously or face a barrier to electronic commerce. But the combination of uncertainty regarding the FTC's evolution of privacy requirements and uncertainty regarding market responses spurred by security breach notifications was central to the striking trend toward corporate reliance on professional privacy management.

Professionalism has long served as an important institution for mediating uncertainty in the face of environmental ambiguity.[73] In the privacy context, increasing ambiguity as to the future behavior of both regulators and market forces prompted a parallel escalation in the reliance on internal corporate experts to guide corporate practices and manage privacy risk.

Our interviews reflect this risk management orientation. The CPOs described a forward-looking focus on identifying future challenges rather than compliance with existing mandates. They also underscore the potential for environmental ambiguity, combined with credible threats of meaningful sanction, to affect the scope of the privacy function within corporate organizations. Our respondents described a broad reach throughout the corporation, authority to participate in strategic decisions about the firm business, and relatively wide latitude to establish corporate practices and define their jobs.

CPOs derived independence and power from their boundary-spanning role, serving both as a voice for privacy and as a trusted insider using a "privacy mindset" to spur mindful internal decision making in the face of pressure to focus on efficiency and profit. The ambiguity of the external environment required this level of outside engagement. Our interviewees spoke of their expertise in two veins: being an effective voice for secondary values; and serving as a trusted internal expert. Our interviewees noted the tension in these two roles, as they both prodded the firm and advised it. Yet the organizational understanding that a larger set of social and market actors were concerned with privacy values and firms' responses strengthened their ability to straddle this conflict. The visibility of privacy failures produced by regulatory and institutional choices, and the traction they receive among various constituents, appears to be key to completing this circle.

11 The Development of the German Privacy Field

Two conundra were raised by the accounts of privacy protection provided by the German privacy leads we interviewed. First, as explored in chapter 9, this account reveals the emergence of patterns quite similar to those in leading U.S. firms, despite the radical divergence between the two countries' formal laws and institutions.

Second, the DPOs noted relatively new corporate behaviors arising against the backdrop of a relatively stable German data protection landscape that existed for decades. These stable elements include the linkage between data protection and a broader human rights framework, the federalist system and behavior of data protection regulators, the influence of court-centered constitutionalism, the participation of works councils in corporate governance of privacy, and legal choices, such as the requirement of a data protection officer itself.

In light of these conundra, this chapter explores the phenomena identified by our respondents and, with the aid of historical and legal texts and further interviews with participants in the German privacy and data protection field, details their development. This history highlights the importance of key governance features put in place as early as 1970, when the State of Hesse enacted the world's first data protection law.[1] Yet it reflects the reality that these foundations were not, in their early years, sufficient to trigger the developments in corporate practice that we witnessed today.

What these elements did, however, was combine to constitute a data protection field that demonstrated striking adaptability in responding to the past decade's rapidly changing threats to data protection and privacy. This chapter explores the factors that generated this adaptability, and the additional legal and social elements that in turn catalyzed the current privacy management practices.

THE FRAMING OF GERMAN DATA PROTECTION

The German DPOs we interviewed conveyed an understanding of data protection that went beyond specific requirements found in law. They explained the way data protection was tied to broader concepts of privacy and dignity, and to an overall human rights framework. They also described the instrumental importance of broader concepts of privacy and dignity to escaping the compliance mentality typical of a "data protection" approach— and for advancing robust, beyond-compliance measures within the firm.

These broader understandings are reflected in the earliest framings of that nation's data protection initiatives. The initiatives defined data protection not as a statutory matter resulting from legislature mandate, but rather in terms that reflect broader political and social concerns, actualized in part by judicial and constitutional contributions to its meaning.

The world's first data protection law in Hesse (initially regulating only treatment of information by the public sector) was a response to fears about the government's use of newly developed mainframe computing power.[2] As one former regulator explained, the notion "that government should be carefully planned," and that "to achieve results you should know far more than you knew at the moment," were "particularly important and characteristic" of administrators' thinking in Hesse. Moves to "rationalize" government through "the automation of registers, new uses of government data," and "new collections" on which to base "social policy" offered administrators new opportunities for more efficient and better-informed public initiatives. Yet news of these planned systems engendered considerable public concern.

While this alarm was not unique to Germany,[3] every member of the German privacy field with whom we spoke cited the significance to the framing of data protection as a matter of broader human rights. This framing reflected the relatively recent experience of Nazi horrors enabled by the collection and use of personal information processed by newly efficient counting and sorting machines.

The human rights-based conception of data protection was extended to the private sector with the passage in 1976 of the Federal Data Protection Act,[4] and received its strongest articulation in the Constitutional Court's 1983 embrace of the constitutional right to "informational self-determination."[5] As one sitting regulator summarized, "the history of the constitution and the guarantee of fundamental rights is a reaction to National Socialism. And the disregard of human dignity has led to the very strong and very eminent position, the guarantee of human dignity in the German constitution. And data protection has been derived by the constitutional court, after the initial legislation [in ways that had] . . . roots in the constitution, human dignity being one of these."[6]

By invoking the right to informational self-determination, the Constitutional Court elevated the concept of data protection in Germany from a statutory creature to a constitutional guarantee, and shifted the onus onto those entities that sought to limit privacy.[7] The decision greatly strengthened the mandate of the federal and state data protection agencies, and governments in turn eventually revised the data protection acts at both levels.[8] Judicial expansion by other courts of principles set out in the German Constitutional Court's foundational Census Decision, which first articulated a right to "informational self-determination" in the German Constitution, further strengthened institutional power to protect privacy and the use of data. Decisions of the Federal Labour Court, for example, extended the constitutional personality right, and the right to privacy flowing from it, to employee information in the workplace.[9] This expanded the opportunities accorded to—and even duties imposed upon—employee works councils to participate in decisions regarding the use of information, as will be discussed further.

INITIAL BUILDING BLOCKS IN THE GERMAN DATA PROTECTION FIELD

Our German respondents further identified a suite of longstanding elements critical to shaping their beliefs about how privacy and data protection should best be translated into firm practices. First, they articulated a sense that the meaning of data protection evolved in part from an ongoing dialogue with data protection authorities. Second, they cited two particular institutional elements: their own roles as independent data protection officers who could access influence at high levels within the firm, engage in strategic discussions about practices and processes necessary to identify and ameliorate privacy risks; and the roles of works councils in negotiating practices involving the use of data. Understanding the history of these salient elements requires examination of a range of forces influencing the German privacy landscape, including legislative choices embodied in statutes, more informal choices by data-protection regulators, decisions by nongovernmental actors in the regulatory field, and legal and structural elements of German law and governance entirely external to data protection.

GERMAN DATA PROTECTION AUTHORITIES (DPAS) AND THE APPROACH TO DATA PROTECTION OVERSIGHT

Multiple State Oversight Authorities in a Federal Scheme   A range of actors in the German field emphasized the federal nature of German political structure as a critical factor shaping privacy and data protection. Some complained about the confusion arising from data protection requirements developed and enforced by multiple regulators. "[The] split of competences," explained one regulator, "makes it not easy to come to common positions, especially in [oversight of the] the private sector. You can question why are there different requirements in Hamburg and Bavaria, [and] it's not easy to answer." In the words of another, "[T]he problem is the oversight conducted for the private sector, [where] the basic requirements are defined by the federal data protection act but the interpretation is different." This hinders deterrence, that regulator believed, because "[y]ou cannot say that there is one very strong authority with very harsh actions." In turn, some authorities "are more flexible than others, so some say 'no we cannot accept this,'" while others "have had a weaker position, [a] more company friendly position."[10]

Many others identified the ways that divergent authorities with different interpretations have proved important in positive ways. Indeed, one leading comparative law scholar told us that federalism was the single most important factor in German "exceptionalism" in data protection leadership.

Most straightforwardly, federalism has facilitated regulatory innovation in data protection. As one regulator explains, "[T]he federal state system has a big advantage, as it's open for different solutions to the same problem in the different federal states, there is competition between the states for the best regulation."[11] Indeed, the enactment of Hesse's pioneering legislation reflects this innovative potential. Spiros Simitis, the author of that legislation, reports that it was drafted in fourteen days, at the request of the state Prime Minister, to take advantage of popular opinion regarding a controversial proposal for governmental use of personal data.[12] Once Hesse's laws were adopted, explained a different regulator, "other states and the federal parliament followed."

Nearly every field leader we interviewed described how such regulatory competition has characterized German data protection's development on issues ranging from "the definition of requirements and technological data protection," "ideas on common procedures of different data controllers," "the status of data protection officials in the public administration," and binding contracts (pioneered by the Berlin DPA), to the initial promotion of "seals and audits" in the state of Schleswig-Holstein,[13] described as "a clear innovation coming at the *Länder* level." From its inception, then, the meaning of data protection in Germany was shaped by a multiplicity of oversight authorities with jurisdiction to arrive at competing interpretations of data protection's requirements, and experiment with different approaches.

Regulatory Style The nature of the power granted to these multiple bodies, their understanding of their role as oversight authorities, and the resulting governance choices, further shaped the German data protection landscape. Most striking in the responses we received was the description of German DPAs as concerned with oversight and guidance rather than prescriptive regulation, a sharp contrast with parallel institutions in other European countries. As one pioneer German regulator described: "[T]o make it clear, German data protection authorities do not speak of themselves as 'regulators.' No data protection authorities say 'we are regulators.' We accept this in the international scope, [but] from the German perspective it is very unusual to use these words for an oversight authority."

Instead, he explained, Germans "see [the role of the DPA] as oversight and giving advice, but there is no power, or in very few fields, to set up rules beyond the specific case." Notably, the rare instances in which such rules arise is under section 38a of the Data Protection Act, involving more bottom-up types of regulation, such as "binding corporate rules and self-regulatory schemes. This is the kind of regulation you can see, but all other fields there is a case by case oversight."

That regulator further linked this arrangement to more general German approaches to governance:

I would say that it's a German tradition. . . . [I]n general, there is a clear distinction between parliament and governments as regulator in their fields. That government has the power to regulate in this range defined by the law. The main decisions have to be done, have to be approved by the parliament, this if the parliament delegates some powers to the government or to specific administrations . . . then they act as regulators. But the data protection authorities are independent, they can make some decisions on very specific cases, they can impose fines—at least the [state-level] authorities have this power.

Another prominent former regulator tied this approach specifically to prevalent elements in German regulatory culture, such as a "certain amount of trust with regards to large companies, that they will make sure rules are followed" (except, he noted, in the banking sector); a faith in the force of reputational concerns in ensuring compliance; a "general atmosphere of mutual respect between control institutions and companies," in which "when companies describe challenges they were facing there is an atmosphere of dialogue; a pattern of "companies and government sitting together to find common solutions"; and, an oversight approach that is generally "not confrontational."

One former regulator understood the role of a data protection commissioner as coordinating or leading a public "discourse." He described especially "a campaign to explain, persuade and achieve" through presence in "the public eye." They held meetings with different parts of the administration, meetings with potential interested parties and allies, such as representatives of works councils, and hosted public meetings, including on weekends and evenings, and in accessible locations, such as state parliament and local universities that could hold from five hundred to six hundred attendees. DPAs also issued publicity materials and reports for coverage in newspapers and television and gave interviews in these venues to "present[ ] what we did."

Another described the way that the role of public discourse was a means for promulgating nonbinding "opinions" and "recommendations . . . to the outside world, to the private sector as well as to the public administration—[such as] what are the requirements for specific levels of security or cryptography? how [do we] deal with specific kinds of data processing?"

In addition to outward-facing publicity efforts, regulators, DPOs and field lawyers also discussed the relative porousness of the DPAs. They cited regular conversations between DPAs and DPOs, and meetings between DPAs and representatives of industry sectors. As one former regulator described: "We accepted informal and formal requests for clarification and guidance on phone and in person. Many of my colleagues, that is what they primarily did."

Finally, those we interviewed described the development of other institutional contexts for negotiations around the meaning of privacy and data protection. Key among these is the *Düsseldorfer Kreis* ("Dusseldorf Circle"), the joint consultative body bringing together state DPAs. Through the *Kreis,* and more recently the conference of the independent data protection commissions, representatives of each *Land*'s authority meet regularly to discuss issues of data protection policy, with the aim of coming to some consensus and common solutions. As one participant explained, the group convenes working groups on the range of relevant cutting-edge issues, including "police justice . . . taxes, statistics, education, health, health and social security." The working groups meet at least twice a year and the members have regular email exchanges. The groups then release public statements or resolutions. Such declarations "have no force of law." As one regulator explains, "[T]hese decisions are not binding, not [even] for the commissioners, because every single commissioner is in fact independent. So he is an independent authority and he has to act independently." Nonetheless, explained another, they serve as "common formulations of what position the regulator authorities take as a composition"—a "kind of statement of how we interpret the law."

These statements operate as a sort of "soft law" guidance. They shape both firm predictions regarding future legal interpretations, and guidance for each individual state commissioner, who then issues "his own statements addressing a specific issues of the data protection law in the private sector."

This process of public dialogue over data governance issues, our respondents described, is in turn furthered by the participation of other third parties over questions of privacy and innovation. As both our DPO and governmental respondents explained, these third parties are, largely, not the sort of independent civil society advocates prominent in the U.S. story. Instead, activists operate from within other politically powerful institutions, such as political parties like "the Green Party or the SDS, or the CDP" or "the trade unions or churches"—or help build other broader-based institutions, like the Pirate Party.

These voices participate in government innovation dialogues convened by parliament, political parties, and government ministries. The dialogues increasingly involve privacy issues at very early stages so as to avoid the backlash against decisions of the type that followed the census, and have prompted discussions about the "RFID passport, health card, and storage of communications data." Through these debates, one prominent member of the privacy field explained, such issues are considered in the context of "social debates" rather than simply "government deciding."

THE LEGAL EMPOWERMENT OF NONGOVERNMENTAL ACTORS IN DATA PROTECTION: DATA PROTECTION OFFICERS AND EMPLOYEE WORKS COUNCILS

Data Protection Officers and the Professionalization of Privacy Nearly every respondent from across the field cited the statutory creation of the position of the data protection officer[14] as the most important regulatory choice for institutionalizing data protection. At the time such a position was mandated in the 1977 Data Protection Act,[15] "the problem under discussion in Germany was very similar to the United States debate," explains one former policymaker. It was "how far data protection should be integrated into daily practices of [regulated] entities, and under the responsibility of such entities. And therefore, data protection officers were seen as a kind of self-organization—not self-regulation, but self-organization."

Indeed, the choice to extend a DPO requirement to the private sector reflected, one regulator explained, a model that had been employed in other sectors of the German industrial economy, such as workplace discrimination and workplace safety. By this choice, policymakers sought "to ensure transformation of rules into everyday practice of companies."

Whether the DPO was a direct employee of the firm or an outside expert,[16] he or she was granted significant independence. The DPO reports directly to the corporate CEO, must be allowed to carry out his or her function free of outside interference, may not be penalized for his or her actions, and can only be fired by the firm in exceptional circumstances.

In terms of responsibilities, The DPO acts as the contact person for the DPA within private firms in a two-way process of translation. In one direction, the DPO provides advice to top firm decision makers, and transforms and interprets the data protection rules into the everyday practice of firms. In the other direction, the DPO monitors the data protection activities in the firm and reports at regular intervals to the DPA. In the end, explains one leading German lawyer, "The underlying rationale was to strengthen effective self-monitoring so as to make state supervision and controls unnecessary as far as possible and thus reduce administrative bureaucracy."[17]

With the passage of the legal requirement, an organization to support the new data protection officer profession, the *Gesellschaft für Datenschutz und Datensicherheit*, or "GDD," was immediately established.[18] According to Christoph Klug, a lawyer who long served in the organization's leadership, the GDD arose explicitly to fill the need created by the absence of specific provisions in the original 1976 federal law setting out the requirements for a DPO.[19] That law contained no detailed definition of the role, or an enumeration of its roles and responsibilities. The law simply provided that the DPO was to work toward ensuring compliance with the Act and any other applicable data protection provisions. Further, the original law contained a requirement that the position may only be filled by "persons with the specialized knowledge and reliability necessary to carry out their duties,[20] but gave no detailed description of what such qualifications might entail.

The GDD began almost immediately, in Klug's words, to "fill in the details and fill in the context," both as to the role of the DPO, and of the best practices that they were to recommend.[21] The association quickly launched comprehensive training and then certification programs, building the identity of the DPO role.[22] Membership in the GDD grew from eight in 1977 to 528 three years later; by 2010, that number exceeded 2000.[23] The association began to develop criteria for DPO qualifications, ultimately engaging in a series of large-scale proposals for, and studies of, the DPO role in Germany.[24] These criteria, in turn, would shape standards eventually adopted by the DPAs.[25]

In its first year, GDD launched an annual conference known as the *Datenschutzfactagung* (DAFTA), which became an opportunity not only for practitioners to meet and share knowledge and ideas, but also for politicians, regulators, and unions to interact with practitioners about current thoughts and concerns.[26] It strengthened local networks through regional groups of DPOs, known as *regionale Erfahrungsaustauschkreise* (Regional Experience-Sharing Circles),[27] which meet three to five times per year. From the beginning, they have featured representatives from the DPAs who discuss their perspectives on the parameters of acceptable data practices. The association worked to assist practitioners, especially those from small- and medium-sized enterprises with limited internal resources, with "nuts and bolts" problems that arise in practice.[28] They also launched a telephone, and then email, hotline where members can ask questions regarding data management.

In the absence of clear mandates from government DPAs, the GDD substantively developed the content and guided the implementation of best practices across the data protection landscape. The association launched working groups[29] to develop approaches and guidelines in different substantive arenas,[30] and published guides for DPOs on issues ranging from treatment of employee data[31] to privacy-enhancing technologies.[32] At regular two-month intervals, the GDD published *Mitteilungen* ("Releases") which reported on the current activities of the GDD and provided members with up-to-date practical information on data protection and data security, developments in legislation, and references to new books and literature about privacy.[33] The GDD also launched the leading German data protection journal, *Recht der Datenverarbeitung*, which includes articles about data protection law and the wider topic of data management.[34]

As a professionalized body of German DPOs developed, data protection became a "business model," in the words of one German regulator. In the words of others, a "culture" of DPOs and a "data protection scene" developed. The inexact nature of the DPO requirement fostered these developments.

Works Councils and Employee Codetermination Our respondents identified works councils as the second key nongovernmental element that contributed to the *sui generis* nature of German data protection as compared to its European counterparts. The German labor movement and its relationship with corporate governance and political and economic rule has stood in marked contrast with that of the United States since World War II.[35] The German Works Constitution Act explicitly creates a system of codetermination by both employers and employee "works councils" over "matters relating to the operation of the establishment,"[36] and authorizes *both* to "safeguard and promote the untrammelled development of the personality of the employees of the establishment."[37] This provision has, in turn, been interpreted by the Federal Labour Court as creating a duty for both employers and works councils to protect intrusions on employee privacy by modern information technology.

Pursuant to this system, works councils are given extensive rights to information, consultation, and codetermination on issues that affect employees. They have the authority to block the introduction or change of internal systems or processes that might have an effect on employees, or demand compensation for employee damages that result from the decisions of firm management.[38]

This "stakeholder governance"[39] model has affected data protection in Germany in a number of different ways throughout the past few decades. Because of the large and powerful role played by works councils in corporate governance, workers' interests have played an important role in discussions about data protection. One such interest has been worker privacy, especially the surveillance of employees and the use of their data to monitor their productivity and effectiveness. On data protection questions within companies, the board, the DPO, and the works council representative must all participate when rules related to employee data are negotiated. Proposals by firms along these lines have been met with resistance by works councils, and sparked a dynamic process of negotiation among corporate stakeholders aimed at demarcating the bounds of employee privacy. At a higher level, DPAs have also engaged in dialogue with works councils, which shaped data protection regulatory policy as well.

Thus the structure of German corporate and labor law created an additional important stakeholder, with divergent perspectives and interests, in the data protection dialogue. As the leading DPOs we interviewed explained, this nexus between privacy and workers' rights stimulates internal conversations regarding more broadly applicable company values, especially those surrounding the appropriate balance between individual rights against company and societal interests. These company values then form part of the backdrop for privacy discussions, including those involving consumer privacy.

TWENTY-FIRST-CENTURY CHANGES: INSTITUTIONAL REVISION AND EFFECTS ON FIRM BEHAVIOR

By the late 1990s, many of the key elements of the German data protection landscape identified in our interviews with leading German DPOs were in place. Information governance was not viewed exclusively through a compliance-oriented data protection lens, but was understood to require consideration and protection of broader privacy, dignity, and human rights values. Multiple oversight authorities within the federal system engaged in governance approaches characterized by dialogue and negotiation—a dialogue that included regulated parties, political groups, industry groups, and labor. And the reliance on required data privacy officers as a "self-organization" mechanism expanded the profession's numbers, networks and associations, and shared commitments.

Despite this, the best practices of contemporary privacy management documented through our interviews had not yet developed. Our respondents described the high level of resources and attention currently devoted to privacy governance in their firms as a relatively recent development. At the turn of the century, data protection and information privacy had not yet commanded a place of prominence on the radar of corporate management.

Furthermore, as one regulator explained, many perceived the choice to employ a data protection officer model over other regulatory schemes, such as the centralized licensing and approval model, as creating more bureaucratic burden than benefit. This view partially explains the reported undercompliance with (and corresponding underenforcement of) DPO requirements, and the tendency toward the use of external DPOs. Indeed, where DPOs were in place within firms, their role was largely seen as low-level, bureaucratic, and inward looking.

As another regulator described in 2002, despite all of the developments noted here, data protection in the end was not approached with a strategic mindset, but with a bureaucratic one. "German privacy law has always been oriented to legislation by the state,"[40] thus "[i]nstead of looking for means to obtain the informed consent of the person concerned, our legislation churned out a great amount of legal provisions which can no longer be kept track of. The result was not—as the Federal Constitutional Court [in the Census Decision] pleaded for—more competence of the law but confusion and non-acceptance."[41]

It would take a suite of new developments, prompted in large part by legislative reform and regulatory adjustment taken after the enactment of the European Data Protection framework, to leverage the key elements of the German privacy landscape and catalyze the firm behaviors described by today's leading DPOs.

KEY FACTORS IN IMPLEMENTING THE 1995 EU DIRECTIVE: SOPHISTICATED REGULATORS ADDRESSING TECHNOLOGICAL CHANGE

These new developments were prompted by both legal and technological change. The passage in 1995 of the EU's Data Protection Directive required updating Germany's existing laws to implement the legal standards in the U.S. framework.

At the same time, there was significant technological change, including new methods to collect data about a wider set of subjects now reachable through the Internet. When coupled with advances in data processing, storage, and retrieval, this meant that companies now had the capability of collecting, holding indefinitely, and using in unexpected ways the personal data of much larger numbers of people. German regulators were acutely aware of the risks and challenges resulting from rapid technological change during the six years it took to agree on amendments to the Federal Data Protection law, ultimately enacted in 2001.

Indeed, those government officials focused on data protection seem to have been particularly sensitized to, and savvy about, the implications of technological change for traditional information risk models, and the need for new approaches to address new threats. Remarks delivered at a conference of the state data protection authority members of the *Düsseldorfer Kreis* considering the twentieth anniversary of the Federal Data Protection Act in 1998—the mid-period between the EU Data Protection Directive's passage and the enactment of the 2001 amendments—reflect this sensitivity.

Bettina Sokol, the Data Protection Commissioner for the state of Nordrhein-Westfalen delivered the opening remarks and set the tone.[42] She began by explicating the shift in the challenges posed by technology. The conditions of the "emerging information society" at the turn of the century, she explained, meant that the traditional data protection approach, by which one could easily enforce prohibitions against controllers' use of data without legitimate purposes, was no longer operative for a variety of reasons.

First, in the networked society a variety of stakeholders take part in data processing. Data processing sites are no longer found only in central state institutions, but potentially with all netizens. Second, personal information is not only consciously and deliberately collected, but also incidentally obtained as a side effect of the use of information and communication services. Even the normal use of the network results in the accrual of personal information in a variety of ways. Third, a kind of "new complexity" results from all of this for those affected. Whether because of the globalization of data flows, the growing information assets held in private hands, or the increasing government desire to use these private information stock-piles, it was no longer easy to understand what happens to the data in every case.

Thus, she continued, "the law must be aware of the limits of its ability to control consciously." Accordingly, "[i]t must provide not only a sovereign regulatory framework that ensures that the hazards to data protection do not arise,"[43] but also "promote through its requirements the development and deployment of, and demand for, privacy-enhancing technology." This way "we can avoid the situation where part of the population falls by the wayside and only the specialists and computer geeks can organize an adequate level of data protection."[44]

At the same conference, Dr. Stefan Walz, Data Protection Commissioner of Bremen, expanded on the approach necessary for the future.[45] He criticized the shortcomings of the EU Data Protection Directive passed only three years before as "built on the background of now-outdated technology scenarios from the seventies and eighties." As an example, he pointed to the framework's general registration requirement for automated processing that "still takes the idea of clearly definable data processing procedures in a mainframe environment."

In the face of technological advances, he argued, privacy will be protected "[o]nly if privacy-friendly process elements are involved as early as possible in system design."[46] He recognized that legal obligations to introduce such technologies and processes face "considerable economic disincentives" within the corporation,[47] but suggested that those disincentives could be overcome by "risk of punishment by the market," in which breaches of confidence are "reinforced by the media coverage." In addition, he maintained, "privacy" must enlist alliances, such as with consumer advocates or others with a market interest in the technologies of privacy promotion, and with "network participants [informed] enough about the risks."[48]

Several years later, Thilo Weichert, deputy privacy protection commissioner of Schleswig-Holstein, echoed these remarks in explaining the change in attitudes necessitated by challenges posed by technological advances. He described a shift from a "data protection" orientation to one of "privacy protection," directed to protecting "the personal or individual rights of people."[49]

"For more than 30 years," he explained, "the focus of German privacy law has been on statutory law, and "[t]he main question was and is, which forms of data processing are legal and which are not."[50] Furthermore: "The emphasis has been on approvals and prohibitions. There are some procedural provisions but a total lack of economic stimulus. Such procedural provisions are, for example, notification of data processing, the obligation to set up a Chief Privacy Officer or Data Protection Officer or the requirement to have special processing procedures approved by a higher-ranking authority."[51]

At the same time, he explained, "there was and still is a lack of incentives for good practice and for good privacy protection concepts."[52]Thus privacy law "has long enough been a matter just between regulatory authorities and the processing body," and produced "a great amount of legal provisions which can no longer be kept track of." As "[d]ata processing has progressed in quantity and quality," he said, "[a]dministrative supervision is no longer capable of keeping the flow of data under control."[53]

Thus, he explained, "[t]here are new ways of controlling data processing which haven't been known before."[54] These involve a strategic approach to privacy protection that focuses on integrating privacy into technical decisions, and harnessing economic and market incentives.

As to the first, whether a consumer "can really exercise [control over his data] depends not only on the good will of the parties involved, but much more on the design of the technical products."[55]As to the second, tools should be leveraged, like audits, certifications, and other "organisational and technological measures" that help make the technical decisions within firms responsive to outside forces. "Since data processing is no longer a strange matter of high-tech competence somewhere far away in a monstrous mainframe computer but an everyday activity pursued by a normal consumer, there should be a way of utilizing this new competence."[56] Privacy protection, he explained, "is just about to enter the market economy."[57]

STATUTORY AMENDMENTS AND PROMINENT DATA SCANDALS
In the context of these understandings by regulators, both top-down regulatory choices and events in the broader market enacted a shift in the German privacy landscape, from a bureaucratic to a strategic orientation,

and to a focus on technological, organizational, and market inputs to privacy decision making.

The 2001 Amendments to the Federal Act   The top-down changes began with Germany's 2001 implementation of the EU Data Protection Directive through amendments to the Federal Data Protection Law. These changes significantly enhanced the investigative, and to some degree the enforcement powers of the supervisory authorities. Previously, DPAs were limited to investigating private-sector firms only if there were specific grounds to believe that a legal violation had occurred. The 2001 amendments created plenary investigative power, and further expanded DPA jurisdiction over compliance not just with the Federal Data Protection Law, but also with "any other data protection rules," including sectoral codes of conduct developed in coordination with industry.[58]

Specifically, the law provided DPAs with authority to demand, without cause, "any information which the supervisory authority needs for the fulfillment of its task"[59] The agency was empowered to access any business premises and offices and to inspect business documents, including the required overview of personal data processing maintained by the company DPO. As to enforcement, the amendments were more limited. DPAs were empowered to order firms to take specific technical or organizational measures, but only to ensure compliance with the legal requirements concerning security and confidentiality, rather than other data protection principles.[60] But the 2001 amendments also introduced the idea of the data protection audit, which set the stage for state authorities to take the lead in developing auditor training and experimenting with "seals of approval" for firms that voluntarily engage in evaluations.[61]

Prominent Data Scandals   These changes in regulatory authority were leveraged by two scandals identified by nearly every single DPO and regulator we interviewed. These involved Deutsche Bahn, the German railway company, and Deutsche Telekom, a formerly state-owned private telecommunications firms.

In the case of Deutsche Bahn, from 2002 to 2005 the company had compared personal data about employees with data about suppliers in an effort to combat internal corruption. It had done so on a general basis, without suspicions about any particular employees. In addition, from 2006 to 2007 the company had monitored employees' external emails sent from the workplace. As the country's largest employer, the scandal affected a high number of German citizens, and as a quasi-national[62] company, it took on shades of the census scandal three decades earlier. After news of the company's conduct became public, an internal corporate shakeup took place, reaching as high as the CEO. Then in 2009, after an investigation, the Berlin DPA imposed a record 1.1 million euro fine, and the company agreed to strengthen its data protection office and policies.[63]

In the Deutsche Telekom case, seventeen million customer records were stolen in 2006, including the addresses, dates of birth, and telephone numbers of several high-profile politicians, an ex–federal president, and other celebrities.[64] It followed a scandal earlier that year where the company admitted to monitoring the communications data of several board members, senior executives, and journalists.[65] These transgressions resulted in criminal charges for several of the employees and contractors involved, as well as large changes to the company's data protection practices and procedures.[66]

In the wake of these and other scandals, and the ensuing media coverage and public debates, many in Germany believed that the existing data-protection regulatory regime and the internal corporate structures developed alongside it were, in the words of one interviewed regulator, "insufficient." As another scholar we interviewed described, this led to a push for increased protection for personal data, both externally and internally to firms.

Further Top-Down Change: The 2009 Amendments to the Federal Act In response to these developments, the federal government in 2009 amended the federal law. In addition to restricting the scope of permissible data collection and use by organizations, these amendments boosted the strength of many of the actors and institutions of the German regulatory field in at least three important ways.

DPAs were strengthened by provisions that gave them the power to order organizations to "remediate compliance, technical, or organizational failures relating to the collection, processing, and use of personal data," to "implement special procedures," or to cease processing personal data completely.[67] The amendments further increased the number and scope of administrative (rather than criminal) offenses. This was of particular importance because now "penalties for such offences can be imposed in summary proceedings."[68] Possible penalties were also increased to as much as 300,000 euros. The amendments doubled the maximum fines for minor offenses and increased them by 20 percent for major offenses, including failure to inform data subjects of security breaches.

The DPO position, too, received more independence and clout. The amendments provided that DPOs could only be fired with cause, and were entitled to training and continuing education paid for by firms.[69] The amendments also encouraged companies, especially small and medium-sized entities, to employ external DPOs.[70]

Finally, the law introduced a security breach notification requirement inspired by similar statutes that had been successfully introduced in the United States. These requirements were meant to provide market transparency about privacy failures and increase publicity and reputational risks, and corresponding costs to firms.[71]

CATALYZING PRIVACY LEADERSHIP

Our informants described how these regulatory, economic, and structural developments combined with the institutions already in place to catalyze the sort of strategic and operational privacy leadership currently evidenced in the top tier of German firms.

As an initial matter, the heightened regulatory vigor among the DPAs, the threat of larger fines and consequential damages, and the increased reputational costs for security breaches drove greater awareness of privacy issues among top managers, who funneled more firm resources toward data protection.

The security breach notification requirement, in the words of one regulator, provides a "very important additional tool." A second explained how enhanced supervisory authority and the security breach notification requirement combined to increase transparency and made the traditional advisory function of the DPAs even more effective. In particular, it has enhanced the role of ex ante consultation with DPA, which now can better leverage the media as a sort of soft-law power. The "press" is now "calling us" about data issues in particular corporate settings, he said. When that happens, "I call [the firm in question] and I want to know what is going on there, and [I say] 'if you need our support please let me know what's really going on before I say something to the press.'" He continued: "[We now] have a very privacy aware public . . . the media are looking into this so [there is] the risk that we get involved and engaged, . . . [that] we give journalists some quotes which the company will not find supportive or positive which will create negative public relations. So that is an educational tool at the same time that you should better talk to us first."

These developments, one privacy leader said, have also brought new entrants into the privacy field, notably consumer protection organizations that supervisory authorities now consult to "try to join forces." A recent proposal to amend the Federal Data Protection Act would go further to empower groups with the authority to sue businesses in court for data protection law breaches.[72]

Combined with the statutory enhancement of their independence, these factors, in the words of one former regulator, "reinforced and strengthened" the preexisting DPO position. "There is both a tougher legal framework and a feeling that the DPAs are getting stricter and stricter," said a leading German privacy lawyer. DPOs "cannot be fired," he added. "So when they go in to try to find out what's going on they have a fair amount of authority." These external developments were further credited with DPOs' growing strategic role within the firm. As one prominent regulator explained, the increase in external regulatory pressure, the need for enhanced risk assessment, the access to greater firm resources, and the ability to tap into existing DPO networks increasingly oriented DPOs toward professionalism and a strategic outlook. This trend was further hastened by the increasing globalization of privacy professional organizing, and the expansion to Europe of the U.S.-based IAPP, which exposes its members to global best practices from a variety of contexts.

The evidence of such a shift was pronounced among the leading DPOs that we interviewed. The change was also echoed by the regulators, academics, and practitioners with whom we spoke. They cited the recent "explosion" of books and treatises that attempt to delineate what data protection law *means* over and above simply setting out what data protection law *is*, as well as the growing number of privacy conferences with greater attendance by the DPOs, particularly those from the larger, multinational firms.

To be sure, the transformations in the role of the DPO have not penetrated throughout all German firms equally. As one leading lawyer made clear, there still remained a division between the leading DPOs we interviewed, many who worked in firms with a multinational presence, and those in smaller, domestic German firms. He explained that while the former group are becoming more strategic, they were "certainly the minority" and "[n]ot fully reflective of the profession." Getting the attention of upper management remained difficult for DPOs in many firms, he said.

At the same time, as one regulator summarized, the combination of the German adoption of the DPO model, the increasing power of that role, the diversity of national and state regulators and the privacy experts who work in them, and the empowerment of a variety of stakeholders in the field, Germany has created a "culture of data protection," where data protection has become "a business model." By creating a system in which "many people specialized on data protection, in turn, Germany has created a circle of people who work on data protection professionally. And I think this is not the case in other states." This, in turn, has a variety of effects: "It's creating the need within the companies to allow these rules and to follow them. Also, it's kind of an interest in those people working on it to keep their business model working." And "because data protection authorities and data protection officers, the whole data protection scene . . . are experts for journalists, and for others . . . they build public opinion on data protection."

V Catalyzing Better Privacy Protection

12 Catalyzing Robust Corporate Privacy Practices: Bringing the Outside In

LESSONS FROM THE UNITED STATES AND GERMANY: BRINGING THE OUTSIDE IN

What can we learn from the histories of privacy in the United States and Germany about what works best to catalyze robust corporate practices? What shared traits of the privacy regimes might explain the orientation and behavior of the firms they govern? How might privacy fields in other countries be shaped to produce similar corporate behavior?

Shared characteristics between the two systems cannot be found in particular formal legal rules, state institutions, or nonstate actors. The different histories of privacy in the United States and Germany reflect different forces, and feature different actors.

The privacy field in the United States, explored in chapter 10, has been positively shaped by the incomplete and comparatively late institutionalization of privacy governance, and has enabled dynamism and adaptability in the face of rapid changes in the use and treatment of personal data. The transparency about technology and industry practices and trends facilitated by Federal Trade Commission processes, combined with the episodic revelation of privacy breaches, opened up the practices of private companies to negative press and vigorous public scrutiny. Transparency fueled debate and enforcement actions aimed at reforming practices and clarifying obligations. As in the Yahoo! case that opens this book, the ensuing dialogue enhanced the role of a cadre of diverse experts, including professional associations and advocates, in defining privacy goals and work. Together, these forces and actors shaped evolving definitions of privacy and dynamic understandings of how those definitions should be reflected in privacy decision making within U.S. firms.

By contrast, the account of data protection in Germany presented in chapter 11 reflects different forces, and features different actors. The German data protection field was first institutionalized nearly three decades before that of the United States, and before the massive shifts in technological capacity and business models that accelerated from the late 1990s into the twenty-first century. The German system featured dedicated data protection authorities, at both the federal and state levels. It included unique structural requirements, notably the appointment of data protection officers for most firms. As a substantive matter, it pioneered an approach to information that was tied to an overall human rights framework, and championed the right to self-determination. And although the variety of nongovernmental advocates that arose in the United States to influence the privacy field was largely absent from much of the history of the German data-protection conversation, the establishment of employee works councils within the corporate structure provided an additional powerful player in the negotiation about information use.

But while the privacy fields in these two jurisdictions reflect diverse legal and institutional choices, as well as culturally distinct nonstate actors, they demonstrate important commonalities. Both feature a set of roles that corporate actors, regulators, and nongovernmental actors were invited, or empowered to play—and the patterns of interaction and relationships required to fulfill those roles.

Most importantly, the U.S. and German systems both catalyzed a powerful approach that we've labeled "bringing the outside in." Regulatory choices and cultural forces aligned to enable "outside" constituencies such as advocacy groups, labor representatives, privacy experts, professional associations, and other elements of civil society to influence corporate behavior meaningfully, and to contest privacy's meaning and application within firms. Public pressure created by breach laws and high-profile investigations and regulatory enforcement actions empowered these nonstate actors and the larger public to discipline corporate behavior in the courts of law and public opinion.

Growing outside pressure, in turn, pushed firms to fund, develop, strengthen, and smarten up their internal privacy operations, especially by appointing chief privacy officers with strategic roles and access to leadership. In their "boundary-spanning" roles, these professionals were increasingly invested with the authority and tools to negotiate privacy norms with both outside and inside players, and to better operationalize privacy protection inside their firms. In both countries, regulation facilitated this virtuous circle of "bringing the outside in" by replacing process-heavy legal requirements with broader, more ambiguous ones that encouraged greater corporate responsibility and accountability for protecting privacy. This, in turn, furthered the growth of chief privacy officers within corporations and, in turn, a robust professional community—including advocates, corporate professionals, academics, and regulators—that tethered the CPOs to external norms, and empowered them within their firms. The privacy community became a stakeholder to which the corporation had to respond. In short, rather than absorbing the full burden of interpreting and policing privacy rules, regulators in the United States and Germany helped facilitate, empower, and leverage a broad *community* invested in protecting privacy.

The country-specific manifestations of "bringing the outside in" can diverge—and do in the U.S. and German experiences. Different institutions served as *functional substitutes*. In Germany, works councils and DPOs are key stakeholders, created by law, that sit within the corporation itself but also bring outside pressure to bear. In the U.S., third-party players, including advocacy organizations and the media, played a larger role. In both fields professional groups were important, and active players. To understand the common successes, it is important to look beyond the identity of specific actors to the shared *properties* of the regulatory fields that enabled these successes.

An exploration of a field's *properties* goes beyond identifying what other scholars have cataloged as privacy "tools."[1] It instead addresses regulatory features at a level of abstraction that allows them to be identified—and, we hope, ultimately cultivated—in different contexts, and in ways reflecting different legal backgrounds and cultures, as they were in Germany and the United States.

Viewed from "from the ground up"—from promising corporate practices, to the actors and roles involved in producing them, to the properties of the privacy field that shape them—the accounts of the U.S. and German privacy fields suggest three common properties important for catalyzing the promising set of common practices that "bring the outside in" to the corporation:

1. ambiguity with accountability;
2. a boundary-spanning community; and
3. disciplinary transparency

A focus on these three properties offers insights into the operation of a strong privacy field and suggests a means to guide the construction of the privacy policy apparatus across national contexts. These properties can be cultivated by regulators through strategic choices at three distinct points in the cycle of governance: agenda setting, interpretation, and enforcement. Recognizing that the unique cultural, political, and economic conditions of a given country will lend themselves to different tools and institutional choices, this focus enables policymakers to recognize the functional substitutes—be they different actors playing particular roles, or different tools deployed in specific ways—that can yield similar properties.

That said, modesty is warranted. Our research underscores the fact that regulatory choices are important but not exclusive inputs into the construction of an effective privacy field. Law and legal institutions matter, both directly and indirectly, but so do other actors and institutions. In fact, we found that the most effective corporate practices evolved in environments where corporate behavior was motivated by the need to satisfy multiple constituencies' perspectives, not just those of the regulator. While formative choices in the substance and form of regulation can encourage, discourage, and shape the participation and even existence of various constituencies, other factors can temper, intensify, or counteract regulatory prerogatives.

AMBIGUITY WITH ACCOUNTABILITY

Privacy leads in both jurisdictions described how ambiguity in regulatory requirements fostered evolution and dynamism in the face of technological and normative developments. It led firms to adopt a broader stance on privacy obligations, going beyond FIPs to rely on and resource a privacy professional to better interpret and act on their obligations. Such "productive ambiguity," they reported, resulted from a range of elements including: broad legal mandates; "activist" regulators; and, stakeholder scrutiny.

In his 1994 work, Smith attributed the corporate neglect of privacy he identified to "ambiguity" regarding the legal meaning of privacy and the requirements governing its protection.[2] Ironically, the histories of the United States and Germany suggest that changes in the field have arisen because of, rather than in spite of, regulatory ambiguity.[3] Incomplete privacy mandates permitted flexibility in the face of uncertainty, and discretion in implementation, permitting heterogeneous methods of compliance in individual firm contexts.[4] At the same time, the enforcement behavior of "activist" regulators, and regulatory modes that enhanced scrutiny of corporate behaviors by other stakeholders in the privacy field, demanded accountability. Together, these elements empowered privacy officers and enlisted the interpretive judgment of firm decision makers, drawing on their superior knowledge about the ways risks manifest themselves in individual firm behaviors and business lines, and about available risk-management capacities and processes.[5]

Broad Legal Mandates and Open Regulatory Approaches   German and U.S. respondents identified the lack of specificity of the governing legal mandates as the most basic level of regulatory choice that drove the high level framing of privacy within the firm from a narrow legal issue to a broader socio-legal concept. A degree of regulatory ambiguity enhanced the CPO's power within the firm to advance a beyond-compliance definition. While German law is more comprehensive and more detailed[6] than the broad "unfair or deceptive practices" mandate that the FTC has used to police privacy in the United States,[7] it nonetheless requires interpretation and adaptation to address issues on the ground. Like the approach to privacy adopted by the FTC,[8] agencies throughout Germany play a significant consultative and advisory role with respect to private sector practices.[9] With a few exceptions, they do not have the authority to issue binding regulations.[10]

This similarity between the two systems is often eclipsed by the loose application of the English term "regulator" to describe German data protection authorities. The DPAs, at least in the first instance, consult with data protection officers within firms to assist them in formulating responses to legal requirements. But they largely engage in "oversight and giving advice." As in the United States, the responsibility for advising the firm leaders of their legal duties falls squarely on the shoulders of the corporate privacy officer as the lead interpreter—an exceedingly important shared property of the actual regulatory landscape.

Contrasting Germany's decision to avoid a "top-heavy licensing and registration system"[11] with France's formal and hierarchical approach underscores the effect of "productive ambiguity" in legal mandates. The French privacy professionals interviewed painted a picture of a national privacy regulator with an enormous regulatory infrastructure, used in part to administer refined registration requirements.[12] In Spain, too, corporations were faced with a detailed set of registration and data-use requirements. In both cases, the task of interpreting and fixing the meaning of regulatory mandates—and the relevant expertise necessary for that process—remained largely in government hands.

A comment by a French DPO highlighted this shared aspect of the German and U.S. systems, and the contrast with France and Spain. The DPO remarked that German DPOs consistently expressed confidence that they can and do comply with privacy mandates, while Spanish and French DPOs often indicated that full compliance was sometimes impossible, no matter how hard their efforts. He suggested that they have traditionally not been "speaking of the same thing" when they use the word "compliance." "[I]t depends on whether you view compliance as a process or as the outcomes," he said. The Germans, he felt, had made a "big move towards . . . the U.S. approach which is really becoming a compliance program like an ethics and compliance program," while the other jurisdictions relied more on formalities as evidence of compliance.

In both the United States and Germany, moreover, the onus for interpreting the more ambiguous regulatory environment fell on privacy professionals. German law, from the outset, envisioned this role, as reflected both in the requirement that firms appoint an independent DPO, and in the practice of negotiating industry codes with regulators to set sector-based standards for behavior.

In the United States, the path to vesting internal subject-matter experts with lead interpretive authority was more circuitous, and less intentional. Powerful CPOs emerged because of a mix of politics—specifically the negotiation of the Safe Harbor agreement—regulatory guidance, and enforcement actions. Best practices and settlement agreements with regulators that include requirements for dedicated management of privacy, while not binding on other companies, are viewed as persuasive by firms seeking to manage their own risk. Thus the United States' more ambiguous privacy field created a need for professionals who could sort out the external signals important to corporate legitimacy.

The firm's responsibility for clarifying its obligations in an ambiguous field was essential to the professional power of the CPO/DPO and to the ongoing resiliency and generativity of privacy. German and U.S. privacy leads found it both necessary and profitable to develop expertise in operationalizing privacy within their own firms. To do so, they engaged peers in dialogue about emerging threats, cultivated the collaborative development of best practices, and evangelized for them.

Activist Regulators In both countries, privacy professionals occupied a robust interpretive role only in the context of activist (and multiple) privacy regulators who demanded forward-looking, dynamic interpretation of privacy mandates, and who were vested with authority to enforce those demands.

Indeed, as discussed in chapter 11, prior to the strengthening of the DPAs' jurisdiction, enforcement authority, and ability to enforce security breach notification failures effected by the 2001 and 2009 amendments to the German Federal Law, mandatory DPOs were far less powerful. In the United States, the FTC's growing exercise of its "roving" authority to police unfair and deceptive practices in the online privacy and security domain—a rise in part due to the legitimacy conferred by their role in the Safe Harbor Agreement—was decisive in moving firms to spend resources "looking around corners" to identify future trouble areas and stay ahead of enforcers. Complying with external law became insufficient to protect privacy and manage risk. This in turn pushed CPOs to become more responsible for identifying what firms must do and may *not* do in the name of information privacy and security.

This history suggests that simply requiring, as a matter of law, that corporations internalize responsibility for sorting out privacy's meaning and implementation may neither be a necessary nor a sufficient condition to produce the meaningful integration of privacy into firm structures. Without activist use of enforcement power by regulators, and (as will be discussed further) approaches that enlist normative pressure by other participants in the privacy field, those requirements may lack the power to push privacy meaningfully into firm practices. The "productive" ambiguity that was typical of both fields, and identified as empowering the CPO/DPO, reflects particular levels of regulatory oversight, and modes of regulatory behavior.

Stakeholder Scrutiny In part because of the legal and regulatory enlistment of outside parties in negotiating privacy's meaning, German and U.S. privacy landscapes both featured ongoing scrutiny of firm choices and practices by third-party stakeholders.

Regulatory choices created the venues and opportunities for this scrutiny. In the United States, interviewees described interactions among regulators, advocates, and academics as routine, and fostered by a suite of ongoing venues provided by regulators, academic institutions, think tanks, and technical standards bodies. In particular, they identified the importance of privacy, civil liberties, and consumer protection advocacy groups that grew in response to the FTC-initiated forums. The FTC forums placed firm practices under the bright light, and invited advocates, academics, and at times other regulators to critique them. The workshops, sweeps, and other fact-gathering exercises destabilized the privacy environment and, importantly, limited the ability of firms to unilaterally construct interpretations of the law. This in turn limited the ability of firms to rely solely on lawyers and compliance to manage privacy risks. Through these fora advocates have arguably exerted more consistent influence on the corporate privacy agenda than they have through courts or legislatures.

The U.S. CPOs largely attributed their prominence and power within the firm to perceptions of the importance of their role in negotiating, interpreting, and integrating the continually moving target of privacy into firm practices. The understanding of privacy that required such activities did not reflect the rules promulgated through various sectoral laws. It grew from consumer expectations and was continually debated and revised at FTC events, as stakeholders picked apart industry practices, examined new business models, and laid bare the growing sea of data in the private sector. Getting this complicated notion of privacy "right" was viewed as essential to cementing the firm's "license to operate." Debates related to the social license place ethics and social obligations—as defined by noncorporate actors—within the scope of firm consideration. Specifically, these CPOs were empowered to ask a wide range of questions about firm activities rather than simply defend such activities as legally permissible.[13] This facet of the CPO's job, they explained, "is of great significance because of the connection between the legitimacy of firm behavior" and a proper understanding of evolving privacy norms. Unlike prescriptive rules, norms are dynamic, are at times contradictory, can diverge both up and down from the law on the books, and vary contextually.

In Germany, corporate interactions with outside stakeholders were less frequent, and less free-wheeling. But our interviewees all stressed the importance of the independent works councils that, along with the embedded data protection officers, brought public concerns over privacy and contests over its requirements into the corporate structure. To a lesser extent, they described the role of industry groups and other nonprivacy institutions like courts, political parties, and even the church, in contributing to public privacy debates. By these means, firms' interpretations of what the law required were constantly scrutinized by representatives of labor and privacy interests. While the two most powerful of these representatives are inside the firm, the statutory requirements and protections for the DPOs and works councils require and empower them to speak forcefully for interests in tension with management. Thus, while they are *in* the firm, they are not fully *of* the firm, but rather channel key values of the outside environment.

In both national contexts, these empowered stakeholders were critical participants in establishing the contours of firms' privacy obligations. In this role, our interviewees suggest they moved corporate behavior away from compliance toward broader objectives of socially and sometimes morally appropriate behavior. In contrast, in the three other countries studied, the regulatory agenda was largely controlled by the relevant data protection authority exclusively. The small professional community was constrained to corporate privacy professionals, and it was generally focused on interfacing with, interpreting, and forecasting the regulators.

The substantive frameworks brought in by other stakeholders attach privacy to other powerful normative and political interests. In the United States, privacy benefits from its relationship to overall issues of marketplace fairness and consumer trust advanced by consumer protection agencies as well as civil society. In Germany, the works councils have brought additional ethical frameworks centered on ethical behavior toward individuals, employees, and citizens, to the table. These sites of contest enable diverse constituencies to attach privacy to their ethical frameworks, and to draw broader rings of society into conversations about privacy protection and corporate responsibility. By creating productive ambiguity about the appropriate application of regulatory requirements in particular contexts, the regulatory choices in Germany and the United States push firms to evolve and revise their understandings of privacy's meaning and expression in corporate practices in the face of technological and normative developments. Ensuring that this interpretation occurs under the steady gaze of other stakeholders who demand sound processes and substantive outcomes limits the ability of firms to reduce privacy protection to a mere process. The dynamic tension over privacy's meaning and firm responsibility toward it created by regular stakeholder scrutiny protects against firm practices that substitute compliance with process for substantive performance on key objectives.

BOUNDARY-SPANNING COMMUNITY

In both the United States and Germany, our respondents situated themselves in a national, and to some extent international community of privacy professionals. This community was broad and inclusive. It was cemented in various venues—such as conferences under the auspices of regulators, activists, and corporate professionals, and in shared reference points, such as the stories circulated among peers to solidify their resolve, scare straight recalcitrant boards, and build a common sense of purpose. And it included relatively powerful third-party stakeholders, from government, the advocacy community, and academia.

The community they spoke of had two interwoven strands. Each is important, in sum, they produce far more than the constituent parts.

First, the CPOs/DPOs spoke of a robust and active community of similarly situated corporate privacy professionals. Corporate privacy professionals collaborated to address new challenges, shared best practices, developed codes of conduct, and assisted each other in numerous other ways.

Second, the CPOs and DPOs were both part of larger communities of privacy professionals that extended beyond the corporate context. The privacy community they described is expansive, including advocates, regulators, academics, as well as privacy professionals in the public and private sector. In the United States, interactions among regulators, advocates, and academics were routine, and were fostered by a suite of ongoing venues provided by regulators, academic institutions, think tanks, and technical standards bodies. Privacy advocates played little role in our German respondents' accounts. At the same time, those accounts described a privacy community rich with academic and regulator participation, connected to civil society interests through labor involvement. In both jurisdictions, active privacy professional associations built community through the provision of intellectual, emotional, and practical support.

Participation in this broader privacy community brings corporate privacy professionals into contact with skeptics and critics about firm behavior, armed with distinct perspectives, commitments, and agendas, but with whom the CPOs/DPOs share some common fealty. Such interactions facilitate new ideas and approaches to problem solving.[14] While the other members of the community often represented interests at odds with the corporations, they were simultaneously supportive and enabling of the corporate privacy professionals. Together, they were embedded in a shared community, tethered to a common logic and shared purposes: privacy and its protection. Accordingly, this community created normative pressure for privacy-protective practices, through negotiation, dialogue, disagreement, as well as advice, encouragement, and constructive criticism.

This broader community, moreover, does not define privacy work as compliance with rules. The privacy that animates this community is the privacy that protects people, avoids creepiness, creates space for self-development and exploration, and limits the gaze of the state. It is an ambiguous and capacious brand of privacy, and it is tied not to legality but privacy's roles in society.

As discussed earlier, our interviews described how the type of "productive ambiguity" produced by creating sites for contest over privacy's meaning and firms' responsibility has been critical to shaping corporate practices in the United States and Germany. But they also suggest that such battles are most fruitful for privacy when they are positioned within a privacy field with a strong, and broad-based privacy community. These sites of contest are a product of legislative choices and regulatory practices, and in both countries create dynamic, nonstate-centered conversations about privacy and corporate practice. The formation of community, however, is less clearly a matter of legislative prerogative. While regulatory choices can create fora for multistakeholder engagement and debate, and can even require joint activities—such as the FTC's advisory committees, and the works councils and DPOs within German firms—it takes more to build community.

DISCIPLINARY TRANSPARENCY

Requiring firms to determine their responsibilities in dialogue with other informed stakeholders provides an infrastructure and orientation for the creation and adoption of robust privacy practices. In the United States and Germany, expanding the cast of stakeholders aware of privacy failures, and therefore able to discipline corporations for missteps, was instrumental in enhancing the influence of CPOs and DPOs, and their ability to marshal resources necessary to support the full adoption of those practices throughout the business.

Greater transparency around privacy failures has enabled nonregulators—and nonexperts—to become credible enforcers. Both our U.S. and German respondents made clear that the regulatory shifts that place privacy in the public eye include not just high-profile enforcement actions, but also the adoption of security breach notification laws. Breach notification laws have empowered a more diverse group of privacy enforcers, and a richer set of penalties. In Germany reported breaches and their backstories travel quickly through works councils inside firms and political venues outside them. In the United States, breach reporting laws have focused boards, shareholders, insurers, business partners, and consumers on privacy. Enforcement has taken direct forms, such as class action lawsuits and shareholder initiatives in the United States, or recent political initiatives in Germany to establish a consumer group cause of action. It has also taken less direct, but nonetheless effective forms, such as a weaker bargaining position in subsequent contract negotiations, customer churn, and reduced brand trust with employees and the public.

Publicity around privacy failures was key to this shift in both the United States and Germany. The public attention connected privacy protection and brand image, resulting in greater deference, authority, and power for privacy professionals within the firm.

Empowering other stakeholders—not just the elite group of privacy professionals—to use their powers of "voice" (ranging from complaints to shareholder actions to labor negotiations to law suits) and "exit"[15] (terminating consumer and business relationships) to discipline corporations for privacy failures contributed to the CPOs' relative power. The addition of these various forms of discipline helped shift corporate perspectives away from privacy as legal compliance, or responsiveness to a small cadre of experts, and toward privacy as a salient and pressing issue of social license.

In an environment where privacy enforcement is shared by multiple parties, and penalties take multiple forms—some of which cannot be decisively settled by lawyers and money, but must be addressed over time by rebuilding trust—corporations responded by interacting more regularly with other stakeholders. They devoted greater attention to maintaining their social license, not just legality. They invested in people and processes to bolster legitimacy, even in the case of a breach.

A jurisdictional comparison helps distinguish forms of transparency that engage this broader community, and promote robust internal privacy practices from those that do not. In a formal sense, much of European privacy regulation has been focused on a *kind* of transparency for decades: database registrations are an entrenched part of the European privacy landscape. Yet while such requirements create a public record about privacy, there is little evidence that they have succeeded in engaging the public. These routine filings are poorly designed to garner public attention or fuel public discourse, and reflect instead what one European scholar characterized as the "bureaucratization of data protection."[16]

Indeed, as late as 1999, even Germany suffered from a process of bureaucratized transparency. Its data protection agencies shifted "uneasily between the image of data protection bureaucratization and an ombudsman role."[17] Events of recent years have shifted the German regulatory field, infusing long-existing regulatory requirements with new meaning. In the United States, this same sort of attention has arisen in a shorter time frame and without similar formal regulatory pressure. Our respondents repeatedly attributed these shifting privacy approaches to more meaningful and attention-focusing forms of informational transparency about privacy threats and risks. Distinct from its bureaucratic relation, this form of transparency encompasses the "external shocks" that organizational theorists describe as particularly useful in focusing attention within firms, and enhancing their institutional capacity to respond to changing situations and risks.[18]

More effective information disclosure regulations share similar properties. They are triggered by instances of corporate failure and require corporations to admit them as such, rather than routinely reporting such activities as part of normal business operations. They also require disclosures to customers, not just regulators. Regulatory tools that enable multiple parties to sanction firms for privacy breaches appear to drive privacy away from legal compliance and toward risk management.

In the United States, CPOs emphasized the importance of the FTC's public statements and enforcement activities in adapting its privacy standards to new contexts, and for creating legal and social pressure on firms to adopt a more forward-looking, dynamic orientation toward privacy protection. The FTC's emphasis on making privacy management practices and failures transparent also yielded metrics for assessing corporate activity over time[19] and benchmarks for improvement.[20] These measures facilitate external accountability and spur changes in organizational management.

Our respondents described how the disciplining force of transparency has contributed to the reconceptualization of privacy as a risk management activity by transforming previously unnoticeable corporate lapses into press events. This, in turn, encouraged multiple actors to police and enforce privacy. The ensuing cycle of highly reported breaches, investigations, and settlements establishing mandatory practices for breaching entities—combined with FTC and high-profile German enforcement actions—made information about privacy risks and best practices publicly available. In both instances, this availability empowered third-party stakeholders and facilitated the shift from compliance to risk management.

Even in France, a number of our respondents described several recent CNIL inspections and enforcement actions, and the negative publicity that resulted, as critical contributions to their decisions to explore more robust ways to consider privacy and implement protections, and to begin the process of designating a chief privacy officer. Spanish respondents also described security breach notification requirements as significant.

In different jurisdictions, news of breaches empowered distinct constituencies: in Spain, by sectoral consumer organizations; in Germany, by labor and data protection officers; and in the United States, by privacy and consumer advocates. But groups in each nation used the information in decidedly different ways, reflecting the different governance roles that these different national actors inhabit.

In Spain, unions and sector-oriented consumer organizations opportunistically used DPA inquiries and fines, as well as data breach incidents, as a way to raise broader grievances, particularly against high-visibility Spanish firms. Companies viewed these actions as manipulative and illegitimate, and even inevitable, and unrelated to the substance of privacy protection per se. Consumer associations did not pressure regulators or companies to reform corporate practices, but rather to extract fines. This cycle of consumer actions and corporate reactions seemed unlikely to deepen institutional commitment to privacy. The Spanish experience suggests that transparency as a regulatory practice may be insufficient on its own to facilitate positive privacy practices. The productive transparency that we observed within given jurisdictions needs to be coupled with other important properties of the privacy regime.

THE THREE PROPERTIES IN ACTION: CPOS BRING THE OUTSIDE IN

The three regulatory properties discussed earlier result in an overarching shift in orientation to privacy defined as legality to privacy defined as a social obligation. Key to that shift, and a metric for it, is the presence of a relatively powerful, to some extent independent, privacy professional tethered to a professional community with a competing, privacy-centered metric of firm success.

Our initial inquiry focused on privacy and data protection leads as a window into corporate behavior, rather than as the prime subject of inquiry. Our goal was to understand privacy work through them, not to study them, per se. In hindsight, we realize that the rapid growth in the number of chief privacy officers, which first stirred us to ask questions, may well be the most significant indicator of strong corporate privacy institutionalization, and the most important artifact of regulatory choices.

We observed corporate privacy professionals realigning staff, instituting new systems, and appropriating and adapting existing systems and processes to advance privacy objectives. We noted the capacity and creativity of these professionals as they seize opportunities both episodic, such as those created by publicity of a peer institution's breach or their own company's missteps, and structural, such as the capacity to "slipstream" privacy into corporate systems and processes built out on other corporate actors' dimes. They have placed old actors in new roles through specialized training and indirect reporting structures that help embed privacy into business units. In some instances they have created spaces for new actors with new voices, including external advisory boards that vet privacy-related decisions, and privacy consultants and auditors. They have created and diffused new tools and practices such as privacy impact assessments that reflect the perspectives of regulators, academics, and advocates. (This signals a shared value framework—a professional logic[21]—across a variety of vantage points and institutional contexts for privacy work.) They have also forged new relationships within firms. Through their work they are "creating, testing, conveying, and applying cultural-cognitive, normative, and/or regulative frameworks"[22] that advance privacy against, between, and intertwined with the larger corporate-profit agenda.

We also noted widespread reliance on other knowledgeable professionals as sources of best practices, sounding boards, and even moral suasion with firm executives. Chief among the diffusion networks cited by our interviewees in every jurisdiction are associations of privacy professionals, including both the IAPP and local privacy professional groups that have developed in strong form over the last two or three years in France, Spain, and Germany. Professional associations, professional titles, and the growth in educational, training, and certificate programs provide evidence of the professionalization of the privacy field.[23] In every jurisdiction, our respondents credited these organizations and the educational fora, conferences, and other shared-learning events they coordinate as critical sources for promulgating international corporate best practices.

Our interviewees' descriptions of the role that professional groups play in fast-tracking best practices (often modeled after the privacy apparatuses in U.S. firms) suggest that they are an essential source of tools and techniques, such as privacy seals and privacy impact assessments. While others have credited regulators and their networks for the spread of self-regulatory practices,[24] our research instead suggests that their focus on regulators and regulatory networks[25] has misled them as to the source of diffusion and change in Europe and elsewhere. Privacy professionals appear to be forcefully diffusing new practices and processes across industries and national borders.

In particular, the privacy professionals in the United States and Germany reported attributes associated with professionalism, including high degrees of autonomy, tacit knowledge and detailed expertise, a professionally defined value system that defines privacy work and goals, and identification with the class and role of privacy professional.[26] Despite the lack of explicit delegation or reference to professional associations, both Germany and the United States have home-grown privacy associations. Further, recent years have seen a growing trend toward an international rather than national professional community, which aligns with the international community of privacy regulators.[27]

New regulations, or new patterns of professional or organizational behavior could alter the environment in ways that shift the relative autonomy and normative force these embedded professionals currently wield. The German story, while ultimately positive, should give us pause, as it highlights the incomplete ability of legal mandates to catalyze this sort of professional activity. Animating the professionals' power required shocks to the corporate system at the level of the board of directors—visible privacy failures that connected with the substantive mission of the works councils and relevant external communities. The comparison between the United States and Germany reveals that less directive and less state-centered forces can produce similarly oriented, and powerful, professionals. The external sources that support the autonomy and power of U.S. privacy professionals are a diverse and fluid group of experts, advocates, academics, and media outlets, with representatives from privacy's professional and advocacy communities. This support is buoyed by the activities of multiple regulators, policy organizations, and in some instances advisory groups handcrafted by corporate privacy professionals to support their work. Despite the less decisive regulatory backstop, and varied corporate activities, these multiple forces act to tether the professionals to concepts, frameworks, and goals distinctly oriented toward privacy protection.

Successful privacy work is a complicated dance. It calls for a balance of insider and outsider perspectives and powers, and a mix of strategic and routine interactions. Influencing policy requires access to high-level policy setting venues typically associated with the upper levels of firm decision making. In these settings privacy professionals must forcefully represent their alternative logic, aiming to tailor or shift firm priorities. Yet doing so can drive home the perception that privacy is a policy decision in conflict with other firm priorities, and this can complicate the day-to-day practice of embedding privacy into firm activities. This day-to-day practice demands that privacy professionals be viewed as one of the team, and on the same page. It requires privacy to be "de-politicized."

Despite these real tensions, we found privacy professionals situated in a manner that enabled them to influence policy and infiltrate operations. These professionals appear ready to assert an alternative framework, setting the content and quality of privacy based on a broad dialogue with peers in the larger corporate enterprise. This is a hopeful development for privacy's protection.

How do the regulatory properties described in the preceding sections help empower privacy field actors to fulfill their roles? Collectively, when these regulatory practices provide opportunities for multistakeholder contests over privacy's meaning and requirements, corporations are driven to perceive privacy as endogenous to the firm. They generate higher-level attention to privacy concerns and require firms, and ultimately the privacy professionals within them, to interpret the demands of the regulatory landscape. This occurs both prior to regulatory direction, through participation in discussions about the business and technical environment, and after rules are proffered, as a result of the more flexible regulatory directives such interactions yield. Finally, disciplinary transparency engages the public and the corporate board by linking the privacy brand with the bottom line. Transparency regulations connect constituencies to the privacy dialogue, which in turn enhances the authority and autonomy of internal privacy professionals, and provides them with greater resources and reach throughout the firm.

CONCLUSION

Taken as a whole, our research highlights salient ways that elements have cohered in both the United States and German privacy fields to "bring the outside in" and spur new forms of privacy's operationalization within corporations. Specifically, it points to regulatory choices that deploy broad legal mandates, and incorporate multistakeholder learning, dialogue, coordination, and process, as well as accountability. These approaches channel the public voice in shaping the law. They promote the "compliance-plus" mindset we found among the interviewed privacy leaders and bolster their resources and power.

The factors that have promoted a more robust sense of professionalism in the United States and Germany were only partly intentional. Important factors, such as the rising connection between brand and privacy and the interpretive role, were produced by legislative and regulatory choices not intentionally aimed at the project of professionalization. Legislators in Germany intended to embed a piece of the regulatory state within firms—with all the normative force and internal tension such a choice reflects—to build a privacy "conscience" into corporate practice. The precipitating factors in the United States show much less intent, yet fueled quicker and *more professional* professionalization than took place in Germany. While German DPOs are a particular class of employees of the firm, with knowledge and expertise requirements, they lack the level of community, cohesion, and external orientation to the profession found among U.S. CPOs. Ambiguity prevalent across the U.S. privacy landscape—at the level of meaning, structures, and processes—can perhaps be credited with the relatively short time span in which privacy professional associations, training programs, conferences, and the wealth of information and practice sharing emerged.

As society becomes more pervasively networked, and privacy protection requires more dynamism, institutional reform efforts should be attentive to preserving the benefits flowing from this embedded class of professionals, and seek to empower them—and the outside forces that keep them on their toes—rather than displace them.

13 Moving Forward

Barely a week goes by without a new privacy revelation or scandal, some of which have shaken entire industries, corroded relations between sovereign nations, and bred distrust between democratic governments and their citizens. During the past year and a half, even as we were researching and writing this book, several high-profile crises made headlines.

One of them convulsed privacy debates. In mid-2013, Edward Snowden released thousands of pages of U.S. National Security Agency documents containing revelations of extensive data collection from telecom and Internet companies.[1] The documents also revealed how the agency, where Snowden worked as a contract employee, used this data to spy on individuals, including foreign leaders. Pundits argued whether Snowden was a hero or a traitor, but everyone agreed that the debate about privacy had taken a new turn. A year later, when Apple released a new iPhone operating system with enhanced privacy features, the *New York Times* declared a "post-Snowden era."[2] The phone encrypts the user's data in such a way that the company—and therefore government agencies—can't get access to it without the owner's help. Apple's design provoked howls of protest from the head of the FBI and other national security officials, who angrily accused the company of protecting criminals and terrorists.[3]

Another privacy earthquake hit the headlines in November 2014. A group of hackers calling themselves the Guardians of Peace had stolen confidential data on thousands of Sony employees, including an estimated 47,000 unique Social Security numbers.[4] (This was arguably minor, given that hackers recently compromised eighty *million* records at Anthem, the health care giant.)[5] The hackers also revealed highly embarrassing correspondence from the company's executives, including a racial reference to

Barack Obama,[6] and even threatened violence if Sony released *The Interview*, a film comedy that depicted the assassination of North Korean leader Kim Jong-un. The FBI and President Obama publicly accused North Korea of the attack and vowed to "respond proportionally."[7] This mixture of a muscular confrontation with a dictator, Hollywood gossip, and free speech issues seized national attention for weeks.

Given the regularity of these high-profile privacy events, it is unsurprising that people express heightened sensitivity and concern about how their personal information is used. A recent Pew survey[8] reported that over nine in ten Americans feel they've lost control over how their personal information is collected and used on the Internet. Eight in ten believe Americans should be concerned about government monitoring of phone calls and Internet communications. At the same time, nearly two-thirds believe the government should do more to regulate advertisers, who they fear are accessing their personal information on social media and other websites. These statistics are concerning to anyone who cares about the future of Internet commerce or democratic government.

At first glance, the survey data appears consistent with the story, calling for greater regulation, that still dominates most legal and scholarly discussion, policy debates in government, and media coverage. People feel they are losing control of their personal information and that it's freely traded on the Internet. As innovations in the realms of big data and the Internet of Things advance, this anxiety only grows. To regain a sense of control, many people naturally look to government for *more* regulation. But they are also leery of their governments, which have their own powerful reasons and mechanisms for collecting and using personal information, as Snowden revealed.

This is a compelling dilemma of our time, and our research points to a promising new direction for addressing it. Our goal is to help broaden privacy's field of vision. In place of oversimplified and increasingly airless discussions of more or less regulation on the books, we argue for carefully searching privacy on the ground for clues to building a more robust field— including but not limited to smarter regulation.

Our own on-the-ground searching began with an observation. We noted the rising number of chief privacy officers at U.S. corporations and wondered what this visible shift in the landscape signaled about corporate attention to privacy—and whether it mattered. We embarked on an initial inquiry to understand how U.S. companies that employed privacy leaders defined, structured, and implemented their privacy practices. Importantly, we also wanted to know what led these firms to hire chief privacy officers, and what factors shaped the overall work they led.

Our interviews with privacy leads yielded startling findings about the limitations of the laws' influence on corporate privacy practices, and the striking importance of nonlegal factors and actors. The research exposed a rift between the dominant story's emphasis on regulation on the books, and the reality of on-the-ground corporate behavior. Indeed, combining our work with a recent analysis of systematic government access to private sector data in thirteen countries[9] suggests that the chasm between privacy law on the books and on the ground is pervasive.

Driven by the findings in the United States, we expanded our research to privacy leads in four more countries, including two—France and Spain—whose strictly defined and enforced privacy regulations seemed most consonant with the dominant story's prescriptions. Again we found revealing results. First, respondents in France and Spain reported that the strict regulatory environments in fact tended to atrophy the internal corporate attention given, resources provided, and expertise gained on privacy issues. Within firms, the "compliance" mentality fostered by stricter regulations and regulatory authorities often relegated privacy concerns to the legal department. This legalistic approach retarded the development of privacy officers who were eager to interact with company leadership, business units, and external stakeholders.

The second finding was more striking. We discovered that the U.S. and German companies—despite widely divergent legal structures, regulatory authorities, and even cultural underpinnings for privacy protection—had remarkably similar and robust privacy practices. In both countries, significant improvements to corporate privacy management had advanced on the ground despite disparate regulatory authority on the books. In the other countries, although sharing a common regulatory framework with Germany, those improvements were nascent or not in evidence. What could account for these results?

To answer, we first worked to define the improvements, as described by our respondents. Analyzing the responses from privacy leads in the five countries, we were able to distill the common successes of the American and German firms into a set of corporate best practices. These practices, described in more detail in chapter 9, are as follows:

1. *Making the Board's Agenda*: a high level of attention, resources, access, and prominence for the privacy function within the firm;

2. *A Boundary-Spanning Privacy Professional*: a high-status privacy lead who mediates between external privacy demands and internal corporate privacy practices; and

3. *The "Managerialization" of Privacy*: the integration of decision making on privacy issues into technology design and business-line processes through the distribution of privacy expertise within business units and assignment of specialized privacy staff to data-intensive processes and systems.

Drilling down, we then identified common features of the U.S. and German privacy fields that pushed corporations toward these best practices. We looked for functional roles and interactions common and critical to both fields, even if performed by different actors. For example, the works councils, although inside German firms, bring in critical perspectives from the outside that may be in tension with standard corporate practices. In the United States that role is generally performed by actors outside the company, such as advocacy and professional groups. We then looked deeper, to consider how regulatory choices shaped these roles and interactions.

RECOMMENDATIONS FOR POLICYMAKERS

Deriving the best practices in the United States and Germany, and analyzing the functional roles that underlie them, in turn suggested ways in which regulatory policy could replicate, encourage, and expand those best practices on the ground. Defined as *properties* of the field rather than hard and fast rules, we distilled three that support the overall approach we've labeled "bringing the outside in."

1. *Ambiguity with Accountability*: broad legal mandates and open regulatory approaches, activist regulators, and meaningful stakeholder scrutiny fostered dynamism in the face of changes and pushed more accountability onto firms;

2. *A Boundary-Spanning Community*: U.S. and German corporate privacy leads situated themselves in a broad and inclusive community of outside

stakeholders, including other corporate privacy professionals as well as those from civil society and government, who both challenge the inside privacy officers and empower their role in the firm;

3. *Disciplinary Transparency*: greater transparency around privacy failures, including data breach laws, enabled nonregulators, such as civil society groups and media, as well as the broader public, to become credible enforcers in the court of public opinion, leading corporations to invest greater resources and authority in internal privacy professionals and processes.

Policy choices that cultivate these properties can leverage, and support, the internal capacity for positive corporate privacy management—the best practices identified in our interviews. Our surveys and analysis of privacy leaders convinced us that the right regulatory choices and institutional practices can push privacy further down the path—from being a regulatory issue of concern to a limited number of technocrats, to a broad-based social concern, a matter of "social license." The time is right. Privacy has begun to transition out of the courts, agencies, and legislatures, into products and services, and public consciousness. Guided by these three regulatory properties, which are described in greater detail in chapter 12, we can harness this moment for positive change.

ENCOURAGING AND EMPOWERING PROFESSIONAL COMMUNITIES

Corporations make a large share of the day-to-day decisions affecting privacy. They collect and process massive amounts of personal information. In the future, more and more information will be collected and processed, from devices embedded in everything from your refrigerator to the ocean floor, and used to make more and more personal and collective decisions, trivial and consequential. Corporations will be making technical and managerial decisions about how to protect that growing trove of data from misuse and theft. Corporate cultures, whether focused on protecting their customers and brands, or exploiting them for quick profit, significantly affect the trust people place in an individual firm, and more broadly in commerce. And they should, because corporate culture affects how businesses respond and embed external values such as privacy.

This information is, as the saying goes, power. It does and will affect critical decisions on what goods and services are available, and to whom, on access to educational and employment opportunities, and on the allocation of vital resources, from medical care to water. The corporations that possess this information, this power, must be subjected to rules that embody human rights and reflect social norms. They must be regulated. But how?

In the 1990s, Smith found corporate managers understandably avoiding responsibility for privacy because there was no metric for success and too much ambiguity in the law. Two decades later, we found privacy professionals empowered by firms desperate to sort out a complicated, chameleon-like set of soft and hard, legal and social constraints and expectations. Under the right conditions, we discovered, ambiguity can fuel a turn to professionals, and maintain space for those professionals to introduce new ways of thinking and acting into the firm.

Doing so requires regulatory structures and practices that demand, or at least enable, firms to engage in interpretive work. Further, regulatory processes that engage firms and other stakeholders in defining privacy norms and making the rules that promote those norms, are more likely to fuel corporate practices that go beyond compliance. The use of collaboration, education, and legal ambiguity makes firms more permeable to external demands and vulnerable to external pressure, particularly when combined with transparency requirements that serve to arouse public concern and discipline corporate behavior. Each of these elements in turn enhances the authority, available resources, and professional development of the "boundary spanning" corporate privacy officers. This mix holds promise for privacy.

The U.S. and German regulatory environments both provide for systematic corporate engagement along these lines. Ironically, perhaps, privacy reforms should aim to develop regulatory powers that support *internal* corporate professionals by empowering *outside* actors—bringing the outside in.

Regulators must possess and use tools that exploit market, corporate, and advocacy capacities to develop collective understandings of risks and solutions to future privacy problems. This collective understanding can reduce needless uncertainty and the associated cost of inconsistent application and redundant regulatory interactions. But narrowly pursuing *regulatory* coherence and uniformity can constrain firm and other stakeholder engagement with risks. More rule-bound governance acts to diminish corporate reliance on high-level internal privacy experts, and in turn reduces these professionals' capacity to embed privacy into corporate culture and business operations.

Transparency requirements are another key tool for regulators to "bring the outside in." Breach laws, high-profile regulatory actions and fines, and the publicity they unleash all bring privacy into the boardroom. Making more information available to outside actors (as breach laws do) increases the pressure on companies to develop the expertise and structures that support better privacy protection. In every country, our respondents reported that increased transparency about privacy failures was essential to promoting a corporate understanding of privacy as more than a regulatory requirement. Instead, making privacy failures public helps position privacy as a risk that must be managed to protect the firm's standing in the community, and it encourages developing corporate structures to engage outside actors. In this way, meaningful transparency—as opposed to simply bureaucratic disclosure—empowers multiple stakeholders to participate in constructing privacy's meaning and debating methods of operationalization and protection. Regulation that promotes meaningful transparency helps position privacy as part of the corporate social "license to operate."

CREATIVE REGULATION

The conventional answer to the growing challenges of privacy protection is to grow the number, specificity and uniformity of regulations, and the concomitant power of regulatory authorities to enforce them. As the amount and variety of data grows exponentially, the number of regulators, agencies, and coordinating bodies would grow in parallel. Regulatory expertise would become more specialized and audits more frequent. As corporate power expands, governments would expand their power to control them.

Unfortunately, as we learned from our respondents, the consequences of this approach are rarely the intended ones. The greater regulatory control is vested in centralized authorities, as in France and Spain, the more likely corporations are to adopt a compliance-only outlook, which is another way of saying they will narrowly seek to avoid fines and punishments rather than attend to overall regulatory aims. Rather than taking greater responsibility for privacy by increasing the attention, resources, and internal reforms to protect customers, corporate legal departments strive to avoid regulatory mishaps and dodge the attention of government. Privacy expertise is lodged outside the company, not in it. Further, this government-centered approach is unlikely to cultivate the corporate incentives or culture or know-how to check *government* privacy abuse.

Our research suggests instead that the countries that pushed more of the responsibility for meaningfully defining, interpreting, and enforcing privacy back toward corporations were rewarded with richer firm practices. Operationally, that's where the action lies—companies continually create new products and services, acquire new data sets, and face down security threats. In short, regulatory authorities that encourage corporate responsibility for privacy do better than those that simply punish bad behavior.

This does not mean just turning over the car keys to private corporations. Bad behavior is still punished—in fact, the punishments that come from market failure, brand tarnishing, and regulatory censure are often more severe. But the role of the regulator becomes far more creative when corporations are ceded greater responsibility for privacy protection. Regulators can use a suite of tools, not just a stick, to push firms to participate with other stakeholders in setting social norms. They can help incentivize corporations to develop strong, flexible structures and internal expertise for responding dynamically to new technologies and new threats. Regulators can facilitate and feed a virtuous circle of activity where more outside voices are heard inside the firm, which in turn strengthens a company's internal capacity to respond to events as it works to maintain its social license to operate.

Our research further suggests that the key role in turning this virtuous circle belongs to the chief privacy officer. Whether mandated, as in the German case, or not, as in the American one, the presence of a CPO emerged as a key indicator of a more robust privacy field, and internal corporate practice. The CPO's expertise and sensitivity to evolving privacy norms grow with greater interaction with corporate peers, including in professional associations, and to outside experts and advocates. These interactions also inform strategic decisions internally, such as designing proactive organizational structures for embedding privacy in firm operations. When crises erupt within a firm or an industry, the CPO has the authority, resources, and social network to protect the company's customers, shareholders, and reputation.

Though some tension between regulators and CPOs is inevitable (and arguably productive), the presence of high-functioning CPOs significantly magnifies the regulators' power to effect change within companies and to protect citizens from privacy abuses. We urge policymakers to evaluate new rules by whether they serve to encourage or discourage firms from investing resources in privacy, and in particular, high-level internal privacy professionals such as chief privacy officers.

We don't contend that these recommendations are the only means through which this amorphous and capacious concept—privacy—can be advanced inside firms. But we do believe that these suggestions, grounded in an all-too-rare examination of how law works on the ground in large corporations, merit consideration and debate.

More broadly, the goal of these recommendations is to encourage the growth of a healthy and vital privacy field in which shared social norms, not just laws on the books, define, interpret, and enforce privacy protection. When law and regulatory authorities overreach or attempt to shoulder the entire responsibility for change, the results are often disappointing or counter-productive. They play a salutary role when they encourage and support positive changes in corporate decision making and the society at large.

POSTSCRIPT: CHARTING THE RIGHT DIRECTION— OPPORTUNITIES AND RISKS FOR NEW REGULATORY POLICY

The current enactment-in-process of an EU-wide Data Protection Regulation presents a significant opportunity to push firms to collaborate with others to identify and solve privacy challenges, and to develop greater internal privacy expertise. Regulatory reform can drive corporations to distribute privacy expertise and accountability throughout the firm, adopt proactive privacy policies based on risk management, and develop outward-looking structures to sensitize the firm to privacy norms.

The draft regulation, indeed, reflects the view that internal expertise and processes that move privacy deeper into the corporate structure are necessary. This trend is evident in proposals requiring firms to conduct privacy impact assessments, engage in privacy by design, and identify and design contextually appropriate information flows. The proposals also envision a greater role for firms in proactive identification and response to privacy issues.

But the current legislative focus on harmonizing, regularizing, and fixing formal regulatory requirements might, at the same time, actually *undermine* the development of structures needed to promote real internal expertise. As the German experience suggests, simply requiring the appointment of data protection or privacy officers is insufficient to deliver a proactive privacy posture. Other aspects of the regulatory environment, and broader privacy field, are essential to trigger firm attention and investment in privacy.

Despite this risk, harmonizing disparate national legal regimes is the foremost goal of the European Union's Data Protection Regulation. The earlier Data Protection Directive required national implementations only. The proposed regulation automatically becomes national law in each member state. Depending upon the specificity with which it is written, this change could foreclose many variations and duplications associated with the current system. Indeed, some states are not happy about this loss of sovereignty to the European Commission.[10] Unfortunately, the desire to constrain country-by-country variation is a key goal, not a byproduct, of data protection reform.

The U.S. Department of Commerce (DOC) initiative to facilitate the creation and adoption of self-regulatory privacy guidelines within specific sectors[11] also seeks to provide greater specificity and clarity about privacy requirements. Here too, the desire is to create certainty regarding industry practice and legality. The initiative hopes to reduce firms' costs and the level of discretion left to potential enforcers on the back end. The guidelines aim to protect firms against accusations of illegality in the courts, through agency actions, and in the media. Although not designed to harmonize a set of fixed regulatory requirements, like the Data Protection Regulation, these self-regulatory guidelines would produce more uniform rules.

Both the U.S. and EU efforts sit uneasily with our findings about promoting responsive corporate practice. As we have shown, more open-textured privacy regimes require firms to engage in interpretative work, which encourages them to hire skilled privacy professionals and develop more robust structures for privacy protection. Less upfront certainty about requirements—productive ambiguity—enables greater flexibility on the ground and discourages a compliance mentality.

Based on our research, regulatory reforms to craft clearer regulatory guidelines[12] may take us down the wrong path. They may reduce costs for corporations, but the short-term benefits of clarity may come at substantial costs to society. Crisp, prescriptive legislative rules offer little room for interpretive work by firms or the broader group of privacy stakeholders. They may also destabilize existing and budding privacy fields by limiting necessary opportunities and sites to contest privacy. When regulation is perceived as being defined by regulators, as we found in Spain and France, corporate privacy protection reverts to a compliance activity. Strategic conversations about privacy recede within firms and in the public dialogue.

Fortunately, the proposed DOC process still demands corporate participation and expertise in rule making, while in the EU regulators would perform this function. The DOC process also seems specifically aimed at engaging multiple stakeholders in setting standards, while the proposed EU process appears regulator driven and state centered at all levels. It includes a set of proposals for sector-specific "codes of conduct"[13] that are "encouraged" to be drawn up through a sort of multi-stakeholder type of consultative process—but with final approval by the regulator. On the positive side, the EU proposal would abolish detailed reporting requirements for every data processing activity, replacing it with privacy impact assessments (PIAs),[14] which also appear to involve a consultative-type process.[15]

There are obvious correlations between regulatory structure and the number of government privacy professionals. Our research, however, suggests less-obvious relationships between regulatory form and the role of such experts within regulated parties in the private sector. Current reform proposals include explicit requirements for placing data protection expertise within firms, conducting privacy impact assessments, and executing privacy through design and defaults, risk management exercises, and codes of conduct. Success at these tasks is premised on the existence of greater internal corporate expertise than most firms we studied possessed. Even in the United States and Germany, where privacy professionals hold relatively high corporate status, manage relatively well-staffed privacy functions, and have relatively sophisticated models for determining and managing privacy obligations, current proposals appear to focus on increased levels of privacy staffing. But, more importantly situating and tethering these professionals to a vibrant privacy community, and supporting external pressure to support their work is vitally important. We urge policymakers to consider the risks and the new possibilities for privacy suggested by our research.

Notes

1 Paradoxes of Privacy on the Books and on the Ground

1. Yahoo! Inc.'s Provision of False Information to Congress, Hearing Before H. Comm. on Foreign Affairs.

2. The Internet in China: A Tool for Freedom or Suppression? Hearing Before H. Subcomm. on Africa, Global Human Rights, and International Operations, and H. Subcomm. Asia and the Pacific, H. Comm. on International Relations, 114 (testimony of Michael Callahan).

3. The Internet in China: A Tool for Freedom or Suppression? Hearing Before H. Subcomm. on Africa, Global Human Rights, and International Operations, and H. Subcomm. Asia and the Pacific, H. Comm. on International Relations.

4. MacKinnon, *Consent of the Networked*.

5. Samway, "Business and Human Rights."

6. "Diverse Coalition Launches New Effort to Respond to Government Censorship and Threats to Privacy."

7. Dredge, "Yahoo Joins Facebook, Google and Others in Revealing US Surveillance Requests"; "Reform Government Surveillance."

8. Schwartz, "First Line of Defense"; IBM, "News Release: IBM Names Harriet P. Pearson as Chief Privacy Officer."

9. Smith, *Managing Privacy*.

10. Ibid., 82.

11. Ibid., 139; see generally ibid., chap. 6 (describing "Ambiguity All Around").

12. Smith, *Managing Privacy*, 207 (emphasis omitted).

13. Ibid., 213; see also ibid., chap. 6 (describing "Ambiguity All Around").

14. Specifically, Smith recommended a Data Protection Board with advisory powers to field complaints and to assist corporations in developing codes of acceptable practice. These codes would be drafted pursuant to a codified set of principles developed through consultation with industry. See Smith, *Managing Privacy*, 217–224.

15. See ibid., 209–224.

16. See ibid., 210.

17. IAPP, "About [The International Association of Privacy Professionals]."

18. This was a study of privacy in several North American and European countries. Flaherty, *Protecting Privacy in Surveillance Societies*.

19. Rubinstein and Lee, *Systematic Government Access to Personal Data*, 2 ("even those nations with otherwise comprehensive data protection laws, access for regulatory, law enforcement, and national security purposes is often excluded from such laws . . . [or] treated as accepted purposes for which access is authorized under separate laws that may or may not provide adequate safeguards against possible abuses.").

20. Ibid. ("almost half the countries studied do not have provisions requiring court orders for surveillance undertaken in the name of national security or for foreign intelligence gathering.").

21. Kuner et al., "Systematic Government Access to Private-Sector Data Redux," 1.

22. Raab and Bennett, "Taking the Measure of Privacy," 553 (discussing the impracticability of measuring outputs or outcomes).

23. Ibid. ("the only reliable criteria are procedural").

24. See Nissenbaum, *Privacy in Context*, 148.

25. Ibid.

26. Lischka and Stöcker, "Data Protection."

2   Literature, Framework, and Methodology

1. The term "information self-determination" was set forth in a German court decision limiting the intrusiveness of the census. See "Bundesverfassungsgericht [BVerfG] [Federal Constitutional Court] Dec. 15, 1983, Entscheidungen Des Bundesverfassungsgerichts [BVerfGE] 65, 1984," 97.

2. Westin, *Privacy and Freedom*, 7.

3. *Records, Computers and the Rights of Citizens, Report of the Secretary's Advisory Committee on Automated Personal Data Systems*.

4. Convention for the Protection of Individuals with Regard to Automatic Processing of Personal Data.

5. OECD, *Guidelines Governing the Protection of Privacy and Transborder Flows of Personal Data*.

6. Directive 95/46/EC of the European Parliament and of the Council of 24 October 1995 on the Protection of Individuals with Regard to the Processing of Personal Data and on the Free Movement of Such Data.

7. Newman, *Protectors of Privacy*, 74–75 ("[T]he EU data privacy directive can be traced to its roots in the historical sequencing of national data privacy regulation and the role that the resulting independent regulatory authorities played in regional politics.").

8. Convention for the Protection of Human Rights and Fundamental Freedoms, 8 (affirming a right to general personal privacy); Cate, *Privacy in the Information Age*, 43–44 (discussing the impact of the experience with Nazi Germany on European privacy laws); Tene, "What Google Knows: Privacy and Internet Search Engines," 1460 ("The prohibition against secret databases is one of the doctrinal foundations of European privacy law, gleaned following decades of totalitarian regimes that used information in secret databases to police and terrorize citizens into conformity and submission.").

9. Convention for the Protection of Individuals with Regard to Automatic Processing of Personal Data.

10. OECD, *Guidelines Governing the Protection of Privacy and Transborder Flows of Personal Data*.

11. Ibid.; see also Bennett, *Regulating Privacy*, 101–111 (describing the OECD principles).

12. OECD, *Guidelines Governing the Protection of Privacy and Transborder Flows of Personal Data*.

13. Ibid.

14. Ibid., pt. P7.

15. Some FIPs proponents consider such access rights to be "the most important privacy protection safeguard." Bennett, *Regulating Privacy*, 103.

16. See chapter 3, this volume.

17. Nissenbaum, *Privacy in Context*.

18. Ibid., 147–150.

19. Gilliom, *Overseers of the Poor*.

20. Lyon, *Surveillance Society*.

21. Stalder, "Privacy Is Not the Antidote to Surveillance," 120–124; Lyon, *Surveillance Society*.

22. Gilliom, "A Response to Bennett's 'In Defence of Privacy.'"

23. Bennett and Raab, *The Governance of Privacy*, 9.

24. Gilliom, "A Response to Bennett's 'In Defence of Privacy.'"

25. Cate, "The Failure of Fair Information Practice Principles," 343.

26. Acquisti, "Privacy in Electronic Commerce and the Economics of Immediate Gratification."

27. Pavlou, Liang, and Xue, "Understanding and Mitigating Uncertainty in Online Environments."

28. Brandimarte, Acquisti, and Loewenstein, "Misplaced Confidences."

29. Privacy Rule Regulation; Harris, *Making Your Privacy Practices Public*; Article 29 Data Protection Working Party, *Opinion 02/2013 on Apps on Smart Devices*; Article 29 Data Protection Working Party, *Opinion 10/2004 on More Harmonised Information Provisions*.

30. Brandimarte, Acquisti, and Loewenstein, "Misplaced Confidences."

31. McDonald and Cranor, "The Cost of Reading Privacy Policies," 17, 19 (reporting ranges of the low-point and high-point estimates the study arrived at for skimming and reading policies). The study ultimately concludes that reading privacy policies costs approximately 201 hours a year at a value of $3,534 annually per American Internet user, or about $781 billion annually for the nation. See also Hoofnagle and King, "Research Report: What Californians Understand about Privacy Offline" (documenting that a majority of adults in California believe that the existence of a privacy policy translates into specific substantive limitations on a company's treatment of information).

32. Koops, "On Decision Transparency"; Crawford and Schultz, "Big Data and Due Process," 201.

33. Regan, *Legislating Privacy*, 241.

34. Ibid., 221.

35. Schwartz, "Privacy and Democracy in Cyberspace."

36. Bennett and Raab, *The Governance of Privacy*, 41–45.

37. Nissenbaum, *Privacy in Context*, 242.

38. Ibid.

39. Jernigan and Mistree, "Gaydar: Facebook Friendships Expose Sexual Orientation."

40. Schwartz, "Internet Privacy and the State."

41. Doe, "With Genetic Testing, I Gave My Parents the Gift of Divorce."

42. After this story 23andMe reversed plans to make participation in this feature a default—it had previously required an opt-in—and announced plans to hire a chief privacy officer. Valby, "23andMe Responds to Controversy over Relative-Finding Tool."

43. Laurie, "Challenging Medical-Legal Norms."

44. Petronio, *Boundaries of Privacy*, 3.

45. Nissenbaum, *Privacy in Context*, 148.

46. Nissenbaum, "Privacy as Contextual Integrity," 138.

47. Ibid. Privacy pluralists who argue against efforts to narrowly, reductively, or rigidly specify privacy instead conceive of privacy as "a set of protections against a plurality of distinct but related problems . . . related by a common denominator or core element . . . (and) share family resemblances with each other." This plurality provides a range of privacy concepts to respond to contextually specific risks. Solove, *Understanding Privacy* (discussing the "benefits of a pluralistic conception of privacy").

48. See generally, Suchman, "On Beyond Interest," 480–482 (describing the normative perspective on decision making, which emphasizes the selection of the applicable norm by first identifying the context as one in which the norm should prevail).

49. Post, "The Social Foundations of Privacy," 959.

50. Nissenbaum, *Privacy in Context*, 148.

51. Scholars have thus noted the need for approaches to privacy that "transcend that of individual benefit" yet do not deny the centrality of the individual in privacy's formulation. Bennett and Raab, *The Governance of Privacy*, 41–45. Another scholar has identified three reasons why "privacy as an individual right . . . provides a weak basis for formulating policy to protect privacy"; namely, "it emphasizes the negative value of privacy; it establishes a conflict between the individual and society; and it fails to take into account the importance of large social and economic organizations." Regan, *Legislating Privacy*, 212, 215. Regan also argues for a definition of privacy based on its benefit to "common, public, and collective purposes." Ibid., 221.

52. Nissenbaum, *Privacy in Context*, 148.

53. See, e.g., ibid., 148–150.

54. Bennett, *The Privacy Advocates*, 16.

55. DeShazo and Freeman, "Public Agencies as Lobbyists," 2219; Bamberger, "Regulation as Delegation."

56. See generally Simon, *Models of Man*, 198 ("The capacity of the human mind for formulating and solving complex problems is very small compared with the size of the problems whose solution is required for objectively rational behavior in the real world" [emphasis omitted].); Arrow, *The Limits of Organization*, 37 ("[T]he scarcity of information-handling ability is an essential feature for the understanding of both individual and organizational behavior.").

57. See Malloy, "Regulation, Compliance and the Firm," 451, 489–490.

58. Walsh, "Managerial and Organizational Cognition," 281; see also Cohen and Bacdayan, "Organizational Routines Are Stored as Procedural Memory," 555. See generally Becker, "Organizational Routines."

59. March, Schultz, and Xueguang, *The Dynamics of Rules*, 186.

60. Weick, "Collective Mind in Organizations."

61. DiMaggio and Powell, "The Iron Cage Revisited," 150.

62. Ibid., 152.

63. Scott and Meyer, "The Organization of Societal Sectors," 140.

64. Pfeffer, *The External Control of Organizations*, 51–52.

65. Vaughan, "The Dark Side of Organizations," 274 ("[T]he same characteristics of a system that produce the bright side will regularly provoke the dark side from time to time.").

66. Feldman and Levy, "Effects of Legal Context on Decision Making Under Ambiguity," 113.

67. Heimer, "Explaining Variation in the Impact of Law," 41.

68. DiMaggio and Powell, "The Iron Cage Revisited," 150–151.

69. Meyer and Rowan, "Institutionalized Organizations," 340–341.

70. Edelman, Erlanger, and Lande, "Internal Dispute Resolution," 529; see also Edelman, Uggen, and Erlanger, "The Endogeneity of Legal Regulation."

71. Heimer, "Explaining Variation in the Impact of Law," 41.

72. See Cunningham, "The Appeal and Limits of Internal Controls to Fight Fraud, Terrorism, Other Ills," 269–270; See generally Power, *The Audit Society*.

73. See below, this chapter.

74. Greening and Gray, "Testing a Model of Organizational Response to Social and Political Issues"; Stevens, Beyer, and Trice, "Managerial Receptivity and Implementation of Policies"; Murray, "The Social Response Process in Commercial Banks."

75. Gunningham, Kagan, and Thornton, "Social License and Environmental Protection," 325.

76. Murray, "The Social Response Process in Commercial Banks," 7.

77. Kagan, Thornton, and Gunningham, "Explaining Corporate Environmental Performance"; Fox-Wolfgramm, Boal, and Hunt, "Organizational Adaptation to Institutional Change."

78. O'Dell and Grayson, "If Only We Knew What We Know"; Gioia and Thomas, "Identity, Image, and Issue Interpretation."

79. Gunningham, Kagan, and Thornton, "Social License and Environmental Protection," 325.

80. Luhmann, "The Unity of the Legal System," 27 (observing that the legal systems must take into account the "normative expectations" of systems outside the law); see also Cerny, "Embedding Global Financial Markets," 67–68.

81. Sitkin and Bies, "The Legalistic Organization."

82. Gunningham and Sinclair, "New Generation Environmental Policy."

83. Lawrence and Lorsch, *Organization and Environment.*

84. Lipshitz et al., "Taking Stock of Naturalistic Decision Making"; Eraut, "Non-Formal Learning and Tacit Knowledge in Professional Work"; Klein, "A Recognition-Primed Decision (PRD) Model of Rapid Decision Making."

85. Argyris, "Good Communication That Blocks Learning," 77–78 (discussing the importance of individual accountability, and communication structures that surface, rather than mask, "the kinds of deep and potentially threatening or embarrassing information" that leads to change, in organizational learning).

86. McAllister, Mitchell, and Beach, "The Contingency Model for the Selection of Decision Strategies"; Tetlock, "Accountability," 316.

87. See Schwartz and Wallin, "Behavioral Implications of Information Systems on Disclosure Fraud" (comparing the decisions to issue fraudulent disclosures, and to allow an information system to issue fraudulent reports at a given rate, and concluding that "making subjects more closely involved with the disclosure reduced the rate of fraudulent disclosures by 30 percent").

88. Tetlock, "Accountability," 314–321 (reviewing research evidence).

89. Bamberger, "Regulation as Delegation," 444.

90. See generally Granovetter, "The Strength of Weak Ties" (hypothesizing, in the context of social networks, that those with "weak ties" in the network provide a bridge between groups with "strong ties"); Granovetter, "The Strength of Weak Ties:

A Network Theory Revisited" (reviewing the empirical studies testing the "weak ties" hypothesis); Scott, *Organizations: Rational, Natural, and Open Systems*, 203–213 (discussing "Bridging Tactics," in the context of "Boundary Setting and Boundary Spanning").

91. Gold, Malhotra, and Segars, "Knowledge Management" (discussing the use of collaboration and benchmarking to assesses the current state of organizational processes and to capture knowledge for use internally).

92. See Menon and Pfeffer, "Valuing Internal vs. External Knowledge," 505 (finding that managers prefer knowledge obtained from outsiders).

93. Bamberger and Mulligan, "PIA Requirements and Privacy Decision-Making in U.S. Government Agencies," 245–247 (discussing how PIA-like environmental impact assessments appear to be more effective when they are required prior to program decisions and are aided by embedded substantive experts).

94. Waters, "Privacy Impact Assessment," 150–151.

95. Ibid., 151.

96. Information and Privacy Commissioner et al., *Privacy by Design*; 32nd International Conference of Data Protection and Privacy Commissioners, "Resolution on Privacy by Design"; Federal Trade Commission, *Protecting Consumer Privacy in an Era of Rapid Change*; Hustinx, "Privacy by Design"; Rubinstein, "Regulating Privacy by Design."

97. Waters, "Privacy Impact Assessment," 150–151.

98. Culnan and Williams, "How Ethics Can Enhance Organizational Privacy."

99. Power, "CyLab Survey Reveals Gap in Board Governance of Cyber Security."

100. Culnan and Williams, "How Ethics Can Enhance Organizational Privacy."

101. Bamberger and Mulligan, "PIA Requirements and Privacy Decision-Making in U.S. Government Agencies."

102. Waters, "Privacy Impact Assessment," 150–151; see also Edwards, "Privacy Impact Assessment in New Zealand," 194–195 ("Once an information system to support the proposal is being designed, or business processes developed, a great many decisions, with varying degrees of impact on privacy, will need to be made.").

103. Waters, "Privacy Impact Assessment," 150–151; see also Edwards, "Privacy Impact Assessment in New Zealand," 194–195 ("Once an information system to support the proposal is being designed, or business processes developed, a great many decisions, with varying degrees of impact on privacy, will need to be made.").

104. Lessig, *Code: Version 2.0*, 5; Bamberger, "Technologies of Compliance."

105. Warren et al., "Privacy Impact Assessments"; Parks et al., "Understanding the Drivers and Outcomes of Healthcare Organizational Privacy Responses"; Bamberger and Mulligan, "PIA Requirements and Privacy Decision-Making in U.S. Government Agencies."

106. See Stewart, "Privacy Impact Assessment Towards a Better Informed Process for Evaluating Privacy Issues Arising from New Technologies" ("PIA needs to be integrated into decision-making processes. For a government proposal, PIA might be integrated into departmental decision-making and appropriate cabinet processes. . . . The important thing is that PIA not be divorced from decision-making processes.").

107. Flaherty, "Privacy Impact Assessments: An Essential Tool for Data Protection."

108. Warren et al., "Privacy Impact Assessments."

109. Wright et al., "Integrating Privacy Impact Assessment in Risk Management." See, for example, the following FTC settlements: In the matter of DSW Inc., F.T.C. No. 052 3096 (Decision and Order 2006) (requiring DSW to maintain a "comprehensive information security program"); In the matter of MySpace LLC, F.T.C. No. 102 3058 (Decision and Order 2012) (requiring a "comprehensive privacy program"); In the matter of Snapchat, Inc., F.T.C. No. 132 3078 (Decision and Order 2014) (requiring a "comprehensive privacy program").

110. Bennett and Raab, *Governance of Privacy*, 30 (exploring the promise of self-regulatory instruments that look "at data protection in wider dimensions: as a social, organizational, political, and technological practice."); Waters, "Privacy Impact Assessment," 149–151.

111. Pound, "Law in Books and Law in Action"; see also Friedman, *The Legal System Perspective* (setting forth a social scientific framework for the study of law in action, by which the legal system is understood to possess three components: social and legal forces that make "the law"; the law itself; and the impact of law on behavior in the outside world).

112. See Kagan, "How Much Do National Styles of Law Matter?," 4–5.

113. Gunningham, Kagan, and Thornton, *Shades of Green*, 147.

114. See Edelman, "Overlapping Fields and Constructed Legalities," 58; see also DiMaggio and Powell, "The Iron Cage Revisited," 148 (defining an organizational field as "those organizations that, in the aggregate, constitute a recognized area of institutional life").

115. Vogel, *National Styles of Regulation*.

116. See generally Coglianese, Nash, and Olmstead, "Performance-Based Regulation"; Parker, "Reinventing Regulation within the Corporation," 547 (discussing "outcome-based" regulation).

117. Sunstein, "Administrative Substance."

118. Lobel, "Orchestrated Experimentalism in the Regulation of Work"; Sturm, "Second Generation Employment Discrimination."

119. Bamberger, "Regulation as Delegation."

120. Merton, *Social Theory and Social Structure*, 199.

121. Marcus, "Implementing Externally Induced Innovations."

122. Bamberger, "Regulation as Delegation"; March and Simon, *Organizations*.

123. Coglianese and Lazer, "Management-Based Regulation," 692 and note 1.

124. See Ayres and Braithwaite, *Responsive Regulation*, 110–113 (describing the public and private benefits of an enforced self-regulation model, which takes advantage of the greater expertise and information of firm insiders).

125. Rakoff, "The Choice between Formal and Informal Modes of Administrative Regulation."

126. Karkkainen, Fung, and Sabel, "After Backyard Environmentalism Toward a Performance-Based Regime of Environmental Regulation"; Sunstein, "Informational Regulation and Informational Standing."

127. Bamberger, "Regulation as Delegation."

128. Coglianese, "Is Consensus an Appropriate Basis for Regulatory Policy?"

129. Rubin, "Images of Organizations and Consequences of Regulation."

130. Edelman and Suchman, *The Legal Lives of Private Organizations*, 1, 8 ("[A]mbiguous mandates and uneven enforcement may actually heighten law's cognitive salience, as organizations struggle to make sense of legal uncertainties and to develop shared definitions of acceptable compliance.").

131. Bamberger and Mulligan, "PIA Requirements and Privacy Decision-Making in U.S. Government Agencies."

132. Black, "The Emergence of Risk Based Regulation and the New Public Management in the UK"; Ayres and Braithwaite, *Responsive Regulation*; Edelman, "Legal Ambiguity and Symbolic Structures."

133. Dowling and Pfeffer, "Organizational Legitimacy," 122.

134. See generally Bevir, *Governance: A Very Short Introduction*; see also Pierre, *Governance, Politics, and the State*.

135. Gunningham, Kagan, and Thornton, *Shades of Green*, 136.

136. Ibid., 147.

137. Kagan, Thornton, and Gunningham, "Explaining Corporate Environmental Performance," 77.

138. Gunningham, Kagan, and Thornton, *Shades of Green*, 147.

139. Rhodes, "Policy Network Analysis."

140. Slaughter, *A New World Order*.

141. Keck and Sikkink, *Activists Beyond Borders*.

142. Linos, *The Democratic Foundations of Policy Diffusion*.

143. Bennett and Raab, *The Governance of Privacy*.

144. Scott, "Lords of the Dance," 223 (arguing that professionals have replace earlier "claimants to wisdom and moral authority—prophets, sages, intellectuals—and currently exercise supremacy in today's secularized and rationalized world").

145. Ibid.

146. Normative isomorphism, institutional entrepreneurship, and institutional work explain how and why professionals spread practices. DiMaggio and Powell, "The Iron Cage Revisited."

147. Adler and Kwon, "The Mutation of Professionalism as a Contested Diffusion Process."

148. Scott, "Evolving Professions," 125.

149. Bamberger and Mulligan, "PIA Requirements and Privacy Decision-Making in U.S. Government Agencies."

150. Scott, "Lords of the Dance" (discussing professionals' role in defining problems, mechanisms of solving, as well as oversight and discipline).

151. Flaherty, *Protecting Privacy in Surveillance Societies*.

152. Bennett, *Regulating Privacy*.

153. See also Rule and Greenleaf, *Global Privacy Protection* (including chapters describing privacy governance in seven jurisdictions).

154. Raab and Koops, "Privacy Actors, Performances and the Future of Privacy Protection," 214; see also Havinga, "Conceptualizing Regulatory Arrangements," 18 ("Knowledge of which particular actors are involved and what their role is in the regulatory social field reveals power relations that may have an effect on the reliability of a certificate, the level of compliance with prescriptions, and the openness of decision making. These insights might trigger government agencies to interfere or to monitor more actively.").

155. Raab and Koops, "Privacy Actors, Performances and the Future of Privacy Protection," 214 ("An important next step in analysis is to look more closely at policy actors and at their different roles. By looking at the various roles and responsibilities that all policy actors are given or take on themselves, we can assess any gaps in the distribution of all aspects of privacy protection across the range of actors.").

156. Bennett and Raab, *The Governance of Privacy*.

157. Bennett, *Privacy Advocates*.

158. See Newman, *Protectors of Privacy*, 2–3; a recent study by Francesca Bignami examining regulatory approaches to privacy in five countries likewise suggests a convergence of European national regulatory styles around regulatory process that combine tough administrative enforcement and pressure for corporate self-regulation. Bignami, "Transgovernmental Networks vs. Democracy," 809–810.

159. See also Bennett and Raab, *The Governance of Privacy*, 27 (exploring transnational policy instruments, demonstrating "a continuing process of policy convergence").

160. Doty and Mulligan, "Internet Multistakeholder Processes and Techno-Policy Standards."

161. Mattei, "Efficiency in Legal Transplants"; Mistelis, "Regulatory Aspects: Globalization, Harmonization, Legal Transplants, and Law Reform"; Schauer, "The Politics and Incentives of Legal Transplantation"; see also Legrand, "The Impossibility of Legal Transplants."

162. Friedman, *The Legal System*, 15

163. Trubek and Galanter, "Scholars in Self-Estrangement."

164. See, e.g., Vogenauer and Weatherill, *The Harmonisation of European Contract Law*; Bignami, "Transgovernmental Networks vs. Democracy."

165. Hesselink, "The New European Legal Culture."

166. Friedman, *The Legal System*, 3, 12.

167. We note that work by Jim Rule engaged in such inquiry twenty years before. See Rule, *Private Lives and Public Surveillance*.

168. Kagan, "How Much Do National Styles of Law Matter?," 7 ("It is far easier to interview or observe public officials in regulatory agencies than to interview or observe regulated businesses that are widely scattered and induce them to disclose how they adapt to the regulatory laws and agencies that they encounter.").

169. See "The World's Biggest Public Companies." On that list appear 88 percent of the U.S. firms, 78 percent of the German firms, 67 percent of the British firms, 62.5 percent of the Spanish firms, and 50 percent of the French firms.

170. Kagan, "How Much Do National Styles of Law Matter?," 19–22.

171. See Mehta and Hawkins, "Integrated Pollution Control and Its Impact," 64.

172. Kagan, "How Much Do National Styles of Law Matter?," 8.

173. Biernacki and Waldorf, "Snowball Sampling."

174. Christopoulos, "Peer Esteem Snowballing."

175. Kagan, "How Much Do National Styles of Law Matter?," 19 (identifying business executives and lawyers as "knowledgeable informants about cross-national differences in legal practices—the methodological equivalent of the village elders interviewed by anthropologists who seek to ascertain the routine norms and practices of a particular community").

176. Dexter, *Elite and Specialized Interviewing*, 5 (describing "elites" as individuals "well-informed or influential on something").

177. Gilding, "Motives of the Rich and Powerful in Doing Interviews with Social Scientists."

178. Mikecz, "Interviewing Elites," 483.

179. Gilding, "Motives of the Rich and Powerful in Doing Interviews with Social Scientists," 765.

180. See, e.g., Kagan, "How Much Do National Styles of Law Matter?," 20–21.

181. Ragin and Becker, *What Is a Case?*, 1–18 (describing how "[b]oundaries around places and time periods define cases").

182. Glaser, *The Discovery of Grounded Theory* (discussing how a "grounded theory" approach, unlike social science research in the positivist tradition, used data to generate concepts and categories that can provide the basis for new theory).

3   Background Law

1. Convention for the Protection of Individuals with Regard to Automatic Processing of Personal Data.

2. The directive provides an omnibus framework prohibiting the processing of personal data within the European Union in the absence of three conditions: (1) Pursuant to a transparency requirement, unless the processing of personal data is deemed "necessary" for a variety of articulated reasons (performing or entering a contract, compliance with a legal obligation or performance of a task carried out in the public interest, to protect the data subject's "vital interests," or for purposes of the legitimate interests of the party to whom the data are disclosed), it may occur only when the subject has given his or her consent. Subjects also have the right to be informed

when personal data are being processed. (2) Personal data can only be processed for "specified, explicit, and legitimate purposes" and may not be processed in a way incompatible with these purposes. (3) Data processing and storage (including length of storage in a form that allows identification of data subjects) must be proportional to the purposes for which the data are collected. See Directive 95/46/EC of the European Parliament and of the Council of 24 October 1995 on the Protection of Individuals with Regard to the Processing of Personal Data and on the Free Movement of Such Data. Pursuant to the directive, moreover, personal data may only be transferred to parties in a third country if that country provides an "adequate level of protection." While the U.S. regime has not been determined to meet that standard, a "safe harbor" framework developed by the Department of Commerce in consultation with the European Union Commission permits individual U.S. firms to self-certify their privacy practices, thereby allowing transfers of personal information from European countries. See Commission Decision of 26 July 2000 pursuant to Directive 95/46/EC of the European Parliament and of the Council on the adequacy of the protection provided by the safe harbor privacy principles and related frequently asked questions issued by the U.S. Department of Commerce, O.J. (L 215) 7 (2000); for a description of the safe harbor principles, see "U.S.-EU Safe Harbor Homepage."

3. Bennett, *Regulating Privacy: Data Protection and Public Policy in Europe and the United States*, 239 (describing the arguments of David H. Flaherty).

4. Newman, *Protectors of Privacy: Regulating Personal Data in the Global Economy*, 23–24.

5. Ibid., 36–37, 98–99.

6. Directive 95/46/EC of the European Parliament and of the Council of 24 October 1995 on the Protection of Individuals with Regard to the Processing of Personal Data and on the Free Movement of Such Data.

7. Newman, *Protectors of Privacy*, 24.

8. See Solove and Hoofnagle, "A Model Regime of Privacy Protection," 358 ("Privacy protection in the United States has often been criticized . . ."). The United States has specifically been criticized for employing self-regulation. See Rubinstein, "Privacy and Regulatory Innovation: Moving beyond Voluntary Codes" ("According to its many critics, privacy self-regulation is a failure. It suffers from an overall lack of transparency, weak or incomplete realization of Fair Information Practice Principles, inadequate incentives to ensure wide scale industry participation, and ineffective compliance and enforcement mechanisms.").

9. Schwartz, "Privacy and Democracy in Cyberspace," 1632.

10. Fair Credit Reporting Act of 1970.

11. Health Insurance Portability and Accountability Act (HIPAA) of 1996 (codified as amended in scattered sections of 42 U.S.C.) (regulating the use and disclosure of protected health information).

12. Gramm-Leach-Bliley Financial Services Modernization Act (GLBA) (empowering various agencies to promulgate data-security regulations for financial institutions).

13. Amendment to the Annual Privacy Notice Requirement under the Gramm-Leach-Bliley Act (Regulation P).

14. See, e.g., Right to Financial Privacy Act (RFPA) of 1978 (protecting the confidentiality of personal financial records by creating a statutory Fourth Amendment protection for bank records); Electronic Communications Privacy Act (ECPA) of 1986 (extending restrictions against wiretaps to include transmissions of electronic data by computer); Video Privacy Protection Act (VPPA) of 1988 (preventing disclosure of personally identifiable rental records of "prerecorded video cassette tapes or similar audio visual materials").

15. Solove and Hartzog, "The FTC and the New Common Law of Privacy." See also chapter 10, this volume.

16. See "Privacy Enforcement and Protection."

17. See "U.S.-EU Safe Harbor Homepage."

18. Privacy Act of 1974.

19. Solove and Hoofnagle, "A Model Regime of Privacy Protection," 359–361; see also ibid., 357 (explaining how "emerging companies known as 'commercial data brokers' have frequently slipped through the cracks" of these laws).

20. Swire, "Trustwrap: The Importance of Legal Rules to Electronic Commerce and Internet Privacy."

21. See, e.g., Clinton and Gore, *A Framework for Global Electronic Commerce*, 4 (promoting self-regulation as the preferred approach to protecting online privacy); Rubinstein, "Privacy and Regulatory Innovation," 360 (explaining that the Clinton administration favored private sector leadership and supported self-regulation, believing it would help electronic commerce flourish: "Clinton officials generally favored the view that private sector leadership would cause electronic commerce to flourish, and specifically supported efforts to 'implement meaningful, consumer-friendly, self-regulatory privacy regimes' in combination with technology solutions.").

22. Cate, "The Changing Face of Privacy Protection in the European Union and the United States," 179.

23. See Regan, "Safe Harbors or Free Frontiers? Privacy and Transborder Data Flows," 275 (referencing "[t]he patchwork of sectoral regulation that has long confused the

Europeans"); Center for Democracy & Technology, "CDT's Guide to Online Privacy" (discussing "the existing motley patchwork of privacy laws and practices"); Dignan, "Senate, Web Ad Titans Joust over Behavioral Targeting" (quoting U.S. Senator Daniel K. Inouye as saying that he "fear[s] that our existing patchwork of sector-specific privacy laws provides American consumers with virtually no protection"); Gellman, "Fragmented, Incomplete, and Discontinuous: The Failure of Federal Privacy Regulatory Proposals and Institutions" 199.

24. See Rotenberg, "Fair Information Practices and the Architecture of Privacy (What Larry Doesn't Get)," pt. 48 ("Technology continued to outpace the law. And the failure to adopt a comprehensive legal framework to safeguard privacy rights could jeopardize transborder data flows with Europe and other regions."); Neil M. Richards argues that patchwork laws in the United States "muddle" privacy and are inconsistent, pointing to the fact that "Facebook can disclose what music we listen to and what news articles we read, but not which films we watch" under the Video Privacy Protection Act, in Richards, "The Perils of Social Reading," 702.

25. See Privacy Rights Clearinghouse, "Privacy Today: A Review of Current Issues"; see also "Federal Agency Protection of Privacy Act: Hearing on H.R. 4561 Before the Subcomm. on Commercial & Admin. Law of the H. Comm. on the Judiciary, 107th Cong. 67–73 (2001) (statement of Edmund Mierzwinski, Consumer Program Director, National Association of State Public Interest Research Groups)" (making a similar assessment).

26. Solove and Hoofnagle, "A Model Regime of Privacy Protection," 358 ("Privacy experts have long suggested that information collection be consistent with Fair Information Practices.").

27. See Hoofnagle, "Privacy Self-Regulation: A Decade of Disappointment," 15 ("Ten years of self-regulation has led to serious failures in this field."); Reidenberg, "Restoring Americans' Privacy in Electronic Commerce" (responding in part to Clinton and Gore, *A Framework for Global Electronic Commerce*, critiquing U.S. reliance on self-regulation, and proposing FIPs-based regulation).

28. See Schwartz, "Privacy and Democracy in Cyberspace," 1682 (arguing that market solutions to privacy devalue the potential for cyberspace to facilitate "democratic self-rule"); see also Reidenberg, "Setting Standards for Fair Information Practice in the U.S. Private Sector," 500–501 (discussing privacy's role in "reflect[ing] specific conceptions of governance" in the public and private sectors); Schwartz, "Privacy and Participation: Personal Information and Public Sector Regulation in the United States," 560 (tying the "individual self-determination" privacy affords to society's capacity for democratic self-governance); Simitis, "Reviewing Privacy in an Information Society," 734 ("[P]rivacy proves to be a prerequisite to the capacity to participate in social discourse. Where privacy is dismantled, both the chance for personal assessment of the political and societal process and the opportunity to develop and maintain a particular style of life fade.").

29. See Newman, *Protectors of Privacy*, 32–33, 94, 125–127; Bignami, "Transgovernmental Networks vs. Democracy," 819 (explaining that the directive requires EU members to enact laws to implement the directive's provisions).

30. Simitis, "Privacy—An Endless Debate."

31. See Newman, *Protectors of Privacy*, 63–70.

32. Burkert, "Privacy—Data Protection," 47, 49.

33. Artikel 30, *Grundgesetz Für Die Bundesrepublik Deutschland* (Basic Law for the Federal Republic of Germany).

34. *Bundesdatenschutzgesetz*, sec. 38(6).

35. "Bundesverfassungsgericht [BVerfG] [Federal Constitutional Court] Dec. 15, 1983, Entscheidungen Des Bundesverfassungsgerichts [BVerfGE] 65, 1984."

36. Ibid.

37. *Bundesdatenschutzgesetz*, sec. 4f(1).

38. Ibid., sec. 4f(2).

39. See Wybitul, "New Requirements for Data Protection Officers in Germany."

40. *Bundesdatenschutzgesetz*, sec. 4f(3).

41. See ibid.

42. Ibid., sec. 4g.

43. Ibid., sec. 43(1), (3).

44. See Bignami, "Cooperative Legalism and the Non-Americanization of European Regulatory Styles," 424–430.

45. Bignami, "Cooperative Legalism and the Non-Americanization of European Regulatory Styles."

46. Ibid.

47. Ibid., 414.

48. Ibid.

49. Ibid.

50. Ibid.

51. Ibid., 426.

52. See Flaherty, *Protecting Privacy in Surveillance Societies*, 25 (discussing the influence of the combination of "exacting legalism" and trust in civil servants on the structure of data protection); Bignami, "Cooperative Legalism and the

Non-Americanization of European Regulatory Styles," 427 (discussing the importance of concepts of "self-responsibility and self-control" in shaping the German data protection field).

53. See chapter 11, this volume.

54. Bignami, "Cooperative Legalism and the Non-Americanization of European Regulatory Styles," 416.

55. OECD, *Better Regulation in Europe: Spain 2010*.

56. Ibid.

57. *Constitución Española* (Spanish Constitution), article 18.4.

58. Klosek, *Data Privacy in the Information Age*, 101; *Ley Orgánica 5/1992* (Organic Law 5/1992).

59. Royal Decree 428/1993.

60. *Ley Orgánica 15/1999, de Protección de Datos de Carácter Personal* (Organic Law 15/1999 for the Protection of Personal Information).

61. Ballon, *E-Commerce & Internet Law: Treatise with Forms* (looseleaf), sec. 26.04[12]; Norton Rose Fulbright, "Global Data Privacy Directory," 42.

62. Norton Rose Fulbright, "Global Data Privacy Directory," 42; Ballon, *E-Commerce & Internet Law*, sec. 26.04[12].

63. Speer et al., "Variable Funding of E.U. Privacy Law Means Uneven Enforcement across European Union."

64. Ramos, *Data Protection in Spain: Overview*; see also DLA Piper and EDRM, *DLA Piper's Data Protection Laws of the World 2013*, 308.

65. "Spanish Data Protection Agency," 2–3.

66. Baker & McKenzie, *Baker & McKenzie's Global Privacy Handbook: 2013 Edition*, 422–423; Financier Worldwide, *Data Protection & Privacy Laws*.

67. Baker & McKenzie, *Baker & McKenzie's Global Privacy Handbook: 2013 Edition*, 422; Financier Worldwide, *Data Protection & Privacy Laws*.

68. Baker & McKenzie, *Baker & McKenzie's Global Privacy Handbook: 2013 Edition*, 422.

69. Ibid.; Financier Worldwide, *Data Protection & Privacy Laws*, 39–40.

70. Baker & McKenzie, *Baker & McKenzie's Global Privacy Handbook: 2013 Edition*, 422.

71. "Spanish Data Protection Agency."

72. Ibid.

73. Thomas and Susnjar, "AEPD Reports an Increase in Complaints with Telecommunications Companies."

74. "Spain Levies Maximum Fine over Google Privacy Policy."

75. Hogan Lovells International LLP, *Data Protection Compliance in Spain: Mission Impossible?*

76. Maillet, "The Historical Significance of French Codifications," 692.

77. Canale et al., *A Treatise of Legal Philosophy and General Jurisprudence*, vol. 9, *A History of the Philosophy of Law in the Civil Law World, 1600–1900*, 149.

78. OECD, *Better Regulation in Europe: France 2010.*

79. Ibid., 50.

80. Ibid., 99.

81. Ibid.

82. *Loi 78-17 du 6 Janvier 1978 Relative à L'informatique, aux Fichiers et aux Libertés* [Law 78-17 of January 6, 1978, regarding Data Processing, Files, and Freedoms].

83. Boucher, "«Safari» ou la chasse aux Français"; "Histoire - Vos Libertés À L'heure de L'informatique (History—Your Freedom in the Information Age)."

84. See articles 22–24, *Loi 78-17 du 6 Janvier 1978 Relative à L'informatique, aux Fichiers et aux Libertés* [Law 78-17 of January 6, 1978 regarding Data Processing, Files, and Freedoms]; CNIL—Commission Nationale de l'Informatique et des Libertés, "Role and Responsabilities [sic]."

85. CNIL—Commission nationale de l'informatique et des libertés, "Role and Responsabilities [sic]"; CNIL—Commission Nationale de l'Informatique et des Libertés, "Les sanctions prononcées par la CNIL."

86. Bignami, "Cooperative Legalism and the Non-Americanization of European Regulatory Styles," 414.

87. Ibid., 423.

88. Ibid., 424.

89. Ibid., 414.

90. See *Loi 2004-801 du 6 août 2004 relative à la protection des personnes physiques à l'égard des traitements de données à caractère personnel et modifiant la loi 78-17 du 6 janvier 1978 relative à l'informatique, aux fichiers et aux libertés* [Law 2004-801 of August 6, 2004, regarding the Protection of Individuals Regarding their Personal Data and modifying Law 78-17 relating to Data Processing, Files, and Freedoms].

91. Bignami, "Cooperative Legalism and the Non-Americanization of European Regulatory Styles," 416.

92. Ibid., 441–442.

93. See CNIL—Commission Nationale de l'Informatique et des Libertés, "Pourquoi désigner un CIL?"

94. Ibid.

95. Ibid.

96. Ibid.; CNIL—Commission Nationale de l'Informatique et des Libertés, "30th Activity Report 2009," 7.

97. Moran, *The British Regulatory State: High Modernism and Hyper-Innovation*, 68.

98. Ibid., 20–22.

99. Levi-Faur and Gilad, "The Rise of the British Regulatory State: Transcending the Privatization Debate," 105–124, 110.

100. Ibid., 105–124, 108.

101. Ibid., 111.

102. Hood et al., *Regulation inside Government: Waste-Watchers, Quality Police, and Sleaze-Busters*, 29–31.

103. Levi-Faur and Gilad, "The Rise of the British Regulatory State," 115.

104. Ibid., 111.

105. Data Protection Act 1984(UK).

106. See below, this chapter.

107. Bignami, "Cooperative Legalism and the Non-Americanization of European Regulatory Styles," 423.

108. "Who We Are."

109. Data Protection Act 1998(UK).

110. Korff, LRDP Kantor Ltd., and Centre for Public Reform, *Comparative Study on Different Approaches to New Privacy Challenges, in Particular in the Light of Technological Developments—A.6 United Kingdom*.

111. Ibid., 1.

112. Ibid., 3. See, for example, *Durant v. Financial Services Authority* [2003], EWCA Civ 1746 (n.d.).

113. Korff, LRDP Kantor Ltd., and Centre for Public Reform, *Comparative Study on Different Approaches to New Privacy Challenges, in Particular in the Light of Technological Developments—A.6 United Kingdom*, 3.

114. UK Information Commissioner's Office, *Guidance on the Rules on Use of Cookies and Similar Technologies*.

115. "The Conditions for Processing: What Is Meant by 'Consent'?"

116. "ICO does not go out of his way to try and uncover breaches of the Act unless they somehow become exposed." Korff, LRDP Kantor Ltd., and Centre for Public Reform, *Comparative Study on Different Approaches to New Privacy Challenges, in Particular in the Light of Technological Developments—A.6 United Kingdom*, 62.

117. Patrikios, "ICO's Enforcement Action: What Do the Cases Tell Us?"

4 Empirical Findings—United States

1. See chapter 3, this volume, under "The United States and Europe."

2. Ubiquitous computing environments are those "in which each person is continually interacting with hundreds of nearby wirelessly interconnected computers. The goal is to achieve the most effective kind of technology, that which is essentially invisible to the user." Weiser, "Some Computer Science Issues in Ubiquitous Computing," 75.

3. See Lisovich, Mulligan, and Wicker, "Inferring Personal Information from Demand-Response Systems," 11.

4. For a thorough examination of the global impact of the EU's Data Protection Directive see Birnhack, "The E.U. Data Protection Directive: An Engine of a Global Regime," 517–518 (concluding that the "adequacy mechanism" in the EU directive has proven an effective tool at spreading the EU framework globally, and discussing its specific impact on the United States through the adoption of the Safe Harbor framework).

5. See below under "Distributed Expertise, Responsibility, and Accountability."

6. See chapter 10, this volume.

7. As of April 11, 2014, "[f]orty-seven states, the District of Columbia, Guam, Puerto Rico and the Virgin Islands have enacted legislation requiring private or government entities to notify individuals of security breaches of information involving personally identifiable information." National Conference of State Legislatures, "Security Breach Notification Laws."

8. See, e.g., *California Civil Code*, sec. §§ 56.06, 1785.11.2, 1798.29, 1798.82. State laws differ to some degree on issues such as permissible delay, penalties, the

existence of private rights of action, and the existence of exemptions for breaches determined immaterial.

9. Robert O'Harrow of the *Washington Post* was a finalist in 2000 for a series of privacy stories that provoked legislative and regulatory action. See "The Pulitzer Prizes | Beat Reporting"; A team of reporters at the *Wall Street Journal* were finalists for the Pulitzer Prize in 2012 for the "What They Know" series, which explored the privacy and surveillance implications of technology. See "Wall Street Journal's 'What They Know' Series—Ashkan Soltani"; in 2014 a team of reporters covering surveillance by the National Security Agency won the Pulitzer Prize for Public Service. See "The Pulitzer Prizes | Public Service."

10. See Arrow, "Uncertainty and the Welfare Economics of Medical Care," 946 (explaining that professionals like doctors sell information to those faced with risk and uncertainty); Edelman, "Legal Ambiguity and Symbolic Structures: Organizational Mediation of Civil Rights Law."

11. See Pfeffer, *The External Control of Organizations: A Resource Dependence Perspective*, xiii.

5 Empirical Findings—Germany

1. A case involving Wikipedia in Germany and the United States illustrates the spectrum. In 1990, two people killed an actor and were sent to prison. When they were released in 2007 and 2008, they sued to have their names removed from prior publications and to prohibit any further published reference to their crime. Their lawyer argued that they should be given an opportunity to rehabilitate and "lead their life without being publicly stigmatized." Wikipedia's German-language version thus deleted all mention of the two men in its article about the murder victim. Similar efforts in the United States have stalled, however, and are unlikely to be successful. Simitis, "Privacy—An Endless Debate," 1994. Similarly, "Google's rollout of its Street View service in North America in 2007 provoked little concern about the privacy implications of private homes and individuals being easily viewed by potentially millions of persons"; see Geissler, "Private Eyes Watching You: Google Street View and the Right to an Inviolate Personality," 897, which states, "In contrast, Street View's reception in Europe, particularly in Germany, has been marked by episodes of both public outrage and government concern."

2. See chapter 4, this volume.

3. See chapters 6 and 7, this volume.

4. See chapter 11, this volume.

5. Ibid.

6. See chapter 5, this volume.

7. Charter of Fundamental Rights of the European Union, Article 7.

8. The 2000 Charter of Fundamental Rights of the European Union differentiates between data protection and privacy. Ibid., see Articles 7–8.

9. See Wiesen, "German Industry and the Third Reich: Fifty Years of Forgetting and Remembering."

10. The Nuremberg Code is a set of research ethics principles for human experimentation set as a result of the subsequent Nuremberg Trials at the end of World War II. See Nuremberg Code.

11. See chapter 11, this volume.

12. Flaherty, *Protecting Privacy in Surveillance Societies*, 22.

13. See chapter 11, this volume.

6 Empirical Findings—Spain

1. If salient, these connections may further suggest the multitude of ways in which nonregulated parties can be empowered by administrative choices and the extent to which the power they wield advances the values the regulation sought to protect or is channeled toward other ends.

2. See chapters 5 and 7, this volume.

3. See chapter 4, this volume, under "The External Orientation of the Strategic CPO" and chapter 5, this volume, under "The Role of the DPO."

4. See chapter 4, this volume, under "Privacy Measured by 'Consumer Expectations.'"

5. See chapter 11, this volume, under "Works Councils and Employee Co-determination."

6. See chapter 3, this volume.

7. Two senior executives, two directors, two managers, and one associate staff. One described his role as "'consultor,' in Spanish. In Spain, middle managers are [at times called] Consultant Manager."

8. Bignami, "Cooperative Legalism and the Non-Americanization of European Regulatory Styles," 427; Flaherty, *Protecting Privacy in Surveillance Societies*, 22; *Bundesdatenschutzgesetz*, 4f(3,5), 4g.

9. See chapter 4, this volume, under "Operationalizing Privacy" and chapter 5, this volume, under "Operationalizing Privacy."

10. Ibid.

11. Ibid.

12. See chapter 4, this volume, under "Media, Advocates, and the Court of Public Opinion."

7   Empirical Findings—France

1. See chapter 3, this volume.

2. Ibid.

3. Bignami, "Cooperative Legalism and the Non-Americanization of European Regulatory Styles," 442–443.

4. These articulations reflect official declarations regarding privacy regulation, as can be found in a recent influential report from the French Senate emphasizing the World War II experience as a ground for "extreme vigilance" regarding privacy protection. Détraigne and Escoffier, *Rapport d'Information fait au nom de la commission des lois constitutionnelles, de législation, du suffrage universel, du Règlement et d'administration générale (1) par le groupe de travail (2) relatif au respect de la vie privée à l'heure des mémoires numériques.*

5. See *Loi 2004-801 du 6 août 2004 relative à la protection des personnes physiques à l'égard des traitements de données à caractère personnel et modifiant la loi 78-17 du 6 janvier 1978 relative à l'informatique, aux fichiers et aux libertés* [Law 2004-801 of August 6, 2004, regarding the Protection of Individuals Regarding their Personal Data and modifying Law 78-17 relating to Data Processing, Files, and Freedoms].

6. Boucher, "«Safari» ou la chasse aux Français."

7. See articles 22–24, *Loi 2004–801 du 6 août 2004 relative à la protection des personnes physiques à l'égard des traitements de données à caractère personnel et modifiant la loi 78–17 du 6 janvier 1978 relative à l'informatique, aux fichiers et aux libertés*; CNIL— Commission Nationale de l'Informatique et des Libertés, "Role and Responsabilities [sic]."

8. CNIL—Commission Nationale de l'Informatique et des Libertés, "Role and Responsabilities [sic]"; CNIL—Commission Nationale de l'Informatique et des Libertés, "Les sanctions prononcées par la CNIL."

9. See chapter 3, this volume.

10. See chapter 10, this volume, under "Regulatory Developments and the Consumer-Oriented Privacy Frame."

11. See chapter 5, this volume.

12. See chapter 6, this volume.

13. Responses included: "there's not this sort of issue"; "the advocacy groups have been quiet"; "in France, this isn't a subject that is handled by consumer associations"; and "it's not a tool that unions will use a lot."

14. See chapter 5, this volume.

15. But see below, this chapter, under "Suggestions of Transition in the French Privacy Field" (discussing a recent trend toward input by professional groups).

16. See CNIL—Commission Nationale de l'Informatique et des Libertés, "Les sanctions prononcées par la CNIL."

17. *Loi 2011-334 du 29 mars 2011 relative au Défenseur des droits* [Law 2011-334 of March 29, 2011 relative to the Defense of Rights], article 8.

18. CNIL—Commission Nationale de l'Informatique et des Libertés, Délibération no. 2010-113 du 22 avril 2010 de la formation restreinte portant avertissement à l'encontre de la société AIS 2 exerçant sous l'enseigne ACADOMIA (CNIL 2010).

19. See, e.g., Chauvel, "Acadomia épinglée par la CNIL."

20. Privacy Laws & Business, "Annual Conference."

8 Empirical Findings—United Kingdom

1. LRDP Kantor Ltd. and Centre for Public Reform, *Final Report: Comparative Study on Different Approaches to New Privacy Challenges, in Particular in the Light of Technological Developments*, 29.

2. Korff, LRDP Kantor Ltd., and Centre for Public Reform, *Comparative Study on Different Approaches to New Privacy Challenges, in Particular in the Light of Technological Developments—A.6 United Kingdom*, 3.

3. Baker & McKenzie, *Baker & McKenzie's Global Privacy Handbook: 2013 Edition*, 476; Data Protection Act 1998.

4. Korff, LRDP Kantor Ltd., and Centre for Public Reform, *Comparative Study on Different Approaches to New Privacy Challenges*, 2; The Privacy and Electronic Communications (EC Directive) Regulations 2003.

5. Schütz, "Comparing Formal Independence of Data Protection Authorities in Selected E.U. Member States."

6. Ibid.

7. Field Fisher Waterhouse, *2012: The Year of the Security Breach Fine*, 2.

8. Data Protection Act 1998; Linklaters LLP, *Data Protected: A Report on Global Data Protection Laws in 2014*, 275–279; Baker & McKenzie, *Baker & McKenzie's Global Privacy Handbook: 2013 Edition*, 486.

9   Identifying Best Practices

1. See chapter 2, this volume, under "Integrating Secondary Goals in the Corporate Context" and "Promise for Secondary Goals in Corporate Decision-Making."

2. See chapter 2, this volume, under "Promise for Secondary Goals in Corporate Decision-making and "The Social License to Operate."

3. Kagan, Thornton, and Gunningham, "Explaining Corporate Environmental Performance: How Does Regulation Matter?," 77.

4. Bamberger, "Regulation as Delegation: Private Firms, Decisionmaking, and Accountability in the Administrative State," 444.

5. See chapter 2, this volume, under "Privacy and Its Protection."

6. Flaherty, "Privacy Impact Assessments: An Essential Tool for Data Protection."

7. See Nissenbaum, *Privacy in Context: Technology, Policy, and the Integrity of Social Life*, 242; (quoting Parfit, *Reasons and Persons*, 86) (explaining that embedded norms create practices "roughly oriented around" societal values and goals); Post, "The Social Foundations of Privacy: Community and Self in the Common Law Tort," 959 (offering a normative account of privacy that does not focus just on the protection of individuals, but also on protection of the community, and finding that privacy torts in the common law uphold social norms, which in turn contribute to both community and individual identity).

10   The U.S. Privacy Field

1. See Bennett and Raab, *The Governance of Privacy*, 52–57 (discussing emergence of trust rhetoric in a range of global venues including the July 1997 EU conference on Global Information Networks and the 1998 OECD Conference in Ottawa).

2. Ibid., 49–50.

3. Clinton and Gore, *A Framework for Global Electronic Commerce*, 16.

4. Bennett and Raab, *The Governance of Privacy*, 52.

5. OECD, *Report of the Ad Hoc Meeting of Experts on Information Infrastructures: Issues Related to Security of Information Systems and Protection of Personal Data and Privacy*, 34.

6. Bennett and Raab, *The Governance of Privacy*, 53 (quoting Gunter Rexrodt and Martin Bangemann, "Theme Paper" [1997]).

7. OECD, *Implementing the OECD "Privacy Guidelines" in the Electronic Environment: Focus on the Internet*.

8. Ibid., 4.

9. Clinton and Gore, *A Framework for Global Electronic Commerce*, 16–18 (describing privacy protection as essential, but noting privacy should not inhibit the free flow of information and arguing that self-regulation is the way).

10. Bennett and Raab, *The Governance of Privacy*, 54.

11. See chapter 2, this volume, under "Privacy and Its Protection"; chapter 3, this volume.

12. Schwartz, "Health Insurance Reform Bill May Undermine Privacy of Patients' Records" (quoting response of Denise Nagel of the National Coalition for Patient Rights to the recently passed Kennedy-Kassebaum health care reform bill, which mandated the creation of a national computer network among health care providers, who were required to participate).

13. O'Harrow Jr., "White House Effort Addresses Privacy; Gore to Announce Initiative Today."

14. Torres and Clark, "Letter from Frank C. Torres, III, Legislative Counsel, Consumers Union, to Donald S. Clark, Secretary, Federal Trade Commission" (arguing for further privacy rules and standards on the grounds of increasing consumer trust).

15. Global Business Dialogue on Electronic Commerce, *The Paris Recommendations*, 6 (presenting further evidence that the business community embraced at least the rhetoric of consumer trust).

16. OECD, *A Global Action Plan for Electronic Commerce*, 22.

17. Federal Trade Commission, "All Events" Public Comments Received, Federal Trade Commission, https://web.archive.org/web/19990829100606/http://www.ftc .gov/bcp/icpw/comments/ (last updated July 8, 1999) (listing all commentators and links to their comments, with nearly every comment making at least a passing mention of consumer trust before launching into the commentator's vision of privacy protection).

18. Horovitz, "AmEx Kills Database Deal after Privacy Outrage" (listing other companies "that recently changed course after consumers balked").

19. Ibid.

20. "American Express Cancels Deal with Database Firm"; Horovitz, "AmEx Kills Database Deal after Privacy Outrage."

21. Clausing, "The Privacy Group That Took on Intel" (describing a successful grassroots campaign to force Intel to reverse its plans to activate an identifying signature in the Pentium III chip).

22. Boal, "Click Back: Privacy Hounds Bring DoubleClick to Heel—for Now," 35 ("Months of backlash from privacy advocates forced DoubleClick to abandon its scheme. CEO Kevin O'Connor said his company was wrong to stake out territory

not yet covered by government and industry standards. 'I made a mistake,' he said."); Vogelstein, "Minding One's Business," 45 (discussing decision to abandon plan to link offline and online data profiles "in the blink of an eye" because "Americans decided DoubleClick's business practices were not to be trusted").

23. The FTC had developed expertise on privacy as the agency responsible for rule-making and enforcement under several sectoral statutes. See Solove and Schwartz, *Information Privacy Law: Cases & Materials*, 776; Turkington and Allen, *Privacy Law: Cases and Materials*, 428, 476, 478, 482, 496–497.

24. See, e.g., Christine A. Varney, Commissioner, Federal Trade Commission, "Privacy in the Electronic Age" (making the point that the FTC is grappling with questions about how best to approach privacy in the information economy).

25. Robert Pitofsky, Former Chairman, Federal Trade Commission, Oral History of Robert Pitofsky (Sixth Interview), 155.

26. Hoofnagle, "Privacy Practices below the Lowest Common Denominator: The Federal Trade Commission's Initial Application of Unfair and Deceptive Trade Practices Authority to Protect Consumer Privacy (1997–2000)."

27. Solove and Hartzog, "The FTC and the New Common Law of Privacy."

28. Federal Trade Commission Act, sec. 45(a).

29. Bernstein, Oral History of Joan Z. Bernstein (Seventh Interview), 240.

30. For an overview of the FTC's activities through 1996, see Federal Trade Commission, "Workshop on Consumer Privacy on the Global Information Infrastructure"; for an overview of completed and planned work as of 1999, see Robert Pitofsky, Former Chairman, Federal Trade Commission, Oral History of Robert Pitofsky (Sixth Interview), 155–165.

31. See Bamberger and Mulligan, "Privacy on the Books and on the Ground," n. 59.

32. For an in-depth discussion of the connection between the EU Directive and privacy developments in the United States and other countries, see Birnhack, "The E.U. Data Protection Directive: An Engine of a Global Regime."

33. Commission Decision of 26 July 2000 pursuant to Directive 95/46/EC of the European Parliament and of the Council on the adequacy of the protection provided by the safe harbor privacy principles and related frequently asked questions issued by the U.S. Department of Commerce, O.J. (L 215) 7 (2000).

34. The European Commission's Decision explicitly provides that the organizations should publicly disclose their privacy policies and be subject to the jurisdiction of the Federal Trade Commission (FTC) under section 5 of the Federal Trade Commission Act, which prohibits unfair or deceptive acts or practices in or affecting

commerce, or that of another statutory body that will effectively ensure compliance with the principles. Ibid.

35. See, e.g., *FTC v. R. F. Keppel & Bro., Inc.*, 291 U.S. 304 (1934), 291:310 ("Neither the language nor the history of the Act suggests that Congress intended to confine the forbidden methods to fixed and unyielding categories."); *FTC v. Raladam Co.*, 283 U.S. 643 (1931), 283:648 ("'Unfair methods of competition' belongs to that class of phrases which do not admit of precise definition, but the meaning and application of which must be arrived at by . . . 'the gradual process of . . . inclusion and exclusion' [citation omitted].").

36. See, e.g., Federal Trade Commission, *Final Report of the FTC Advisory Committee on Online Access and Security*.

37. Federal Trade Commission, "All Events." The FTC held fourteen public workshops on matters related to privacy between 1995 and 2004. Twelve related to unfairness and deception, one concerned financial privacy, and one concerned credit reporting. See Credit Reporting: Workshops, Federal Trade Commission, https://web.archive.org/web/20100527091247/http://www.ftc.gov/privacy/privacy initiatives/credit_wkshp.html (last visited May 1, 2015); Financial Privacy: Financial Privacy Rule: Workshops, Federal Trade Commission, https://web.archive.org/ web/20100527091520/http://www.ftc.gov/privacy/privacyinitiatives/financial_rule_ wkshp.html (last visited May 1, 2015); Unfairness and Deception: Workshops, Federal Trade Commission, https://web.archive.org/web/20100527091112/http://www .ftc.gov/privacy/privacyinitiatives/promises_wkshp.html (last visited May 1, 2015).

38. See, e.g., Ad-Hoc Working Group on Unsolicited Commercial Email, *Report to the Federal Trade Commission*.

39. Since 1996, the FTC has issued seventeen reports relating to privacy: seven staff reports and ten reports to Congress. See Federal Trade Commission, "Legal Resources—Children's Privacy"; Federal Trade Commission, "All Events"; Financial Privacy: Pretexting: Reports and Testimony, https://web.archive.org/web/ 20100307172831/http://www.ftc.gov/privacy/privacyinitiatives/pretexting_reptest .html (last visited May 1, 2015); Unfairness and Deception: Reports and Testimony, https://web.archive.org/web/20100307172727/http://www.ftc.gov/privacy/privacy initiatives/promises_reptest.html (last visited May 1, 2015).

40. See Federal Trade Commission, *Individual Reference Services—A Report to Congress*; Network Advertising Initiative, "2008 NAI Principles—The Network Advertising Initiative's Self-Regulatory Code of Conduct."

41. See generally Hoofnagle, "Privacy Practices below the Lowest Common Denominator: The Federal Trade Commission's Initial Application of Unfair and Deceptive Trade Practices Authority to Protect Consumer Privacy (1997–2000)" (discussing the initial five cases brought by the FTC under their "deceptive practices or acts" jurisdiction).

42. See generally Bamberger, "Normative Canons in the Review of Administrative Policymaking," 99 (discussing the capacity of agencies to provide a site for norm elaboration through deliberative and participatory processes outside the APA rule-making or adjudication processes).

43. The need to demonstrate the "adequacy" of U.S. companies' privacy practices for purposes of the Safe Harbor guideline—which permit individual U.S. firms to transfer personal information from European countries after a self-certification process—also contributed to the creation of the privacy seal programs. To be eligible to participate in the Safe Harbor guidelines, corporations must provide both recourse mechanisms to consumers and a process for verifying company adherence to privacy commitments. The seal programs provided one mechanism for meeting these obligations. See generally "Safe Harbor Workbook."

44. See Better Business Bureau, "Welcome to BBBOnline"; TRUSTe, "Powering Trust in the Data Economy—TRUSTe."

45. Berman and Mulligan, Letter to Federal Trade Commission (discussing the Platform for Privacy Preferences (P3P) Project and requesting participation in FTC Workshop on Consumer Information Privacy); Cranor, *Web Privacy with P3P*, 43–57 (discussing P3P's origin and relation to other external policy activities).

46. See Hetcher, "The FTC as Internet Privacy Norm Entrepreneur," 2046 (arguing that the FTC's promotion of privacy policies was a means for "the Agency to sink its jurisdictional hooks more firmly into the Internet privacy debate, and therefore the Internet").

47. See, e.g., Federal Trade Commission, "Press Releases" (offering press releases discussing four FTC enforcement actions—against CVS Caremark, Microsoft, Eli Lilly, and Lisa Frank—initiated after privacy advocates or the media brought the matter to the FTC's attention); Bennett, *The Privacy Advocates: Resisting the Spread of Surveillance*, 124–125, 152, 155, 160–161 (discussing five other actions triggered by complaints from advocacy groups).

48. See, e.g., Federal Trade Commission, *Final Report of the FTC Advisory Committee on Online Access and Security* (discussing mechanisms to afford consumers access to personal information collected and maintained by commercial websites—mechanisms that are being designed by, among others, representatives from Consumers Union, the Electronic Privacy Information Center, the Center for Democracy & Technology, and the Electronic Frontier Foundation, as well as several privacy academics).

49. Ad-Hoc Working Group on Unsolicited Commercial Email, *Report to the Federal Trade Commission*; Center for Media Education, *Web of Deception: Threats to Children from Online Marketing*.

50. For example, Jason Catlett, president of Junkbusters, a for-profit company that helped consumers reduce unwanted marketing communications, positioned himself

as a privacy advocate for purposes of participating in FTC proceedings. See Catlett to Federal Trade Commission, "Letter from Jason Catlett, President, Junkbusters Corp., to Federal Trade Commission"; see also Borrus, "The Privacy War of Richard Smith" (containing an FTC associate director's comments on the importance of independent privacy expert Richard Smith's work).

51. This level of activity contrasts starkly with advocates' pursuits in the far more costly realm of litigation; indeed, privacy organizations have rarely led court challenges to remedy privacy wrongs in the corporate sector. See Bennett, *The Privacy Advocates*, 118–120.

52. See generally Olson, *The Logic of Collective Action*, 44 (articulating the public-choice insight that concentrated groups enjoy a comparative advantage with respect to their ability to organize to advance group interests compared to groups facing diffuse, individually small benefits); Stigler, "The Theory of Economic Regulation," 3 (setting forth a model of interest groups and regulatory agencies by which "regulation is acquired by the industry and is designed and operated primarily for its benefit").

53. National Conference of State Legislatures, "Security Breach Notification Laws."

54. This approach, ironically, may have created a perverse disincentive for corporations to post privacy policies. See Reidenberg, "Privacy Wrongs in Search of Remedies," 886 ("A company risks liability by making a disclosure, but does not risk accountability by remaining silent.").

55. See, e.g., Federal Trade Commission, Complaint for Permanent Injunction and Other Equitable Relief, *Federal Trade Commission v. Reverseauction.com, Inc.* (United States District Court, District of Columbia 2000) (alleging that violating a user agreement in order to send unsolicited and misleading commercial advertisements was likely to cause substantial, unavoidable harm to consumers, and thus constituted an unfair trade practice).

56. See, e.g., *FTC v. Seismic Entertainment Productions, Inc.*, 441 F. Supp. 2d 349 (Dist. Court, D. New Hampshire 2006), 441: 2–3; Advertising.com, Inc., and John Ferber; Analysis of Proposed Consent Order to Aid Public Comment, 70 Fed. Reg. 46175 (2005), 70: 175–177. Several of the FTC's spyware actions were informed by complaints filed by the Center for Democracy & Technology, which leads a group of anti-spyware software companies, academics, and public interest groups dedicated to defeating spyware called the Anti-Spyware Coalition (ASC). See Combating Spyware: H.R. 964, The Spy Act: Hearing Before the Subcomm. on Commerce, Trade, & Consumer Prot. of the H. Comm. on Energy & Commerce, 42 (statement of Ari Schwartz, deputy director, Center for Democracy & Technology).

57. In "bundled" software offerings, the users understand that they are installing one program, but because they fail to read the EULA and the software attempts to hide itself in other ways, they fail to understand that they are in fact installing

several different software programs and often creating relationships with several different companies. Typically these programs engage in invasive activities (pop-up or other forms of push advertising) or extractive activities (monitoring and data collection) which users presumably would avoid if given appropriate notice. Re: Advertising.com, Inc. dba Teknosurf.com, and John Ferber, 140 F.T.C. 220 (2005), 140: 222 (declaring failure to adequately disclose bundled software that traced browsing "deceptive").

58. "Best Practices" and other documents of the Anti-Spyware Coalition similarly propose a richer contextual understanding of privacy issues based on "risk factors—those that increase the potential concern about a technology—and consent factors, basic notice, consent, and user control—that mitigate the risks." See Anti-Spyware Coalition, "Best Practices: Factors for Use in the Evaluation of Potentially Unwanted Technologies," 1.

59. See Mulligan and Perzanowski, "The Magnificence of the Disaster: Reconstructing the Sony BMG Rootkit Incident," 1205–1211.

60. See Re: Sony BMG Music Entertainment, Agreement Containing Consent Order (2007) (requiring that installation of software from a CD and the transfer of information by such software meets a heightened "clear and prominent" standard for notice and consent).

61. See, e.g., Re: BJ's Wholesale Club, Inc., 140 F.T.C. 465 (2005); Re: Cardsystems Solutions, Inc., Complaint P9, No. C-4168 (2006); Re: DSW Inc., Complaint P10, No. C-4168 (2006).

62. See Re: BJ's Wholesale Club, Inc., 140 F.T.C. 465 (2005), 140: 468–472 (alleging unfairness where no statements were made about security); see also Scott, "The FTC, the Unfairness Doctrine and Data Security Litigation: Has the Commission Gone Too Far?" (discussing and criticizing the FTC's data security cases under the unfairness doctrine); Serwin, "The FTC's Increased Focus on Protecting Personal Information: An Overview of Enforcement and Guidance," 2 (discussing impact of FTC's corporate data security actions and promulgation of guidelines).

63. Sunstein, "Informational Regulation and Informational Standing: Akins and Beyond," 613 (describing the shift in informational regulation as "one of the most striking developments in the last generation of American law").

64. Ibid., 614.

65. Privacy Rights Clearinghouse, "Chronology of Data Breaches."

66. Consumers Union of U.S., Inc. and State Public Interest Research Groups, "The Clean Credit and Identity Theft Protection Act: Model State Law."

67. See Acquisti, Friedman, and Telang, "Is There a Cost to Privacy Breaches? An Event Study," 1573 (discussing the impact of a short-duration, 0.6 percent reduction in stock price on the day the breach is reported).

68. See Evers, "Break-in Costs ChoicePoint Millions."

69. Ponemon Institute LLC, "2014 Cost of Data Breach Study: United States."

70. Ibid.

71. See Mulligan and Simitian, "Assessing Security Breach Notification Laws" (identifying similar impact of SBN laws in areas such as asset management, portable media encryption, and the development of best practices).

72. Samuelson Law, Technology & Public Policy Clinic, "Security Breach Notification Laws: Views from Chief Security Officers," 13–21 (discussing internal impact of breach letters from the perspective of chief information security officers).

73. See, e.g., Arrow, "Uncertainty and the Welfare Economics of Medical Care," 947, 965 (describing how physician professionalism was an intermediating "nonmarket social institution" that compensated for uncertainty in the context of the severe information asymmetry between market actors); Edelman, "Legal Ambiguity and Symbolic Structures: Organizational Mediation of Civil Rights Law," 1531 (discussing the importance of professional organizations in mediating legal ambiguity).

11   The Development of the German Privacy Field

1. Simitis, "Privacy—An Endless Debate."

2. See ibid., 1995.

3. Ibid., 1995–1996 (describing similar discussions in the U.S. Congress).

4. Burkert, "Privacy—Data Protection," 47, 49.

5. "Bundesverfassungsgericht [BVerfG] [Federal Constitutional Court] Dec. 15, 1983, Entscheidungen Des Bundesverfassungsgerichts [BVerfGE] 65, 1984."

6. To be sure, not every one of the field leaders viewed this in an entirely positive light. In the words of one regulator, "Because of the experience with the two regimes, with the Nazis and the Stasi, [the data protection discourse is] always fear-dominated—[the fear that] that the state takes your data and is doing something, [a] company is doing something with your data. It's fear-dominated. And it's not hope-dominated."

7. Burkert, "Privacy—Data Protection," 54–55.

8. Ibid., 55.

9. See, e.g., *Bundesverfassungsgericht* (expanding the general right of privacy to cover telephone calls in the workplace) and *Bundesarbeitsgericht* (extending a presumption that hidden video surveillance in the workplace is an inadmissible infringement on the personality rights of employees). See also chapter 3, this volume, under "Germany."

10. A third described the complexities arising from the activity of single firms in multiple state jurisdictions. While the DPAs of the *Länder* think that the situs of jurisdiction arises from the location of a firm's "main establishment," "if you go in a pedestrian area through [any] city . . . all these chains . . . have establishments—one in Hamburg, one in Munich, one in Berlin, then it's [really] the data protection authority in Berlin and Hamburg and Munich [who] are responsible."

11. Weichert, "Privacy Protection Audit and IT Security Problems in Germany" (written by the Deputy Privacy Protection Commissioner of the state of Schleswig-Holstein).

12. Interview with Kenneth A. Bamberger and Deirdre K. Mulligan.

13. See generally Weichert, "Privacy Protection Audit and IT Security Problems in Germany."

14. See chapter 3, this volume, under "Germany."

15. *Bundesdatenschutzgesetz*, sec. 4f(1).

16. Ibid., sec. 4f(2).

17. Klug, "Improving Self-Regulation through (Law-Based) Corporate Data Protection Officials."

18. GDD e.V., "The German Association for Data Protection and Data Security (GDD)."

19. Interview with Kenneth A. Bamberger and Deirdre K. Mulligan.

20. *Bundesdatenschutzgesetz*, sec. 4f, paragraph 2, sentence 1.

21. Interview with Kenneth A. Bamberger and Deirdre K. Mulligan.

22. See, e.g., "Schulungen Bei Der GDD—GDD e.V."; "GDDCert.—GDD e.V."; Grassel, "GDD Datenschutz-Training: PC-gestützte Datenschutz Schulung für Mitarbeiter die mit personenbezogenen Daten umgehen [GDD Data Protection Training: PC-based data-protection training for employees who handle personal data]."

23. GDD e.V., "Membership."

24. See, e.g., Institute für Datenschutzbeauftragte der Gesellschaft für Datenschutz und Datensicherung, "Anforderungen an die Fachkunde und Zuverlässigkeit des betrieblichen Datenschutzbeauftragten gemäß §36 Abs. 2 BDSG [Requirements as to the 'expertise and reliability' of the corporate data protection officer pursuant to § 36 of the Federal Data Protection Act]"; Herwig and Jaspers, *Datenschutz in Deutschland: Ergebnisse der Umfrage zur Datenschutzpraxis und zur Stellung des Datenschutzbeauftragten von 1996* [Privacy in Germany: Results of the 1996 survey on data protection practices and the Data Protection Officer Position].

25. See, for example, Hunton & Williams LLP, "German DPAs Set Minimum Qualification and Independence Requirements for Company Data Protection Officers."

26. "38. Datenschutzfachtagung (DAFTA) und 33. RDV-Forum—GDD e.V."

27. "Erfa-Kreise—GDD e.V."

28. GDD e.V., *Datenschutz und Datensicherung in kleineren und mittleren Unternehmen: Eine Arbeitshilfe für die betriebliche Datenschutzpraxis* [Privacy and Data Protection in Small and Medium-Sized Enterprises: A Working Guide for Company Privacy Practices].

29. "GDD-Arbeitskreise—GDD e.V."

30. See, e.g., GDD e.V., *Bildschirmtext und Datenschutz* [The *Bidschirmtext* (Screentext) On-line Service and Data Protection]; GDD e.V., *Datensicherung im Unternehmen: Sicherheit bei dezentralen Systemen* [Backing up Company Information: Security in Decentralized Systems].

31. GDD e.V., *BDSG: Unterlage zur mitarbeiterinformation, Einführung in das Bundesdatenschutzgesetz* [A Guide to Employee Information under the Federal Data Protection Act].

32. "GDD-Ratgeber—GDD e.V."; Hermann and Münch, *Software-Tools zur Unterstützung der Tätigkeit von Datenschutzbeauftragten im Vergleich* [Software Tools to Support the Activities of Data Protection Officers: A Comparison].

33. "Mitteilungen der GDD—GDD e.V."

34. "RDV Online."

35. Cioffi, "Corporate Governance Reform, Regulatory Politics, and the Foundations of Finance Capitalism in the United States and Germany," 540.

36. *Betriebsverfassungsgesetz* [Works Constitution Act], sec. 87.

37. Ibid., sec. 75.

38. Cioffi, "Corporate Governance Reform," 542.

39. Ibid.

40. Weichert, "Privacy Protection Audit and IT Security Problems in Germany."

41. Ibid.

42. Sokol, "Eröffnung [Opening Remarks], 20 Jahre Datenschutz—Individualismus Oder Gemeinschaftssinn?" (translation by the authors).

43. Ibid.

44. Ibid.

45. Walz, "Datenschutz-Herausforderung Durch Neue Technik Und Europarecht" (translation by the authors).

46. Ibid.

47. Ibid.

48. Ibid.

49. Weichert, "Privacy Protection Audit and IT Security Problems in Germany."

50. Ibid.

51. Ibid.

52. Ibid.

53. Ibid.

54. Ibid.

55. Ibid.

56. Ibid.

57. Ibid.

58. LRDP Kantor Ltd. and Centre for Public Reform, *Final Report: Comparative Study on Different Approaches to New Privacy Challenges, in Particular in the Light of Technological Developments*, 52.

59. *Bundesdatenschutzgesetz*, sec. 38(3).

60. LRDP Kantor Ltd. and Centre for Public Reform, *Final Report: Comparative Study on Different Approaches to New Privacy Challenges, in Particular in the Light of Technological Developments*, 53.

61. Ibid., 53–54.

62. It is a private company whose majority shareholder is the Federal Republic of Germany. See "Members to the Supervisory Board of Deutsche Bahn AG."

63. Hunton & Williams LLP, "Deutsche Bahn Accepts € 1.1 Million Fine Imposed for Violation of Data Protection Law."

64. Landler, "Phone Giant in Germany Stirs a Furor."

65. Oates, "Deutsche Telecom Caught Doing an HP."

66. Deutsche Telekom, *Report Data Privacy and Data Security 2010*.

67. Jones Day Publications, "Germany Strengthens Data Protection Act, Introduces Data Breach Notification Requirement."

68. Korff, LRDP Kantor Ltd., and Centre for Public Reform, *Comparative Study on Different Approaches to New Privacy Challenges, in Particular in the Light of Technological Developments—A.6 United Kingdom.*

69. Jones Day Publications, "Germany Strengthens Data Protection Act, Introduces Data Breach Notification Requirement."

70. Ibid.

71. Ibid.

72. Gabel, "Germany to Tighten Data Protection Laws: Consumer Protection Associations Shall Be Granted Right to Take Businesses to Court."

12 Catalyzing Robust Corporate Privacy Practices

1. See Bennett and Raab, *The Governance of Privacy*, 207–208 ("How the instruments, or ingredients, actually mix or combine . . . ; what kinds of combination are best, which one must be added before another one can be added, and whether the 'mix' can be designed from the start as a comprehensive privacy protection regime, are questions.").

2. Smith, *Managing Privacy*: Information Technology and Corporate America, 213; See also ibid., chapter 6 (describing "Ambiguity All Around").

3. Edelman and Suchman, *The Legal Lives of Private Organizations*, 1, 8.

4. See ibid.

5. See Ayres and Braithwaite, *Responsive Regulation: Transcending the Deregulation Debate*, 110–113 (describing the public and private benefits of an enforced self-regulation model, which takes advantage of the greater expertise and information of firm insiders).

6. See *Bundesdatenschutzgesetz*; Wybitul, "New Requirements for Data Protection Officers in Germany."

7. See Bamberger and Mulligan, "Privacy on the Books and on the Ground."

8. The FTC has instead used enforcement mechanisms and other regulatory tools. See chapter 10, this volume, under "Regulatory Developments and the Consumer-Oriented Privacy Frame."

9. See Flaherty, *Protecting Privacy in Surveillance Societies*, 28; Bignami, "Cooperative Legalism and the Non-Americanization of European Regulatory Styles," 429 (explaining that German privacy authorities have limited powers and can issue only nonbinding recommendations).

10. See Flaherty, *Protecting Privacy in Surveillance Societies*, 28, 52 (describing the attitude and approach of the federal Data Protection Commissioner ("DPC") as emphasizing "mediation, conciliation, and education" and explaining that the responsibility of the State Ministries of the Interior is implementation of data protection in the private sector, while the DPC has no direct role but "may express opinions"); Bignami, "Cooperative Legalism and the Non-Americanization of European Regulatory Styles," 424, 429–430 (discussing that in Germany regulators were styled as ombudsmen who wielded soft powers of persuasion and describing the German system as one in which "self-regulation was central," and "rulemaking power was retained by the government").

11. Bignami, "Cooperative Legalism and the Non-Americanization of European Regulatory Styles," 426.

12. See chapter 7, this volume, under "The French Understanding of Privacy's Meaning and the Limited Privacy Field."

13. See chapter 4, this volume, under "Privacy Leadership from the Top: The Role of the CPO."

14. Zietsma et al., "The War of the Woods: Facilitators and Impediments of Organizational Learning Processes"; Hart and Sharma, "Engaging Fringe Stakeholders for Competitive Imagination."

15. Hirschman, *Exit, Voice, and Loyalty*.

16. See Burkert, "Privacy—Data Protection" (discussing the way agencies sometimes "convey the feeling that [they] regard themselves as being judged by the amount of pages they produce in these reports").

17. Ibid., 63 (internal citation omitted).

18. Bamberger, "Regulation as Delegation: Private Firms, Decisionmaking, and Accountability in the Administrative State," 439–440 (discussing the value of such external shocks in promoting organizational accountability).

19. See Dorf and Sabel, "A Constitution of Democratic Experimentalism," 314–323, 403 (discussing how agencies can take advantage of their vantage point on the behavior of multiple firms to develop "rolling best practices" by collecting data from regulated entities about what works and what does not, and then disseminating that information back through education and capacity building); see also Karkkainen, Fung, and Sabel, "After Backyard Environmentalism: Toward a Performance-Based Regime of Environmental Regulation" (providing, in the environmental context, a model in which administrative agencies develop the architecture for gathering and analyzing information across local contexts as a part of the regulatory and education process).

20. See Sturm, "Second Generation Employment Discrimination," 492–519 (discussing the importance of benchmarks in fostering meaningful organizational change and improvement).

21. Scott, "Evolving Professions: An Institutional Field Approach," 120 ("a professional logic attempt(s) to ward off both control by customers (in markets) and control by managers (in organizations), insisting that it should rightfully reside in providers oriented to serving client needs, subject on to the oversight of similarly oriented and trained colleagues"); see also Freidson, *Professionalism, the Third Logic: On the Practice of Knowledge.*

22. Scott, "Lords of the Dance: Professionals as Institutional Agents," 233.

23. See Raab and Koops, "Privacy Actors, Performances and the Future of Privacy Protection," 212 (describing the proliferation of new privacy actors including "data protection or privacy officers" "who are charged with responsibility for the legal compliance and good practice of their organisations and who have developed institutional bases for their training, common learning, interest co-ordination and representation" and whose "activities emanate from organisations . . . and represent a movement towards professionalism" and noting that "[t]here are now many thousand such persons on the scene.").

24. Francesca Bignami's nuanced treatment of privacy policy concludes that "European regulatory styles are converging . . . on a regulatory process that combines tough, legalistic administrative enforcement of government rules, extensive public pressure on industry actors to self-regulate, and low levels of litigation," which she calls "cooperative legalism." In particular, Bignami credits regulators in Northern European Union member states for the diffusion of self-regulatory approaches, including the adoption of corporate compliance officers and industry codes of conduct, and techniques such as privacy seals and privacy impact statements: see Bignami, "Cooperative Legalism and the Non-Americanization of European Regulatory Styles," 412, 435–440; Abraham Newman, too, has centered his examination of policy diffusion on a strong network of data protection authorities, suggesting their importance in the formulation of a unified privacy framework in the EU as well as changes in regulatory procedures and instruments in recent years: see Newman, *Protectors of Privacy*, 95 (documenting the formidable, and indeed outsized role, member state data protection authorities played in the creation of the structure and requirements of the EU Directive).

25. See Bignami, "Cooperative Legalism and the Non-Americanization of European Regulatory Styles," 418 ("Within the European Union, the diffusion of policy ideas among national regulators is particularly intense because of the dense set of transnational policymaking networks that exist in virtually every area of social and economic governance.").

26. See, for example, In the Matter of Google Inc., F.T.C. No. 102 3136 (Decision and Order 2011) (setting out the requirement to establish, implement, and maintain, a comprehensive privacy program that addresses privacy risks, protects the privacy and confidentiality of covered information, and is coordinated and overseen by an employee[s]).

27. Raab and Koops, "Privacy Actors, Performances and the Future of Privacy Protection," 210 (describing "long-standing network . . . of the world's privacy commissioners who've met annually . . . going back some thirty years").

13   Moving Forward

1. Greenwald, MacAskill, and Poitras, "Edward Snowden: The Whistleblower behind the NSA Surveillance Revelations."

2. Sanger and Chen, "Signaling Post-Snowden Era, New iPhone Locks Out N.S.A."

3. Ibid.

4. Serrano and Hennessey, "Sony 'Made a Mistake' in Canceling Release of 'Interview,' Obama Says."

5. Munro, "Health Data Breach at Anthem Is a Blockbuster That Could Affect 80 Million."

6. Caulfield and Siemaszko, "Sony Email Hack Shows Scott Rudin, Amy Pascal Making Racist Jokes about Obama; Producer Apologizes."

7. Serrano and Hennessey, "Sony 'Made a Mistake' in Canceling Release of 'Interview,' Obama Says."

8. Pew Research Center, *Public Perceptions of Privacy and Security in the Post-Snowden Era.*

9. Rubinstein, Nojeim, and Lee, "Systematic Government Access to Personal Data: A Comparative Analysis."

10. Rittweger and Molloy, "E.U. Data Protection Reform: An Overview of the European Commission's Proposed Regulation," 1.

11. The intention was to provide privacy some level of contextualization by focusing on discrete challenges, however, the meaning of "context" has been lost in translation and it seems that economic sectors are the most apt definition of the scope of various initiatives.

12. While technically nonbinding and therefore more likely providing a safe harbor like protection against claims of illegality, companies sometimes make choices that minimize legal exposure over those that might best advance the substantive goal of the regulatory scheme. See Thaw, "The Efficacy of Cybersecurity Regulation"

(explaining how the encryption safe harbor in security breach notification laws spurs CEOs to support the adoption of encryption, even though corporate information security officers might choose to invest in other options).

13. European Commission, *Proposal for a Regulation of the European Parliament and of the Council on the Protection of Individuals with Regard to the Processing of Personal Data and on the Free Movement of Such Data (General Data Protection Regulation),* preamble (76), article 38.

14. Ibid., preamble (70), article 33.

15. Ibid., article 33(4).

Glossary and Abbreviations

Association Française des Correspondants à la protection des Données à caractère Personnel (AFCDP). The French professional association for CILs and other privacy practitioners, providing training, information, networking, standardization, and other professional resources.

Binding corporate rules (BCR). A mechanism under the EU Data Protection Law that allows for multinational corporations, groups of companies, and other international organizations to make intra-organizational data transfers in compliance with the law.

Chief privacy officer (CPO). The lead individual in an organization responsible for privacy and data protection functions within the organization. This person may or may not be a data protection officer.

Commission Nationale de l'Informatique et des Libertés (CNIL). The French government authority tasked with the responsibilities of informing, advising and educating the public about data protection rights; protecting those rights; and regulating, controlling, inspecting and if necessary, penalizing data processors.

Computers, Freedom and Privacy Conference. An annual academic conference for issues at the intersection of computer technology, freedom, and privacy.

Correspondant informatique et libertés (CIL). A French data protection officer. See also **Data protection officer.**

Council of Europe. An independent, international organization, separate and distinct from the European Union, whose member states promote cooperation and harmonization in several areas, including legal standards, human rights, democratic development, the rule of law, and culture. The European Court of Human Rights, which enforces the European Convention on Human Rights, is a body of the Council of Europe.

Council of Europe Convention. The 1981 Convention for the Protection of Individuals with Regard to Automatic Processing of Personal Data, adopted by the Council of Europe.

c-suite. A colloquial term for the set of top executives at an organization, usually those with "C" or "chief" in their titles. For example, the c-suite usually consists of, at least, a chief executive officer (CEO) and a chief financial officer (CFO).

Data protection authority (DPA). Generic term for the European regulatory body responsible for privacy/data protection functions. See also **Commission nationale de l'informatique et des libertés** and **Information Commissioner's Office.**

Data protection officer (DPO). An individual appointed and registered as the person who is responsible, in an independent manner, for the internal application of the provisions of the European Data Protection Regulation in an organization. See also **Chief privacy officer** and **Correspondant informatique et libertés.**

Data Protection Registrar. The predecessor organization to the Information Commissioner's Office.

Director of the Area (Spain). The leader of a department.

DPA (UK). Data Protection Act of 1998 (United Kingdom).

European Charter of Fundamental Rights. Enshrines certain political, social, and economic rights into EU law. The charter applies to the seven principal bodies of the European Union and its member states.

European Commission (EC). The executive body of the European Union that has EU-level legislative authority. It is tasked with upholding EU treaties, proposing legislation, and implementing decisions.

The 1995 European Union Data Protection Directive. Directive 95/46/EC on the protection of individuals with regard to the processing of personal data and on the free movement of such data is an EU directive adopted in 1995 that regulates the processing of personal data within the European Union.

euros (EUR). The common currency of the European Union.

Fair Information Practices (FIPs). Guidelines that reflect widely accepted concepts concerning regarding the fair handling, storage, and management of information in an electronic marketplace.

Federal Trade Commission (FTC). An independent agency of the U.S. government, established in 1914 by the Federal Trade Commission Act. Its mission includes the promotion of consumer protection and the elimination and prevention of anti-competitive business practices.

German Association for Data Protection and Data Security. A nonprofit organization that promote practicable and effective data protection.

Gramm-Leach-Bliley Act (GLBA). U.S. legislation enacted in 1999 that requires financial institutions—companies that offer consumers financial products or services like loans, financial or investment advice, or insurance—to explain their information-sharing practices to their customers and to safeguard sensitive data.

Health Insurance Portability and Accountability Act of 1996 (HIPAA). Title II of the act requires the department of Health and Human Services to implement rules governing the use and disclosure of protected health information

Information Commissioner's Office (ICO). The British regulatory agency responsible for privacy and data protection matters. Formerly known as the **Data Protection Registrar.**

International Association of Privacy Professionals (IAPP). A professional association providing resources, training, professional development, networking, certification, and standardization for privacy practitioners around the world.

London Interbank Offered Rate (LIBOR). An estimate of the average rate paid by leading banks in London to borrow from other banks. Between 2008 and 2012 several studies and news articles revealed that this benchmark figure was regularly manipulated by traders.

Organisation for Economic Co-operation and Development (OECD). An international organization that has the self-declared aim of stimulating economic progress and world trade, through a commitment to principles of democracy and the market economy.

Privacy and Electronic Communications (EC Directive) Regulations 2003. A British legislative instrument that implements the European e-Privacy Directive (Directive 2002/58/EC).

Privacy Law Scholars Conference. An annual conference bringing together privacy law scholars and privacy law practitioners.

Security breach notifications. Legislation requiring private or government entities to notify individuals of security breaches of information involving personally identifiable information.

Système automatisé pour les fichiers administratifs et le répertoire des individus (SAFARI). A database of personal information on citizens that was proposed by the French government in the early 1970s, was the subject of a massive public outcry, and then was ultimately canceled.

Trans-substantive corporate committee. A group within a business organization that is assembled from a diverse set of members, each of whom is responsible for different substantive roles.

U.S.-EU Safe Harbor. A program that permits U.S. companies to comply with EU privacy requirements for sending protected information to countries outside the European Union.

WikiLeaks. A nonprofit organization that publishes secret and classified information and media from anonymous sources.

Bibliography

32nd International Conference of Data Protection and Privacy Commissioners. "Resolution on Privacy by Design," October 27, 2010. https://secure.edps.europa .eu/EDPSWEB/webdav/shared/Documents/Cooperation/Conference_int/10-10-27 _Jerusalem_Resolutionon_PrivacybyDesign_EN.pdf.

"38. Datenschutzfachtagung (DAFTA) und 33. RDV-Forum—GDD e.V." Accessed August 13, 2014. https://www.gdd.de/seminare/dafta.

Acquisti, Alessandro. "Privacy in Electronic Commerce and the Economics of Immediate Gratification." In *Proceedings of the 5th ACM Conference on Electronic Commerce (EC '04)*, 21–29. New York: ACM, 2004. http://doi.acm.org/10.1145/988772.988777.

Acquisti, Alessandro, Allan Friedman, and Rahul Telang. "Is There a Cost to Privacy Breaches? An Event Study." In *ICIS 2006 Proceedings*, 1563. Milwaukee, 2006. http:// www.heinz.cmu.edu/~acquisti/papers/acquisti-friedman-telang-privacy-breaches .pdf.

Ad-Hoc Working Group on Unsolicited Commercial Email. *Report to the Federal Trade Commission*, 1998. http://theory.stanford.edu/~matias/papers/cdt-spam.PDF.

Adler, Paul S., and Seok-Woo Kwon. "The Mutation of Professionalism as a Contested Diffusion Process: Clinical Guidelines as Carriers of Institutional Change in Medicine." *Journal of Management Studies* 50, no. 5 (July 2013): 930–962.

Advertising.com, Inc., and John Ferber; Analysis of Proposed Consent Order to Aid Public Comment, 70 Fed. Reg. 46175 (2005).

Amendment to the Annual Privacy Notice Requirement under the Gramm-Leach-Bliley Act (Regulation P). 79 FR 27214, 2014.

"American Express Cancels Deal with Database Firm." *Plain Dealer*. July 16, 1998.

Anti-Spyware Coalition. "Best Practices: Factors for Use in the Evaluation of Potentially Unwanted Technologies," 2007. http://www.antispywarecoalition.org/ documents/BestPractices.htm.

Argyris, Chris. "Good Communication That Blocks Learning." *Harvard Business Review* 72, no. 4 (1994): 77–85.

Arrow, Kenneth J. "Uncertainty and the Welfare Economics of Medical Care." *American Economic Review* 53, no. 5 (December 1963): 941–973.

Arrow, Kenneth Joseph. *The Limits of Organization.* 1st ed. The Fels Lectures on Public Policy Analysis. New York: Norton, 1974.

Article 29 Data Protection Working Party. *Opinion 02/2013 on Apps on Smart Devices.* Brussels: European Commission: Directorate-General Justice, February 27, 2013. http://ec.europa.eu/justice/data-protection/article-29/documentation/opinion -recommendation/files/2013/wp202_en.pdf.

Article 29 Data Protection Working Party. *Opinion 10/2004 on More Harmonised Information Provisions.* Brussels: European Commission: Directorate-General Justice, November 25, 2004. http://ec.europa.eu/justice/policies/privacy/docs/wpdocs/2004/ wp100_en.pdf.

Ayres, Ian, and John Braithwaite. *Responsive Regulation: Transcending the Deregulation Debate.* Oxford: Oxford University Press, 1992.

Baker & McKenzie. *Baker & McKenzie's Global Privacy Handbook: 2013 Edition*, 2013. http://www.bakermckenzie.com/files/Uploads/Documents/North%20America/ DoingBusinessGuide/Houston/bk_globalprivacyhandbook_13.pdf.

Ballon, Ian C. *E-Commerce & Internet Law: Treatise with Forms* (looseleaf). 2nd ed. Eagan, MN: West, 2009.

Bamberger, Kenneth A. "Normative Canons in the Review of Administrative Policymaking." *Yale Law Journal* 118, no. 1 (2008): 64–125.

Bamberger, Kenneth A. "Regulation as Delegation: Private Firms, Decisionmaking, and Accountability in the Administrative State." *Duke Law Journal* 56 (2) (2006): 377–468.

Bamberger, Kenneth A. "Technologies of Compliance: Risk and Regulation in a Digital Age." *Texas Law Review* 88, no. 4 (2010): 669–739.

Bamberger, Kenneth, and Deirdre Mulligan. "PIA Requirements and Privacy Decision-Making in U.S. Government Agencies." In *Privacy Impact Assessment*, ed. David Wright and Paul de Hert, 225–249. Dordrecht: Springer, 2012.

Bamberger, Kenneth, and Deirdre Mulligan. "Privacy on the Books and on the Ground." *Stanford Law Review* 63, no. 2 (2011): 247–316.

Becker, Markus C. "Organizational Routines: A Review of the Literature." *Industrial and Corporate Change* 13, no. 4 (August 1, 2004): 643–678.

Bennett, Colin J. *Regulating Privacy: Data Protection and Public Policy in Europe and the United States.* Ithaca, NY: Cornell University Press, 1992.

Bennett, Colin J. *The Privacy Advocates: Resisting the Spread of Surveillance*. Cambridge, MA: MIT Press, 2008.

Bennett, Colin J., and Charles Raab. *The Governance of Privacy: Policy Instruments in Global Perspective*. Cambridge, MA: MIT Press, 2006.

Berman, Jerry, and Deirdre K. Mulligan. Letter to Federal Trade Commission. "Letter from Jerry Berman & Deirdre K. Mulligan, Internet Privacy Working Grp., to Federal Trade Commission," April 15, 1997. http://www.ftc.gov/bcp/privacy/wkshp97/comments2/ipwg049.htm.

Bernstein, Joan Z. "Oral History of Joan Z. Bernstein (Seventh Interview)." Interview by Vicki Jackson, May 1, 2000. http://dcchs.org/JoanZBernstein/050100.pdf.

Betriebsverfassungsgesetz [Works Constitution Act], 1972. http://www.gesetze-im-internet.de/englisch_betrvg/englisch_betrvg.html.

Better Business Bureau. "Welcome to BBBOnline." Accessed May 27, 2014. http://www.bbb.org/online/.

Bevir, Mark. *Governance: A Very Short Introduction*. 1st ed. Very Short Introductions. Oxford: Oxford University Press, 2012.

Biernacki, Patrick, and Dan Waldorf. "Snowball Sampling: Problems and Techniques of Chain Referral Sampling." *Sociological Methods & Research* 10, no. 2 (November 1, 1981): 141–163.

Bignami, Francesca. "Cooperative Legalism and the Non-Americanization of European Regulatory Styles: The Case of Data Privacy." *American Journal of Comparative Law* 59 (2) (April 1, 2011): 411–461.

Bignami, Francesca. "Transgovernmental Networks vs. Democracy: The Case of the European Information Privacy Network." *Michigan Journal of International Law* 26 (2004): 807–868.

Birnhack, Michael D. "The E.U. Data Protection Directive: An Engine of a Global Regime." *Computer Law & Security Report* 24, no. 6 (2008): 508–520.

Black, Julia. "The Emergence of Risk Based Regulation and the New Public Management in the UK." *Public Law* (Autumn 2005): 512–549.

Boal, Mark. "Click Back: Privacy Hounds Bring DoubleClick to Heel—for Now." *Village Voice*, March 7, 2000.

Borrus, Amy. "The Privacy War of Richard Smith." *Businessweek Online*, February 14, 2000. http://www.businessweek.com/2000/00_07/b3668067.htm.

Boucher, Phillipe. "«Safari» ou la chasse aux Français." *Le Monde*, March 21, 1974.

Brandimarte, L., A. Acquisti, and G. Loewenstein. "Misplaced Confidences: Privacy and the Control Paradox." *Social Psychological & Personality Science* 4, no. 3 (May 1, 2013): 340–347.

Bundesarbeitsgericht. AP Nr. 15 zu § 611 BGB Persönlichkeitsrecht, 1987.

Bundesdatenschutzgesetz. RGBl I, 2003.

Bundesverfassungsgericht, 1991.

"Bundesverfassungsgericht [BVerfG] [Federal Constitutional Court] Dec. 15, 1983, Entscheidungen Des Bundesverfassungsgerichts [BVerfGE] 65, 1984." *Human Rights Law Journal* 5 (1984): 94–116.

Burkert, Herbert. "Privacy—Data Protection: A German/European Perspective." In *Governance of Global Networks in the Light of Differing Local Values*, ed. Christoph Engel and Kenneth H. Keller, 43–70. Baden-Baden: Nomos Verlagsgesellschaft, 2000.

California Civil Code, 2010.

Canale, D., E. Pattaro, H. Rottleuthner, R. A. Shiner, A. Peczenik, and G. Sartor, eds. *A Treatise of Legal Philosophy and General Jurisprudence*. Vol. 9, *A History of the Philosophy of Law in the Civil Law World, 1600–1900*. Dordrecht, The Netherlands; New York: Springer, 2005.

Cate, Fred H. *Privacy in the Information Age*. Washington, DC: Brookings Institution Press, 1997.

Cate, Fred H. "The Changing Face of Privacy Protection in the European Union and the United States." *Indiana Law Review* 33 (1999): 173–232.

Cate, Fred H. "The Failure of Fair Information Practice Principles." In *Consumer Protection in the Age of the Information Economy*, ed. Jane K. Winn, 341–378. Aldershot: Ashgate Publishing, Ltd, 2006.

Catlett, Jason. Letter to Federal Trade Commission. "Letter from Jason Catlett, President, Junkbusters Corp., to Federal Trade Commission," October 18, 1999. http://www.ftc.gov/bcp/workshops/profiling/comments/catlett.htm.

Caulfield, Philip, and Corky Siemaszko. "Sony Email Hack Shows Scott Rudin, Amy Pascal Making Racist Jokes about Obama; Producer Apologizes." *New York Daily News*, December 11, 2014. http://www.nydailynews.com/entertainment/gossip/rudin-pascal-made-racist-jokes-obama-sony-hacks-article-1.2041618.

Center for Democracy & Technology. "CDT's Guide to Online Privacy." Accessed May 24, 2014. http://www.cdt.org/privacy/guide.

Center for Media Education. *Web of Deception: Threats to Children from Online Marketing*. Washington, DC. 1996. http://legacy.library.ucsf.edu/documentStore/j/j/a/jja14j00/Sjja14j00.pdf.

Cerny, Philip G. "Embedding Global Financial Markets: Securitization and the Emerging Web of Governance." In *Private Organisations in Global Politics*, ed. Karsten

Ronit and Volker Schneider, 59–82. New York: Routledge, 2000. http://site.ebrary
.com/lib/berkeley/Doc?id=10054255.

Charter of Fundamental Rights of the European Union. 2000 O.J. (364) 10, 2000.

Chauvel, Corentin. "Acadomia épinglée par la CNIL." *20minutes.fr*, May 27, 2010.
http://www.20minutes.fr/societe/407540-acadomia-epinglee-cnil.

Christopoulos, D. "Peer Esteem Snowballing: A Methodology for Expert Surveys."
In *Eurostat Conference for New Techniques and Technologies for Statistics*, 171–179.
Brussels, 2009. http://ec.europa.eu/eurostat/documents/1001617/4398464/POSTER
-2P-PEER-ESTEEM-SNOWBALLING-CHROSTOPOULOS.pdf.

Cioffi, John W. "Corporate Governance Reform, Regulatory Politics, and the Foundations of Finance Capitalism in the United States and Germany." *German Law
Journal* 7, no. 6 (2006): 533–562.

Clausing, Jeri. "The Privacy Group That Took on Intel." *New York Times*, February 1,
1999.

Clinton, William J., and Albert Gore Jr. *A Framework for Global Electronic Commerce*,
1997. Accessed May 20, 2015. http://clinton4.nara.gov/WH/New/Commerce/.

CNIL—Commission Nationale de l'Informatique et des Libertés. "30th Activity
Report 2009." Direction de l'information légale et administrative. Paris, 2010. http://
www.cnil.fr/fileadmin/documents/en/CNIL-30e_rapport_2009-EN.pdf.

CNIL—Commission Nationale de l'Informatique et des Libertés. Délibération no.
2010–113 du 22 avril 2010 de la formation restreinte portant avertissement à
l'encontre de la société AIS 2 exerçant sous l'enseigne ACADOMIA (CNIL 2010).

CNIL—Commission Nationale de l'Informatique et des Libertés. "Les sanctions
prononcées par la CNIL." Accessed June 4, 2014. http://www.cnil.fr/linstitution/
missions/sanctionner/les-sanctions-prononcees-par-la-cnil/.

CNIL—Commission Nationale de l'Informatique et des Libertés. "Pourquoi désigner
un CIL?" Accessed June 4, 2014. http://www.cnil.fr/linstitution/missions/informer
-conseiller/correspondants/pourquoi-designer-un-cil/.

CNIL—Commission Nationale de l'Informatique et des Libertés. "Role and Responsabilities [sic]." Accessed June 4, 2014. http://www.cnil.fr/english/the-cnil/role-and
-responsabilities/.

Coglianese, Cary. "Is Consensus an Appropriate Basis for Regulatory Policy?" In
*Environmental Contracts: Comparative Approaches to Regulatory Innovation in the United
States and Europe*, ed. Eric W. Orts and Kurt Deketelaere, 93–113. The Hague: Kluwer
Law International, 2001.

Coglianese, Cary, and David Lazer. "Management-Based Regulation: Prescribing Private Management to Achieve Public Goals." *Law & Society Review* 37, no. 4 (2003):
691–730.

Coglianese, Cary, Jennifer Nash, and Todd Olmstead. "Performance-Based Regulation: Prospects and Limitations in Health, Safety, and Environmental Protection."
Administrative Law Review 55, no. 4 (October 1, 2003): 705–729.

Cohen, Michael D., and Paul Bacdayan. "Organizational Routines Are Stored as Procedural Memory: Evidence from a Laboratory Study." *Organization Science* 5, no. 4
(November 1, 1994): 554–568.

Combating Spyware: H.R. 964, The Spy Act: Hearing Before the Subcomm. on Commerce, Trade, & Consumer Prot. of the H. Comm. on Energy & Commerce. 110th
Cong. 40, 2007.

Commission Decision of 26 July 2000 pursuant to Directive 95/46/EC of the European Parliament and of the Council on the adequacy of the protection provided by
the safe harbour privacy principles and related frequently asked questions issued by
the U.S. Department of Commerce, O.J. (L 215) 7 (2000). 2000.

"The Conditions for Processing: What Is Meant by 'Consent'?" *ICO—Information
Commissioner's Office*, November 20, 2014. https://ico.org.uk/for-organisations/
guide-to-data-protection/conditions-for-processing/#consent.

Constitución Española (Spanish Constitution). 1978.

Consumers Union of U.S., Inc., and the State Public Interest Research Groups. "The
Clean Credit and Identity Theft Protection Act: Model State Law," January 2011.
http://consumersunion.org/wp-content/uploads/2013/02/model.pdf.

Convention for the Protection of Human Rights and Fundamental Freedoms. 213
U.N.T.S. 221. 1950.

Convention for the Protection of Individuals with Regard to Automatic Processing
of Personal Data. E.T.S. No. 108. 1981. http://conventions.coe.int/Treaty/en/
Treaties/Html/108.htm.

Cranor, Lorrie Faith. *Web Privacy with 3P3*. Beijing; Sebastopol, CA: O'Reilly Media,
2002.

Crawford, Kate, and Jason Schultz. "Big Data and Due Process: Toward a Framework
to Redress Predictive Privacy Harms." *Boston College Law Review* 55, no. 1 (2014):
93–128.

Culnan, Mary J., and Cynthia Clark Williams. "How Ethics Can Enhance Organizational Privacy: Lessons from the Choicepoint and TJX Data Breaches." *Management
Information Systems Quarterly* 33, no. 4 (December 2009): 673–687.

Cunningham, Lawrence A. "The Appeal and Limits of Internal Controls to Fight
Fraud, Terrorism, Other Ills." *Journal of Corporation Law* 29 (2004): 267–336.

Data Protection Act 1984 (UK). 1984, C. 35 (repealed 2000). Accessed May 20, 2015.
http://www.legislation.gov.uk/ukpga/1984/35/contents.

Data Protection Act 1998 (UK), C. 29. 1998. Accessed January 11, 2015. http:// www.legislation.gov.uk/ukpga/1998/29/contents.

DeShazo, J. R., and Jody Freeman. "Public Agencies as Lobbyists." *Columbia Law Review* 105, 8 (2005): 2217–2309.

Détraigne, Yves, and Anne-Marie Escoffier. *Rapport d'Information fait au nom de la commission des lois constitutionnelles, de législation, du suffrage universel, du Règlement et d'administration générale (1) par le groupe de travail (2) relatif au respect de la vie privée à l'heure des mémoires numériques.* Sénat, May 27, 2009. http://www.senat.fr/rap/ r08-441/r08-4411.pdf.

Deutsche Telekom. *Report Data Privacy and Data Security 2010,* 2010. www.telekom .com/static/-/15426/3/report-datasecurity-2010-si.

Dexter, Lewis Anthony. *Elite and Specialized Interviewing. Handbooks for Research in Political Behavior.* Evanston, IL: Northwestern University Press, 1970.

Dignan, Larry. "Senate, Web Ad Titans Joust over Behavioral Targeting." *Between the Lines,* July 9, 2008. http://www.zdnet.com/blog/btl/senate-web-ad-titans-joust-over -behavioral-targeting/9280.

DiMaggio, Paul J., and Walter W. Powell. "The Iron Cage Revisited: Institutional Isomorphism and Collective Rationality in Organizational Fields." *American Sociological Review* 48 (1983): 147–160.

Directive 95/46/EC of the European Parliament and of the Council of 24 October 1995 on the Protection of Individuals with Regard to the Processing of Personal Data and on the Free Movement of Such Data. O.J. (L 281) 31, 1995. http://eur-lex .europa.eu/LexUriServ/LexUriServ.do?uri=CELEX:31995L0046:en:HTML.

"Diverse Coalition Launches New Effort to Respond to Government Censorship and Threats to Privacy." *Global Network Initiative,* October 26, 2008. https://www .globalnetworkinitiative.org/newsandevents/Diverse_Coalition_Launches_New _Effort_To_Respond_to_Government_Censorship_and_Threats_to_Privacy.php.

DLA Piper, and EDRM. *DLA Piper's Data Protection Laws of the World 2013.* 2nd ed.DLA Piper UK LLP, 2013.

Doe, George. "With Genetic Testing, I Gave My Parents the Gift of Divorce." *Vox,* September 9, 2014. http://www.vox.com/2014/9/9/5975653/with-genetic-testing-i -gave-my-parents-the-gift-of-divorce-23andme.

Dorf, Michael C., and Charles F. Sabel. "A Constitution of Democratic Experimentalism." *Columbia Law Review* 98 (2) (1998): 267–473.

Doty, Nick, and Deirdre K. Mulligan. "Internet Multistakeholder Processes and Techno-Policy Standards: Initial Reflections on Privacy at the World Wide Web Consortium." *Journal on Telecomm. &. High Tech. L.* 11 (2013): 135–325.

Dowling, John, and Jeffrey Pfeffer. "Organizational Legitimacy: Social Values and Organizational Behavior." *Pacific Sociological Review* 18, no. 1 (January 1975): 122–136.

Dredge, Stewart. "Yahoo Joins Facebook, Google and Others in Revealing US Surveillance Requests." *The Guardian—Technology*, June 18, 2013. http://www.theguardian .com/technology/2013/jun/18/yahoo-reveals-us-surveillance-requests-nsa.

Durant v. Financial Services Authority [2003], EWCA Civ 1746, n.d.

Edelman, Lauren B. "Legal Ambiguity and Symbolic Structures: Organizational Mediation of Civil Rights Law." *American Journal of Sociology* 97, no. 6 (May 1992): 1531–1576.

Edelman, Lauren B. "Overlapping Fields and Constructed Legalities: The Endogeneity of Law." In *Private Equity, Corporate Governance and the Dynamics of Capital Market Regulation*, ed. Justin O'Brien, 55–90. London: Imperial College Press, 2007.

Edelman, Lauren B., Howard S. Erlanger, and John Lande. "Internal Dispute Resolution: The Transformation of Civil Rights in the Workplace." *Law & Society Review* 27 (1993): 497–534.

Edelman, L. B., and M. C. Suchman, eds. *The Legal Lives of Private Organizations*. Aldershot: Ashgate, 2007.

Edelman, Lauren B., Christopher Uggen, and Howard S. Erlanger. "The Endogeneity of Legal Regulation: Grievance Procedures as Rational Myth." *American Journal of Sociology* 105 (2) (1999): 406–454.

Edwards, John. "Privacy Impact Assessment in New Zealand—A Practitioner's Perspective." In *Privacy Impact Assessment*, ed. David Wright and Paul de Hert, 149–160. London: Springer, 2012.

Electronic Communications Privacy Act (ECPA) of 1986. 18 U.S.C. §§2510–2522, 2006.

Eraut, Michael. "Non-Formal Learning and Tacit Knowledge in Professional Work." *British Journal of Educational Psychology* 70, no. 1 (2000): 113–136.

"Erfa-Kreise—GDD e.V." Accessed August 13, 2014. https://www.gdd.de/eforen.

European Commission. *Proposal for a Regulation of the European Parliament and of the Council on the Protection of Individuals with Regard to the Processing of Personal Data and on the Free Movement of Such Data (General Data Protection Regulation)*. Brussels, January 25, 2012.

Evers, Joris. "Break-in Costs ChoicePoint Millions." *CNET News*, July 20, 2005. http://news.cnet.com/Break-in-costs-ChoicePoint-millions/2100-7350_3-5797213 .html.

Fair Credit Reporting Act of 1970. Pub. L. No. 91–508, 84 Stat. 1128 (codified as Amended at 15 U.S.C. §§1681–1681x), 2006.

"Federal Agency Protection of Privacy Act: Hearing on H.R. 4561 Before the Subcomm. on Commercial & Admin. Law of the H. Comm. on the Judiciary, 107th Cong. 67–73 (2001) (statement of Edmund Mierzwinski, Consumer Program Director, National Association of State Public Interest Research Groups)," 2002. http://commdocs.house.gov/committees/judiciary/hju79365.000/hju79365_0f.htm.

Federal Trade Commission. "All Events." Accessed May 27, 2014. http://www.ftc.gov/news-events/events-calendar/all.

Federal Trade Commission. Complaint for Permanent Injunction and Other Equitable Relief, Federal Trade Commission v. Reverseauction.com, Inc. (United States District Court, District of Columbia, 2000).

Federal Trade Commission. Final Report of the FTC Advisory Committee on Online Access and Security, May 15, 2000. http://govinfo.library.unt.edu/acoas/papers/finalreport.htm.

Federal Trade Commission. Individual Reference Services—A Report to Congress, December 1997. http://www.ftc.gov/reports/individual-reference-services-report-congress.

Federal Trade Commission. "Legal Resources—Children's Privacy." BCP Business Center. Accessed May 27, 2014. https://www.ftc.gov/tips-advice/business-center/privacy-and-security/children%27s-privacy.

Federal Trade Commission. "Press Releases." Accessed May 27, 2014. http://www.ftc.gov/news-events/press-releases.

Federal Trade Commission. Protecting Consumer Privacy in an Era of Rapid Change: Recommendations for Businesses and Policymakers, March 2012. http://www.ftc.gov/sites/default/files/documents/reports/federal-trade-commission-report-protecting-consumer-privacy-era-rapid-change-recommendations/120326privacyreport.pdf.

Federal Trade Commission. "Workshop on Consumer Privacy on the Global Information Infrastructure," June 4, 1996. http://www.ftc.gov/news-events/events-calendar/1996/06/consumer-privacy-global-information-infrastructure.

Federal Trade Commission Act. 15 U.S.C. §§41–58, 2006.

Federal Trade Commission Act. 15 U.S.C. §§45(a)(2), 2013.

Feldman, Martha S., and Alan J. Levy. "Effects of Legal Context on Decision Making Under Ambiguity." In The Legalistic Organization, ed. Sim B. Sitkin and Robert J. Bies, 109–136. Thousand Oaks, CA: Sage Publications, 1994.

Field Fisher Waterhouse. 2012—The Year of the Security Breach Fine. ICO Enforcement Action Tracker, 2012. https://privacyassociation.org/media/pdf/knowledge_center/FFW-ICO_Enforcement_Action_Tracker_2012.PDF.

Financier Worldwide. *Data Protection & Privacy Laws*. Annual Review. Birmingham, UK, December 2012. http://www.ssek.com/download/document/FW_DataProtection_73 .pdf.

Flaherty, David H. "Privacy Impact Assessments: An Essential Tool for Data Protection." Presented at the 22nd Annual Meeting of Privacy and Data Protection Officials. Venice, September 27, 2000. http://aspe.hhs.gov/datacncl/flaherty.htm.

Flaherty, David H. *Protecting Privacy in Surveillance Societies: The Federal Republic of Germany, Sweden, France, Canada, and the United States*. Chapel Hill: University of North Carolina Press, 1989.

Fox-Wolfgramm, Susan J., Kimberly B. Boal, and G. James Hunt. "Organizational Adaptation to Institutional Change: A Comparative Study of First-Order Change in Prospector and Defender Banks." *Administrative Science Quarterly* 43, no. 1 (March 1998): 87–126.

Freidson, Eliot. *Professionalism, the Third Logic: On the Practice of Knowledge*. Chicago: University of Chicago Press, 2001.

Friedman, Lawrence M. *The Legal System: A Social Science Perspective*. New York: Russell Sage Foundation, 1975.

FTC v. Raladam Co., 283 U.S. 643 (1931).

FTC v. R. F. Keppel & Bro., Inc., 291 U.S. 304 (1934).

FTC v. Seismic Entertainment Productions, Inc., 441 F. Supp. 2d 349 (Dist. Court, D. New Hampshire, 2006).

Gabel, Detlev. "Germany to Tighten Data Protection Laws: Consumer Protection Associations Shall Be Granted Right to Take Businesses to Court." *White & Case Technology Newsflash*, March 2014. http://www.whitecase.com/articles/032014/ germany-tighten-data-protection-laws-consumer-protection-associations-granted -right-businesses-court/.

"GDD-Arbeitskreise—GDD e.V." Accessed August 13, 2014. https://www.gdd.de/ ueber-uns/gdd-arbeitskreise.

"GDDCert.—GDD e.V." Accessed January 15, 2015. https://www.gdd.de/seminare/ gddcert.

GDD e.V. *BDSG: Unterlage zur mitarbeiterinformation, Einführung in das Bundesdatenschutzgesetz* [A Guide to Employee Information under the Federal Data Protection Act], 1992.

GDD e.V. *Bildschirmtext und Datenschutz* [The *Bidschirmtext* (Screen-text) On-line Service and Data Protection], 1984.

GDD e.V. *Datenschutz und Datensicherung in kleineren und mittleren Unternehmen: Eine Arbeitshilfe für die betriebliche Datenschutzpraxis* [Privacy and Data Protection in Small and Medium-Sized Enterprises: A Working Guide for Company Privacy Practices], 1991.

GDD e. V. *Datensicherung im Unternehmen: Sicherheit bei dezentralen Systemen.* [Backing Up Company Information: Security in Decentralized Systems]. PC-Security Working Group, 1995. Bonn: GDD.

GDD e.V. "Membership." Accessed February 12, 2015. https://www.gdd.de/interna tional/english/membership.

GDD e.V. "The German Association for Data Protection and Data Security (GDD)." Accessed June 3, 2014. https://www.gdd.de/international/english.

"GDD-Ratgeber—GDD e.V." Accessed August 13, 2014. https://www.gdd.de/gdd -arbeitshilfen/gdd-ratgeber.

Geissler, Roger C. "Private Eyes Watching You: Google Street View and the Right to an Inviolate Personality." *Hastings Law Journal* 63 (2012): 897–926.

Gellman, Robert M. "Fragmented, Incomplete, and Discontinuous: The Failure of Federal Privacy Regulatory Proposals and Institutions." *Software Law Journal* 6 (1993): 199–238.

Gilding, Michael. "Motives of the Rich and Powerful in Doing Interviews with Social Scientists." *International Sociology* 25, no. 6 (November 1, 2010): 755–777.

Gilliom, John. "A Response to Bennett's 'In Defence of Privacy.'" *Surveillance & Society* 8, no. 4 (2011): 500–504.

Gilliom, John. *Overseers of the Poor: Surveillance, Resistance, and the Limits of Privacy.* Chicago: University of Chicago Press, 2001.

Gioia, Dennis A., and James B. Thomas. "Identity, Image, and Issue Interpretation: Sensemaking During Strategic Change in Academia." *Administrative Science Quarterly* 41 (1996): 370–403.

Glaser, Barney G. *The Discovery of Grounded Theory; Strategies for Qualitative Research. Observations.* Chicago: Aldine Pub. Co., 1967.

Global Business Dialogue on Electronic Commerce. *The Paris Recommendations*, September 13, 1999. http://www.gbd-e.org/pubs/Paris_Recommendations_1999.pdf.

Gold, Andrew H., Arvind Malhotra, and Albert H. Segars. "Knowledge Management: An Organizational Capabilities Perspective." *Journal of Management Information Systems* 18, no. 1 (2001): 185–214.

Gramm-Leach-Bliley Financial Services Modernization Act (GLBA). 15 U.S.C. §§6801–6809, 6821–6827, 2006.

Granovetter, Mark. "The Strength of Weak Ties: A Network Theory Revisited." *Sociological Theory* 1 (1983): 201–233.

Granovetter, Mark S. "The Strength of Weak Ties." *American Journal of Sociology* 78 (6) (May 1973): 1360–1380.

Grassel, Rudolf. "GDD Datenschutz-Training: PC-gestützte Datenschutz Schulung für Mitarbeiter die mit personenbezogenen Daten umgehen [GDD Data Protection Training: PC-Based Data-Protection Training for Employees Who Handle Personal Data]," 1995.

Greening, D. W., and B. Gray. "Testing a Model of Organizational Response to Social and Political Issues." *Academy of Management Journal* 37, no. 3 (June 1, 1994): 467–498.

Greenwald, Glenn, Ewen MacAskill, and Laura Poitras. "Edward Snowden: The Whistleblower behind the NSA Surveillance Revelations." *The Guardian*, June 11, 2013. http://www.theguardian.com/world/2013/jun/09/edward-snowden-nsa -whistleblower-surveillance.

Grundgesetz Für Die Bundesrepublik Deutschland (Basic Law for the Federal Republic of Germany), 1949.

Gunningham, Neil, Robert A. Kagan, and Dorothy Thornton. *Shades of Green: Business, Regulation, and Environment.* Stanford, CA: Stanford University Press, 2003.

Gunningham, Neil, Robert A. Kagan, and Dorothy Thornton. "Social License and Environmental Protection: Why Businesses Go Beyond Compliance." *Law & Social Inquiry* 29, no. 2 (2004): 307–341.

Gunningham, N., and D. Sinclair. "New Generation Environmental Policy: Environmental Management Systems and Regulatory Reform." *Melbourne University Law Review* 22 , no. 3 (1999): 592–616.

Harris, K. D.*Making Your Privacy Practices Public.* California Department of Justice, May 2014. https://oag.ca.gov/sites/all/files/agweb/pdfs/cybersecurity/making_your _privacy_practices_public.pdf.

Hart, Stuart L., and Sanjay Sharma. "Engaging Fringe Stakeholders for Competitive Imagination." *Academy of Management Executive* 18, no. 1 (2004): 7–18.

Havinga, Tetty. "Conceptualizing Regulatory Arrangements: Complex Networks of Actors and Regulatory Roles." *Nijmegen Sociology of Law Working Paper* No. 2012/01, September 14, 2012. http://ssrn.com/abstract=2189471.

Health Insurance Portability and Accountability Act (HIPAA) of 1996. Pub. L. No. 104–191, 110 Stat. 1936, 1996.

Heimer, Carol A. "Explaining Variation in the Impact of Law: Organizations, Institutions, and Professions." In *Studies in Law, Politics, and Society*, ed. Austin Sarat and Susan S. Silbey, 15–29. Greenwich, CT: JAI Press, 1995.

Hermann, Jana, and Peter Münch. *Software-Tools zur Unterstützung der Tätigkeit von Datenschutzbeauftragten im Vergleich* [Software Tools to Support the Activities of Data Protection Officers: A Comparison]. GDD e.V., 1995.

Herwig, Ralf, and Andreas Jaspers. *Datenschutz in Deutschland: Ergebnisse der Umfrage zur Datenschutzpraxis und zur Stellung des Datenschutzbeauftragten von 1996* [Privacy in Germany: Results of the 1996 Survey on Data Protection Practices and the Data Protection Officer Position], 1997.

Hesselink, Martijn W. "The New European Legal Culture." In *The New European Private Law: Essays on the Future of Private Law in Europe*, ed. Martijn W. Hesselink, 11–75. The Hague; London: Kluwer Law International, 2002.

Hetcher, Steven. "The FTC as Internet Privacy Norm Entrepreneur." *Vanderbilt Law Review* 53 (2000): 2041–2062.

Hirschman, Albert O. *Exit, Voice, and Loyalty: Responses to Decline in Firms, Organizations, and States.* Cambridge, MA: Harvard University Press, 1970.

"Histoire—Vos libertés à l'heure de l'informatique (History—Your Freedom in the Information Age)." *CNIL—Commission Nationale de l'Informatique et des Libertés.* Accessed February 11, 2015. http://www.cnil.fr/vos-droits/histoire/.

Hogan Lovells International LLP. *Data Protection Compliance in Spain: Mission Impossible?* Madrid, May 2012. http://www.hoganlovells.com/files/Publication/f2f84282-b813-4fd0-97bf-d6a204649c5d/Presentation/PublicationAttachment/d3471979-a610-4f77-b60c-d73f25a5632d/Data_Protection_In_Spain-May%202012.pdf.

Hood, Christopher, Colin Scott, Oliver James, George Jones, and Tony Travers. *Regulation inside Government: Waste-Watchers, Quality Police, and Sleaze-Busters.* Oxford; New York: Oxford University Press, 1999.

Hoofnagle, Chris Jay. "Privacy Practices below the Lowest Common Denominator: The Federal Trade Commission's Initial Application of Unfair and Deceptive Trade Practices Authority to Protect Consumer Privacy (1997–2000)," January 1, 2001. http://papers.ssrn.com/sol3/papers.cfm?abstract_id=507582.

Hoofnagle, Chris Jay. "Privacy Self-Regulation: A Decade of Disappointment." *Electronic Privacy Information Center*, 2005. http://epic.org/reports/decadedisappoint.pdf.

Hoofnagle, Chris Jay, and Jennifer King. "Research Report: What Californians Understand about Privacy Offline." SSRN Scholarly Paper. Rochester, NY: Social Science Research Network, May 15, 2008. http://papers.ssrn.com/abstract=1133075.

Horovitz, Bruce. "AmEx Kills Database Deal after Privacy Outrage." *USA Today*, July 15, 1998.

Hunton & Williams LLP. "Deutsche Bahn Accepts € 1.1 Million Fine Imposed for Violation of Data Protection Law." *Privacy and Information Security Law Blog*. Accessed August 21, 2014. https://www.huntonprivacyblog.com/2009/10/articles/deutsche -bahn-accepts-e-1-1-million-fine-imposed-for-violation-of-data-protection-law/.

Hunton & Williams LLP. "German DPAs Set Minimum Qualification and Independence Requirements for Company Data Protection Officers." *Privacy and Information Security Law Blog*, December 17, 2010. https://www.huntonprivacyblog.com/ 2010/12/articles/german-dpas-set-minimum-qualification-and-independence -requirements-for-company-data-protection-officers/.

Hustinx, Peter. "Privacy by Design: Delivering the Promises." *Identity in the Information Society* 3, no. 2 (May 7, 2010): 253–255.

IAPP. "About." [The International Association of Privacy Professionals] Privacyassociation.org. Accessed May 25, 2014. https://www.privacyassociation.org/about _iapp.

IBM. "News Release: IBM Names Harriet P. Pearson as Chief Privacy Officer," November 29, 2000. http://www-03.ibm.com/press/us/en/pressrelease/1464.wss.

Information and Privacy Commissioner, Ontario, Canada, Hydro One, and Toronto Hydro Corporation. *Privacy by Design: Achieving the Gold Standard in Data Protection for the Smart Grid*, June 2010. https://www.ipc.on.ca/images/Resources/achieve -goldstnd.pdf.

Institute für Datenschutzbeauftragte der Gesellschaft für Datenschutz und Datensicherung. "Anforderungen an die Fachkunde und Zuverlässigkeit des betrieblichen Datenschutzbeauftragten gemäß §36 Abs. 2 BDSG [Requirements as to the 'expertise and reliability' of the corporate data protection officer pursuant to § 36 of the Federal Data Protection Act]." *Recht der Datenverarbeitung* 10, no. 1 (1994).

The Internet in China: A Tool for Freedom or Suppression? Hearing before H. Subcomm. on Africa, Global Human Rights, and International Operations, and H. Subcomm. Asia and the Pacific, H. Comm. on International Relations. 109th Cong. 2006.

In the matter of DSW Inc., F.T.C. No. 052 3096 (Decision and Order 2006).

In the matter of Google Inc., F.T.C. No. 102 3136 (Decision and Order 2011).

In the matter of MySpace LLC, F.T.C. No. 102 3058 (Decision and Order 2012).

In the matter of Snapchat, Inc., F.T.C. No. 132 3078 (Decision and Order 2014).

Jernigan, Carter, and Behram F. T. Mistree. "Gaydar: Facebook Friendships Expose Sexual Orientation." First Monday 14, no. 10 (September 25, 2009). http://firstmonday.org/ojs/index.php/fm/article/view/2611.

Jones Day Publications. "Germany Strengthens Data Protection Act, Introduces Data Breach Notification Requirement," October 2009. http://www.jonesday.com/germany-strengthens-data-protection-act-introduces-data-breach-notification-requirement-10-26-2009/#_edn18.

Kagan, Robert A. "How Much Do National Styles of Law Matter?" In *Regulatory Encounters: Multinational Corporations and American Adversarial Legalism*, ed. Lee Axelrad and Robert A. Kagan, 253–255. Berkeley; Los Angeles: University of California Press, 2000.

Kagan, Robert A., Dorothy Thornton, and Neil Gunningham. "Explaining Corporate Environmental Performance: How Does Regulation Matter?" *Law & Society Review* 37 (1) (March 2003): 51–90.

Karkkainen, Bradley C., Archon Fung, and Charles F. Sabel. "After Backyard Environmentalism: Toward a Performance-Based Regime of Environmental Regulation." *American Behavioral Scientist* 44 (4) (2000): 692–711.

Keck, Margaret E., and Kathryn Sikkink. *Activists Beyond Borders: Advocacy Networks in International Politics*. 1st ed. Ithaca, NY: Cornell University Press, 1998.

Klein, Gary A. "A Recognition-Primed Decision (PRD) Model of Rapid Decision Making." In *Decision Making in Action: Models and Methods*, ed. Gary A. Klein, Judith Orasanu and Roberta Calderwood, 138–147. Norwood, CT: Ablex Publishing Corporation, 1993.

Klosek, Jacqueline. *Data Privacy in the Information Age*. Westport, CT: Greenwood Publishing Group, 2000.

Klug, Christoph. "Improving Self-Regulation through (Law-Based) Corporate Data Protection Officials." *Privacy Laws & Business International Newsletter*, no. 63 (June 2002).

Koops, Bert-Jaap. "On Decision Transparency, or How to Enhance Data Protection after the Computational Turn." In *Privacy, Due Process and the Computational Turn*, ed. M. Hildebrandt and K. De Vries, 196–220. Abingdon: Routledge, 2013.

Korff, Douwe, LRDP Kantor Ltd., and Centre for Public Reform. *Comparative Study on Different Approaches to New Privacy Challenges, in Particular in the Light of Technological Developments—A.6 United Kingdom*. Country Studies. European Commission: Directorate-General Justice, Freedom and Security, June 2010. http://ec.europa.eu/justice/policies/privacy/docs/studies/new_privacy_challenges/final_report_country_report_A6_united_kingdom.pdf.

Kuner, Christopher, Fred H. Cate, Christopher Millard, and Dan Jerker B. Svantesson. "Systematic Government Access to Private-Sector Data Redux." *International Data Privacy Law* 4, no. 1 (2014): 1.

Landler, Mark. "Phone Giant in Germany Stirs a Furor." *New York Times*, May 27, 2008. http://www.nytimes.com/2008/05/27/business/worldbusiness/27tapes.html.

Laurie, Graeme T. "Challenging Medical-Legal Norms: The Role of Autonomy, Confidentiality, and Privacy in Protecting Individual and Familial Group Rights in Genetic Information." *Journal of Legal Medicine* 22, no. 1 (2001): 1–54.

Lawrence, Paul R., and Jay William Lorsch. *Organization and Environment: Managing Differentiation and Integration*. Boston: Division of Research, Graduate School of Business Administration, Harvard University, 1967.

Legrand, Pierre. "The Impossibility of Legal Transplants." *Maastricht Journal of European and Comparative Law* 4 (1997): 111–124.

Lessig, Lawrence. *Code: Version 2.0*. New York: Basic Books, 2006.

Levi-Faur, David, and Sharon Gilad. "The Rise of the British Regulatory State: Transcending the Privatization Debate." *Comparative Politics* 37, no. 1 (October 1, 2004): 105–124.

Ley Orgánica 15/1999, de Protección de Datos de Carácter Personal [Organic Law 15/1999 for the Protection of Personal Information], 1999.

Ley Orgánica 5/1992 [Organic Law 5/1992], 1992.

Linklaters LLP. *Data Protected: A Report on Global Data Protection Laws in 2014*, June 2014. https://clientsites.linklaters.com/Clients/dataprotected/Pages/UnitedKingdom.aspx.

Linos, Katerina. *The Democratic Foundations of Policy Diffusion: How Health, Family, and Employment Laws Spread Across Countries*. Oxford; New York: Oxford University Press, 2013.

Lipshitz, Raanan, Gary Klein, Judith Orasanu, and Eduardo Salas. "Taking Stock of Naturalistic Decision Making." *Journal of Behavioral Decision Making* 14, no. 5 (December 2001): 331–352.

Lischka, Konrad, and Christian Stöcker. "Data Protection: All You Need to Know about the EU Privacy Debate." *Spiegel Online*, January 18, 2013. http://www.spiegel.de/international/europe/the-european-union-closes-in-on-data-privacy-legislation-a-877973.html.

Lisovich, Mikhail A., Deirdre K. Mulligan, and Stephen B. Wicker. "Inferring Personal Information from Demand-Response Systems." *Security & Privacy, IEEE* 8, no. 1 (2010): 11–20.

Lobel, Orly. "Orchestrated Experimentalism in the Regulation of Work." *Michigan Law Review* 101, no. 6 (May 2003): 2146–2162.

Loi 78–17 du 6 Janvier 1978 Relative à L'informatique, aux Fichiers et aux Libertés [Law 78–17 of January 6, 1978 regarding Data Processing, Files, and Freedoms]. *Journal Officiel de la République Française* [J.O.] [Official Gazette of France], 1978.

Loi 2004–801 du 6 août 2004 relative à la protection des personnes physiques à l'égard des traitements de données à caractère personnel et modifiant la loi 78–17 du 6 janvier 1978 relative à l'informatique, aux fichiers et aux libertés [Law 2004–801 of August 6, 2004 regarding the Protection of Individuals Regarding their Personal Data and modifying Law 78–17 relating to Data Processing, Files, and Freedoms]. *Journal Officiel de la République Française* [J.O.] [Official Gazette of France], 2004.

Loi 2011–334 du 29 mars 2011 relative au Défenseur des droits [Law 2011–334 of March 29, 2011 relative to the Defense of Rights]. *Journal Officiel de la République Française* [J.O.] [Official Gazette of France], 2011.

LRDP Kantor Ltd., and Centre for Public Reform. *Final Report: Comparative Study on Different Approaches to New Privacy Challenges, in Particular in the Light of Technological Developments*. European Commission: Directorate-General Justice, Freedom and Security, January 20, 2010. http://ec.europa.eu/justice/policies/privacy/docs/studies/new_privacy_challenges/final_report_en.pdf.

Luhmann, Niklas. "The Unity of the Legal System." In *Autopoietic Law: A New Approach to Law and Society*, ed. Gunther Teubner, 12–35. Berlin; New York: W. de Gruyter, 1988.

Lyon, David. *Surveillance Society: Monitoring Everyday Life. Issues in Society*.Buckingham, UK; Philadelphia: Open University, 2001.

MacKinnon, Rebecca. *Consent of the Networked: The World-Wide Struggle for Internet Freedom*. New York: Basic Books, 2012.

Maillet, Jean. ""The Historical Significance of French Codifications." *Tulane Law Review* 44 (1970): 681–692.

Malloy, Timothy F. "Regulation, Compliance and the Firm." *Temple Law Review* 76 (2003): 451–531.

March, James G., Martin Schultz, and Xueguang Zhou. *The Dynamics of Rules: Change in Written Organizational Codes*. Stanford, CA: Stanford University Press, 2000.

March, James G., and Herbert Alexander Simon. *Organizations*. New York: Wiley, 1958.

Marcus, A. A. "Implementing Externally Induced Innovations: A Comparison of Rule-Bound and Autonomous Approaches." *Academy of Management Journal* 31, no. 2 (June 1, 1988): 235–256.

Mattei, Ugo. "Efficiency in Legal Transplants: An Essay in Comparative Law and Economics." International Review of Law and Economics 14 (1994): 3–19. http://works.bepress.com/ugo_mattei/14.

McAllister, Daniel W., Terence R. Mitchell, and Lee Roy Beach. "The Contingency Model for the Selection of Decision Strategies: An Empirical Test of the Effects of Significance, Accountability, and Reversibility." Organizational Behavior and Human Performance 24, no. 2 (1979): 228–244.

McDonald, Aleecia M., and Lorrie Faith Cranor. "The Cost of Reading Privacy Policies." I/S: A Journal of Law and Policy for the Information Society 4, no. 3 (2008): 540–565.

Mehta, Alex, and Keith Hawkins. "Integrated Pollution Control and Its Impact: Perspectives from Industry." Journal of Environmental Law 10, no. 1 (1998): 61–77.

"Members to the Supervisory Board of Deutsche Bahn AG." Deutsche Bahn. Accessed January 17, 2015. http://www.deutschebahn.com/en/group/ataglance/supervisory_board.html.

Menon, Tanya, and Jeffrey Pfeffer. "Valuing Internal vs. External Knowledge: Explaining the Preference for Outsiders." Journal of Management Science 49, no. 4 (April 2003): 497–513.

Merton, Robert K. Social Theory and Social Structure. Glencoe, IL: Free Press, 1957.

Meyer, John W., and Brian Rowan. "Institutionalized Organizations: Formal Structure as Myth and Ceremony." American Journal of Sociology 83, no. 2 (1977): 340–363.

Mikecz, Robert. "Interviewing Elites: Addressing Methodological Issues." Qualitative Inquiry 18, no. 6 (2012): 482–493.

Mistelis, Loukas A. "Regulatory Aspects: Globalization, Harmonization, Legal Transplants, and Law Reform—Some Fundamental Observations." International Lawyer 34 (2000): 1055–1069.

"Mitteilungen der GDD—GDD e.V." Accessed August 13, 2014. https://www.gdd.de/service/gdd-mitteilungen/mitteilungen-der-gdd.

Moran, Michael. The British Regulatory State: High Modernism and Hyper-Innovation. Oxford; New York: Oxford University Press, 2003.

Mulligan, Deirdre K., and Aaron Perzanowski. "The Magnificence of the Disaster: Reconstructing the Sony BMG Rootkit Incident." Berkeley Technology Law Journal 22 (2007): 1157–1232.

Mulligan, Deirdre K., and Joseph Simitian. "Assessing Security Breach Notification Laws." On file with authors, n.d.

Munro, Dan. "Health Data Breach at Anthem Is a Blockbuster That Could Affect 80 Million." *Forbes—Pharma & Healthcare*, February 5, 2015. http://www.forbes.com/sites/danmunro/2015/02/05/health-data-breach-at-anthem-is-a-blockbuster-could-affect-80-million/.

Murray, Edwin A., Jr. "The Social Response Process in Commercial Banks: An Empirical Investigation." *Academy of Management Review* 1, no. 3 (July 1, 1976): 5–15.

National Conference of State Legislatures. "Security Breach Notification Laws," April 11, 2014. http://www.ncsl.org/research/telecommunications-and-information-technology/security-breach-notification-laws.aspx.

Network Advertising Initiative. "2008 NAI Principles—The Network Advertising Initiative's Self-Regulatory Code of Conduct," 2008. http://www.networkadvertising.org/principles.pdf.

Newman, Abraham L. *Protectors of Privacy: Regulating Personal Data in the Global Economy*. Ithaca, NY: Cornell University Press, 2008.

Nissenbaum, Helen. "Privacy as Contextual Integrity." *Washington Law Review* 79, no. 1 (2004): 119–158.

Nissenbaum, Helen. *Privacy in Context: Technology, Policy, and the Integrity of Social Life*. Palo Alto, CA: Stanford University Press, 2009.

Norton Rose Fulbright. "Global Data Privacy Directory," June 2013. http://www.nortonrosefulbright.com/files/global-data-privacy-directory-52687.pdf.

"Nuremberg Code." United States Holocaust Memorial Museum website. Accessed February 11, 2015. http://www.ushmm.org/information/exhibitions/online-features/special-focus/doctors-trial/nuremberg-code.

Oates, John. "Deutsche Telecom Caught Doing an HP." *The Register*, May 27, 2008. http://www.theregister.co.uk/2008/05/27/dt_des_hp/.

O'Dell, Carla, and C. Jackson Grayson. "If Only We Knew What We Know: Identification and Transfer of Internal Best Practices." *California Management Review* 40, no. 3 (1998): 154–174.

O'Harrow, Robert, Jr. "White House Effort Addresses Privacy; Gore to Announce Initiative Today." *The Washington Post*, May 14, 1998.

Olson, Mancur. *The Logic of Collective Action*. Cambridge, MA: Harvard University Press, 1965.

OECD. *A Global Action Plan for Electronic Commerce*. OECD Digital Economy Papers, October 1, 1999. http://www.oecd-ilibrary.org/science-and-technology/a-global-action-plan-for-electronic-commerce_236544834564.

OECD. Better Regulation in Europe: France 2010. Paris: OECD, 2010. http://public
.eblib.com/choice/publicfullrecord.aspx?p=605877.

OECD. *Better Regulation in Europe: Spain 2010.* Paris: OECD, 2010.

OECD. *Guidelines Governing the Protection of Privacy and Transborder Flows of Personal
Data,* 1980. http://www.oecd.org/sti/ieconomy/oecdguidelinesontheprotectionofpri
vacyandtransborderflowsofpersonaldata.htm.

OECD. *Implementing the OECD "Privacy Guidelines" in the Electronic Environment: Focus
on the Internet,* 1998. http://www.oecd.org/dataoecd/33/43/2096272.pdf.

OECD. *Report of the Ad Hoc Meeting of Experts on Information Infrastructures: Issues
Related to Security of Information Systems and Protection of Personal Data and Privacy.*
Paris, 1996. http://www.oecd.org/internet/ieconomy/2094252.pdf.

Parfit, Derek. *Reasons and Persons.* Oxford: Oxford University Press, 1984.

Parker, Christine. "Reinventing Regulation within the Corporation: Compliance-
Oriented Regulatory Innovation." *Administration & Society* 32, no. 5 (November 1,
2000): 529–565.

Parks, Rachida, Chao Chu, Heng Xu, and Lascelles Adams. "Understanding the Drivers and Outcomes of Healthcare Organizational Privacy Responses." Shanghai, 2011.
http://aisel.aisnet.org/icis2011/proceedings/IThealthcare/8/.

Patrikios, Antonis. "ICO's Enforcement Action: What Do the Cases Tell Us?" *Field
Fisher—Privacy and Information Law Blog,* March 1, 2013. http://privacylawblog
.fieldfisher.com/2013/icos-enforcement-action-what-do-the-cases-tell-us.

Pavlou, Paul A., Huigang Liang, and Yajiong Xue. "Understanding and Mitigating
Uncertainty in Online Environments: A Principal-Agent Perspective." *Management
Information Systems Quarterly* 31, no. 1 (2007): 105–136.

Petronio, Sandra. *Boundaries of Privacy: Dialectics of Disclosure.* Albany: State University of New York Press, 2002.

Pew Research Center. *Public Perceptions of Privacy and Security in the Post-Snowden
Era,* November 2014. http://www.pewinternet.org/2014/11/12/public-privacy-
perceptions/.

Pfeffer, Jeffrey. *The External Control of Organizations: A Resource Dependence Perspective.* New York: Harper & Row, 1978.

Pierre, Jon. *Governance, Politics, and the State: Political Analysis.* New York: St. Martin's
Press, 2000.

Pitofsky, Robert, and Former Chairman, and the Federal Trade Commission. "Oral
History of Robert Pitofsky (Sixth Interview)." Interview by Brooksley Born, March
30, 2004. http://dcchs.org/RobertPitofsky/3_30_04.pdf.

Ponemon Institute LLC. "2014 Cost of Data Breach Study: United States," May 2014.

Post, Robert C. "The Social Foundations of Privacy: Community and Self in the Common Law Tort." *California Law Review* 77, no. 5 (1989): 957–1010.

Pound, Roscoe. "Law in Books and Law in Action." *American Law Review* 44 (1910): 12–36.

Power, Michael. *The Audit Society: Rituals of Verification.* Oxford; New York: Oxford University Press, 1997.

Power, Richard. "CyLab Survey Reveals Gap in Board Governance of Cyber Security." *Carnegie Mellon University CyLab*, August 22, 2008. https://www.cylab.cmu .edu/news_events/news/2008/governance.html.

Privacy Act of 1974. Pub. L. No. 93–579, 88 Stat. 1896 (codified at 5 U.S.C. §552a), 2006.

The Privacy and Electronic Communications (EC Directive) Regulations 2003. 2003 No. 2426, 2003. http://www.legislation.gov.uk/uksi/2003/2426/contents/made.

"Privacy Enforcement and Protection." State of California Department of Justice, Office of the Attorney General. Accessed February 11, 2015. http://oag.ca.gov/ privacy.

Privacy Laws & Business. "Annual Conference." Accessed June 4, 2014. http://www .privacylaws.com/annual_conference/.

Privacy Rights Clearinghouse. "Chronology of Data Breaches," December 31, 2013. http://www.privacyrights.org/data-breach.

Privacy Rights Clearinghouse. "Privacy Today: A Review of Current Issues," May 2013. https://www.privacyrights.org/ar/Privacy-IssuesList.htm.

Privacy Rule Regulation. 16 C.F.R. § 313.3(d), n.d.

"The Pulitzer Prizes | Beat Reporting." Accessed February 11, 2015. http://www .pulitzer.org/bycat/Beat-Reporting.

"The Pulitzer Prizes | Public Service." Accessed February 11, 2015. http://www .pulitzer.org/bycat/Public-Service.

Raab, Charles D., and Colin J. Bennett. "Taking the Measure of Privacy: Can Data Protection Be Evaluated?" *International Review of Administrative Sciences* 62, no. 4 (1996): 535–556.

Raab, C., and B.-J. Koops. "Privacy Actors, Performances and the Future of Privacy Protection." In *Reinventing Data Protection?* ed. S. Gutwirth, Y. Poullet, P. De Hert, C. de Terwangne and S. Nouwt, 207–221. Dordrecht: Springer, 2009.

Ragin, C. C., and H. S. Becker, eds. *What Is a Case? Exploring the Foundations of Social Inquiry*. Cambridge, UK; New York:Cambridge University Press, 1992.

Rakoff, Todd D. "The Choice between Formal and Informal Modes of Administrative Regulation." *Administrative Law Review* 52, no. 1 (2000): 159–174.

Ramos, Diego. *Data Protection in Spain: Overview*. Data Protection. Practical Law—Multi-Jurisdictional Guide 2014/15. Association of Corporate Counsel; Thomson Reuters, July 1, 2014. http://uk.practicallaw.com/1-520-8264.

"RDV Online." Accessed August 13, 2014. http://www.rdv-online.com/.

Re: Advertising.com, Inc. dba Teknosurf.com, and John Ferber, 140 F.T.C. 220 (2005).

Re: BJ's Wholesale Club, Inc., 140 F.T.C. 465 (2005).

Re: Cardsystems Solutions, Inc., Complaint P9, No. C-4168 (2006).

Records, Computers and the Rights of Citizens, Report of the Secretary's Advisory Committee on Automated Personal Data Systems, July 1973. https://www.epic.org/privacy/hew1973report/.

Re: DSW Inc., Complaint P10, No. C-4168 (2006).

"Reform Government Surveillance." Accessed February 12, 2015. https://www.reformgovernmentsurveillance.com/?redirection=combiner.

Regan, Priscilla M. *Legislating Privacy: Technology, Social Values, and Public Policy*. Chapel Hill: University of North Carolina Press, 1995.

Regan, Priscilla M. "Safe Harbors or Free Frontiers? Privacy and Transborder Data Flows." *Journal of Social Issues* 59, no. 2 (2003): 263–282.

Reidenberg, Joel R. "Privacy Wrongs in Search of Remedies." *Hastings Law Journal* 54 (2002): 877–898.

Reidenberg, Joel R. "Restoring Americans' Privacy in Electronic Commerce." *Berkeley Technology Law Journal* 14 (1999): 771–792.

Reidenberg, Joel R. "Setting Standards for Fair Information Practice in the U.S. Private Sector." *Iowa Law Review* 80 (1995): 497–552.

Re: Sony BMG Music Entertainment, Agreement Containing Consent Order, 2007.

Rhodes, R. A. W. "Policy Network Analysis." In *The Oxford Handbook of Public Policy*, ed. Michael Moran, Martin Rein, and Robert E. Goodin, 425–447.Oxford; New York: Oxford University Press, 2008.

Richards, Neil. "The Perils of Social Reading." *Georgetown Law Journal* 101 (2013): 689–724.

Right to Financial Privacy Act (RFPA) of 1978. 12 U.S.C. §§3401–3422, 2006.

Rittweger, Christoph, and Claire Molloy. "E.U. Data Protection Reform: An Overview of the European Commission's Proposed Regulation." *Bloomberg BNA—World Data Protection Report*, February 24, 2012.

Rotenberg, Marc. "Fair Information Practices and the Architecture of Privacy (What Larry Doesn't Get)." *Stanford Technology Law Review* 2001 (2001): 1–4.

Royal Decree 428/1993, 1993.

Rubin, Edward L. "Images of Organizations and Consequences of Regulation." *Theoretical Inquiries in Law* 6, no. 2 (2005): 347–390.

Rubinstein, Ira S. "Privacy and Regulatory Innovation: Moving beyond Voluntary Codes." I/S: A Journal of Law and Policy for the Information Society 6 (2011): 356–423.

Rubinstein, Ira S. "Regulating Privacy by Design." *Berkeley Technology Law Journal* 26 (2011): 1409–1456.

Rubinstein, Ira S., and Ronald Lee. *Systematic Government Access to Personal Data: A Comparative Analysis.* Center for Democracy & Technology, November 13, 2013. https://www.cdt.org/files/pdfs/govaccess2013/government-access-to-data-compara tive-analysis.pdf.

Rubinstein, Ira S., Gregory T. Nojeim, and Ronald D. Lee. "Systematic Government Access to Personal Data: A Comparative Analysis." *International Data Privacy Law* 4, no. 2 (2014): 96–119.

Rule, James B. *Private Lives and Public Surveillance: Social Control in the Computer Age.* New York: Schocken Books, 1974.

Rule, J. B., and G. W. Greenleaf, eds. *Global Privacy Protection: The First Generation.* Cheltenham, UK; Northhampton, MA: Edward Elgar, 2008.

"Safe Harbor—U.S.-European Union—Self-Certification." *Export.gov.* Accessed May 25, 2014. https://new.export.gov/community/pages/71-u-s-eu-safe-harbor-self -certification.

"Safe Harbor Workbook." *Export.gov.* Accessed May 27, 2014. http://export.gov/ safeharbor/eg_main_018238.asp.

Samuelson Law, Technology & Public Policy Clinic. "Security Breach Notification Laws: Views from Chief Security Officers." UC Berkeley School of Law, December 2007. http://www.law.berkeley.edu/files/cso_study.pdf.

Samway, Michael. "Business and Human Rights." *Yahoo! Yodel*, May 7, 2008. https:// yodel.yahoo.com/blogs/yahoo-americas/business-human-rights-870.html.

Sanger, David E., and Brian X. Chen. "Signaling Post-Snowden Era, New iPhone Locks Out N.S.A." *New York Times*, September 26, 2014. http://www.nytimes .com/2014/09/27/technology/iphone-locks-out-the-nsa-signaling-a-post-snowden -era-.html.

Schauer, Frederick. "The Politics and Incentives of Legal Transplantation." In *Governance in a Globalizing World*, ed. Joseph S. Nye and John D. Donahue, 253–268. Washington, DC: Brookings Institution Press; Cambridge, MA: Visions of Governance in the 21st Century, 2000.

"Schulungen Bei Der GDD—GDD e.V." Accessed August 13, 2014. https://www.gdd .de/seminare.

Schütz, Philip. "Comparing Formal Independence of Data Protection Authorities in Selected E.U. Member States." University of Exeter, 2012. http://regulation.upf.edu/ exeter-12-papers/Paper%20265%20-%20Schuetz%202012%20-%20Comparing%20 formal%20independence%20of%20data%20protection%20authorities%20in%20 selected%20EU%20Member%20States.pdf.

Schwartz, John. "First Line of Defense; Chief Privacy Officers Forge Evolving Corporate Roles." *New York Times*, February 12, 2001. http://www.nytimes.com/2001/ 02/12/business/first-line-of-defense-chief-privacy-officers-forge-evolving-corporate -roles.html.

Schwartz, John. "Health Insurance Reform Bill May Undermine Privacy of Patients' Records." *The Washington Post*, August 4, 1996.

Schwartz, Paul M. "Internet Privacy and the State." *Connecticut Law Review* 32 (1999): 815–859.

Schwartz, Paul M. "Privacy and Democracy in Cyberspace." *Vanderbilt Law Review* 52 (1999): 1607–1701.

Schwartz, Paul M. "Privacy and Participation: Personal Information and Public Sector Regulation in the United States." *Iowa Law Review* 80 (1995): 553–618.

Schwartz, Steven T., and David E. Wallin. "Behavioral Implications of Information Systems on Disclosure Fraud." *Behavioral Research in Accounting* 14 (1) (February 1, 2002): 197–221.

Scott, Michael D. "The FTC, the Unfairness Doctrine and Data Security Litigation: Has the Commission Gone Too Far?" August 21, 2007. http://papers.ssrn.com/sol3/ papers.cfm?abstract_id=1012232.

Scott, W. Richard. "Evolving Professions: An Institutional Field Approach." In *Organisation Und Profession*, ed. Thomas Klatetzki and Veronika Tacke, 119–141. Organisation Und Gesellschaft. VS Verlag für Sozialwissenschaften, 2005. http:// link.springer.com/chapter/10.1007/978-3-322-80570-6_5.

Scott, W. Richard. "Lords of the Dance: Professionals as Institutional Agents." *Organization Studies* 29 (2) (February 2008): 219–238.

Scott, W. Richard. *Organizations: Rational, Natural, and Open Systems*. 5th ed. Upper Saddle River, NJ: Prentice Hall, 2002.

Scott, W. Richard, and John W. Meyer. "The Organization of Societal Sectors." In *Organizational Environments: Ritual and Rationality*, ed. W. Richard Scott and John W. Meyer, 129–153. Newbury Park, CA: Sage Publications, 1992.

Serrano, Richard A., and Kathleen Hennessey. "Sony 'Made a Mistake' in Canceling Release of 'Interview,' Obama Says." *Los Angeles Times*. December 19, 2014. http://www.latimes.com/world/asia/la-fg-fbi-sony-norkor-20141219-story.html#page=1.

Serwin, Andrew B. "The FTC's Increased Focus on Protecting Personal Information: An Overview of Enforcement and Guidance," November 22, 2008. http://papers.ssrn.com/sol3/papers.cfm?abstract_id=1305669.

Simitis, Spiros. "Privacy—An Endless Debate." *California Law Review* 98 (2010): 1989–2007.

Simitis, Spiros. "Reviewing Privacy in an Information Society." *University of Pennsylvania Law Review* 135 (1987): 707–746.

Simon, Herbert A. *Models of Man: Social and Rational; Mathematical Essays on Rational Human Behavior in a Social Setting*. New York: Wiley, 1957.

Sitkin, Sim B., and Robert J. Bies. "The Legalistic Organization: Definitions, Dimensions, and Dilemmas." *Organization Science* 4, no. 3 (August 1, 1993): 345–351.

Slaughter, Anne-Marie. *A New World Order*. Princeton, NJ: Princeton University Press, 2005.

Smith, H. Jeff. *Managing Privacy: Information Technology and Corporate America*. Chapel Hill: University of North Carolina Press, 1994.

Sokol, Bettina. "Eröffnung [Opening Remarks], 20 Jahre Datenschutz—Individualismus Oder Gemeinschaftssinn?" Presented at the 1998 Conference of State (Land) Data Protection Authorities, Düsseldorf, 1998. https://www.ldi.nrw.de/mainmenu_Service/submenu_Tagungsbaende/Inhalt/20_Jahre_Datenschutz/20_Jahre_Datenschutz1.pdf.

Solove, Daniel J. *Understanding Privacy*. Cambridge, MA: Harvard University Press, 2008.

Solove, Daniel J., and Woodrow Hartzog. "The FTC and the New Common Law of Privacy." *Columbia Law Review* 114 (2014): 583–676.

Solove, Daniel J., and Chris Jay Hoofnagle. "A Model Regime of Privacy Protection." *University of Illinois Law Review*, no. 2 (2006): 357–403.

Solove, Daniel J., and Paul Schwartz. *Information Privacy Law: Cases & Materials.* 3rd ed. Austin; New York: Aspen Publishers, 2008.

"Spain Levies Maximum Fine over Google Privacy Policy." *BBC News—Technology*, December 20, 2013. http://www.bbc.com/news/technology-25461353.

"Spanish Data Protection Agency," n.d. http://www.agpd.es/portalwebAGPD/canaldocumentacion/publicaciones/common/pdfs/AEPD_en.pdf.

Speer, Lawrence J., "Variable Funding of E.U. Privacy Law Means Uneven Enforcement Across European Union." *[BNA] Privacy & Security Law Report* 7 (January 8, 2007): 49–54.

Stalder, Felix. "Privacy Is Not the Antidote to Surveillance." *Surveillance & Society* 1, no. 1 (2009): 120–124.

Stevens, John M., Janice M. Beyer, and Harrison M. Trice. "Managerial Receptivity and Implementation of Policies." *Journal of Management* 6, no. 1 (March 1, 1980): 33–54.

Stewart, Blair. "Privacy Impact Assessment Towards a Better Informed Process for Evaluating Privacy Issues Arising from New Technologies." [BNA] *Privacy Law & Policy Report* 5 (1999): 147–149.

Stigler, George J. "The Theory of Economic Regulation." *Bell Journal of Economics and Management Science* 2 (1971): 3–21.

Sturm, Susan. "Second Generation Employment Discrimination: A Structural Approach." *Columbia Law Review* 101 (2001): 458–568.

Suchman, Mark C. "On Beyond Interest: Rational, Normative and Cognitive Perspectives in the Social Scientific Study of Law." *Wisconsin Law Review* 1997 (1997): 475–501.

Sunstein, Cass R. "Administrative Substance." *Duke Law Journal* 1991 (1991): 607–646.

Sunstein, Cass R. "Informational Regulation and Informational Standing: Akins and Beyond." *University of Pennsylvania Law Review* 147 (1999): 613–675.

Swire, Peter P. "Trustwrap: The Importance of Legal Rules to Electronic Commerce and Internet Privacy." *Hastings Law Journal* 54 (2003): 847–873.

Tene, Omer. "What Google Knows: Privacy and Internet Search Engines." *Utah Law Review* 2008 (2008): 1433–1492.

Tetlock, Philip E. "Accountability: The Neglected Social Context of Judgment and Choice." *Research in Organizational Behavior* 7 (1985): 297–332.

Thaw, David. "The Efficacy of Cybersecurity Regulation." *Georgia State University Law Review* 30, no. 2 (2014): 1.

Thomas, Liisa M., and Sara Susnjar. "AEPD Reports an Increase in Complaints with Telecommunications Companies." *Winston & Strawn LLP—Privacy Law Corner*, November 6, 2013. http://www.winston.com/en/privacy-law-corner/aepd-reports -an-increase-in-complaints-with-telecommunications.html.

Torres, Frank C., III, and Donald S. Clark. "Letter from Frank C. Torres, III, Legislative Counsel, Consumers Union, to Donald S. Clark, Secretary, Federal Trade Commission," March 26, 1999. http://www.ftc.gov/bcp/icpw/comments/conunion.htm.

Trubek, David M., and Marc Galanter. "Scholars in Self-Estrangement: Some Reflections on the Crisis in Law and Development Studies in the United States." *Wisconsin Law Review* 1974 (1974): 1062–1102.

TRUSTe. "Powering Trust in the Data Economy—TRUSTe." Accessed May 27, 2014. http://www.truste.com/.

Turkington, Richard C., and Anita L. Allen. *Privacy Law: Cases and Materials*. 2nd ed., St. Paul, MN: West Group, 2002.

UK Information Commissioner's Office. *Guidance on the Rules on Use of Cookies and Similar Technologies*. Privacy and Electronic Communications Regulations, May 2012. https://ico.org.uk/media/for-organisations/documents/1545/cookies _guidance.pdf.

"U.S.–EU Safe Harbor Homepage." Export.gov. Accessed May 26, 2014. http:// export.gov/safeharbor/eu/index.asp.

Valby, Karen. "23andMe Responds to Controversy over Relative-Finding Tool." *Fast Company*, September 17, 2014. http://www.fastcompany.com/3035812/healthware/ 23andme-responds-to-controversy-over-relative-finding-tool.

Varney, Christine A. Commissioner, Federal Trade Commission. "Privacy in the Electronic Age." Presented at the Privacy and American Business Conference, November 1, 1995. http://www.ftc.gov/public-statements/1995/11/privacy-electronic -age.

Vaughan, Diane. "The Dark Side of Organizations: Mistake, Misconduct, and Disaster." *Annual Review of Sociology* 25, no. 1 (1999): 271–305.

Video Privacy Protection Act (VPPA) of 1988. 18 U.S.C. §§2710–2712, 2006.

Vogel, David. *National Styles of Regulation: Environmental Policy in Great Britain and the United States*. Ithaca, NY: Cornell University Press, 1986.

Vogelstein, Fred. "Minding One's Business." U.S. News & World Report (March 2000): 45.

Vogenauer, Stefan, and Stephen Weatherill, eds.*The Harmonisation of European Contract Law: Implications for European Private Laws, Business and Legal Practice*. (Studies of the Oxford Institute of European and Comparative Law). Oxford; Portland, OR: Hart Publishing, 2006.

"Wall Street Journal's 'What They Know' Series—Ashkan Soltani." Accessed February 11, 2015. http://ashkansoltani.org/work/what-they-know/.

Walsh, James P. "Managerial and Organizational Cognition: Notes from a Trip Down Memory Lane." *Organization Science* 6, no. 3 (May 1, 1995): 280–321.

Walz, Stephan. "Datenschutz-Herausforderung Durch Neue Technik Und Europarecht." Presented at the 1998 Conference of State (Land) Data Protection Authorities, Düsseldorf, 1998. https://www.ldi.nrw.de/mainmenu_Service/submenu_Tagungs baende/Inhalt/20_Jahre_Datenschutz/20_Jahre_Datenschutz1.pdf.

Warren, Adam, Robin Bayley, Colin Bennett, Andrew Charlesworth, Roger Clarke, and Charles Oppenheim. "Privacy Impact Assessments: International Experience as a Basis for UK Guidance." *Computer Law & Security Report* 24, no. 3 (January 2008): 233–242.

Waters, Nigel. "Privacy Impact Assessment—Great Potential Not Often Realized." In *Privacy Impact Assessment*, ed. David Wright and Paul de Hert, 149–160. Dordrecht: Springer, 2012.

Weichert, Thilo. "Privacy Protection Audit and IT Security Problems in Germany." Presented at the 4th International Conference "Infobalt," Vilnius, Lithuania, October 21, 2002. https://www.datenschutzzentrum.de/material/themen/divers/ audgs_en.htm.

Weick, Karl E. "Collective Mind in Organizations: Heedful Interrelating on Flight Decks." *Administrative Science Quarterly* 38 (1993): 357–381.

Weiser, Mark. "Some Computer Science Issues in Ubiquitous Computing." *Communications of the ACM* 36, no. 7 (1993): 75–84.

Westin, Alan F. *Privacy and Freedom*. 1st ed. New York: Atheneum, 1967.

"Who We Are." ICO.Information Commissioner's Office, December 4, 2014. https:// ico.org.uk/about-the-ico/who-we-are/.

Wiesen, S. Jonathan. "German Industry and the Third Reich: Fifty Years of Forgetting and Remembering." *Dimensions: A Journal of Holocaust Studies* 13, 1999. http:// archive.adl.org/braun/dim_13_2_forgetting.html#.U43ydxaxNj4.

"The World's Biggest Public Companies." *Forbes*, May 2014. http://www.forbes.com/ global2000/list/.

Wright, David, Kush Wadhwa, Monica Lagazio, Charles Raab, and Eric Charikane. "Integrating Privacy Impact Assessment in Risk Management." *International Data Privacy Law* 4, no. 2 (May 1, 2014): 155–170.

Wybitul, Tim. "New Requirements for Data Protection Officers in Germany." *Mayer Brown Business & Technology Sourcing Review* 16 (2011): 19–23.

Yahoo! Inc.'s Provision of False Information to Congress, Hearing before H. Comm. on Foreign Affairs. 110th Cong. (November 6, 2007).

Zietsma, C., M. Winn, O. Branzei, and I. Vertinsky. "The War of the Woods: Facilitators and Impediments of Organizational Learning Processes." *British Journal of Management* 13 (2002): S61–S74.

Index